... One of them created our
Dominican H. Upmann, so you
could forget Havana.
That's One-Upmannship

HENNESSY
Martini

CIGAR
Aficionado's

BUYING GUIDE TO
PREMIUM
CIGARS

1996 EDITION

M. SHANKEN COMMUNICATIONS, INC.
NEW YORK

CIGAR AFICIONADO'S
BUYING GUIDE TO PREMIUM CIGARS
1996 EDITION

Editor & Publisher .... Marvin R. Shanken

Executive Editor .... Michael Moaba
Managing Editor .... Gordon Mott
Editorial Director, Books .... Ann Berkhausen
Assistant Editors .... Amy Lyons, Tara Collins,
Shandana Durrani
Editorial Assistant .... Alan Richtmyer

Creative Director .... Martin Leeds
Art Director................... Kathy McGilvery
Cover Design Director .... Ken Newbaker
Cover Designer .... Diane Miljat

Director of Business Development .. George Brightman
Marketing Manager .... Connie McGilvray
Advertising Director, Luxury Goods. . James J. Archambault Jr.
Associate, Business Development ... Britta Jensen

Director of Advertising Services .... Elizabeth Ferrero
Advertising Services Manager...... Virginia Juliano

Director of Retail Sales........... Christine Carroll
Director of Circulation .... Laura Zandi

Published by M. SHANKEN COMMUNICATIONS, INC.
387 Park Avenue South, New York, New York 10016
Telephone: 212-684-4224 Telefax: 212-684-5424

ISBN 1-881659-32-1

Manufactured in the United States of America

The Macanudo Crown

Of all premium-cigar makers, only Macanudo crowns the head of every one of its cigars. Unlike a flat head, a crowned cigar head does not bend or break under pressure. Perfectly rounded and supported by the tobacco beneath the cigar's wrapper leaf, a crowned head makes a cigar easier to cut, smoother to draw and more satisfying to smoke.

BREITLING

1884

CHRONOMAT

When *Concorde* climbs to its cruising altitude of 16,000 m, it demonstrates its unique manner of fusing advanced aerodynamics and unrivalled performance with pure beauty. Swiftly, unerringly, it will cover an ocean's breadth at 2,200 k.p.h., leaving all other civil airliners far behind.

Prized by pilots the world over, BREITLING's mechanical CHRONOMAT chronograph truly deserves the finest of everything – a case in solid 18K gold for instance. Generously proportioned and totally impervious to the effects of water and air, it adds a touch of luxury to the watch's functional excellence.

There is, after all, more to time measurement than technology. The subtleties of an intricate mechanical movement or the rich gleam of a hand-polished case provide enduring satisfactions that even time itself can never alter.

Selfwinding mechanical chronograph with $\frac{1}{5}$th second graduations.

30-minute and 12-hour totalizers.

Oversized calendar digits. Power reserve in excess of 42 hours.

Unidirectional ratcheted rotating bezel with marker tabs.

Case water-resistant to 100 m with glare-proofed cambered sapphire crystal.

Case in 18K yellow or white gold. Also available in steel, with two-tone finish and 18K gold rider tabs or in steel with 18K gold bezel.

Available with three types of leather strap with either tang-type buckle or folding clasp, or else with PILOT or ROULEAUX bracelet.

INSTRUMENTS   FOR   PROFESSIONALS

Foreword

Welcome to *Cigar Aficionado*'s 1996 Buying Guide to Premium Cigars.

This guide contains ratings for nearly 800 cigars, organized according to their scores into listings by size, country and brand. You will find the complete tasting notes with each cigar. Preceding this is some general information which will help you to purchase, understand and enjoy your cigars.

In addition, we have compiled a list of over 2,000 leading tobacconists around the world where *Cigar Aficionado* is sold. That list now includes virtually every major cigar retailer across the United States, and in the major foreign capitals.

The cigar-friendly restaurant guide focuses specifically on places that have responded to our questionnaires; the list includes 1200 restaurants. We ask that you please let us know immediately if a restaurant's cigar policy has changed.

We hope this guide enhances your smoking pleasure. Enjoy.

Marvin R. Shanken
Editor & Publisher

Table of

DAN WAGNER

Contents

COURTNEY GRANT WINSTON

Shape, Size and Color

The popularity of cigars in recent years has triggered a whole new set of concerns for smokers. There are more cigars, more brands, more sizes within each brand and, seemingly, more ways to describe cigars that from the outside look identical. And it's always been true that one company's double corona may be another company's Churchill size. It's not really a conspiracy to confuse consumers, but it does make for a complicated buying decision.

Fortunately, there is an accepted vocabulary and certain basic criteria that apply to all hand-rolled cigars. The parameters are fairly simple: brand, wrapper color, and size and shape. Of course, country of manufacture is important too, but today tobacco is a global commodity and cigars made in the Dominican Republic may contain tobacco from Cameroon, Mexico and Nicaragua. Therefore, it may be important to you to understand the origins of tobacco in your cigar because a particular type may create a certain flavor that you like.

Let's start with the brand name. The brand is the designation given by the manufacturer to a particular line of cigars. Punch, Partagas, Macanudo, Montecristo and Davidoff are just a few well-known names. You'll find these names on the cigar band, which is generally wrapped around the "head," or the closed end, of the cigar.

However, depending on which country you're in, even these well-known names can be a source of confusion. Some brands were first produced in Cuba; after Castro's revolution in 1959, many cigar manufacturers fled, believing they could take their brand names with them. The Cubans argued the brands belonged

Double Claro

Claro

Colorado Claro

to the country. So today, you have a Punch made in Cuba and one made in Honduras; a Partagas in Cuba and a Partagas in the Dominican Republic. The dual origin problem also affects Romeo y Julieta, La Gloria Cubana, Fonseca, H. Upmann and El Rey del Mundo, Cohiba and Montecristo. You can usually determine which is which by a small Habano or Havana inscribed on the band.

Color refers to the shade of the outer wrapper leaf. In the past, manufacturers used dozens of terms for the wrapper leaves which were grown in Cuba, Sumatra, Brazil and the United States; U.S. cigar makers often described eight to ten different shades. Today, there are six major color grades in use. And wrapper leaf is grown today not only in the countries mentioned above, but in Ecuador, Nicaragua, Honduras and Cameroon as well.

Here are the six basic shades:

• **Double Claro:** Light green, and often called candela. The leaves are cured with heat to fix the chlorophyll in the leaf. They often taste slightly sweet. At at one time a majority of American market cigars came with

a light-green wrapper, but claro claro is not as popular today.

• **Claro:** A light tan color, usually grown under shade tents. Claro is prized for its neutral flavor qualities.

• **Colorado Claro:** Light brown to brown. It is most often sun-grown.

• **Colorado - Colorado Maduro:** Brown to reddish brown. It is also usually shade-grown and has rich flavor and a subtle aroma.

• **Maduro:** From the Spanish word for "ripe," it refers to the extra length of time needed to produce a rich, dark-brown wrapper. A maduro should be silky and oily, with a rich strong flavor and mild aroma. There are several processes used to create maduro: one involves "cooking" the leaves in a pressure chamber; the other uses long, hotter-than-normal fermentation in huge bulks. A maduro wrapper usually produces a slightly sweet taste.

• **Oscuro:** Meaning dark, it is also called negro or black in tobacco-producing countries. It usually is left on the plant the longest, and it is matured or sweated the longest.

You've seen the brand you're looking for, you've spotted the color

Colorado

Colorado Maduro

Maduro

Oscuro

Corona

Corona Gorda

Panatela

Double Corona

Culebra

Diademas

Pyramid

13

Robusto

Petit Corona

Belicoso

Lonsdale

ILLUSTRATIONS BY ROBERT TRONDSEN

Churchill

Perfecto

wrapper you like to smoke, now it's time to get down to choosing a size and shape. In Spanish, the word *vitola* conveniently covers both concepts, but in English we're left describing both size (girth and length) and shape. Most cigars come in boxes with a front mark that tells you the shape of the cigar such as Punch Double Corona or H. Upmann Lonsdale. As you come to know shapes, you also can make some assumptions about size, such as knowing that a double corona is not a short, thin cigar.

It's unfortunate that there is so much confusion about size and shape when there needn't be. But after several generations of every manufacturer independently deciding which size name went with which length and girth, there is no simple logic to the definitions. In fact, haphazard naming conventions have resulted in the same word, such as Churchill, being used by different manufacturers for cigars of different sizes. If any single statement can be made about the standards of different countries, it is that Cuban standards tend to be more uniform. That's because there is one body governing the state-owned tobacco company in Cuba, and it oversees the entire industry there.

The basic measurement standard, however, is the same. The only variations are whether it is expressed in metric or U.S. customary systems. Length, therefore, is listed in inches or centimeters and thickness or diameter, or ring gauge as it commonly known, is in 64ths of an inch or millimeters. A classic corona size, for example, is 6 by 42, which means it is six inches long and 42/64ths of an inch thick.

If you're searching for common denominators to use as a starting point for shape, it helps to know that all cigars can be divided into two categories: parejos, or straight cigars, and figurados, or irregular shapes.

Simply put, parejos are straight-sided cigars, the kind with which most smokers are familiar. There are three basic groups in this category: coronas, panatelas and lonsdales.

Listed below are some standard size names with their standard sizes in parentheses.

• **Coronas** (6 inches by 42/44 ring gauge) have traditionally been the manufacturer's benchmark against which all other cigars are measured. Coronas have an open "foot" (the end you light) and a closed "head" (the end you smoke); the head is most often rounded. A Churchill normally measures 7 by 47. A robusto is 5 by 50. A double corona is 7 1/2 by 49. In other words, these are all variations on the corona theme.
• **Panatelas** (7 x 38) are usually longer than coronas, but they are dramatically thinner. They also have an open foot and closed head.
• **Lonsdales** (6 3/4 by 42) are thicker than panatelas, but longer than coronas.

The irregular shapes, or figurados, encompass every out-of-the-ordinary-shaped cigar. The following list comprises the major types:

• **Pyramid:** It has a pointed, closed head and widens to an open foot.
• **Belicoso:** A small pyramid-shaped cigar with a rounded head rather than a point.
• **Torpedo:** A shape with a pointed head, a closed foot and a bulge in the middle.
• **Perfecto:** This looks like the cigar in cartoons with two closed rounded ends and a bulge in the middle.
• **Culebra:** Three panatelas braided together.
• **Diademas:** A giant cigar 8 inches or longer. Most often it has an open foot, but occasionally it will come with a perfecto or closed foot.

Remember, even with these "classic" irregular shapes, there are variations among manufacturers. Some cigars called belicosos look like pyramids, and some called torpedos look like pyramids because they do not have a perfecto tip. Confusing? Yes, it is.

Unfortunately, it really is self-defeating to try to talk about "classic" or "normal" ranges for any cigars on the market today. The basic shape designations can vary so greatly from company to company that they make little sense. Once you've become comfortable with the terminology, however, ask your tobacconist what the exact dimensions are of the cigar you like to smoke. Use that as your

GREAT CIGARS
DON'T MAKE THEMSELVES,
IT TAKES
A. FUENTE.

ARTURO FUENTE

IMPORTED

"We will never rush the hands of time."

ARTURO FUENTE
The Reigning Family Of Premium Cigars

base to branch out to bigger or smaller, longer or shorter cigars. And, don't assume because you like a Churchill from one company that you're going to get the same-size cigar with that name from another manufacturer.

There are some other designations that are worth knowing because they refer to the style of packing. An 8-9-8 designation, for instance, simply means that the cigars are stacked in three rows inside the box, eight on the bottom, nine in the middle and eight on top. They usually come in a distinctive round-sided box. Amatista refers to a glass jar of 50 cigars, originally packaged by H. Upmann, which was developed for smokers who wanted a "factory fresh" smoke. Finally, there are tubos, cigars that are packed in aluminum, glass or even wooden tubes; a tightly sealed tube will keep cigars fresh for a long period of time. Some cigars are also box-pressed, meaning they are put inside a box so tightly that they acquire a soft, squarish appearance.

The Grande Réserve of Cigars.

Some of life's great pleasures require both time and
skill in their making.

The Dunhill Aged Cigar is one such example,
a fine spirit such as Cognac another.

From manufacture to the appreciation of the
intrinsic qualities of each, the Dunhill Aged Cigar
and the finest Cognacs have much in common.

Both have roots in the soil culminating in the
harvest of tobacco leaf or grape.

Both require the attentions of a Master Blender
to ensure the end result consistently yields the
highest standards of quality.

And both are aged and matured in wood to
impart their unique and individual character.

A smoothness and mellowness of
taste is also common to both, as
is a subtlety of aroma.

Perhaps that's why, enjoyed
together, they provide a perfect partnership.

And why the Dunhill Aged Cigar deserves
to share Cognac's highest appellation –
The Grande Réserve of Cigars.

IMPORTED AND DISTRIBUTED BY LANE LIMITED
2280 Mountain Industrial Boulevard, Tucker, Georgia, U.S.A. 30084
Telephone: 800 - 221 - 4134

CALLE OCHO
HOT PLACE
COOL CIGAR!

From the largest Cuban cigar factory north of Havana, Caribbean Cigar Factory introduces "CALLE OCHO" [Kai-a-ocho]. Available in eleven popular sizes, arriving where fine cigars are sold.

Taste

Every cigar smoker has experienced the displeasure of lighting up, pulling a big draw of smoke into their mouth and wondering what on God's earth they were smoking. Of course, for every unpleasant taste experience there are dozens of pleasurable ones—when the cigar takes on a character beyond mere tobacco and becomes something more complex. Any such foray into new taste territory is part of what becoming an aficionado is all about.

While smoking a cigar is the central act in appreciating it, there's more to it than just putting it in your mouth and puffing away. Professional

Jack Nicholson

STEVE WAYDA

tobacco experts and experienced smokers practice some basic steps in connoisseurship that are worth every cigar lover's effort to master.

Forming an overall impression of a cigar means using all of your senses: sight, touch, smell, taste and even your hearing. First, sight and touch go hand in hand. The first thing that you do when you remove a cigar from a box, or from your humidor, is inspect it. Even if this act is only subconscious, the appearance and feel of the cigar wrapper tell a story, and several lessons about taste can be learned from the outside of any cigar. Then, listen to it. Roll the cigar between fingers in order to determine the moisture content of the wrapper and the filler. It should be firm, but should give a little when squeezed, and there shouldn't be any rustling or crackling of the leaves.

A wrapper does not make or break a cigar. But it plays an important role because it provides texture and beauty, and is your first contact with the personality and character of a cigar. Even before you light up, seeing and feeling a wrapper with nice silky oil and without visual blemishes should give you certain expectations. Wrapper appearance will vary depending upon where the leaf was grown.

Linda
Evangelista

The best wrappers from Cuba are indeed like silk, with exceedingly close cell structure—they don't feel like vegetable matter because their surface is so smooth. These wrappers have an elasticity and strength often lacking in wrapper leaves from other countries.

By contrast, a Cameroon wrapper shows oil in its bumpy surface, called "tooth" in the tobacco industry. These bumps are a good sign that great taste and aroma will follow, even if the texture of the leaf isn't silky. Wrappers from Connecticut and Ecuador are somewhat close in surface texture, though not in color. Better Ecuadoran leaf has less tooth, is smooth to the touch, and has a mattelike appearance. The Connecticut wrapper shows more color depth, a bit more tooth and a nice shine.

Despite the differences in oils, seeing oil in any wrapper leaf indicates that the cigar has been well-humidified (oil secretes from tobacco at 70 to 72 percent humidity) and that the smoke should be relatively cool. A cool smoke is a tastier one, because it means the tobacco isn't carbonizing or overheating, which can limit the flavors.

If you see cracks or ripples in the surface of the wrapper leaf, you know

STEVE WAYDA

22

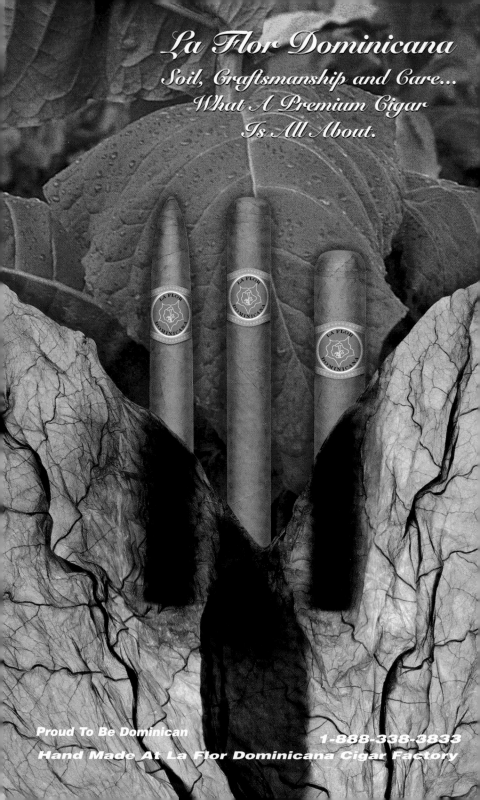

that the cigar was exposed to cycles of over-humidification and excessive dryness. This, too, is important. If the cigar is forced through rapid cycles of expansion and contraction, the internal construction is destroyed. A cigar with internal damage will smoke unevenly, or "plug," drawing unevenly. This may still occur due to faulty construction, but your chances are better with a perfect wrapper than with a broken one.

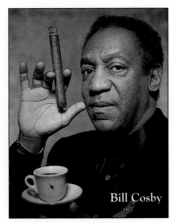

Bill Cosby

After lighting your cigar, look at the ash. According to most cigar experts, a white ash is better than a gray one. This is not merely an aesthetic issue; better soil produces whiter ash and more taste. Soil can be manipulated through fertilization, but if too much magnesium (a key ingredient in producing white ash) is added to the mix, the ash will flake, and nobody wants a messy cigar, even if the ash is white. Gray ash may hint at deficiencies in the soil, thus in the flavor.

A final visual cue is the burn rate. You can taste a cigar that is burning improperly because an uneven burn distorts the flavor of the blend. Simply put, a cigar is designed to burn different tobaccos evenly throughout the length of the smoke. A cigar may start off mild and grow stronger or change in some other way; these changes can be attributed to the location of the tobaccos. Thus, if a cigar burns unevenly, the delicate balance designed to produce a particular flavor or taste is disturbed, and the cigar will not taste right.

The sense of taste is located mainly on the tongue and to a lesser degree on the roof of the mouth. There exist only four basic tastes: sweet, sour, salty and bitter. Everything else is either a combination of these four or a combination of taste and aroma. Although food flavor descriptors are now being used, most tobacco men stick with words like acidic, salty, bitter, sweet, bite, sour, smooth, heavy, full-bodied, rich and balanced. Aroma too is important, and most cigar makers not only taste for flavors, but smell for aroma at the same time.

To come up with a blend of tastes that works, it takes many different types of tobacco. And to reach a consistent taste, one that stays the same year after year, is the most difficult task for any cigar maker. No two leaves of tobacco are the same, and no two cigars can be the same year to year.

Cigar makers utilize different tobaccos to try to compensate for nature. They continually seek a blend that will achieve consistency and at the same time create some flavor complexity. A

COURTNEY GRANT WINSTON

good blend uses tobaccos from different geographic zones, varieties, grades and harvests, so that the cigar will be complete and balanced.

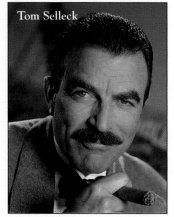

Tom Selleck

Achieving this balance is difficult. There are an infinite number of variables that can alter the taste of any blend: soil, tobacco variety, climate, ground condition, curing, the harvester, fermentation, manufacturing process and the humidity of the cigar.

Two especially important factors in taste are aging and construction. Aging provides smoothness, richness and roundness—qualities you won't find in a cigar right from the roller's table.

Even with the finest blend in the world, a poorly constructed cigar will be less enjoyable than a perfectly made cigar of only modest blend. A loose draw (a cigar that burns fast, letting a lot of smoke pass through quickly because it is underfilled) will increase smoking temperature, destroying taste. A tight draw, on the other hand, reduces the sensitivity of the taste buds; drawing less smoke means having less to taste. Moreover, a tight draw may extinguish more frequently, and relighting makes a cigar harsh.

The variability of cigars may be one of the most essential things a consumer should remember. Cigars are handmade products, produced by skilled artisans in quantities of anywhere from 100 to 300 a day, depending on the size of the cigar and the manufacturing process.

Like any handmade item, cigars are subject to human error. A bit too much tobacco here, a bit too little there, or a fatigued hand applying the wrong amount of pressure can completely alter the final product. All manufacturers inadvertantly let the occasional faulty cigar slip through their quality control system and reach the marketplace. What should a consumer do? Accept the reality, throw out the cigar and light up a new one. It's extremely unlikely that the next one will be flawed unless you are smoking a second-rate brand.

And, once you're smoking your favorite cigar, you won't even have to think about the complex set of processes that brought the cigar to your hand. It will most likely taste as great as the last one, and you'll already be looking forward to the next one.

STEVE WAYDA

"Agnes, have you seen my Don Diegos?"

CHAPTER 3

Cutting and Lighting

One of the greatest joys in cigar smoking comes at the beginning of the ritual: cutting and lighting the cigar. It is a rite of connoisseurship, no doubt. But more important, it is an essential step in the overall process of cigar enjoyment. A bad cut can seal a cigar's fate. If attention is not paid, or the proper procedure not followed, the cigar can smoke hot, the wrapper leaf can unravel and leave a flap hanging off the cigar, or the smoker's teeth will get covered with tobacco. A correct cut is like a perfect golf swing; all you know in the end is that the ball flies down the center of fairway like it had wings.

Each smoker has a favorite way to snip off the end of a cigar. A ritual so personal is subject to inflexible opinions about right and wrong methods, and the choice of method is often

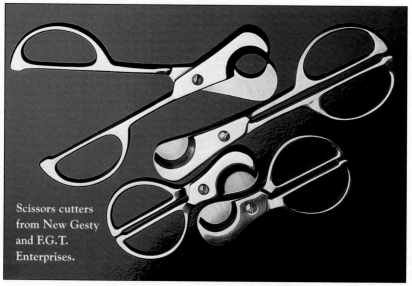

Scissors cutters from New Gesty and F.G.T. Enterprises.

GENE COLEMAN

28

Rated "A+" by Cigar Aficionado

Winter 1995/96

J.C. Pendergast Humidified Display & Storage Systems

For Proper Storage of Your Premium Cigars

CHAIR: #773 French Smoking Chair
Shown in Don Juan Hand-Distressed Leather.
Matching Ottoman and Sofa are also available.

HUMIDOR: Model HC3630
Shown in Honduras Mahogany

Model DC1503D
Shown in
Honduras Mahogany

All J.C. Pendergast systems feature automatic humidification systems with natural Spanish Cedar interiors.

Other Products include Built-In Humidified Cigar Display Cases, Walk-In Humidors and Commercial Humidification Systems for storage facilities.

Model CA4868
Shown in Cherry

Model CA3668
Shown in Spanish Cedar

Model CA2468
Shown in Honduras Mahogany

Model HC3668
Shown in Honduras Mahogany

DESIGN & MANUFACTURING
414-634-2388 FAX: 414-634-7791
2909 Wolff St. Racine, WI 53404

SALES, FULFILLMENT & DISTRIBUTION
1-800-634-1855 414-884-3500 FAX: 414-884-0926
1333 N. Grandview Pkwy. Sturtevant, WI 53177

traceable to the mentor who taught a given smoker to appreciate cigars. Regardless of method, though— whether wedge, guillotine, scissors, bull's-eye, piercer, knife or teeth—the quality of the cutting tool often relates directly to the quality of the cut. And there are a few basic rules that can lead to a perfect cut.

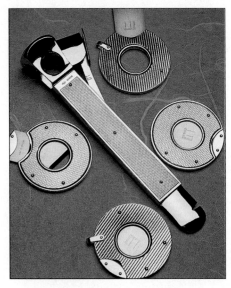

Guillotine cutters and a wedge table cutter from Dunhill.

flag, the leaf is twisted off in a pigtail. In all cases, the cap or flag closes off the wrapper and binder leaves that hold the filler leaves together in the "bunch."

The goal of a guillotine or scissors cut is to clip off enough of the end to expose the filler leaves, but to leave enough of the cap or flag on to keep the

If mistakes are made in the cut, it may be because the smoker doesn't understand how cigars are made. All premium handmade cigars are closed off at one end (called the "head") in the manufacturing process. In some cases, this closure is made with a separate piece of the tobacco leaf called a "cap," usually cut from the same wrapper leaf that's on the cigar. It is secured with a special vegetable-base glue. Others are finished off with a "flag," a piece of leaf that is part of the same wrapper leaf but has been shaped with a knife to be wrapped around the head end of the cigar, which is secured with the same kind of glue. The latter technique is obvious in some cigars because instead of being smoothed out underneath the

wrapper on the cigar. That usually means a cut of about two millimeters, or about one-sixteenth of an inch. If you're not into metrics or rulers, another safe gauge is to look for the "shoulder" of the cigar. In a flat-end cigar, it may be quite noticeable; in a rounded end, it's a little harder to find but basically it's where the curve of the end straightens out. In a well-made cigar, the cap or flag usually extends over the shoulder. A cut made at the shoulder, or just a touch above, may be perfect.

Guillotine cutters must be kept sharp. Once they become dull, the blade begins to "push" the tobacco leaves, often tearing the side of the cigar away from the blade. To achieve a clean cut with a single-blade guillo-

tine, the cigar should be positioned against the far side of the opening, the blade brought to rest against the cigar, and the end snipped with a sharp or quick thrust. Most single-blade guillotines also have a pocket for the blade; these must be regularly cleaned of tobacco pieces, or the blade may jam. Beware of inexpensive guillotine cutters with a single blade; they can damage cigars.

Double-bladed guillotines eliminate the problem of the cigar's far side being torn by an improper stroke of the blade. Be sure the cigar is flush against one blade before attempting to make a cut. The cutting motion should be crisp. These cutters should also be cleaned, but their design usually prevents jamming; an annual cleaning should be enough.

Scissors are more problematic. A good scissors must be properly balanced between the handles and the clipping edges. If not, it is very hard to hold the cigar steady against one of the cutting blades to get a clean cut. Also, if the hinge doesn't allow for a long movement of your fingers, it can be very hard to get a straight cut across the end of the cigar. But again, the same principle applies—you want to cut off enough of the cigar to expose the filler leaves without removing all of the cap.

One of the most popular cutters today leaves a V-shaped wedge in the end of the cigar. A greater surface area of the filler bunch is exposed than in a straight cut across the end.

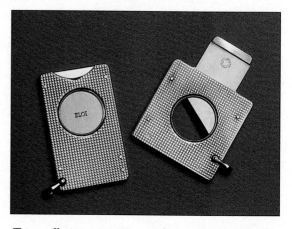

Two guillotine cutters in stainless steel and gold plate from Eloi.

But smokers who like to chew the end of their cigars should be wary of a wedge cut. If too much pressure is applied to the end of the cigar, the wedge can collapse. This causes an accumulation of moisture and tars, and can make the draw tighter. If you pull too hard on the cigar, it can make the cigar smoke hotter and harsher.

Two other types of cutters, a bull's-eye and a piercer, accomplish the same basic cut: putting a hole in the end of the cigar without damaging the cap's adhesion to the cigar. The bull's-eye uses a hollow-tip cutter that is turned in a quick circular motion. Experts advise against mak-

GENE COLEMAN

CIGAR Introductory Offer

Aficionado

- ☐ 4 issues (1 year) $16.95
- ☐ 8 issues (2 years) $31.95

Name (please print)

Address

City _____ State _____ Zip

☐ Check enclosed ☐ Bill me

Charge to: ☐ VISA ☐ MasterCard ☐ Amex

Card # _____ Exp. Date

Signature _____ 46DX4

CIGAR
Aficionado

WINTER 1994

TOM
SELLECK
HUNGRY FOR MORE

TASTING
69 TORPEDOS
PLUS
CIGY TALESE; MELBO'S
GULF PARADISE; DIAMONDS;
BORDEAUX WINES; A HOLIDAY
GIFT GUIDE AND MUCH MUCH MORE

Call Toll Free
1-800-992-2442

Please allow 4-6 weeks for delivery of first issue. Canada: $20.95 including GST, in U.S. funds.
All other foreign: $26.95 in U.S. funds.

ing the hole too deep; a too-deep cut can draw the air and smoke down toward the middle of the cigar, making it smoke hotter. The same caution should be used with the piercer, which often looks like an auger.

Many people swear by a simple knife or one-sided razor blade. Although the free blade requires a steady hand, the depth and angle of the cut, especially in a V-shaped wedge, can be gauged precisely according to the smoker's preference. The key to a successful knife cut is the sharpness of the blade. But unlike some guillotine cutters, a knife blade can be sharpened on a whetstone.

No article on cutting would be complete without the simplest cutting device of all: your teeth. This way is certainly convenient—you always have your teeth with you. But experts, many of whom incidentally make a living selling fancy cutters in addition to cigars, argue that only the very skilled teeth cutter can ensure a good, clean cut every time. They argue you can't see the cigar, you don't know exactly where the cut is being made, and you run the risk of tearing the cap and wrapper. There is also an element of bad manners; spitting out the tobacco

Lighter by Dunhill.

can be unsightly. But in a pinch, teeth always work.

Let's dispel a few myths about lighting cigars. Yes, the use of a wooden match or a cedar strip called a "spill" is elegant, and it can be effective. But it's often time-consuming and unwieldy because it takes more than one match to properly light a cigar. Therefore, any good butane lighter is an efficient cigar smoker's companion. The one caveat concerns fluid lighters. While lighter manufacturers dispute this, it is a fact that oil-based fluids can impart a taste to a cigar, so you must be careful not to draw too heavily when using this type of lighter. Fluid lighters are dependable, though, and tend to have a lot of lights in them.

Now you're ready to light. Cool smoke is the goal of a perfect light. There is a simple rule to follow: Never let the cigar touch the flame. When you light up, hold the cigar at a 45-degree angle above the flame, just far enough away so that the tip of the flame dances up to the cigar but never quite touches it. Then, to assure a proper light, rotate the cigar in your hand so that the foot of the cigar lights all the way around. When a lightly burning ring surrounds the tip of the cigar and begins to creep toward the center of the foot, blow out lightly through the cigar. Not everyone does this, but it makes sense; rather than breathing a first puff of lighter (or match-born sulfur) gases into the cigar, your first exhalation will rid the tobacco of these unwanted flavors.

Then you are ready to begin smoking. Do so by continuing to rotate the cigar as you take your first few puffs. This will regulate the burn, ensure that it is even and prevent "tunneling," which is when one side of the cigar burns faster than the other. This technique applies to all forms of lighting: matches, cedar strips or lighters.

Some people wonder if a cigar should be relit if it goes out. Even with a perfect lighting job, a cigar may go out occasionally. While smoking a cigar at a rate of one puff a minute can ensure a smooth, cool smoke, sometimes that isn't feasible. You may be on the telephone, or in a conversation with someone, and just forget to keep puffing. If your cigar goes out, by all means, relight it—just use the same caution in lighting it as you would with a fresh cigar. However, be aware that after a couple of relights, a cigar can begin to get harsh.

If you insist on spills or matches, there are a few rules to follow. You may use a candle to light a spill, but never use a candle to light a cigar; wax vapors can ruin its taste. If you're using matches, long ones are preferable. If you use short ones, strike two at one time, let the sulfur burn off and then commence lighting—by using two, you get a broader flame and make it easier to get an even light.

Lighters are the most portable source of fire, and most can be lit with one hand while the other holds the cigar. A good lighter should have a certain heft; some are cut from solid blocks of brass and feel like it. But as important as the weight is the feel in your hand, like a good knife. It should be balanced and fit the size of your palm.

Opening the lighter should be effortless. The cap should swing open smoothly, and the hinge mechanism should be silent. (A hollow or clunky sound can indicate inferior materials.) Once it is opened, the cap should swing fully away from the body of the lighter; otherwise the flame may not be accessible, especially if you're lighting a bigger cigar. The flame should be adjustable, and should be fat, again something that is more important for a cigar smoker than a cigarette smoker. Some cigar lighters actually have two flames.

In the end, the goal is to have a trouble-free light. Since you'll be using it frequently, look for a lighter that feels comfortable and works in all situations including windy ones. If a lighter is not only functional but attractive, you'll be carrying it around like a pocket watch forever.

Storing and Carrying Cigars

Humidors have become almost as popular as cigars. Retailers everywhere remember selling only a few every year; today, they talk about a few a day. There's a simple reason: A well-made humidor is essential to the care and conditioning of a cigar, which by its nature is entirely dependent on the surrounding environment.

A humidor should maintain a cigar at its peak of "smokability." This isn't simple, because a humidor must re-create the tropical or semitropical environment in which most cigar tobacco is grown and where most fine, hand-rolled premium cigars are manufactured and aged. Makeshift tropical environments—like a steamy bathroom or a zippered plas-

Elie Bleu Burl Cabinet humidor.

tic bag with a moist paper towel—don't work well.

A cigar is composed of multiple layers of tobacco. In an inconsistently humid environment like a shower stall, the outside of the cigar will dry once the mist is cut off, but the inside of the cigar will still be damp. The inside "bunch" of tobacco will swell while the wrapper contracts and splits open, destroying your investment.

The most crucial characteristic of a fine humidor is that it provides a consistently tropical environment (about 68-70 degrees Fahrenheit and 70-72 percent humidity) over a long period of time. Remember, this doesn't only mean how often you need to add water to the

humidification system; it also means that 20 years from now the box lid hasn't warped and the hinges still open easily and quietly. Reputable humidor manufacturers include Davidoff, Danny Marshall, Dunhill, Elie Bleu, Michel Perrenoud and Savinelli. Excellent larger humidors, really standing floor cases and even credenza size boxes, are also being made today by manufacturers such as J. Pendergast, Kreitman-Thelan, Vinotemp and others.

The components of a good humidor can be judged easily. Starting from the inside of the box, look for details like perfectly squared and fitted seams. You shouldn't see any glue, and a gap in a joint spells trouble because it provides an exit for moisture, eventually resulting in warping. Cedar is the best wood for the inside of a humidor because of its ability to enhance the aging process. It allows the various tobaccos in a cigar the chance to "marry" so that the cigar is not composed of separate tobacco flavors, but of subtle nuances of taste.

The rim of the box should be constructed uniformly, with tight tolerances, so that the lid closes with the solid feel of a Mercedes Benz car door. An inner lip, especially a lower one, will protect cigars from dry outside air. This is all the more necessary in a box without a lock, because only the weight of the lid will keep it tightly shut. A humidor lid should never close like a safe, however, because if no air were allowed to circulate, musty smells would destroy your cig-

ars. The entire box should be balanced, both when left closed and when opened. (The last thing you want is to have your box tumble off the desk because the lid is too heavy or bounces when lifted.)

Of course, a perfectly constructed box is worthless if it has no means of providing humidity. At one time old apple cores were thought to do this nicely, but modern humidification systems are more reliable. Most humidifiers rely on some variety of sponges, chemical compounds or plain bottles to provide moisture. However, remember that prime cigar aging demands constant humidity levels. Usually, humidor instruction manuals proclaim low maintenance. But once you've prepared the humidor for use—try wiping the interior with a damp cloth before loading it up with cigars—you should rely as much on the "feel" of the cigars inside as on the humidification system. If the cigars feel dry even though the humidity gauge reads 70 percent, you should check the device.

Other practical features, in order of importance, are: a tray, which pro-

Elie Bleu Medal Series humidors.

the surface where it sits. Handles are often helpful additions, especially on larger units.

Keep in mind that in a home or office, a humidor shouldn't overwhelm its surroundings. Deciding where to put your new purchase before buying it might help you find a humidor that will both look good and function well. If you made the right choice, twenty years from now—when your son starts to covet your humidor—you will know for certain that your investment was worthwhile. You didn't buy a mere "box."

Another key question is what to do with cigars when you travel across the country, or across town for a big dinner. The best travel humidors and cigar cases are designed to keep cigars in perfect, smokable condition. Constructed of little more than metal, wood, leather and thread, they are just as simple and refined as what they protect. Do not ignore this parallel truth: your cigars and what you put them in should both be well-conceived products of a basic but nearly flawless design.

Cases, whether telescoping, multifingered, open (without separate cigar dividers), tubular or some combination of the above, should always do at least two things exceptionally well: protect and hold your cigars. The equation is simple—you want whatever cigars you smoke most often to fit easily into your cigar case.

If you smoke a longer cigar, a telescoping case will be necessary. And if

vides the owner the option of storing cigars at more than one level so that they are exposed to varying degrees of humidity (always place parched cigars as far as possible from the humidification device so they will regain humidity slowly, then move them closer to the device); slots or wells drilled into box sides, allowing a unit to breath while preventing separation and warping of veneer; and lid magnets for holding cutting instruments, which are occasionally added to humidors. A hygrometer, while fancy-looking, is seldom accurate even in the most expensive desk-top models.

The appearance of your humidor is entirely up to you. A deep, rich lacquer finish is beautiful and functional and should be judged as you would the finish of a dining-room table. Also, a felt bottom will serve as protection for both the box and

GENE COLEMAN

Ashton leather pocket cigar cases.

you smoke various ring gauges during the course of the same day, avoid fingered cases which are constructed to hold specific ring gauges and will not stretch to hold larger sizes.

If you smoke the same ring gauge consistently, a fingered case is a good bet because it will keep your cigars from rolling around or rubbing against the interior of the case, especially when you get down to the last cigar. Open cases have no safeguards to prevent your cigars from rattling around once you've removed one or two.

If you'll be stowing a two-, three- or four-fingered case in your glove compartment for your drive to and from the office or for weekend jaunts in the country, any good quality case will do. Thick leather, of almost any hide, is tough and will resist the minor jostling caused by potholes and traffic jams.

If upon your arrival at work you're going to remove the case from the car and stow it in your coat pocket, be sure that it will fit. Most four-fingered models are very wide, and unless your chest size and tailor are cooperative, you might look like you're packing a weapon.

Aside from a standard check for stitch quality and uniform construction—with no rough edges showing— picking out a leather case that will

protect your cigars is an easy task. A good case should slide open with minimal effort (test this by putting some of your own cigars into the case), and should be lined, to protect your cigars from leathery aromas and prevent the wrapper leaf from catching on any rough inner hide. Choosing a cigar case is much like buying new shoes: quality (which includes durability), fit, ease of use and style are the most important factors, in that order.

If your travel entails bumping (literally) into strangers, take more care in selecting a case—or consider a wooden or silver tube. Tubes are both bulky and heavy, but they can certainly take more abuse than leather, and they will keep a cigar fresh for up to 72 hours. If you mind the extra weight but still need heavy-duty protection, opt for a telescoping case with very thick leather.

Once you've selected a case or tube suitable for your needs, use it wisely. Slide fresh cigars into your case in the morning, and be sure to remove any unsmoked cigars at night, returning them to storage in your humidor. Most cases will not keep cigars fresh for more than a day. And whatever you do, never store a partially smoked cigar in a case—the aroma will linger, affecting every cigar placed in the case long after this careless mistake.

Unlike cases, travel humidors are too big for local commuting. The smallest models hold five Churchill-size cigars (one more cigar than the largest standard case), and are much too big to fit in a jacket pocket. The advantage to this bulk is that a travel humidor will keep cigars fresh much longer than all pocket-sized cases because it comes with a humidification unit.

Even though a travel humidor is designed for a multiday trip and a case is not, your expectations for both products should be similar. Again, remember the size and shape of your cigars, and be certain that the box will accommodate them. Then inspect the details. Look for features like solid rear hinges, preferably of the "piano" variety, which stretch the length of the box. Also, be certain that the humidification unit inside the box will stay put while you sprint to catch a plane or toss your luggage into the back of a taxicab.

If all goes well, both you and your cigars will arrive in fine condition, ready to smoke away the troubles of an all-too-fast modern age.

PETERSON OF DUBLIN INTRODUCE A NEW RANGE OF HANDMADE CIGARS FROM THE DOMINICAN REPUBLIC

Buying Cigars

In the old days, a tobacconist was like a barber. He knew his clientele. He knew what each customer liked to smoke. And, more often than not, he had the time to discuss everything from the relative pleasures of a Connecticut Shade versus a Cuban seed cigar wrapper, to the World Series or the Presidential race.

Times have changed. Most tobacconists today say they have so many new customers that they don't know any of them very well. And they are always so busy that the time spent with each customer is limited. If you're finding it hard to establish a relationship with a retailer—keep trying. They are still one of the best resources a cigar smoker can have. So take the time to get to know your tobacconist. Make sure that he knows what you like to smoke. Maybe over

DAN WAGNER

44

"Fidel Castro thought I had left Cuba with only the clothes on my back. But my secrets were locked in my heart."

After Fidel Castro came to power, Ramón Cifuentes could no longer make his Partagas® cigars in Cuba. Skilled hands and the Cuban leaf were far too scarce. In contrast, the Dominican Republic now has the Caribbean's finest cigar-makers and richest soil. And only Partagas cigars are still made under the watchful eyes of the same man who made them long ago in Cuba.

PARTAGAS

The cigar that knew Cuba when.

time you'll get lucky; when he receives a shipment of hard-to-get cigars, he might put aside a few for you.

Having a hometown tobacconist doesn't solve the question of what you do when you're on the road. Being in a strange city without cigars can be frustrating. What should you look for when judging whether a tobacconist has his act together?

If you ask a tobacconist for cigars and he shows you into a walk-in humidor where moist air caresses your face, and you almost need a sweater because the temperature is right around 70 degrees, you know you're in the right place. Tobacconists who take the time, trouble and expense to construct a properly humidified environment where cigars are kept in perfect smoking condition are definitely worth the detour. If you are at all in doubt about the storage conditions, ask to pick up a cigar. Feel it. If it is supple and its oils are clearly intact, then you can pretty much rest assured that the cigar you buy will be ready to smoke.

What are some of the trouble signs? First of all, if you are shown a glass counter display case that looks like it's been there forever, be sure to check out the cigars. Some of the humidification units in this type of display case are not very efficient, or they require regular maintenance that they may not always get. The evidence will be in the cigars themselves. Again, there is no substitute for asking to feel a cigar. If you're not allowed to touch, be suspicious.

You may also want to ask about the freshness of the cigars. If the store looks as if it pays more attention to

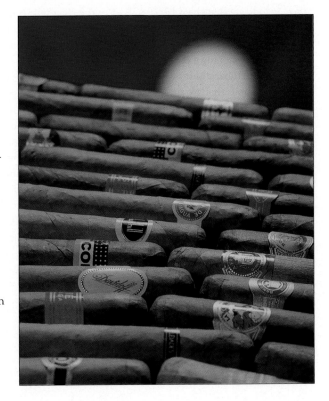

DAN WAGNER

47

gifts and magazines than to smok-
ables, you may not have any idea how
long the cigars in the display case
have been there. A store with heavy
traffic will turn over its inventory
more frequently. In high-volume outlets, even counter-style humidification
units may be completely satisfactory
because consumer demand forces the
owner to pay attention to his cigars.

Some additional factors are
important if you are trying to establish a long-term relationship with a
tobacconist. Is he willing to entertain
your requests for special orders, or
does he insist that you try one of his
"store brands"? The latter phenomenon may indicate that the tobacconist is most interested in selling
what he has in stock. On the other
hand, if you're smoking a particular
brand, and the tobacconist says he
has several brands that are similiar to
your favorite, try them out. You're
likely to get a cigar that you like, and
in the future you'll have an alterna-
tive if for some reason the store runs
out of your preferred smoke.

Today, it's important to find a
tobacconist who is following the cigar
market closely. Because of the boom
in cigar sales in the last few years,

new brands and sizes are coming on
the market monthly. A good tobacconist will know what's available and
what kind of tobacco is being used in
the cigar, and if he or she knows your
preferences, he may be able to recommend some new cigars that suit your
taste.

There's another new factor to
consider in any visit to a retailer.
Around the country, one of the most
common retailer complaints is how
customers treat cigars on the shelf.
Although we do recommend that you
ask to touch cigars, touching does
not require squeezing so hard the
wrapper breaks. A gentle pressure on
the cigar tells you all you need to
know about its condition. You should
also be considerate of the shopper
behind you. You may have seen
tobacco men breathe deeply from the
open foot of a cigar, but don't try it
yourself. First of all, the average consumer doesn't have a clue what he's
smelling for. And if you have the
urge to try the smell test in a retail
environment, think about the guy
coming in after you or the dozens
who've been there before you. It's not
necessary to determine the quality or
condition of the cigar.

When You Find Fonseca, You've Found the Best.

Cognacs and Brandies

Somewhere in the medieval past, a distiller took grapes—the fruit of the vine—and transformed them into a fine distilled spirit. Today, that spirit is known as Cognac when it comes from a small, clearly defined area known by that name in France; Armagnac when it's from the region of that name near Cognac; or simply brandy when it comes from anywhere else.

Cognac is considered the pinnacle of grape brandies. On its label you may find a variety of designations indicating origin, aging and blend. If the town of Cognac is the center of a bull's-eye, then the six areas where grapes for use in Cognac can be grown extend in roughly concentric circles out from the

center. At the center is Grande Champagne, a small area from which the best Cognacs are considered to come. Then there is Petit Champagne, which despite its name is larger than Grande Champagne. The other four

COURTNEY GRANT WINSTON

50

There are three designations which indicate length of aging: V.S., which is aged less than four and a half years; V.S.O.P., is aged more than four and a half years; and X.O., or Napoleon, which indicates Cognacs aged more than six and a half years. After aging, one of the real arts of Cognac comes into play—the blending. A master blender will often use grapes from a variety of regions or sources to arrive at a consistent final product. A designation of "Fine Champagne" means 50 percent of the grapes come from the Grande Champagne. If all the grapes are from either the Grande or Petite Champagne regions, the Cognac label may state this.

areas in descending order of quality are Borderies, Fins Bois, Bons Bois and Boi Communs or Ordinaries.

Today, most Cognac comes from a single grape variety, Ugni Blanc, and after fermentation the grapes go through a double distillation. Then Cognac is aged in French oak barrels.

Some Cognac makers also produce extra special Cognacs with names like Martell Extra, Rémy

BERING GRANDE

THE PERFECT COMPANION
FOR A GOOD MATCH.

THIS IS A FINE HANDMADE, FULL-SIZED (8½" X 52) CIGAR IMPORTED FROM
HONDURAS. EACH CIGAR IS CAREFULLY ROLLED USING ONLY LONG FILLER
TOBACCOS, A NATURAL LEAF BINDER AND CONNECTICUT WRAPPER. THE RESULT
IS A CIGAR WITH AN EASY DRAW AND A ROBUST TASTE. AND, TO SET THESE FINE
NEW CIGARS OFF, THEY COME IN A HINGED, FIFTEEN-COUNT WOODEN BOX.
WITH THE ADDITION OF THE GRANDE, BERINGS NOW COME IN THIRTEEN
POPULAR SHAPES. AVAILABLE AT YOUR FAVORITE TOBACCONIST.

IMPORTED BY SWISHER INTERNATIONAL, INC.

Martin Louis XIII, Hennessey Paradis, Courvoisier Initiale Extra and Hine Triomphe. While all of these contain Cognacs that are aged considerably longer than six and a half years, even up to 70 years in some cases, they are legally bound only to have no Cognac less than six and a half years old. Names of other outstanding producers include Delamain, Frapin, Pierre Ferrand, A.E. Dor, A. de Fussigny, A. Hardy and Louis Royer.

Armagnac is similar to Cognac but only goes through a single distillation. It is considered a bit rougher than Cognac but purists believe it has a truer "grapey" flavor. It is also aged in oak barrels, and unlike Cognac, it can be bottled with a specific vintage date. Some brands to consider are Sempe, Larressingle, Darroze and Marquis de Caussade.

Spanish brandy is also a fine spirit. These brandies use a different grape variety, and are often richer and darker in appearance with a sweeter flavor on the palate. Top brands include Cardenal Mendoza, Lepanto, Duque de Alba and Carlos X.

American brandy has made huge strides in the last 10 years. Two producers, Carneros Alambic and Germain-Robin, are producing pot still products; as the brandies get more barrel aging, they are being blended into top quality products. Recently, Paul Masson also launched an aged brandy into the U.S. market.

The simple grape-based spirits that do not undergo significant barrel aging include grappa, a clear liquid, and various forms of marc, a spirit made from the leftover grape must after the harvest. Grappas are primarily Italian, although some American producers, such as Sebastiani, have been creating fine grappas. They have strong grape flavors, and are clean, striking spirits. In recent years, grappas made from single grape varieties, often with even more pronounced flavors, have arrived on the market.

Cognac, though, is the traditional choice in many countries for the perfect accompaniment to a great cigar. The intensity of the spirit is an especially good match for a robust hand-rolled cigar. Add a cup of coffee, and you have what the French call the "Three C's": Coffee, Cognac and Cigars.

CHAPTER 7

Port

It's almost a standard scene in any Victorian novel or play: the English gentlemen retire to the drawing room for a glass of Port and a cigar. A reflection of the cigar's glowing ember shimmers in the dark, nearly black, liquid in their glasses.

Port is a fortified wine. Port begins like any other wine—on a grapevine. But to be called Port, the vineyards, known as quintas, must be located in Portugal's Upper Douro Valley. The grapes are harvested and then crushed in shallow open concrete containers called lagars or in stainless steel vats. The wines are fermented to about 5 percent alcohol and then brandy is added to bring the solution to about 20 percent alcohol. The fortification process preserves the natural sweetness in the wine.

There are several different types of Port. Vintage Port is designated by the producer or shipper, and is a statement on the overall quality of the vintage. The decision is made in the spring following the second winter of the harvest. For instance, the 1985 vintage was declared in the spring of 1987. The

producers taste the wine frequently. If a vintage is declared, the wines must be aged in wood casks for two years before bottling.

Vintage years are usually declared two or three times a decade, although not all the major houses agree on any single year. In the '60s, vintages were declared in 1960, 1963, 1966 and by a few houses in 1967; the '70s brought 1970, 1975 and 1977 and two houses in 1978; in the '80s, a banner decade, vintages were declared in 1980, 1982, 1983 and 1985. A dry spell of six years followed. Now, both 1991 and 1992 have been declared vintage years.

The top producers of vintage Port are Graham, Fonseca, Taylor and Quinta do Noval, although the latter is better known for its rare Nacional. Other producers include Cockburn, Croft, Dow, Ferreira, Sandeman and Warre. Great Ports can last a lifetime. Ports from the 1963 vintage, for instance, have not reached their peak, and 1955 and 1945 are still drinking marvelously.

If a vintage is not declared, then the fortified wine may be used in

Presenting

THE **Cuesta-Rey** DOMINICAN CABINET SELECTION

Cabinet 8-9-8

Cabinet #2

CUESTA-REY Hand Made REPÚBLICA DOMINICANA

Cabinet #2

'95

Cabinet 8-9-8

Cabinet #1 Hand Made

CUESTA-REY Hand Made REPÚBLICA DOMINICANA

Cabinet #1

CUESTA-REY Hand Made REPÚBLICA DOMINICANA

Cabinet #1

CUESTA-REY Hand Made REPÚBLICA DOMINICANA

1884

...From the cigar maker to the cabinet maker...

"Unsurpassed for Quality and Craftsmanship"

CABINET SIZES

No. 1	8½" x 52
No. 898	7" x 49
No. 2	7" x 36
No. 1884	6¾" x 44
No. 95	6¼" x 42

Natural and Maduro Wrappe

Quinta do Seixo 1983, Offley Boa Vista 1983 and the 1987 and 1991 Taylor Quinta de Vargellas.

In addition, Port producers make tawny Ports that have received even more wood-aging. They are designated as 10-year-old, 20-year-old and 40-year-old, although this refers to the average age of the fortified wines used in the blend, not the absolute age of the blend. They tend to be lighter and show a nuttier, more mature character. Finally,

Ports known as "late bottled vintage" or "vintage character" or saved for nonvintage or tawny Ports. "Late bottled vintage port" carries a vintage date, and receives more barrel-aging before bottling so that it is ready to drink sooner than the classic vintage Port. Most Ports may be blended from the wines of several different vineyards, but single vineyard Ports have also become common on the market. Some of the better ones are Ferreira's

there is the nonvintage Port category, which is much less expensive. It's hard to separate the various designations in this category; some producers call it "ruby Port," others "vintage character." In general, it should have about five years of barrel-aging to smooth it out. Nearly every Port producer makes a nonvintage port, and most cost less than $15 a bottle. Look for Churchill's Finest Reserve, Noval LB and Fonseca Bin 27.

Scotch and Irish Whiskey

I f there is a spirit that "marries" its flavors perfectly with cigars, Scotch is certainly the top candidate. This concoction of water and peat-smoked, malted barley is often redolent of smoky, charcoal-like flavors that go well with a fine cigar.

Most Scotch whisky is blended, often using dozens of fine malt spirits from distinct distilleries that are then blended with neutral grain spirits. The proportion of nonbarley grain spirits in a blended Scotch is a closely guarded secret, often passed down from one family generation or master blender to the next. Blends can vary in taste, and descriptors such as dry, sweet, smooth, smoky, peaty, salty, complex, balanced, clean and soft are used to describe the taste. The exact character of blended Scotch is determined by the barley malt, the

ratio of malt to neutral spirits and the length and type of aging. Some blended Scotch brands include Chivas Regal; Crown Royal; Dewars; J&B; Cutty Sark; Johnnie Walker Red, Black and Blue; White Horse; Grants; Clan MacGregor; Passport and Teacher's.

A real phenomenon in the United States is the rise in popularity of single malt Scotch whiskies.

KENT HANSON

You never know where you'll find our Havana Classico.

Taste the Havana Classico Experience.

Introducing the Havana Classico. A cigar created by a select cache of very experienced Cuban master rollers who consider cigar making an artform. Our **Havana Classicos** are totally hand made, one at a time using traditional Cuban methods that have been passed down through the generations. Each **Havana Classico** is created from a blend of the most distinct tobaccos in the world. The wrapper is grown and aged especially for this cigar. A rich, full bodied masterpiece of unequaled flavor and construction that you expect from Caribbean Cigar Factory, Little Havana, makers of *outstanding* cigars. Give your favorite tobacconist a call and ask for the new definitive Cuban cigar, because you never know where **Havana Classicos** will turn up. For information on where to find **Havana Classicos** call 305-267-3911.

Havana Classico and Caribbean Cigar Factory are registered trademarks of Caribbean Cigar Co. Miami, Florida

Several brands are part of any well-stocked bar today: Glenfiddich, Glenlivet, The Macallan, Highland Park, Glenmorangie, Aberlour, the Dalmore, Cardhu and Laphroaig. A host of others, rarer and harder to find, evoke images of ancient Scotland: Talisker, Lagavulin, Bunnahabhain, Bruichladdich, Oban and Edradour. Single malts differ from blended Scotches in that they are the product of a single distillery, so the inherent character of that distillery shines through. The distillery's home region is also a contributing factor; the big five are Islay, Speyside, Lowlands, Highlands and Campbeltown, and each is considered to have its own distinguishing features. Single malts also exhibit the differences between the two different types of barrels used in aging Scotch: old Sherry barrels or Bourbon barrels. Each imparts its own character, but it is generally agreed that Sherry casks impart a slight sweetness to a Scotch whisky while Bourbon is more neutral.

Irish whiskey also occupies a favorite niche in the world of grain-based spirits. In the United States, the two most widely available are Jameson's and Old Bushmills. Most Irish whiskey is triple-distilled, creating a more neutral-tasting spirit than most Scotch whisky. Also, Old Bushmills is primarily a grain spirit with only a small touch of malt. Recently, Old Bushmills created an all single malt product called Bushmills Malt.

Serious Scotch drinkers, especially single malt aficionados, prefer their beverage neat or at most, on the rocks. But Scotch and water or Scotch and soda are certainly accepted drinks. Given Scotch's popularity in the postwar years, bartenders also created a host of exotic Scotch-based cocktails: Rob Roy (Scotch and sweet vermouth) and Rusty Nail (Scotch and Drambuie) are just two.

But if you're intent on exploring the marriage of peat-smoked barley and a fine hand-rolled cigar, stick to the unadulterated versions.

Rum

Like a great cigar, rum is a child of the tropics. But its origins are at least 3,000 years older. The fermented juice of sugar cane was produced first in Asia, made its way through North Africa to Spain and finally arrived in the New World. It was a barter commodity that helped drive the slave trade and much of commerce in the seventeenth and eighteenth centuries.

The majority of rum is of the clear or white variety. It is the fuel for a host of fun cocktails that starts with rum and cola, moves on through Daiquiris, Planter's Punch and Pina Coladas, and ends with mixtures of just about any fruit juice known to man. Rum is the ultimate mixable.

But in recent years, the world has discovered what Latins have known for centuries: a dark, aged rum offers the same enjoyment and smooth character as an aged Cognac, single malt Scotch or Bourbon. After about

A SOMEWHAT SURPRISING COMPARISON

It may seem a bit presumptuous to compare our moderately priced Don Tomás Special Edition with the legendary Cohiba of Cuba.

On the other hand, think of it this way: Although you may have a few Cohibas hidden away in your humidor, you can't replace them easily. When you do find one, it can arrive with a twenty dollar price tag. But you're a cigar lover. What do you do for that exquisite pleasure everyday? We suggest you try a Don Tomás Special Edition. Rolling a Don Tomás gently between the fingers, we think you will find that it feels very much like the Cohiba. Upon lighting up,

you will be pleasantly surprised at the smoothness of its draw. Don Tomás grows all of our own long leaf tobaccos in the rich soil of Honduras.

As you approach the midpoint of your Don Tomás experience, you will notice the length of ash and the evenness with which it burns. Very much like that of the other cigar.

Now as you lean back into your easy chair, take a sip of single malt scotch, a puff of your Don Tomás and close your eyes, you will experience the satisfaction of a great cigar at a price that's equally satisfying.

DON TOMÁS®
More than an everyday cigar.

COHIBA ESPLENDIDO
(PRICE N/A)

DON TOMÁS S.E.200
(APPROX. $4.50)

five years of aging in charred oak barrels, the natural molasses colors turn amber and golden, and the flavors of maturity—vanilla, nuts, spices—come out on the palate.

Rum begins as molasses, using the by-product that remains after the crystallized sugar has been removed from sugar cane stalk. (There are other methods using cane juice and syrup, but they tend not to produce a product of equal quality.) This fact puts rum producers one step ahead of whiskey or vodka makers; in these grain-based products, starches from the grains must first be transformed into sugar.

The range of fermentation and distillation techniques that follows is remarkably diverse, making the word rum almost impossible to define. Some rum makers use a natural, slow fermentation of up to 12 days; others use a controlled fermentation with a secret yeast that produces results in a couple of days. Some use pot stills, much like Cognac stills, to refine their raw spirits; others use modern column stills that tend to produce cleaner, more neutral spirits.

Rum is then aged in used white-oak Bourbon barrels, with some charring of the insides to add color and flavor to the rum; the length of aging is determined by the maker's taste preferences. Almost all of the so-called aged or dark rums are blends of rums of different ages. United States law requires that any age statement on the label must refer to the youngest rum used in the blend, so a five-year-old rum cannot contain rums with less than five years of aging, but could include rums up to eight or ten years old.

Some of the aged rums available in America are Appleton Estate (Jamaica), Bacardi Añejo and Bacardi Gold Reserve (Puerto Rico), Bermúdez Aniversario (Dominican Republic), Ron Botran (Guatemala), Brugal (Dominican Republic), Flor de Caña (Nicaragua), Gosling's Black Seal (Bermuda), Mount Gay (Barbados), Myers's Rum (Jamaica), Pampero Aniversario (Venezuela) and Zacapa Centenario (Guatemala).

Connoisseurs can often identify rums based on their country of origin. Puerto Rican rums tend to be light. Barbados, Martinique, Nicaragua, Trinindad and the Virgin Islands produce medium-bodied rums. And the rums from Bermuda, Guatemala and Jamaica are usually the heaviest and darkest. The best rums are slow-fermented, distilled in pot stills and aged a long time.

Some professional cigar tasters in the Caribbean use rum to cleanse their palates between cigars. The reason is simple: the flavors and aromas of the tropics enhance the overall experience of smoking a cigar.

DANNEMANN

THE AROMA OF SUCCESS
...a truly international brand.

20 SMALL CIGARS. DANNEMANN

DANNEMANN

MOODS

El noble cigarillo

MOODS.
THE CIGARILLO WITH THE UNIQUE TOBACCO BLEND.

Perhaps the most successful cigarillo launched in Europe in the past decade. Moods is a premium cigarillo with a unique filler blend and rich sumatra wrapper. The Moods blend delivers a smooth taste and an exciting aroma that enhances your surroundings.

DANNEMANN

El noble cigarillo

Bourbon

Bourbon is America's own, a homegrown whiskey that was invented in frontier-era Kentucky. Legend has it that a "white lightning" maker, Elijah Craig, suffered a warehouse fire that charred some of his shipping barrels. He filled them with freshly distilled spirit anyway. When the shipment arrived in New Orleans, the liquid had an amber color and a noticeably softer flavor.

Bourbon is a strictly regulated spirit. To be called Bourbon, it must be made from at least 51 percent corn; most distillers use 65 to 75 percent with a percentage of wheat or other grains often included in the fermentation mash. Bourbon must age a minimum of two years in new white-oak barrels that have

been charred. No additives or colors are permitted. Though Bourbon can be made anywhere in the United States, only that made in Kentucky can have Bourbon on the label. Names like Jim Beam, Heaven Hill, Ancient Age, Early Times, Old Crow, Old Grand-Dad and Wild Turkey are engraved in Bourbon drinkers' minds.

Some other great American

whiskeys aren't called Bourbon, but are made in similar fashion, and often taste very much the same, too. Jack Daniel's and George Dickel are two Tennessee whiskeys. Jack Daniel's differs from Bourbon in that it is charcoal-filtered; its upscale brother, Gentleman Jack, receives two charcoal filterings. Both have a sweeter, smokier taste.

There's been a revolution in Bourbon-making during recent years: small-batch and single-barrel products are the fashion of the day. Most Bourbons are blends of several hundred different barrels that have been aged in huge warehouses and then mixed together to get a uniform taste. But "boutique" Bourbons may be a blend of only 20 barrels, or in several cases, are bottled from only one barrel. They usually carry a premium price, although some, like Maker's Mark, are around $20 in most markets. Other well-known brands are Basil Hayden, Booker's 107, Blanton's, Elijah Craig, Hancock's Reserve, Knob Creek, Rock Hill Farms and

Wild Turkey Rare Breed. You'll also find some "cask-strength" Bourbons in this group; they are bottled straight from the barrel without being cut with water, and the proofs may range up to 126.

Drinking Bourbon, whatever its origin, is a ritual that is as personal as shaving. Some people swear Bourbon should be consumed straight, others say cut with water, others insist that a couple of cubes of ice is all you need. The character of the Bourbon will change depending on the amount of water mixed in; some open up with floral and spice flavors, while others just taste watered down. Try your brand each way, and you'll find the right way for you. As for other drinks, Bourbon and ginger ale and the Whiskey Sour (shaken with sugar and lemon juice) are old favorites. And don't forge the Mint Julep, not really much more than Bourbon poured over cracked ice and mint leaves with a little sugar. Purists, however, reject anything but straight, pure Bourbon in their glass.

CHAPTER 11

Cigar Tasting Notes

Listed By Size *and* Score

I n this section you will find complete descriptions and tasting notes for the 800 cigars rated by *Cigar Aficionado* since its founding in 1992: double coronas, Churchills, corona gordas, lonsdales, coronas, robustos, petit coronas, panatelas, and unusually shaped cigars such as torpedos and pyramids (grouped together in the figurado category here). There is also a separate listing for the dark-wrapped cigars known as maduros. Of course, the cigar's score, arrived at by a panel of senior editors of *Cigar Aficionado* in blind tastings, is also listed here.

All cigars are rated on a 100 point scale. The scoring system is as follows: 95–100 — classic; 90–94 — outstanding; 80–89 — very good to excellent; 70–79 — average to good commercial quality; below 70 — don't waste your money; N/A = Not Available.

A cigar's final score reflects judgments made in four categories:

Appearance and Construction. The cigar is examined for quality of the wrapper and construction. The testers look for things like oiliness, firmness and overall consistency of wrapper color. Bulging veins, excessive spotting, marks and a rough finish are defects.

Smoking Characteristics. The way the cigar burns is evaluated; this includes the evenness of the burn and the color of the ash. The cigar's draw is also judged here.

Flavor. The tasters look for mild-, medium- and full-bodied characteristics. A description is then written about the taste of the cigar, which may include everything from cocoa beans and coffee to wet hay and grass. Spiciness is also a key factor. The "finish," or length of time that the flavors stay in the mouth, is noted as well.

Overall Impression. This is the taster's own opinion based on his summary of the cigar's characteristics.

The guide is formatted in three different ways. Following the tasting notes, you will find a section with the cigars listed by country of origin and then by score within each size category, and then an alphabetical listing by brand.

Cigar Tasting Notes

Listed By Size *and* Score

DOUBLE CORONA

**HOYO DE MONTERREY DOUBLE 96
CORONA**
Cuba
Ring Gauge: 49 • *Length:* 7⅝"
Filler: Cuba • *Binder:* Cuba •
Wrapper: Cuba
An extraordinary full-bodied smoke.
This cigar is filled with cocoa and
coffee bean flavors backed up by
smooth woody and leathery notes. It
has a perfect draw, and a toast-like
aroma.
U.S.: N/A • U.K.: £10.10

RAMON ALLONES GIGANTES 94
Cuba
Ring Gauge: 49 • *Length:* 7⅝"
Filler: Cuba • *Binder:* Cuba •
Wrapper: Cuba
This cigar has a smooth, creamy tex-
ture with strong pepper and spice
notes. It has a sweet, intense, nutty
character on the finish.
U.S.: N/A • U.K.: £9.90

OPUS X DOUBLE CORONA 93
Dominican Republic
Ring Gauge: 49 • *Length:* 7⅝"
Filler: Dom. Rep. • *Binder:* Dom.
Rep. • *Wrapper:* Dom. Rep.

A beautiful reddish-brown wrapper
delivers flavors of spices, leather and
coffee beans. It has a very earthy,
perfumed aroma.
U.S.: $9.00 • U.K.: N/A

CUBA ALIADOS CHURCHILL 92
Honduras
Ring Gauge: 54 • *Length:* 7¼"
Filler: Dom. Rep. • *Binder:* Ecuador
Wrapper: Ecuador
A cigar with a beautiful, dark-brown
wrapper. It has strong flavors of spice
and cocoa beans with solid, earthy
tobacco characteristics. Some incon-
sistency was noted.
U.S.: $3.00 • U.K.: £4.10

DAVIDOFF DOUBLE "R" 92
Dominican Republic
Ring Gauge: 50 • *Length:* 7½"
Filler: Dom. Rep. • *Binder:* Dom.
Rep. • *Wrapper:* U.S.A./Conn.
Shade
This very spicy cigar also has strong
flavors of cedar wood and coffee
beans, and a smooth, creamy finish
that lingers on the palate.
U.S.: $16.50 • U.K.: £19.00

PARTAGAS LUSITANIA 92
Cuba
Ring Gauge: 49 • *Length:* 7 ⅝"
Filler: Cuba • *Binder:* Cuba •
Wrapper: Cuba

A rich, full-bodied cigar that has cedar and leathery flavors with strong hints of chestnuts and cinnamon.
U.S.: N/A • U.K.: £9.90

BELINDA PRIME MINISTER   91
Honduras
Ring Gauge: 50 • *Length:* 7½"
Filler: Dom. Rep., Honduras •
Binder: Honduras • *Wrapper:*
Ecuador
An excellent draw supports this smooth-tasting cigar. It has flavors of spice and nuts, and there is cedar taste that rounds out the solid tobacco core.
U.S.: $2.25 • U.K.: N/A

LA GLORIA CUBANA   91
SOBERANOS
U.S.A.
Ring Gauge: 52 • *Length:* 8"
Filler: Dom. Rep, Nicaragua •
Binder: Dom. Rep. • *Wrapper:*
Ecuador
This cigar has strong flavors of spice and leather, and delivers a smooth, medium-bodied smoke.
U.S.: $2.60 • U.K.: N/A

PUNCH DOUBLE CORONA   91
Cuba
Ring Gauge: 49 • *Length:* 7⅜"
Filler: Cuba • *Binder:* Cuba •
Wrapper: Cuba
This is a strong cigar with excellent tobacco character and a long finish. It has flavors of spice and leather that give it an earthy, almost herbal, complexity.
U.S.: N/A • U.K.: £10.10

LA UNICA NO. 100   90
Dominican Republic
Ring Gauge: 52 • *Length:* 8½"
Filler: Dom. Rep. • *Binder:* Dom. Rep. • *Wrapper:* U.S.A./Conn. Shade

A well-balanced cigar with an earthy character. It has sweet spice flavors like nutmeg and a pleasant nutty component.
U.S.: $2.55 • U.K.: N/A

MACANUDO VINTAGE CABINET   90
SELECTION NO. 1
Jamaica
Ring Gauge: 49 • *Length:* 7½"
Filler: Dom. Rep., Jamaica • *Binder:*
Mexico • *Wrapper:* U.S.A./Conn.
Shade
A medium-bodied smoke with woody, leathery characteristics, and some mild spicy flavors.
U.S.: $8.50 • U.K.: N/A

HOYO DE MONTERREY   89
EXCALIBUR NO. 1
Honduras
Ring Gauge: 54 • *Length:* 7¼"
Filler: Nica., Hon., Dom. Rep. •
Binder: Ecuador • *Wrapper:*
U.S.A./Conn. Shade
A really gorgeous cigar, with a medium-brown wrapper and an oily sheen. It smokes like a dream, with delicious coffee and tobacco flavors and a long, rich finish.
U.S.: $2.80 • U.K.: N/A

PAUL GARMIRIAN P.G.   89
RESERVE GOURMET
Dominican Republic
Ring Gauge: 50 • *Length:* 7⅜"
Filler: Dom. Rep. • *Binder:* Dom. Rep • *Wrapper:* U.S.A./Conn. Shade
This cigar is beautiful, with an oily brown wrapper that smokes at an even, steady pace. The aromas and flavors are reminiscent of coffee and cream, and last for a long time on the palate.
U.S.: $8.60 • U.K.: £7.95

PRIMO DEL REY SOBERANO   **89**
Dominican Republic
Ring Gauge: 50 • *Length:* 7½"
Filler: Dom. Rep. • *Binder:* U.S.A.
Wrapper: Brazil
A solid full-bodied smoke that has
strong elements of coffee, and sweet
spices such as nutmeg that give it a
refined character.
U.S.: $2.50 • U.K.: N/A

ROMEO & JULIETA   **89**
VINTAGE NO. 5
Dominican Republic
Ring Gauge: 50 • *Length:* 7½"
Filler: Dom. Rep. • *Binder:* Mexico
Wrapper: U.S.A./Conn. Shade
A medium-bodied cigar that has a
light nutty character with some fla-
vors of mild sweet spices like nutmeg.
U.S.: $6.50 • U.K.: N/A

DON JUAN PRESIDENTE   **88**
Nicaragua
Ring Gauge: 50 • *Length:* 8½"
Filler: Nicaragua, Dom. Rep. •
Binder: Nicaragua • *Wrapper:*
U.S.A/Connecticut Shade
A mild, smooth cigar. It has sweet fla-
vors of vanilla and cinnamon with
some nuttiness.
U.S.: $2.65 • U.K.: N/A

JOYA DE NICARAGUA   **88**
VIAJANTE
Nicaragua
Ring Gauge: 52 • *Length:* 8½"
Filler: Nicaragua • *Binder:*
Nicaragua • *Wrapper:* Nicaragua
A solid cigar with rich, sweet spice
flavors of cinnamon and chocolate
and a creamy finish.
U.S.: $3.05 • U.K.: N/A

LA GLORIA CUBANA   **88**
CHURCHILL
U.S.A.
Ring Gauge: 50 • *Length:* 7"
Filler: Dom. Rep., Brazil, Mexico •
Binder: Dom. Rep. • *Wrapper:*
Ecuador
Rich and decadent smoke. The wrap-
per is dark brown, with a great sheen.
It is a full-bodied, powerful cigar with
fascinating caramel and chocolate fla-
vors and a mouth-filling texture.
U.S.: $1.75 • U.K.: N/A

OSCAR SUPREME   **88**
Dominican Republic
Ring Gauge: 48 • *Length:* 8"
Filler: Dom. Rep. • *Binder:* Dom.
Rep. • *Wrapper:* U.S.A./Conn.
Shade
This cigar has solid tobacco flavors,
and a steely, mineral characteristic
that is backed up by a solid spiciness.
U.S.: $7.15 • U.K.: £7.50

PAUL GARMIRIAN GOURMET   **88**
DOUBLE CORONA
Dominican Republic
Ring Gauge: 50 • *Length:* 7⅝"
Filler: Dom. Rep. • *Binder:* Dom.
Rep. • *Wrapper:* U.S.A./Conn.
Shade
A very pleasant, attractive, medium-
bodied smoke with mild sweet spice
flavors and a creamy aftertaste.
U.S.: $9.50 • U.K.: £8.95

POR LARRAÑAGA FABULOSO   **88**
Dominican Republic
Ring Gauge: 50 • *Length:* 7"
Filler: Dom. Rep. • *Binder:*
Dom. Rep. • *Wrapper:*
U.S.A./Conn. Shade
A mellow, medium-bodied cigar
that has some earthy elements,
almost flintlike, but with good
solid depth of spicy flavors.
U.S.: $4.50 • U.K.: N/A

SOSA SOBERANO **88**
Dominican Republic
Ring Gauge: 52 • *Length:* 7½"
Filler: Dom. Rep., Brazil • *Binder:*
Honduras • *Wrapper:* Ecuador
A rich, chocolate brown wrapper.
This cigar delivers a very spicy and
nutty smoke, but our tasters noted
some young tobacco that diminished
the cigar's complexity.
U.S.: $2.85 • U.K.: N/A

8-9-8 COLLECTION CHURCHILL **87**
Jamaica
Ring Gauge: 49 • *Length:* 7½"
Filler: Jamaica, Dom. Rep. • *Binder:*
Mexico • *Wrapper:* U.S.A./Conn.
Shade
This is a well-made, mild cigar with a
smooth wrapper and a good draw. It
has a rich taste with some mild spice
and nut flavors.
U.S.: $6.75 • U.K.: N/A

CRUZ REAL CHURCHILL NO.14 **87**
Mexico
Ring Gauge: 50 • *Length:* 7½"
Filler: Mexico • *Binder:* Mexico •
Wrapper: Mexico
A rustic cigar with an easy draw. It is
medium-bodied and has good spicy
aroma and flavors.
U.S.: $3.88 • U.K.: £3.00

DUNHILL PERAVIAS **87**
Dominican Republic
Ring Gauge: 50 • *Length:* 7"
Filler: Dom. Rep., Brazil • *Binder:*
Dom. Rep. • *Wrapper:*
U.S.A./Conn. Shade
This is a very enjoyable cigar with
intriguing leafy, nutty aromas and fla-
vors and a velvety mouth-feel. It
burns extremely well, with a nearly
perfect, even draw.
U.S.: $4.75 • U.K.: £6.30

EL REY DEL MUNDO FLOR **87**
DEL MUNDO
Honduras
Ring Gauge: 54 • *Length:* 7½"
Filler: Dom. Rep, Honduras •
Binder: Honduras • *Wrapper:*
Honduras
Inconsistent. Several tasters had cig-
ars with too tight a draw. It does have
some smooth spicy flavors and a
woody, earthy aftertaste, but may
need more aging.
U.S.: $3.50 • U.K.: N/A

LICENCIADOS PRESIDENTE **87**
Dominican Republic
Ring Gauge: 50 • *Length:* 8"
Filler: Dom. Rep. • *Binder:* Dom.
Rep. • *Wrapper:* U.S.A./Conn.
Shade
This is a good, medium-bodied cigar
with an earthy element that com-
bines with smooth nut and mild
spice flavors.
U.S.: $2.40 • U.K.: N/A

NAT SHERMAN DAKOTA **87**
Dominican Republic
Ring Gauge: 49 • *Length:* 7½"
Filler: Dom. Rep., Mexico • *Binder:*
Mexico • *Wrapper:* Cameroon
A full-bodied cigar that has strong
pepper flavors, and a woody, earthy
character.
U.S.: $4.90 • U.K.: N/A

ROYAL JAMAICA CHURCHILL **87**
Dominican Republic
Ring Gauge: 51 • *Length:* 8"
Filler: Jamaica, Dom. Rep. Indonesia
Binder: Indonesia • *Wrapper:*
Cameroon
An interesting medium-bodied cigar
with a smooth creaminess, and solid
flavors of mild chocolate and spice.
U.S.: $4.60 • U.K.: N/A

SANTA CLARA 1830 NO. 1   **87**
Mexico
Ring Gauge: 52 • *Length:* 7½"
Filler: Mexico • *Binder:* Mexico •
Wrapper: Mexico
A straightforward, medium-bodied
cigar with flavors of mild spices and a
bit of nuttiness.
U.S.: $2.50 • U.K.: £4.00

THOMAS HINDS HONDURAN   **87**
SELECTION PRESIDENTE
Honduras
Ring Gauge: 52 • *Length:* 8½"
Filler: Honduras • *Binder:*
Honduras • *Wrapper:* Ecuador
A brownish-green wrapper offers a
rather firm draw. It has mild, smooth
flavors of creamy spice and a solid
tobacco core.
U.S.: $4.30 • U.K.: N/A

ASHTON AGED MADURO   **86**
NO. 60
Dominican Republic
Ring Gauge: 52 • *Length:* 7½"
Filler: Dom. Rep. • *Binder:* Dom.
Rep. • *Wrapper:* U.S.A./Conn.
Broadleaf
This maduro-style cigar has a mild,
smooth character with a backbone of
sweet spices and pepper.
U.S.: $5.00 • U.K.: N/A

BAUZA FABULOSO   **86**
Dominican Republic
Ring Gauge: 50 • *Length:* 7½"
Filler: Dom. Rep., Nicaragua •
Binder: Mexico • *Wrapper:*
Cameroon
A smooth-tasting cigar with some
exotic floral aromas and flavors. It has
some unusual herbal, earthy tones on
the palate.
U.S.: $2.55 • U.K.: N/A

DON LINO HABANO RESERVE   **86**
Honduras
Ring Gauge: 50 • *Length:* 7½"
Filler: Honduras • *Binder:*
Honduras • *Wrapper:*
U.S.A./Conn. Shade
This is a smooth-tasting cigar with
some perfumed aromas, but with a
slightly dry, straw-like finish.
U.S.: $5.35 • U.K.: N/A

NAT SHERMAN TRIBUNE   **86**
Dominican Republic
Ring Gauge: 50 • *Length:* 7½"
Filler: Dom. Rep. • *Binder:* Dom.
Rep. • *Wrapper:* Mexico
This maduro cigar offers plenty of
sweet spice flavors, and some choco-
late and chocolate elements. It is
medium-bodied with a rich finish.
U.S.: $4.35 • U.K.: N/A

PARTAGAS NO. 10   **86**
Dominican Republic
Ring Gauge: 49 • *Length:* 7½"
Filler: Dom. Rep., Mexico • *Binder:*
Mexico • *Wrapper:* Cameroon
A mild cigar with spicy, dry woody
flavors. It also has some solid tobacco
notes.
U.S.: $4.00 • U.K.: N/A

PETRUS DOUBLE CORONA   **86**
HAVANA
Honduras
Ring Gauge: 50 • *Length:* 7¾"
Filler: Honduras • *Binder:*
Honduras • *Wrapper:* Honduras
Young tobacco may have affected this
cigar. It has good flavors of spice, nuts
and coffee, but it was a little rough.
U.S.: $4.25 • U.K.: N/A

ENGLAND

98

JOHN COURAGE
PREMIUM AMBER LAGER

RING GAUGE: 470
LENGTH: 8"
FILLER: ONLY THE BEST
BINDER - GLASS
WRAPPER - PAPER AND FOIL

A well-made, full-bodied amber lager with a crisp, bold flavor. The finish is pleasant, made even more so by the prompt ordering of another bottle.

John Courage is proudly served at many cigar-friendly restaurants. Ask for it.

TAKE COURAGE. THE ORIGINAL AMBER SINCE 1787.

ZINO VERITAS   **86**
Honduras
Ring Gauge: 50 • *Length:* 7"
Filler: Honduras • *Binder:*
Honduras • *Wrapper:* Honduras
This cigar has a lovely medium-
brown wrapper with an oily texture.
It is medium-bodied with flavors of
nutmeg and chocolate and a delicious
aftertaste.
U.S.: $6.40 • U.K.: N/A

ASHTON CHURCHILL   **85**
Dominican Republic
Ring Gauge: 50 • *Length:* 7½"
Filler: Dom. Rep. • *Binder:* Dom.
Rep. • *Wrapper:* U.S.A./Conn.
Shade
This is delicate and light, with lovely
creamy and floral flavors, and a
refreshing aftertaste. An attractive
afternoon cigar.
U.S.: $3.25 • U.K.: N/A

CUESTA-REY DOMINICAN   **85**
No. 2
Dominican Republic
Ring Gauge: 48 • *Length:* 7¼"
Filler: Dom. Rep. • *Binder:* Dom.
Rep. • *Wrapper:* U.S.A./Conn.
Shade
This cigar is finished a bit roughly,
and it has a dry, sandy taste with a
woody, grassy finish.
U.S.: $2.75 • U.K.: £4.25

DON LINO CHURCHILL   **85**
Honduras
Ring Gauge: 50 • *Length:* 8"
Filler: Dom. Rep. • *Binder:* Dom.
Rep. • *Wrapper:* U.S.A./Conn. Shade
This is a very light-wrapped cigar
with a nice creamy nuttiness and
some solid tobacco flavors.
U.S.: $2.65 • U.K.: N/A

EL RICO HABANO   **85**
GRAN HABANERO
U.S.A.
Ring Gauge: 50 • *Length:* 7¾"
Filler: Dom. Rep., Nica., Hon., Ecu.
Binder: Dom. Rep. • *Wrapper:*
Ecuador
A superbly constructed cigar, the El
Rico double corona burns beautifully
and is a joy to smoke. It is medium-
bodied with mild, lovely spicy flavors
and a long aftertaste.
U.S.: $1.80 • U.K.: N/A

EL SUBLIMADO CHURCHILL   **85**
Dominican Republic
Ring Gauge: 50 • *Length:* 8"
Filler: Dom. Rep. • *Binder:* Dom.
Rep. • *Wrapper:* U.S.A./Conn.
Shade
This cigar has a medium body, and
some spicy flavors, but an unusual
and pleasant perfumed, herbal taste.
U.S.: $12.00 • U.K.: N/A

JOSE BENITO PRESIDENTE   **85**
Dominican Republic
Ring Gauge: 50 • *Length:* 7¼"
Filler: Dom. Rep. • *Binder:* Central
America • *Wrapper:* Cameroon
This is a rich-tasting, medium-bodied
cigar that has some creamy coffee fla-
vors and a core of spiciness.
U.S.: $3.60 • U.K.: N/A

LA FINCA BOLIVARES   **85**
Nicaragua
Ring Gauge: 50 • *Length:* 7½"
Filler: Nicaragua • *Binder:*
Nicaragua • *Wrapper:* Nicaragua
This cigar burned a little hot, but it
has some pepper and nutmeg flavors,
with a rustic edge to them.
U.S.: $2.00 • U.K.: N/A

LA HOJA SELECTA COSIAC **85**
U.S.A.
Ring Gauge: 49 • *Length:* 7"
Filler: Dom. Rep., Nicaragua •
Binder: Dom. Rep. • *Wrapper:*
U.S.A./Conn. Shade
This is a wonderfully constructed
cigar, with an attractive medium-
brown wrapper. It is mild with pretty,
nutty flavors and a slightly bitter
aftertaste.
U.S.: $1.95 • U.K.: N/A

MACANUDO PRINCE PHILIP **85**
Jamaica
Ring Gauge: 49 • *Length:* 7½"
Filler: Dom. Rep., Jamaica • *Binder:*
Mexico • *Wrapper:* U.S.A./Conn.
Shade
This cigar seemed to have some
immature tobacco. It was a little sour,
but with some nice wood and nut
flavors.
U.S.: $4.00 • U.K.: N/A

PLEIADES ALDEBARAN **85**
Dominican Republic
Ring Gauge: 50 • *Length:* 8½"
Filler: Dom. Rep. • *Binder:* Dom.
Rep. • *Wrapper:* U.S.A./Conn.
Shade
This is a mild cigar with light, creamy
tobacco character, and some mild
spicy flavors.
U.S.: $10.06 • U.K.: N/A

PUNCH DIADEMAS **85**
Honduras
Ring Gauge: 50 • *Length:* 7½"
Filler: Hon., Nica., Dom. Rep. •
Binder: Ecuador • *Wrapper:*
Ecuador
A very good-looking cigar with a
smooth finish and fine texture. The
Diademas smokes steady and easy,
with light, grassy, earthy flavors and a
slightly bitter finish.
U.S.: $3.40 • U.K.: N/A

PUNCH CHATEAU L **85**
Honduras
Ring Gauge: 52 • *Length:* 7½"
Filler: Honduras • *Binder:*
Honduras • *Wrapper:* Honduras
A dark-brown wrapper. It has rich,
spicy flavors with solid cocoa bean
notes, but there is a woodsy-earthy
tone that detracts in this cigar.
U.S.: $2.90 • U.K.: N/A

THE GRIFFIN'S PRESTIGE **85**
Dominican Republic
Ring Gauge: 48 • *Length:* 8"
Filler: Dom. Rep. • *Binder:* Dom.
Rep. • *Wrapper:* U.S.A./Conn.
Shade
A cigar with some solid tobacco char-
acteristics and some spiciness but also
with vegetal flavors that detract.
U.S.: $5.45 • U.K.: N/A

AVO NO. 3 **84**
Dominican Republic
Ring Gauge: 52 • *Length:* 7½"
Filler: Dom. Rep. • *Binder:* Dom.
Rep. • *Wrapper:* U.S.A./Conn.
Shade
This is a cigar with a dry taste on the
finish, but some nutty, mild spice fla-
vors.
U.S.: $6.25 • U.K.: N/A

CASA BLANCA PRESIDENTE **84**
Dominican Republic
Ring Gauge: 50 • *Length:* 7½"
Filler: Dom. Rep. • *Binder:* Mexico
Wrapper: U.S.A./Conn. Shade
A very mild cigar with a solid grassy,
dry paper character, but it has a light
creamy finish.
U.S.: $2.15 • U.K.: N/A

DON LINO COLORADO 84
Honduras
Ring Gauge: 50 • *Length:* 7½"
Filler: Honduras, Nicaragua •
Binder: Honduras • *Wrapper:*
U.S.A./Conn. Shade
A very mild, light cigar with some
sweet, dry aromas and flavors.
U.S.: $8.00 • U.K.: N/A

JOYA DE NICARAGUA 83
CHURCHILL
Nicaragua
Ring Gauge: 49 • *Length:* 6⅞"
Filler: Nicaragua • *Binder:*
Nicaragua • *Wrapper:* Nicaragua
This is not the most complex cigar,
but it has plenty of flavor. The medi-
um-brown wrapper with a slightly
rough finish is a little underfilled.
Nonetheless, it shows a nutty, coffee
character and lovely, velvety texture.
U.S.: $2.20 • U.K.: £3.00

LA FONTANA MICHELANGELO 83
Honduras
Ring Gauge: 52 • *Length:* 7½"
Filler: Honduras • *Binder:* Mexico
Wrapper: U.S.A./Conn. Shade
This is a very loosely filled cigar with
a hot draw. It has dry, straw-like fla-
vors and a very dry, papery finish.
U.S.: $3.15 • U.K.: N/A

LEON JIMENES NO. 1 83
Dominican Republic
Ring Gauge: 50 • *Length:* 7½"
Filler: Dom. Rep. • *Binder:* Dom.
Rep. • *Wrapper:* U.S.A./Conn.
Shade
A very light, mellow smoke with
some creamy, mild spice flavors but a
flat, neutral finish.
U.S.: $5.50 • U.K.: N/A

ROMEO & JULIETA 83
CHURCHILL
Dominican Republic
Ring Gauge: 50 • *Length:* 7"
Filler: Brazil, Dom. Rep. • *Binder:*
U.S.A./Conn. Broadleaf • *Wrapper:*
Cameroon
This cigar has interesting earthy, rich
flavors, but it is a little overfilled and
hard. While smoking, it has nutty,
coffee, earthy aromas and flavors with
a long aftertaste.
U.S.: $2.30 • U.K.: N/A

ROYAL JAMAICA 83
GIANT CORONA
Dominican Republic
Ring Gauge: 49 • *Length:* 7½"
Filler: Jamaica • *Binder:* Java •
Wrapper: Cameroon
This cigar is lovely to look at with a
fine, medium-brown wrapper and firm
construction. Lots of walnut and cof-
fee character.
U.S.: $3.10 • U.K.: £7.00

V CENTENNIAL PRESIDENTE 83
Honduras
Ring Gauge: 50 • *Length:* 8"
Filler: Dom. Rep., Honduras,
Nicaragua • *Binder:* Mexico •
Wrapper: U.S.A./Conn. Shade
A mild cigar with a rough, light-
brown wrapper. It has a grassy, dry
paper taste with a hint of spice.
U.S.: $5.75 • U.K.: N/A

VUELTABAJO GIGANTE 83
Dominican Republic
Ring Gauge: 52 • *Length:* 8½"
Filler: Dom. Rep. • *Binder:* Dom.
Rep. • *Wrapper:* U.S.A./Conn. Shade
This mild cigar has very simple light
flavors that tend toward dry wood
and paper; has some sour notes.
U.S.: $2.75 • U.K.: N/A

TE-AMO CHURCHILL   **82**
Mexico
Ring Gauge: 50 • *Length:* 7½"
Filler: Mexico • *Binder:* Mexico •
Wrapper: Mexico
An extremely mild cigar with a very
hot, loose draw that has grassy and
vegetal flavors.
U.S.: $3.05 • U.K.: N/A

TROYA EXECUTIVE NO. 72   **82**
Dominican Republic
Ring Gauge: 50 • *Length:* 7¼"
Filler: Dom. Rep. • *Binder:* Dom.
Rep. • *Wrapper:* U.S.A./Conn.
Shade
A mild cigar with a very yellow-
brown wrapper. It is medium-bodied
with some creamy flavors. A very
simple smoke.
U.S.: $3.70 • U.K.: N/A

EL RICO HABANO   **80**
GRAN HABANERO DELUXE
U.S.A.
Ring Gauge: 50 • *Length:* 7¼"
Filler: Nicaragua, Ecuador, Dom. Rep.
Binder: Dom. Rep. • *Wrapper:*
Ecuador
A medium-bodied cigar with decent,
earthy flavor, but it lacks complexity.
U.S.: $2.35 • U.K.: N/A

BACCARAT CHURCHILL   **79**
Honduras
Ring Gauge: 50 • *Length:* 7"
Filler: Honduras • *Binder:* Mexico
Wrapper: U.S.A./Conn. Shade
Rather unusual in style, the Baccarat
has light chocolate and tobacco fla-
vors although its sweet wrapper may
not be to everyone's liking. It is well-
constructed and extremely firm.
U.S.: $1.75 • U.K.: N/A

CHURCHILL

ROMEO Y JULIETA CHURCHILL   **92**
Cuba
Ring Gauge: 47 • *Length:* 7"
Filler: Cuba • *Binder:* Cuba •
Wrapper: Cuba
This remains the benchmark Cuban
Churchill. It is filled with a deep, rich
spiciness and strong cocoa bean fla-
vors, and has a lingering rich finish.
U.S.: N/A • U.K.: £9.70

PUNCH CHURCHILL   **91**
Cuba
Ring Gauge: 47 • *Length:* 7"
Filler: Cuba • *Binder:* Cuba •
Wrapper: Cuba
A very smooth, full-bodied cigar with
a rich earthiness, flavors of leather
and sweet spices like nutmeg, and a
pleasing woody finish.
U.S.: N/A • U.K.: £9.70

BOLIVAR CORONA GIGANTES   **90**
Cuba
Ring Gauge: 47 • *Length:* 7"
Filler: Cuba • *Binder:* Cuba •
Wrapper: Cuba
A cigar filled with spices, including
cinnamon and nutmeg, and a pleas-
ant sweetness that finishes in a com-
plex earthiness.
U.S.: N/A • U.K.: £9.70

DON JUAN CHURCHILL   **90**
Nicaragua
Ring Gauge: 49 • *Length:* 7"
Filler: Nicaragua • *Binder:* Dom.
Rep. • *Wrapper:* Nicaragua
A very smooth-tasting cigar with fla-
vors of toasts and nuts and a strong
spicy tobacco finish with a nutmeg
quality.
U.S.: $2.30 • U.K.: N/A

QUAI D'ORSAY IMPERIALES 90
Cuba
Ring Gauge: 47 • *Length:* 7"
Filler: Cuba • *Binder:* Cuba •
Wrapper: Cuba
A rich-tasting cigar with toasted
bread and cinnamon flavors and a lin-
gering finish.
U.S.: N/A • France: 54.90FF

ARTURO FUENTE 89
DOUBLE CHATEAU
Dominican Republic
Ring Gauge: 50 • *Length:* 6¾"
Filler: Dom. Rep. • *Binder:* Dom.
Rep. • *Wrapper:* U.S.A./Conn.
Shade
A beautifully made cigar with an
even brown color and good draw. It
has medium- to full-bodied quality
with pepper and spice flavors and a
slightly dry finish.
U.S.: $2.65 • U.K.: N/A

ARTURO FUENTE CHURCHILL 89
Dominican Republic
Ring Gauge: 48 • *Length:* 7¼"
Filler: Dom. Rep. • *Binder:* Dom.
Rep. • *Wrapper:* Cameroon
A rich, medium-bodied cigar with a
solid, sweet spiciness and a strong
component of coffee beans that fin-
ishes just a touch dry.
U.S.: $2.50 • U.K.: N/A

COHIBA ESPLENDIDOS 89
Cuba
Ring Gauge: 47 • *Length:* 7"
Filler: Cuba • *Binder:* Cuba •
Wrapper: Cuba
A full-bodied cigar with fruity, black
cherry-like notes, and a woody spici-
ness on the palate. A firm, almost
tough draw.
U.S.: N/A • U.K.: £17.60

CUBA ALIADOS VALENTINO 89
NO. 1
Honduras
Ring Gauge: 47 • *Length:* 7"
Filler: Honduras, Dom. Rep. •
Binder: Honduras, Dom. Rep. •
Wrapper: Ecuador
This medium-bodied cigar has rich,
flavorful character with a smooth,
toasty texture and includes a spiciness
and a cedar-box quality.
U.S.: $2.95 • U.K.: N/A

FLOR DE CANO DIADEMAS 89
Cuba
Ring Gauge: 47 • *Length:* 7"
Filler: Cuba • *Binder:* Cuba •
Wrapper: Cuba
A full-bodied cigar with an earthy
character, and a full range of leather
and sweet spice flavors like nutmeg.
U.S.: N/A • U.K.: £9.70

MONTECRISTO CHURCHILL 89
Dominican Republic
Ring Gauge: 48 • *Length:* 7"
Filler: Dom. Rep. • *Binder:* Dom.
Rep. • *Wrapper:* U.S.A./Conn.
Shade
A very well-made medium-bodied
cigar with a creamy character, flavor
notes of leather and light spices, and
a toasted butter finish.
U.S.: $6.95 • U.K.: N/A

PARTAGAS NO. 10 89
Dominican Republic
Ring Gauge: 49 • *Length:* 7½"
Filler: Dom. Rep., Mexico • *Binder:*
Mexico • *Wrapper:* Cameroon
A well-made cigar with a solid
medium-bodied smoke. It has nutty
flavors around a very spicy core and a
nice coffee-bean finish.
U.S.: $4.25 • U.K.: N/A

SAINT LUIS REY CHURCHILL **89**
Cuba
Ring Gauge: 47 • *Length:* 7"
Filler: Cuba • *Binder:* Cuba •
Wrapper: Cuba
This is a powerful cigar with a rich cocoa bean character and a touch of leather and nuts, but with a short finish.
U.S.: N/A • U.K.: £9.00

8-9-8 COLLECTION CHURCHILL **88**
Jamaica
Ring Gauge: 49 • *Length:* 7½"
Filler: Jamaica, Dom. Rep. • *Binder:* Mexico • *Wrapper:* U.S.A./Conn. Shade
A well-made cigar with a some fruit notes on the palate, and a nice spiciness with an elegant finish.
U.S.: $6.75 • U.K.: N/A

DIANA SILVIUS CHURCHILL **88**
Dominican Republic
Ring Gauge: 50 • *Length:* 7"
Filler: Dom. Rep. • *Binder:* Dom. Rep. • *Wrapper:* U.S.A./Conn. Shade
A medium-bodied cigar with a spicy, peppery flavor and a long spicy finish. Some inconsistency.
U.S.: $5.80 • U.K.: N/A

HOYO DE MONTERREY **88**
CHURCHILL
Cuba
Ring Gauge: 47 • *Length:* 7"
Filler: Cuba • *Binder:* Cuba •
Wrapper: Cuba
This cigar has some exotic spice flavors including nutmeg and cinnamon, but it has a dry finish.
U.S.: N/A • U.K.: £9.70

JUAN CLEMENTE CHURCHILL **88**
Dominican Republic
Ring Gauge: 46 • *Length:* 6⅛"
Filler: Dom. Rep. • *Binder:* Dom. Rep. • *Wrapper:* U.S.A./Conn. Shade
This is a rich-tasting but medium-bodied cigar with earthy flavors and a decent spicy character.
U.S.: $4.90 • U.K.: N/A

LA UNICA NO. 200 **88**
Dominican Republic
Ring Gauge: 49 • *Length:* 7"
Filler: Dom. Rep. • *Binder:* Dom. Rep. • *Wrapper:* U.S.A./Conn. Shade
A nice medium-bodied cigar with complex flavors including nuts, sweet spices and black pepper.
U.S.: $2.40 • U.K.: £4.00

LOS LIBERTADORES MAMBISE **88**
Dominican Republic
Ring Gauge: 48 • *Length:* 6⅞"
Filler: Dom. Rep. • *Binder:* Dom. Rep. • *Wrapper:* U.S.A./Conn. Shade
A mild- to medium-bodied cigar with a light woody spiciness, and some espresso coffee bean on an otherwise woody finish.
U.S.: $6.95 • U.K.: N/A

MONTECRUZ SUN GROWN **88**
NO. 200
Dominican Republic
Ring Gauge: 46 • *Length:* 7¼"
Filler: Dom. Rep., Brazil • *Binder:* Dom. Rep. • *Wrapper:* Indonesia
A well-made cigar with some leather notes and earthy complexity and a smooth, creamy finish.
U.S.: $3.70 • U.K.: N/A

NAT SHERMAN EXCHANGE SELECTION OXFORD NO. 5   88
Dominican Republic
Ring Gauge: 49 • *Length:* 7"
Filler: Dom. Rep., Mexico, Jamaica •
Binder: Mexican • *Wrapper:*
U.S.A./Conn. Shade
This is a good solid cigar with some
earthiness, spicy flavors and a nice
woody finish.
U.S.: $5.85 • U.K.: N/A

OLOR COLOSSOS   88
Dominican Republic
Ring Gauge: 48 • *Length:* 7½"
Filler: Dom. Rep. • *Binder:* Dom.
Rep. • *Wrapper:* U.S.A./Conn.
Shade
A spicy cigar with a very nice silky
pepper quality that otherwise leads
into a fairly neutral finish.
U.S.: $2.60 • U.K.: N/A

SAVINELLI E.L.R. CHURCHILL   88
Dominican Republic
Ring Gauge: 48 • *Length:* 7¼"
Filler: Dom. Rep. • *Binder:* Dom.
Rep. • *Wrapper:* U.S.A./Conn.
Shade
A medium-bodied cigar with a
smooth nutty character and a creamy
texture that leads into a soft spicy fin-
ish.
U.S.: $7.50 • U.K.: N/A

SOSA CHURCHILL   88
Dominican Republic
Ring Gauge: 49 • *Length:* 6¹⁵⁄₁₆"
Filler: Dom. Rep. • *Binder:*
Honduras • *Wrapper:* Ecuador
This is a spicy and pepper-tasting
cigar with hints of mild cocoa flavors
that end up with a nutty, but slightly
dry finish.
U.S.: $2.85 • U.K.: N/A

THOMAS HINDS HONDURAN CHURCHILL   88
Honduras
Ring Gauge: 49 • *Length:* 7"
Filler: Honduras • *Binder:*
Honduras • *Wrapper:* Ecuador
This is a well-made cigar with a rich
spiciness that has a bit of young tobac-
co, but is a solid tasting cigar.
U.S.: $3.45 • Canada: $3.85

AVO NO. 5   87
Dominican Republic
Ring Gauge: 46 • *Length:* 6¼"
Filler: Dom. Rep. • *Binder:* Dom.
Rep. • *Wrapper:* U.S.A./Conn.
Shade
An elegant smoke with a rich, spicy
component that includes flavors of
nutmeg and other sweet spices. A
slightly dry finish.
U.S.: $6.05 • U.K.: N/A

CARRINGTON NO. 5   87
Dominican Republic
Ring Gauge: 46 • *Length:* 6⅛"
Filler: Dom. Rep. • *Binder:* Dom.
Rep. • *Wrapper:* U.S.A./Conn.
Shade
A mild- to medium-bodied cigar with
a solid core of spice, and a good toasty
flavor.
U.S.: $4.20 • U.K.: N/A

EL REY DEL MUNDO TAINOS   87
Cuba
Ring Gauge: 47 • *Length:* 7"
Filler: Cuba • *Binder:* Cuba •
Wrapper: Cuba
Uneven construction hurts this sim-
ple, mild cigar with a grassy taste and
a light spicy finish.
U.S.: N/A • U.K.: £8.36

NAT SHERMAN DAKOTA   **87**
Dominican Republic
Ring Gauge: 49 • *Length:* 7½"
Filler: Jam., Mex., Dom. Rep. •
Binder: Mexico • *Wrapper:*
Cameroon
This uncomplicated cigar with a
medium-brown wrapper delivers a
taste of dark-roasted coffee and a mild
spiciness.
U.S.: $4.30 • U.K.: N/A

NAT SHERMAN GOTHAM   **87**
SELECTION NO. 500
Dominican Republic
Ring Gauge: 50 • *Length:* 7"
Filler: Dom. Rep. • *Binder:* Dom.
Rep. • *Wrapper:* U.S.A./Conn.
Shade
A pleasant medium- to full-bodied
cigar with a good spiciness on the
palate and an earthy creaminess on
the finish.
U.S.: $6.35 • U.K.: N/A

POR LARRAÑAGA FABULOSO   **87**
Dominican Republic
Ring Gauge: 50 • *Length:* 7"
Filler: Dom. Rep. • *Binder:*
Dom. Rep. • *Wrapper:*
U.S.A./Conn. Shade
A smooth and creamy cigar
with a good balance and a core
of spice and coffee notes that
finishes with a slightly dry wood
and earth taste.
U.S.: $4.50 • U.K.: N/A

PUNCH GRAN CRU MONARCH   **87**
Honduras
Ring Gauge: 48 • *Length:* 6¾"
Filler: Nicaragua, Dom. Rep. •
Binder: U.S.A./Conn. Broadleaf •
Wrapper: Ecuador, Honduras
An attractive cigar with a light floral
character, but several tasters noted a
hot, slightly harsh finish.
U.S.: $5.00 • U.K.: N/A

SANTA ROSA CHURCHILL   **87**
Honduras
Ring Gauge: 49 • *Length:* 7"
Filler: Nicaragua, Honduras, Dom.
Rep. • *Binder:* Nicaragua •
Wrapper: U.S.A. Shade
A good, solid medium-bodied cigar
with a spicy core of flavors, a smooth
texture and a spicy finish.
U.S.: $2.90 • U.K.: N/A

V CENTENNIAL CHURCHILL   **87**
Honduras
Ring Gauge: 48 • *Length:* 7"
Filler: Dom. Rep, Honduras,
Nicaragua • *Binder:* Mexico •
Wrapper: U.S.A./Conn. Shade
A medium-bodied cigar that has a
solid spicy core and an overall
smooth, creamy character with a
cedar wood finish.
U.S.: $5.25 • U.K.: N/A

ASHTON PRIME MINISTER   **86**
Dominican Republic
Ring Gauge: 48 • *Length:* 6⅛"
Filler: Dom. Rep. • *Binder:* Dom.
Rep. • *Wrapper:* U.S.A./Conn.
Shade
An elegant cigar that looks as good as
it tastes. It has creamy coffee flavors
and a mild spicy finish laced with
white pepper.
U.S.: $3.10 • U.K.: N/A

AVO XO MAESTOSO   **86**
Dominican Republic
Ring Gauge: 48 • *Length:* 7"
Filler: Dom. Rep. • *Binder:* Dom.
Rep. • *Wrapper:* U.S.A./Conn.
Shade
A medium-bodied cigar that has mild
flavors of nuts, leather backed up by a
bit of spiciness.
U.S.: $8.80 • U.K.: N/A

CACIQUE NO. 7   86
Dominican Republic
Ring Gauge: 46 • *Length:* 6⅛"
Filler: Dom. Rep. • *Binder:* Dom.
Rep. • *Wrapper:* U.S.A./Conn.
Shade
A medium-bodied cigar with some
pleasant, toasty notes, and an earthy
quality of woods and mushrooms.
U.S.: $2.60 • U.K.: N/A

CUESTA-REY CABINET 8-9-8   86
Dominican Republic
Ring Gauge: 49 • *Length:* 7"
Filler: Dom. Rep. • *Binder:* Dom.
Rep. • *Wrapper:* U.S.A./Conn.
Shade
This is a nice, medium-bodied smoke
with some nutty flavors and a slightly
dry, woody finish.
U.S.: $2.50 • U.K.: £5.50

DAVIDOFF ANIVERSARIO NO. 2   86
Dominican Republic
Ring Gauge: 48 • *Length:* 7"
Filler: Dom. Rep. • *Binder:* Dom.
Rep. • *Wrapper:* U.S.A./Conn.
Shade
This cigar offers up a range of cream
and nut flavors and a firm draw, but it
has a bit of sourness on the finish.
U.S.: $14.10 • U.K.: £15.40

DON DIEGO MONARCH   86
Dominican Republic
Ring Gauge: 47 • *Length:* 7¼
Filler: Dom. Rep. • *Binder:* Dom.
Rep. • *Wrapper:* U.S.A./Conn.
Shade
This mellow, straightforward cigar has
a beautiful dark-brown wrapper and
rich flavors of mild coffee and nuts.
U.S.: $3.40 • U.K.: N/A

DUNHILL CABRERAS   86
Dominican Republic
Ring Gauge: 48 • *Length:* 7"
Filler: Dom. Rep., Brazil • *Binder:*
Dom. Rep. • *Wrapper:*
U.S.A./Conn. Shade
This is a mild, creamy cigar with a
mild coffee flavor and a smooth char-
acter overall. It has a mild finish.
U.S.: $6.30 • U.K.: N/A

EL REY DEL MUNDO DOUBLE   86
CORONA
Honduras
Ring Gauge: 48 • *Length:* 7"
Filler: Honduras, Dom. Rep. •
Binder: Honduras • *Wrapper:*
Ecuador
A medium-bodied cigar. It has a
strong woody component with a bal-
ance of coffee-like flavors.
U.S.: $3.00 • U.K.: N/A

FONSECA 10-10   86
Dominican Republic
Ring Gauge: 50 • *Length:* 7"
Filler: Dom. Rep. • *Binder:* Mexico
Wrapper: U.S.A./Conn. Shade
This is a medium-bodied cigar with
smooth flavors that include cream
and sweet nuts, but with a somewhat
tight draw.
U.S.: $4.25 • U.K.: N/A

JOSÉ MARTI MARTI   86
Dominican Republic
Ring Gauge: 50 • *Length:* 7¼"
Filler: Dom. Rep. • *Binder:* Dom.
Rep. • *Wrapper:* U.S.A./Conn.
Shade
This is a mild- to medium-bodied
cigar. It has some light spiciness, an
overall woody character and a dry
finish.
U.S.: $3.00 • U.K.: N/A

LA RESERVA NO. 2   **86**
Honduras
Ring Gauge: 48 • *Length:* 6½"
Filler: Dom. Rep., Honduras •
Binder: Ecuador • *Wrapper:*
U.S.A./Conn. Shade
A straightforward, smooth-smoking
cigar with an attractive dark-brown
wrapper. It has ample mild spice and
pepper flavors.
U.S.: $2.75 • U.K.: N/A

LEMPIRA CHURCHILL   **86**
Honduras
Ring Gauge: 48 • *Length:* 7"
Filler: Honduras, Dom. Rep. •
Binder: Honduras • *Wrapper:*
U.S.A./Conn. Shade
A cigar with good balance and a
smooth taste backed up by spice and
pepper flavors.
U.S.: $3.25 • U.K.: N/A

LEON JIMENES NO. 2   **86**
Dominican Republic
Ring Gauge: 47 • *Length:* 7"
Filler: Dom. Rep. • *Binder:* Dom.
Rep. • *Wrapper:* U.S.A./Conn.
Shade
A cigar with a firm draw and a very
pronounced nutty taste that opens up
to a solid tobacco flavor.
U.S.: $4.25 • U.K.: N/A

MONTESINO GRAN CORONA   **86**
Dominican Republic
Ring Gauge: 48 • *Length:* 6¼"
Filler: Dom. Rep., Brazil • *Binder:*
Dom. Rep. • *Wrapper:*
U.S.A./Conn. Sun-Grown
This well-made, light-bodied cigar
comes on quickly with a mild creami-
ness, but overall it is slightly grassy
and has a tangy finish.
U.S.: $1.85 • U.K.: N/A

PUNCH DOUBLE CORONA   **86**
Honduras
Ring Gauge: 48 • *Length:* 6¾"
Filler: Nicaragua, Honduras, Dom.
Rep. • *Binder:* Ecuador •
Wrapper: U.S.A./Conn. Shade
A mild, middle-of-the-road cigar with
a creamy smooth smoke and tastes of
nuts and spices.
U.S.: $2.20 • U.K.: N/A

TROYA NO. 63   **86**
Dominican Republic
Ring Gauge: 46 • *Length:* 6⅛"
Filler: Dom. Rep. • *Binder:* Dom.
Rep. • *Wrapper:* U.S.A./Conn.
Shade
A very nicely balanced, medium-bod-
ied smoke with a firm draw, earthy
aroma and a mix of flavors including
toast and sweet spices.
U.S.: $2.85 • U.K.: N/A

ZINO VERITAS   **86**
Honduras
Ring Gauge: 50 • *Length:* 7"
Filler: Honduras • *Binder:*
Honduras • *Wrapper:* Honduras
An attractive cigar with a floral
aroma and flavor notes of spice and
leather on the palate that extend into
the finish.
U.S.: $7.10 • U.K.: N/A

BACCARAT CHURCHILL   **85**
Honduras
Ring Gauge: 50 • *Length:* 7"
Filler: Honduras • *Binder:* Mexico
Wrapper: Honduras
Despite a touch of sweet gum on the
wrapper, this cigar still has solid
tobacco flavors, a bit of spice and a
nice tanginess.
U.S.: $2.05 • U.K.: N/A

BANCES CORONA INMENSA   **85**
Honduras
Ring Gauge: 48 • *Length:* 6¼"
Filler: Honduras, Dom. Rep.
Nicaragua • *Binder:* Honduras •
Wrapper: Ecuador
This is a spicy cigar with a solid core
of earthy flavors that end up with a
slightly dry finish.
U.S.: $2.55 • U.K.: N/A

CABALLEROS CHURCHILL   **85**
Dominican Republic
Ring Gauge: 50 • *Length:* 7"
Filler: Dom. Rep. • *Binder:* Dom.
Rep. • *Wrapper:* U.S.A./Conn.
Shade
A cigar with strong herbal notes and
a smooth balance with a creamy char-
acter and a fairly spicy finish.
U.S.: $3.50 • U.K.: N/A

CAMACHO CHURCHILL   **85**
Honduras
Ring Gauge: 48 • *Length:* 7"
Filler: Honduras • *Binder:*
Honduras • *Wrapper:* Honduras
A cigar with a fine floral aroma, and
flavors of toasts and nuts, but with a
fairly flat, dry finish.
U.S.: $2.75 • U.K.: N/A

EL RICO HABANO   **85**
DOUBLE CORONA
U.S.A.
Ring Gauge: 47 • *Length:* 7"
Filler: Dom. Rep., Ecuador, Nicaragua
Binder: Ecuador • *Wrapper:*
Ecuador
This oily, dark-brown wrapper gives a
full-bodied smoke with an earthy
aroma. It has some spice but also has
a youthful harshness.
U.S.: $2.35 • U.K.: N/A

JOYA DE NICARAGUA   **85**
CHURCHILL
Nicaragua
Ring Gauge: 49 • *Length:* 6⅞"
Filler: Nicaragua • *Binder:*
Nicaragua • *Wrapper:* Nicaragua
Showed some inconsistency, but it
has a nice spicy character with a
nutty aroma and a slightly dry finish.
U.S.: $2.40 • U.K.: N/A

LOS LIBERTADORES   **85**
RESERVE SPECIAL CHURCHILL
Dominican Republic
Ring Gauge: 49 • *Length:* 6⅞"
Filler: Dom. Rep. • *Binder:* Dom.
Rep. • *Wrapper:* U.S.A./Conn.
Shade
This cigar tastes of young tobacco,
but has a nice creaminess and a touch
of pepper on a dry finish.
U.S.: $7.20 • U.K.: N/A

MACANUDO VINTAGE NO. 1   **85**
Jamaica
Ring Gauge: 49 • *Length:* 7½"
Filler: Jamaica, Dom. Rep. Mexico •
Binder: Mexico • *Wrapper:*
U.S.A./Conn. Shade
This is a well-made, medium-bodied
cigar with some flavors of nuts and a
light spiciness.
U.S.: $8.75 • U.K.: N/A

MAYA CHURCHILL   **85**
Honduras
Ring Gauge: 49 • *Length:* 6⅞"
Filler: Honduras, Dom. Rep. •
Binder: Honduras • *Wrapper:*
U.S.A./Conn. Shade
This mild cigar has a nice woody fin-
ish that comes out of good, solid,
nutty flavors.
U.S.: $2.50 • U.K.: N/A

ONYX 646   **85**
Dominican Republic
Ring Gauge: 46 • *Length:* 6⅛"
Filler: Dom. Rep., Mexico • *Binder:*
Indonesia • *Wrapper:* Mexico
A maduro cigar with roasted nut and
coffee bean flavors that finishes with
sweet spice notes.
U.S.: $2.30 • U.K.: N/A

PRIMO DEL REY ARISTOCRAT   **85**
Dominican Republic
Ring Gauge: 48 • *Length:* 6¼"
Filler: Dom. Rep., Mexico, Brazil •
Binder: Indonesia • *Wrapper:*
U.S.A./Conn. Shade
A rustic-looking cigar. It is a medium-
bodied smoke with creamy, dark cof-
fee flavors.
U.S.: $1.70 • U.K.: N/A

PUNCH CHATEAU L   **85**
Honduras
Ring Gauge: 54 • *Length:* 7¼"
Filler: Honduras, Nicaragua, Dom.
Rep. • *Binder:* Honduras •
Wrapper: Ecuador
This cigar has a good draw with a
nice rich spicy taste, and a slightly
woody finish.
U.S.: $3.05 • U.K.: N/A

RAMON ALLONES REDONDOS   **85**
Dominican Republic
Ring Gauge: 49 • *Length:* 7½"
Filler: Dom. Rep., Mexico • *Binder:*
Mexico • *Wrapper:* Cameroon
This is a well-balanced cigar with a
toasty character and a nice solid spici-
ness on the palate.
U.S.: $3.95 • U.K.: N/A

ROMEO & JULIETA   **85**
VINTAGE NO. 4
Dominican Republic
Ring Gauge: 48 • *Length:* 7"
Filler: Dom. Rep. • *Binder:* Mexico
Wrapper: U.S.A./Conn. Shade

This is a nice, mild cigar that has
some mild spice and coffee flavors,
but with a slightly dry finish.
U.S.: $6.00 • U.K.: N/A

ASHTON CHURCHILL   **84**
Dominican Republic
Ring Gauge: 52 • *Length:* 7½"
Filler: Dom. Rep. • *Binder:* Dom.
Rep. • *Wrapper:* U.S.A./Conn.
Shade
This is a very well-made mild cigar
that has some spicy flavors but with
some young tobacco tastes.
U.S.: $4.50 • U.K.: N/A

ASHTON PRIME MINISTER   **84**
Dominican Republic
Ring Gauge: 48 • *Length:* 7"
Filler: Dom. Rep. • *Binder:* Dom.
Rep. • *Wrapper:* U.S.A./Conn.
Shade
A nice-looking cigar with a touch of
spice and dried fruit, but has a flinty
finish, and the bite of young tobacco.
U.S.: $3.90 • U.K.: N/A

BACCARAT CHURCHILL   **84**
Honduras
Ring Gauge: 48 • *Length:* 7
Filler: Honduras • *Binder:* Mexico
Wrapper: Honduras/Conn. Shade
A cigar for smokers who like a sweet-
ened wrapper. It is a mild smoke with
light tobacco flavors and a mild after-
taste.
U.S.: $1.75 • U.K.: N/A

BAUZA CASA GRANDE   **84**
Dominican Republic
Ring Gauge: 48 • *Length:* 6¼
Filler: Dom. Rep., Nicaragua •
Binder: Mexico • *Wrapper:*
Cameroon

A well-made cigar that has a sweetish tobacco character with some sweet spices, but shows some young tobacco notes.
U.S.: $2.75 • U.K.: N/A

CREDO MAGNIFICAT 84
Dominican Republic
Ring Gauge: 46 • *Length:* 6⅛"
Filler: Dom. Rep. • *Binder:* Dom. Rep. • *Wrapper:* U.S.A./Conn. Shade
A well-made cigar that suffers somewhat from young tobacco. A bit raw but with some solid flavors of nuts and wood on the palate.
U.S.: $4.95 • U.K.: N/A

CUBA ALIADOS CHURCHILL EXTRA 84
Honduras
Ring Gauge: 54 • *Length:* 7¼"
Filler: Dom. Rep • *Binder:* Ecuador
Wrapper: Ecuador
This cigar has a very firm draw and a cedary character. Overall, it lacks depth and complexity.
U.S.: $3.25 • U.K.: £4.30

CUESTA-REY DOMINICAN NO. 2 84
Dominican Republic
Ring Gauge: 48 • *Length:* 7¼"
Filler: Dom. Rep. • *Binder:* Dom. Rep. • *Wrapper:* U.S.A./Conn. Shade
A nice, light, spicy cigar with some nuttiness. It shows a bit of youth with a slightly green wood finish.
U.S.: $2.95 • U.K.: £6.20

DON JUAN CHURCHILL 84
Nicaragua
Ring Gauge: 46 • *Length:* 7"
Filler: Nicaragua • *Binder:* Nicaragua • *Wrapper:* Nicaragua
A medium-bodied cigar with very light, creamy and grassy flavors.
U.S.: $1.50 • U.K.: N/A

H. UPMANN MONARCH 84
Dominican Republic
Ring Gauge: 47 • *Length:* 7"
Filler: Dom. Rep. • *Binder:* Dom. Rep. • *Wrapper:* Indonesia
This cigar has a rough wrapper and a firm draw. It has a slightly sour taste with a core of spicy and nutty flavors.
U.S.: $4.00 • U.K.: N/A

HABANA GOLD CHURCHILL 84
Honduras
Ring Gauge: 46 • *Length:* 7½"
Filler: Nicaragua, Honduras • *Binder:* Nicaragua • *Wrapper:* Ecuador
This easy-drawing cigar has some spice on the palate and a flinty finish that ends a bit dry.
U.S.: $5.00 • U.K.: N/A

JOSE BENITO CHURCHILL 84
Dominican Republic
Ring Gauge: 50 • *Length:* 7"
Filler: Dom. Rep. • *Binder:* Central America • *Wrapper:* Cameroon
A nice, medium-bodied cigar with a floral aroma, and a sweet tobacco character with good balance.
U.S.: $2.85 • U.K.: N/A

LA AURORA BRISTOL ESPECIAL 84
Dominican Republic
Ring Gauge: 48 • *Length:* 6⅜"
Filler: Dom. Rep. • *Binder:* Dom. Rep. • *Wrapper:* Cameroon
A slightly tight, mild cigar with a pleasant earthy quality and some nutty flavors. Some inconsistency noted.
U.S.: $2.10 • U.K.: N/A

LA FONTANA DA VINCI 84
Honduras
Ring Gauge: 48 • *Length:* 6⅛
Filler: Honduras • *Binder:* Honduras • *Wrapper:* U.S.A./Conn. Shade
This cigar's sweet wrapper isn't for everybody, but it is a well-made, light,

mild smoke with a slightly grassy and creamy flavor.
U.S.: $2.25 • U.K.: N/A

SANTA DAMIANA CABINET SELECTION NO. 800   84
Dominican Republic
Ring Gauge: 50 • *Length:* 7"
Filler: Dom. Rep. • *Binder:* Dom. Rep. • *Wrapper:* U.S.A./Conn. Shade
A pleasant mild- to medium-bodied cigar with a creamy, smooth character and flavors of nuts, with a touch of spice and a dry finish.
U.S.: $8.00 • U.K.: N/A

TE-AMO PRESIDENTE   84
Mexico
Ring Gauge: 50 • *Length:* 7"
Filler: Mexico • *Binder:* Mexico • *Wrapper:* Mexico
A distinct, peppery cigar with a mineral-like finish.
U.S.: $2.90 • U.K.: N/A

TEMPLE HALL 700   84
Jamaica
Ring Gauge: 49 • *Length:* 7½"
Filler: Jamaica, Dom. Rep., Mexico • *Binder:* Mexico • *Wrapper:* Cameroon
This is a pleasant, mild- to medium-bodied cigar with a touch of spice and vanilla.
U.S.: $5.50 • U.K.: N/A

HOYO DE MONTERREY DOUBLE CORONA   83
Honduras
Ring Gauge: 48 • *Length:* 6¾"
Filler: Honduras, Nicaragua, Dom. Rep. • *Binder:* Honduras • *Wrapper:* Ecuador
An oily wrapper with some strong spicy elements and a creamy character with slightly dry finish.
U.S.: $2.50 • U.K.: N/A

LAS CABRILLAS DESOTO   83
Honduras
Ring Gauge: 50 • *Length:* 6⅛"
Filler: Mexico, Nicaragua • *Binder:* Mexico • *Wrapper:* U.S.A./Conn. Shade
A smooth-tasting cigar with a good balance of creaminess and a soft, leathery taste.
U.S.: $1.85 • U.K.: N/A

MACANUDO PRINCE PHILIP   83
Jamaica
Ring Gauge: 49 • *Length:* 7½"
Filler: Jamaica, Dom. Rep., Mexico • *Binder:* Mexico • *Wrapper:* U.S.A./Conn. Shade
A mild cigar with an earthy quality and a creamy texture.
U.S.: $4.20 • U.K.: N/A

PRIMO DEL REY CLUB SELECCION REGAL   83
Dominican Republic
Ring Gauge: 50 • *Length:* 7"
Filler: Dom. Rep. • *Binder:* Dom. Rep. • *Wrapper:* U.S.A./Conn. Shade
Inconsistency noted. This cigar had some good spicy character but also had a dry, slightly papery finish.
U.S.: $2.10 • U.K.: N/A

ROYAL JAMAICA GIANT CORONA   83
Dominican Republic
Ring Gauge: 49 • *Length:* 7½"
Filler: Dom. Rep., Jamaica, Sumatra • *Binder:* Cameroon • *Wrapper:* Indonesia
This cigar showed some tightness in the draw and had a sweet nut flavor and a mild coffee bean finish.
U.S.: $3.70 • U.K.: N/A

SANTA DAMIANA
SELECCION NO. 100   **83**
Dominican Republic
Ring Gauge: 48 • *Length:* 6¼"
Filler: Dom. Rep. • *Binder:* Dom.
Rep. • *Wrapper:* U.S.A./Conn.
Shade
A cigar with some cedary compo-
nents. Overall it has a dry, woody
character.
U.S.: $7.00 • U.K.: N/A

TRESADO SELECCION NO. 200   **83**
Dominican Republic
Ring Gauge: 48 • *Length:* 7"
Filler: Dom. Rep. • *Binder:*
Cameroon • *Wrapper:* Indonesia
A mild, smooth cigar with a floral
character and a woody finish.
U.S.: $1.85 • U.K.: N/A

VUELTABAJO CHURCHILL   **83**
Dominican Republic
Ring Gauge: 48 • *Length:* 7"
Filler: Dom. Rep. • *Binder:* Dom.
Rep. • *Wrapper:* U.S.A./Conn.
Shade
A medium-bodied cigar with a
smooth, nutty character and a pleas-
ing, mildly earthy finish.
U.S.: $2.80 • U.K.: N/A

CUBITA 2000   **82**
Dominican Republic
Ring Gauge: 50 • *Length:* 7"
Filler: Dom. Rep. • *Binder:* Dom.
Rep. • *Wrapper:* U.S.A./Conn.
Shade
While this cigar is well-made, it
begins with a sharp peppery taste that
turns into a sweetish flavor.
U.S.: $5.00 • U.K.: N/A

HOYO DE MONTERREY   **82**
EXCALIBUR BANQUET
Honduras
Ring Gauge: 48 • *Length:* 6¼"
Filler: Nicaragua, Honduras, Dom.
Rep. • *Binder:* Honduras •
Wrapper: U.S.A./Conn. Shade
Showed inconsistency. This cigar has
a mild spiciness but was hampered by
apparently young tobacco and a
slightly hot finish.
U.S.: $5.55 • U.K.: £5.29

HOYO DE MONTERREY SULTAN   **82**
Honduras
Ring Gauge: 54 • *Length:* 7¼"
Filler: Honduras, Nicaragua, Dom.
Rep. • *Binder:* Honduras •
Wrapper: Ecuador
This medium- to full-bodied cigar has
some spiciness, but is dominated by
dry, balsa-wood flavors that have a
faint vegetal quality.
U.S.: $3.05 • U.K.: N/A

PAUL GARMIRIAN CHURCHILL   **82**
Dominican Republic
Ring Gauge: 48 • *Length:* 7"
Filler: Dom. Rep. • *Binder:* Dom.
Rep • *Wrapper:* U.S.A./Conn.
Shade
This medium-bodied cigar has a very
mild, spicy note, but ends up with a
relatively flat finish.
U.S.: $8.00 • U.K.: £7.90

PETRUS CHURCHILL   **82**
Honduras
Ring Gauge: 50 • *Length:* 7"
Filler: Honduras • *Binder:*
Honduras • *Wrapper:* Ecuador
A fairly rough-looking cigar with
some nut and mild spice notes, and a
dry, woody finish.
U.S.: $3.50 • U.K.: £7.50

PRIMO DEL REY SOBERANOS   82
Dominican Republic
Ring Gauge: 50 • *Length:* 7½"
Filler: Dom. Rep. • *Binder:* U.S.A.
Wrapper: Indonesia
A mild cigar with some nutty flavors,
but an inconsistent construction and
an unattractive wrapper.
U.S.: $2.50 • U.K.: N/A

PUNCH GRAN CRU DIADEMAS   82
Honduras
Ring Gauge: 54 • *Length:* 7¼"
Filler: Honduras, Nicaragua, Dom.
Rep • *Binder:* Honduras •
Wrapper: Ecuador
This cigar has some peppery and spicy
notes, but ends on the vegetal side
with a dry finish.
U.S.: $4.05 • U.K.: N/A

PLEIADES SIRIUS   81
Dominican Republic
Ring Gauge: 46 • *Length:* 6⅛"
Filler: Dom. Rep. • *Binder:* Dom.
Rep. • *Wrapper:* U.S.A./Conn.
Shade
This cigar had draw problems. It
also had very dry flavors including
orange peel, and a touch of spice on
the finish.
U.S.: $5.25 • U.K.: N/A

PRIMO DEL REY ARISTOCRAT   81
Dominican Republic
Ring Gauge: 48 • *Length:* 6¼"
Filler: Dom. Rep. • *Binder:* Dom.
Rep. • *Wrapper:* U.S.A./Conn. Shade
A veiny, rough wrapper produces
slightly dried out flavors that hint at
cocoa beans, with a sharp finish.
U.S.: $1.95 • U.K.: N/A

PUNCH DOUBLE CORONA   81
Honduras
Ring Gauge: 48 • *Length:* 6¼"
Filler: Honduras, Nicaragua, Dom.
Rep. • *Binder:* Honduras •
Wrapper: Ecuador
This cigar has some coffee and pepper
flavors, but ends with a neutral, flat taste.
U.S.: $2.50 • U.K.: N/A

HOYO DE MONTERREY   80
EXCALIBUR NO. 1
Honduras
Ring Gauge: 54 • *Length:* 7¼"
Filler: Honduras, Nicaragua, Dom.
Rep • *Binder:* Honduras •
Wrapper: U.S.A./Conn. Shade
This cigar had an unusual flower-like
aroma, a very grassy flavor element
and a dry finish.
U.S.: $3.40 • U.K.: £3.80

ORNELAS CHURCHILL   79
Mexico
Ring Gauge: 49 • *Length:* 7"
Filler: Mexico • *Binder:* Mexico •
Wrapper: Mexico
An unusually green wrapper. It has
some sweet tobacco quality but shows
evidence of young tobacco, and an
overall vegetal quality.
U.S.: $5.00 • U.K.: N/A

SANTA CLARA 1830 NO. 2   78
Mexico
Ring Gauge: 48 • *Length:* 6½"
Filler: Mexico • *Binder:* Mexico •
Wrapper: Mexico
This cigar has an extremely rough,
sandpapery wrapper. It also has a very
dry character, with a balsa-wood fla-
vor and a papery finish.
U.S.: $2.20 • U.K.: £3.50

CORONA GORDA

LICENCIADOS TORO   **93**
Dominican Republic
Ring Gauge: 50 • *Length:* 6"
Filler: Dom. Rep. • *Binder:*
Honduras • *Wrapper:*
U.S.A./Conn. Shade
This is a medium-bodied cigar packed
with flavors of nuts, coffee and a solid
cedar finish. It is very well-made with
a beautiful dark-brown wrapper.
U.S.: $1.70 • U.K.: N/A

HOYO DE MONTERREY   **92**
EPICURE NO. 1
Cuba
Ring Gauge: 46 • *Length:* 5¼"
Filler: Cuba • *Binder:* Cuba •
Wrapper: Cuba
A well-made, full-bodied cigar with
chocolate and coffee flavors. A solid,
spicy smoke with a long finish.
U.S.: N/A • U.K.: £7.12

ROMEO Y JULIETA   **91**
EXHIBICION NO. 3
Cuba
Ring Gauge: 46 • *Length:* 5½"
Filler: Cuba • *Binder:* Cuba •
Wrapper: Cuba
A full-bodied cigar loaded with cocoa
bean and nut aromas and complex,
spicy flavors. It has a rich finish.
U.S.: N/A • U.K.: £6.64

BELINDA CABINET   **89**
Honduras
Ring Gauge: 45 • *Length:* 5⅝"
Filler: Dom. Rep., Honduras •
Binder: Honduras • *Wrapper:*
Ecuador
An attractive, medium-bodied cigar
with a smooth spiciness and a creamy
coffee flavor.
U.S.: $1.65 • U.K.: N/A

COHIBA SIGLO IV   **89**
Cuba
Ring Gauge: 46 • *Length:* 6"
Filler: Cuba • *Binder:* Cuba •
Wrapper: Cuba
This full-bodied cigar has rich flavors
of dark chocolate and a leathery spici-
ness, but a tough draw limits it.
U.S.: N/A • U.K.: £9.68

HOYO DE MONTERREY   **89**
EXCALIBUR NO. 3
Honduras
Ring Gauge: 50 • *Length:* 6¼"
Filler: Honduras • *Binder:*
Honduras • *Wrapper:*
U.S.A./Conn. Shade
A good, solid smoke with toasty aro-
mas and nice flavors of coffee and
roasted nuts that finish on a cedary
note.
U.S.: $2.80 • U.K.: £4.00

PUNCH PUNCH   **89**
Cuba
Ring Gauge: 46 • *Length:* 5½"
Filler: Cuba • *Binder:* Cuba •
Wrapper: Cuba
Inconsistent. A full-bodied cigar with
nutty, spicy, flowery flavors. But tight-
ness and a short aftertaste hurt this
cigar.
U.S.: N/A • U.K.: £6.64

SOSA GOVERNOR   **89**
Dominican Republic
Ring Gauge: 50 • *Length:* 6"
Filler: Brazil, Dom. Rep. • *Binder:*
Honduras • *Wrapper:* Ecuador
This cigar has a dark-brown wrapper
with plenty of spicy, chocolaty notes,
and a smooth, medium body.
U.S.: $2.45 • U.K.: N/A

AVO NO. 2   88
Dominican Republic
Ring Gauge: 50 • *Length:* 6"
Filler: Dom. Rep. • *Binder:* Dom.
Rep. • *Wrapper:* U.S.A./Conn.
Shade
A simple, well-made cigar with nut-
meg and cedary flavors and a nice,
medium-length finish.
U.S.: $5.50 • U.K.: N/A

H. UPMANN MAGNUM   88
Cuba
Ring Gauge: 46 • *Length:* 5½"
Filler: Cuba • *Binder:* Cuba •
Wrapper: Cuba
A cigar with plenty of nuts and spici-
ness on the palate, with a clean, lin-
gering tobacco aftertaste.
U.S.: N/A • U.K.: £7.04

MACANUDO HYDE PARK   88
Jamaica
Ring Gauge: 49 • *Length:* 5½"
Filler: Mex., Jam., Dom. Rep. •
Binder: Mexico • *Wrapper:*
U.S.A./Conn. Shade
A mild, medium-bodied cigar with
smooth, creamy flavors.
U.S.: $3.20 • U.K.: N/A

PARTAGAS LIMITED   88
RESERVE REGALE
Dominican Republic
Ring Gauge: 47 • *Length:* 6¼"
Filler: Mex., Jam., Dom. Rep. •
Binder: Mexico • *Wrapper:*
Cameroon
A well-made cigar that has a solid
tobacco core with mild, spicy flavors
and finish.
U.S.: $8.50 • U.K.: N/A

CASA BLANCA DELUXE   87
Dominican Republic
Ring Gauge: 50 • *Length:* 6"
Filler: Dom. Rep. • *Binder:* Mexico
Wrapper: U.S.A./Conn. Shade

A somewhat spicy, solid cigar with
creamy, peppery flavors on the palate
and a nice, long finish.
U.S.: $1.70 • U.K.: £3.00

CUBA ALIADOS NO. 4   87
Honduras
Ring Gauge: 46 • *Length:* 5½"
Filler: Dom. Rep., Brazil • *Binder:*
Ecuador • *Wrapper:*
Ecuador/Sumatra
A smooth-tasting cigar with some
herbal and earthy flavors and a mild,
spicy undertone.
U.S.: $2.00 • U.K.: N/A

DUNHILL CONDADO   87
Dominican Republic
Ring Gauge: 48 • *Length:* 6"
Filler: Dom. Rep. • *Binder:* Dom.
Rep. • *Wrapper:* U.S.A./Conn.
Shade
A nice, brownish-yellow wrapper
with slightly rough construction, but
it has light coffee and spice flavors.
U.S.: $4.05 • U.K.: £5.25

LA GLORIA CUBANA EXTRA   87
U.S.A.
Ring Gauge: 46 • *Length:* 6¼"
Filler: Dom. Rep., Nica. • *Binder:*
Nicaragua • *Wrapper:* Ecuador
A toasty, floral aroma with a solid
pepper-spice core of flavors that give
character to this full-bodied cigar.
U.S.: $1.75 • U.K.: N/A

MACANUDO VINTAGE NO. 5   87
Jamaica
Ring Gauge: 49 • *Length:* 5½"
Filler: Jam., Mex., Dom. Rep. •
Binder: Mexico • *Wrapper:*
U.S.A./Conn. Shade
A well-made smoke with creamy,
smooth tobacco flavors.
U.S.: $7.00 • U.K.: N/A

ONYX NO. 650   **87**
Dominican Republic
Ring Gauge: 50 • *Length:* 6"
Filler: Dom. Rep., Mexico • *Binder:*
Indonesia • *Wrapper:* Mexico
A medium-bodied cigar with a
maduro-style wrapper. The Onyx has
solid flavors of chocolate and an even
burn.
U.S.: $2.35 • U.K.: N/A

OSCAR NO. 500   **87**
Dominican Republic
Ring Gauge: 50 • *Length:* 5½"
Filler: Dom. Rep. • *Binder:* Dom.
Rep. • *Wrapper:* U.S.A./Conn.
Shade
A well-made cigar with a good draw.
The Oscar has roasted coffee-bean
flavors and a rich, cedary finish.
U.S.: $6.15 • U.K.: £5.30

PARTAGAS ALMIRANTE   **87**
Dominican Republic
Ring Gauge: 47 • *Length:* 6¼"
Filler: Jam., Dom. Rep., Mex. •
Binder: Mexico • *Wrapper:*
Cameroon
A flavorful cigar with a medium-bod-
ied spiciness. It has a slightly dry finish.
U.S.: $3.40 • U.K.: N/A

ROMEO & JULIETA   **87**
VINTAGE NO. 2
Dominican Republic
Ring Gauge: 46 • *Length:* 6"
Filler: Dom. Rep. • *Binder:* Mexico
Wrapper: U.S.A./Conn. Shade
This is a medium-bodied cigar that
has solid tobacco flavors and hints of
cedar and coffee.
U.S.: $4.75 • U.K.: N/A

ROYAL JAMAICA DIRECTOR   **87**
Dominican Republic
Ring Gauge: 45 • *Length:* 6"
Filler: Jamaica • *Binder:* Indonesia
Wrapper: Cameroon

This cigar has straightforward flavors
of cedar and herbs, with a medium-
length finish.
U.S.: $3.10 • U.K.: N/A

SANTA ROSA TORO   **87**
Honduras
Ring Gauge: 50 • *Length:* 6"
Filler: Honduras • *Binder:*
Honduras • *Wrapper:* Honduras
A well-made, spicy cigar with inter-
esting chocolate and cedar flavors
and a smooth finish.
U.S.: $3.00 • U.K.: N/A

ARTURO FUENTE 8-5-8   **86**
Dominican Republic
Ring Gauge: 47 • *Length:* 6"
Filler: Dom. Rep. • *Binder:* Dom.
Rep. • *Wrapper:* Cameroon
This is an attractive, dark-wrapped
cigar with some sweet, spicy flavors,
but it finishes a bit dry and woody.
U.S.: $1.90 • U.K.: N/A

DON TOMAS CORONA   **86**
Honduras
Ring Gauge: 50 • *Length:* 5½"
Filler: Honduras • *Binder:*
Honduras • *Wrapper:* Honduras
A nice brown wrapper on a cigar that
has pleasant cinnamon-spice and
cedar flavors with a smooth aftertaste.
U.S.: $1.90 • U.K.: N/A

NAT SHERMAN CARNEGIE   **86**
Dominican Republic
Ring Gauge: 48 • *Length:* 6"
Filler: Dom. Rep. • *Binder:* Dom.
Rep. • *Wrapper:* U.S.A./Conn.
Shade
An earthy cigar with solid spice and
roasted coffee-bean flavors. It burns
well and has a good draw.
U.S.: $4.40 • U.K.: N/A

NAT SHERMAN GOTHAM   **86**
SELECTION NO. 711
Dominican Republic
Ring Gauge: 50 • *Length:* 7"
Filler: Dom. Rep. • *Binder:* Dom.
Rep • *Wrapper:* U.S.A./Conn.
Shade
A well-made cigar with rich, spicy
flavors; finishes with a light, mellow
taste.
U.S.: $6.50 • U.K.: N/A

PRIMO DEL REY ALMIRANTE   **86**
Dominican Republic
Ring Gauge: 50 • *Length:* 6"
Filler: Dom. Rep. • *Binder:* Dom.
Rep. • *Wrapper:* Brazil
A pleasant cigar with mild, spicy fla-
vors and a cedary aroma, but it has a
bit of a tough draw.
U.S.: $1.80 • U.K.: N/A

PUNCH SUPER ROTHSCHILD   **86**
Honduras
Ring Gauge: 50 • *Length:* 5¼"
Filler: Honduras • *Binder:* Ecuador
Wrapper: Ecuador
A cigar with spiciness on the palate,
but it finishes with a slightly vegetal
character.
U.S.: $2.00 • U.K.: N/A

BERING HISPANOS   **85**
Honduras
Ring Gauge: 50 • *Length:* 6"
Filler: Mex., Dom. Rep., Hon. •
Binder: Honduras • *Wrapper:*
Mexico
A mild, flavorful smoke with some
cinnamon-spice flavors and a medi-
um-rich finish.
U.S.: $1.20 • U.K.: N/A

CANARIA D'ORO INMENSO   **85**
Dominican Republic
Ring Gauge: 49 • *Length:* 5½"
Filler: Mexico, Dom. Rep. • *Binder:*
Mexico • *Wrapper:* Mexico

A medium-bodied cigar with nut and
cedar flavors and a short, herbal finish.
U.S.: $1.85 • U.K.: N/A

DAVIDOFF 5000   **85**
Dominican Republic
Ring Gauge: 46 • *Length:* 5⅜"
Filler: Dom. Rep. • *Binder:* Dom.
Rep. • *Wrapper:* U.S.A./Conn.
Shade
A pleasant, light cigar with green,
herbal characteristics and a cedary
finish.
U.S.: $8.50 • U.K.: £9.75

DON LINO HAVANA   **85**
RESERVE TORO
Honduras
Ring Gauge: 46 • *Length:* 5½"
Filler: Honduras • *Binder:*
Honduras • *Wrapper:* Honduras
A mild cigar that has some spicy
notes, but lacks complex depth of fla-
vor. A pleasant smoke.
U.S.: $3.85 • U.K.: N/A

H. UPMANN CHURCHILL   **85**
Dominican Republic
Ring Gauge: 46 • *Length:* 5⅝"
Filler: Dom. Rep. • *Binder:* Dom.
Rep. • *Wrapper:* Cameroon
This cigar starts slow with a bit of
harshness, but ends smoothly with a
solid core of dried spice and herbal
flavors.
U.S.: $2.60 • U.K.: N/A

JUAN CLEMENTE CLUB   **85**
SELECTION NO. 1
Dominican Republic
Ring Gauge: 50 • *Length:* 6"
Filler: Dom. Rep. • *Binder:* Dom.
Rep. • *Wrapper:* U.S.A./Conn.
Shade
A straightforward cigar with solid
tobacco flavors. Finishes with a slight
bite.
U.S.: $6.50 • U.K.: N/A

MONTECRUZ NO. 201 SUN GROWN   85
Dominican Republic
Ring Gauge: 46 • *Length:* 6¼"
Filler: Dom. Rep., Brazil • *Binder:*
Dom. Rep. • *Wrapper:* Cameroon
This cigar is a bit rough, but it delivers a spicy, medium-bodied flavor and a slightly hot finish.
U.S.: $3.00 • U.K.: N/A

PAUL GARMIRIAN EPICURE   85
Dominican Republic
Ring Gauge: 50 • *Length:* 5½"
Filler: Dom. Rep. • *Binder:* Dom.
Rep. • *Wrapper:* U.S.A./Conn.
Shade
This mild, light-bodied cigar has a spicy character, but is dominated by woody flavors and a dry finish.
U.S.: $6.80 • U.K.: £6.75

PETRUS CORONA SUBLIME   85
Honduras
Ring Gauge: 50 • *Length:* 6"
Filler: Honduras • *Binder:*
Honduras • *Wrapper:* Honduras
This is a decent smoke with hints of chocolate and spice, but it finishes a bit dry.
U.S.: $2.95 • U.K.: N/A

SANTA CLARA 1830 NO. 1830   85
Mexico
Ring Gauge: 50 • *Length:* 6"
Filler: Mexico • *Binder:* Mexico •
Wrapper: Mexico
A rough wrapper didn't detract from this earthy, spicy smoke. It has a medium-length spicy finish.
U.S.: $1.75 • U.K.: N/A

TEMPLE HALL NO. 550   85
Jamaica
Ring Gauge: 50 • *Length:* 5½"
Filler: Dom. Rep., Mexico • *Binder:*
Mexico • *Wrapper:* U.S.A./Conn.
Shade
A loosely filled cigar that burned slightly hot, but with some light pepper flavors and a cedary finish.
U.S.: $5.20 • U.K.: N/A

H. UPMANN CORSARIO   84
Dominican Republic
Ring Gauge: 50 • *Length:* 5½"
Filler: Dom. Rep. • *Binder:* Dom.
Rep. • *Wrapper:* Cameroon
Inconsistent. Rough flavors marred several tasters' cigars; sweet, dried citrus notes were evident in others.
U.S.: $4.50 • U.K.: N/A

HOYO DE MONTERREY GOVERNORS   84
Honduras
Ring Gauge: 48 • *Length:* 6"
Filler: Honduras • *Binder:*
Honduras • *Wrapper:*
U.S.A./Conn. Shade
A cigar with some earthy characteristics and a medium body. Some spiciness on the palate, but a dry finish.
U.S.: $2.10 • U.K.: N/A

NAT SHERMAN TRAFALGAR NO. 4   84
Dominican Republic
Ring Gauge: 47 • *Length:* 6"
Filler: Dom. Rep., Mex., Jam. •
Binder: Mexico • *Wrapper:*
U.S.A./Conn. Shade
A smooth, almost delicate cigar with light, mellow flavors of nuts and creamy coffee.
U.S.: $5.00 • U.K.: N/A

BOLIVAR CORONA EXTRA   83
Cuba
Ring Gauge: 46 • *Length:* 5¾"
Filler: Cuba • *Binder:* Cuba •
Wrapper: Cuba
A slight sourness detracts from a mellow nutty and peppery flavor with a dry finish.
U.S.: N/A • U.K.: £6.25

CABAÑAS ROYALE **83**
Dominican Republic
Ring Gauge: 46 • *Length:* 5⅞"
Filler: Dom. Rep. • *Binder:* Dom.
Rep. • *Wrapper:* Mexico
A rough, dark wrapper produces a
spicy smoke with solid tobacco fla-
vors, but a slightly vegetal finish.
U.S.: $2.20 • U.K.: N/A

DON DIEGO GRANDE **83**
Dominican Republic
Ring Gauge: 50 • *Length:* 6"
Filler: Dom. Rep. • *Binder:* Dom.
Rep. • *Wrapper:* U.S.A./Conn.
Shade
A very light yellow wrapper delivers a
mild, creamy taste with some herbal
characteristics.
U.S.: $3.00 • U.K.: N/A

DON LINO ORO TORO **83**
Honduras
Ring Gauge: 46 • *Length:* 5½"
Filler: Honduras • *Binder:*
Honduras • *Wrapper:* Honduras
A sweet, herbal flavor in a medium-
bodied cigar, but with a burnt citrus
aroma and finish.
U.S.: $2.50 • U.K.: N/A

EL REY DEL MUNDO ROBUSTO **83**
LARGA
Honduras
Ring Gauge: 50 • *Length:* 6"
Filler: Dom. Rep., Honduras •
Binder: Honduras • *Wrapper:*
Honduras
Inconsistent. A medium-bodied cigar
with a dried herbal, tobacco charac-
ter.
U.S.: $3.00 • U.K.: N/A

PUNCH SUPERIOR **83**
Honduras
Ring Gauge: 48 • *Length:* 5½"
Filler: Honduras • *Binder:*
Honduras • *Wrapper:* Honduras

A cigar with some harshness on the
palate and vegetal flavors, but an
earthy aroma and finish provide some
character.
U.S.: $2.90 • U.K.: N/A

TE-AMO TORO **83**
Mexico
Ring Gauge: 50 • *Length:* 6"
Filler: Mexico • *Binder:* Mexico •
Wrapper: Mexico
A rough, dark wrapper. A medium-
bodied cigar that smokes well with
some herbal and vegetal flavors.
U.S.: $2.35 • U.K.: N/A

EL REY DEL MUNDO CHOIX **82**
SUPREME
Honduras
Ring Gauge: 49 • *Length:* 6"
Filler: Dom. Rep., Honduras •
Binder: Honduras • *Wrapper:*
Honduras
A tight draw with some sourness,
although several tasters noted nutty
flavors.
U.S.: $3.00 • U.K.: N/A

LA FINCA JOYAS **82**
Nicaragua
Ring Gauge: 50 • *Length:* 6"
Filler: Nicaragua • *Binder:*
Nicaragua • *Wrapper:* Nicaragua
A roughly constructed cigar with
some pleasant herbal and cedary fla-
vors and a light body.
U.S.: $1.60 • U.K.: N/A

SANTA DAMIANA NO. 300 **81**
Dominican Republic
Ring Gauge: 46 • *Length:* 5½"
Filler: Dom. Rep. • *Binder:* Dom.
Rep. • *Wrapper:* U.S.A./Conn.
Shade
A cigar with very light, woody, almost
stemmy flavors, and a dry, woody finish.
U.S.: $5.00 • U.K.: N/A

NAT SHERMAN SUTTON 80
Dominican Republic
Ring Gauge: 49 • *Length:* 5½"
Filler: Dom. Rep. • *Binder:* Mexico
Wrapper: Mexico
Rough construction. This cigar has a stemmy, vegetal character and a fast burn that finishes harshly.
U.S.: $3.20 • U.K.: N/A

TRESADO NO. 300 78
Dominican Republic
Ring Gauge: 46 • *Length:* 6"
Filler: Dom. Rep. • *Binder:*
Cameroon • *Wrapper:* Indonesia
This cigar burned hot with a loose fill. Flavors are in the vegetal, grassy range and lack real tobacco character.
U.S.: $1.60 • U.K.: N/A

LONSDALE

COHIBA SIGLO V 96
Cuba
Ring Gauge: 43 • *Length:* 6¾"
Filler: Cuba • *Binder:* Cuba •
Wrapper: Cuba
It's a shame when you finish this cigar; you can't get enough of it. It is full-bodied and rich, yet maintains superb harmony. A truly refined cigar.
U.S.: N/A • U.K.: £13.50

COHIBA SIGLO III 95
Cuba
Ring Gauge: 42 • *Length:* 6"
Filler: Cuba • *Binder:* Cuba •
Wrapper: Cuba
A great addition to a great line of cigars. It is gorgeous to look at, with its smooth, rich brown wrapper, and it gives loads of pleasure with every puff. An opulent smoke with great finesse and class.
U.S.: N/A • U.K.: £10.00

PARTAGAS NO. 1 92
Cuba
Ring Gauge: 42 • *Length:* 6½"
Filler: Cuba • *Binder:* Cuba •
Wrapper: Cuba
An excellent, spicy cigar filled with a core of cocoa and coffee flavors, with a long, almost leathery finish.
U.S.: N/A • U.K.: £6.95

QUINTERO CHURCHILL 92
Cuba
Ring Gauge: 42 • *Length:* 6½"
Filler: Cuba • *Binder:* Cuba •
Wrapper: Cuba
A powerful, full-bodied cigar with a deep nutty aroma and strong flavors of clove and nutmeg, with a cocoa-like finish.
U.S.: N/A • Switzerland: 6SF

CUBA ALIADOS LONSDALE 91
Honduras
Ring Gauge: 42 • *Length:* 6½"
Filler: Dom. Rep. • *Binder:* Ecuador
Wrapper: Ecuador
A rich, powerful cigar packed with spice, cocoa and coffee flavors and an exotic floral finish. A great dark-brown wrapper.
U.S.: $2.20 • U.K.: N/A

EL REY DEL MUNDO LONSDALE 91
Cuba
Ring Gauge: 42 • *Length:* 6½"
Filler: Cuba • *Binder:* Cuba •
Wrapper: Cuba
This is a mellow smoke with medium-bodied, flavorful character and a long, clean aftertaste.
U.S.: N/A • U.K.: £6.75

A bond as
old as history and
deep as Caribbean
tradition.

*Bacardi rum and
a fine cigar.*

Savor the richness.
Bacardi Select
& La Gloria Cubana.

Ron
**BACARDI
SELECT**

*A select blend
of the world's richest rums
slowly aged in oak barrels.
The rums are charcoal-filtered
before their marriage
in the oak, resulting in a
distinctly smooth dark rum.*

PUERTO RICAN RUM

MEDALS AWARDED TO BACARDI

PARTAGAS LIMITED RESERVE ROYALE   **91**
Dominican Republic
Ring Gauge: 43 • *Length:* 6¼"
Filler: Mex., Dom. Rep., Jamaica •
Binder: Mexico • *Wrapper:*
Cameroon
This cigar is packed with spice and pepper flavors. It is well-made and has a lingering finish.
U.S.: $8.00 • U.K.: N/A

RAFAEL GONZALES LONSDALE   **91**
Cuba
Ring Gauge: 42 • *Length:* 6½"
Filler: Cuba • *Binder:* Cuba •
Wrapper: Cuba
A dark-brown wrapper burns evenly on this full-bodied cigar, which has flavors of coffee and cocoa and a solid spicy core.
U.S.: N/A • U.K.: £6.95

BOLIVAR GOLD MEDAL   **90**
Cuba
Ring Gauge: 42 • *Length:* 6½"
Filler: Cuba • *Binder:* Cuba •
Wrapper: Cuba
A full-flavored cigar with a toasty aroma and a nutty spiciness that ends with a bit of cedary aftertaste.
U.S.: N/A • U.K.: £7.40

H. UPMANN LONSDALE   **90**
Cuba
Ring Gauge: 42 • *Length:* 6½"
Filler: Cuba • *Binder:* Cuba •
Wrapper: Cuba
A well-made, full-bodied cigar that has an earthy aroma and complex flavors of spice and dried fruits.
U.S.: N/A • U.K.: £6.95

MONTECRISTO NO. 1   **90**
Cuba
Ring Gauge: 42 • *Length:* 6½"
Filler: Cuba • *Binder:* Cuba •
Wrapper: Cuba

This cigar showed inconsistency. At its best, it has a beautiful wrapper and nutty aromas with sweet spice flavors.
U.S.: N/A • U.K.: £7.85

TROYA CETRO   **90**
Dominican Republic
Ring Gauge: 44 • *Length:* 6¼"
Filler: Dom. Rep. • *Binder:* Dom. Rep. • *Wrapper:* U.S.A./Conn. Shade
This cigar has a medium body with a solid spicy flavor and a rich, almost leathery mouth feel on the finish.
U.S.: $2.45 • U.K.: N/A

DAVIDOFF 4000   **89**
Dominican Republic
Ring Gauge: 42 • *Length:* 6"
Filler: Dom. Rep. • *Binder:* Dom. Rep. • *Wrapper:* U.S.A./Connecticut
A firm cigar with attractive aromas and elegant coffee and nut flavors.
U.S.: $7.60 • U.K.: £9.10

DAVIDOFF GRAN CRU NO. 1   **89**
Dominican Republic
Ring Gauge: 42 • *Length:* 6"
Filler: Dom. Rep. • *Binder:* Dom. Rep. • *Wrapper:* U.S.A./Conn. Shade
A beautiful brown wrapper on a finely constructed cigar that delivers a spicy pepper flavor and a cedary finish.
U.S.: $7.90 • U.K.: £8.70

HOYO DE MONTERREY LE HOYO DES DIEUX   **89**
Cuba
Ring Gauge: 42 • *Length:* 6"
Filler: Cuba • *Binder:* Cuba •
Wrapper: Cuba
A spicy, well-rolled cabinet cigar with rich flavors and an earthy aftertaste.
U.S.: N/A • U.K.: £6.96

LICENCIADOS EXCELENTES   89
Dominican Republic
Ring Gauge: 43 • *Length:* 6¼"
Filler: Dom. Rep. • *Binder:*
Honduras • *Wrapper:*
U.S.A./Conn. Shade
A rich-tasting smoke with creamy
butterscotch notes. A spicy under-
tone comes through a slightly tight
draw.
U.S.: $1.50 • U.K.: N/A

MACANUDO AMATISTA   89
Jamaica
Ring Gauge: 42 • *Length:* 6¼"
Filler: Mex., Jamaica, Dom. Rep. •
Binder: Mexico • *Wrapper:*
U.S.A./Conn. Shade
A very well-balanced cigar with
medium-bodied flavors, including
cocoa and mild spices, and a long,
mild finish.
U.S.: $4.05 • U.K.: N/A

V CENTENNIAL CETRO   89
Honduras
Ring Gauge: 44 • *Length:* 6½"
Filler: Dom. Rep., Mex., Nica., Hon.
Binder: Dom. Rep. • *Wrapper:*
U.S.A./Conn. Shade
A medium-bodied cigar with a core of
earthy flavors that have a hint of
spiciness. It finishes smoothly.
U.S.: $3.75 • U.K.: N/A

ARTURO FUENTE   88
RESERVA NO. 1
Dominican Republic
Ring Gauge: 42 • *Length:* 6½"
Filler: Dom. Rep. • *Binder:* Dom.
Rep. • *Wrapper:* Cameroon
A very well-balanced cigar with
sweetish, round tobacco aromas that
turn to aged spice flavors on the
palate.
U.S.: $5.75 • U.K.: N/A

ARTURO FUENTE SPANISH   88
LONSDALE
Dominican Republic
Ring Gauge: 42 • *Length:* 6½"
Filler: Dom. Rep. • *Binder:* Dom.
Rep. • *Wrapper:* Cameroon
A cigar filled with earthy, spicy fla-
vors. It's well-made and has a long,
smooth finish.
U.S.: $1.65 • U.K.: N/A

ASHTON 8-9-8   88
Dominican Republic
Ring Gauge: 44 • *Length:* 6½"
Filler: Dom. Rep. • *Binder:* Dom.
Rep. • *Wrapper:* U.S.A./Conn. Shade
This cigar has an oily reddish-brown
wrapper. It delivers a rich mix of fla-
vors including spices and nuts.
U.S.: $3.35 • U.K.: £3.60

BAUZA JAGUAR   88
Dominican Republic
Ring Gauge: 42 • *Length:* 6½"
Filler: Dom. Rep., Nica. • *Binder:*
Mexico • *Wrapper:* Cameroon
A rich, peppery cigar with full-bodied
flavors of tobacco and aged cedar wood.
U.S.: $1.50 • U.K.: N/A

CUESTA-REY DOMINICAN NO. 4   88
Dominican Republic
Ring Gauge: 42 • *Length:* 6½"
Filler: Dom. Rep. • *Binder:* Dom.
Rep. • *Wrapper:* U.S.A./Conn. Shade
A nutty aroma comes from this mild
cigar, which also has some nutty fla-
vors and a moderate finish.
U.S.: $2.25 • U.K.: N/A

CUESTA-REY NO. 95   88
Dominican Republic
Ring Gauge: 42 • *Length:* 6¼"
Filler: Dom. Rep. • *Binder:* Dom.
Rep. • *Wrapper:* Cameroon
An attractive dark-brown wrapper
that has an earthy depth of pepper
flavor. It finishes with a cedary note.
U.S.: $1.65 • U.K.: N/A

DON TOMAS SUPREMO 88
Honduras
Ring Gauge: 42 • *Length:* 6¼"
Filler: Honduras • *Binder:*
Honduras • *Wrapper:* Honduras,
Sumatra
A well-made cigar with a good draw, a
rich aroma and a nutty flavor.
U.S.: $1.60 • U.K.: N/A

DUNHILL DIAMANTE 88
Dominican Republic
Ring Gauge: 42 • *Length:* 6⅝"
Filler: Dom. Rep. • *Binder:* Dom.
Rep. • *Wrapper:* U.S.A./Conn.
Shade
A medium-bodied cigar with floral
aromas and flavors of nuts and sweet
woods like cedar.
U.S.: $3.40 • U.K.: £5.20

FONSECA 8-9-8 88
Dominican Republic
Ring Gauge: 43 • *Length:* 6"
Filler: Dom. Rep. • *Binder:* Mexico
Wrapper: U.S.A./Conn. Shade
A mild cigar that has a hint of dry
wood on the palate, but also tastes of
coffee and spice.
U.S.: $3.00 • U.K.: N/A

LA GLORIA CUBANA 88
MEDAILLE D'OR NO. 1
U.S.A.
Ring Gauge: 43 • *Length:* 6¼"
Filler: Dom. Rep., Nicaragua •
Binder: Dom. Rep. • *Wrapper:*
Ecuador
A rich, full-bodied smoke with leath-
ery, earthy notes and a solid spicy and
coffee core of flavors.
U.S.: $1.70 • U.K.: N/A

OSCAR NO. 300 88
Dominican Republic
Ring Gauge: 44 • *Length:* 6¼"
Filler: Dom. Rep. • *Binder:* Dom.
Rep. • *Wrapper:* U.S.A./Conn. Shade

A full-bodied, mouth-filling smoke
with spicy, coffee and earthy flavors
but with a short finish.
U.S.: $4.65 • U.K.: £6.30

PRIMO DEL REY NO. 2 88
Dominican Republic
Ring Gauge: 42 • *Length:* 6¼"
Filler: Dom. Rep. • *Binder:*
U.S.A./Conn. Broadleaf • *Wrapper:*
Brazil
A spicy, medium-bodied cigar with
flavors of pepper and toasted nuts. It
has a slightly vegetal character on the
finish.
U.S.: $1.50 • U.K.: N/A

ROYAL JAMAICA 88
CORONA GRANDE
Dominican Republic
Ring Gauge: 42 • *Length:* 6½"
Filler: Jamaica • *Binder:* Indonesia
Wrapper: Cameroon
A dark-wrapped cigar with creamy
pepper flavors. It has a medium body
and is very well balanced.
U.S.: $2.65 • U.K.: N/A

BERING PLAZA 87
Honduras
Ring Gauge: 43 • *Length:* 6"
Filler: Mex., Dom. Rep., Hon. •
Binder: Honduras • *Wrapper:*
Mexico
A solid-smoking cigar with pepper
flavors that come through a good,
easy draw.
U.S.: $ .95 • U.K.: N/A

CASA BLANCA LONSDALE 87
Dominican Republic
Ring Gauge: 42 • *Length:* 6½"
Filler: Dom. Rep. • *Binder:* Mexico
Wrapper: U.S.A./Conn. Shade
A smooth-tasting, mild cigar that is
creamy with light pepper flavors.
U.S.: $2.15 • U.K.: £4.00

JOSE BENITO PALMA 87
Dominican Republic
Ring Gauge: 43 • *Length:* 6"
Filler: Dom. Rep. • *Binder:*
Honduras • *Wrapper:* Cameroon
A spicy aroma on this well-made,
medium-bodied cigar leads to smooth,
mild flavors of nutmeg and pepper.
U.S.: $2.00 • U.K.: N/A

MONTECRUZ NO. 210 87
SUN GROWN
Dominican Republic
Ring Gauge: 42 • *Length:* 6½"
Filler: Dom. Rep., Brazil • *Binder:*
Dom. Rep. • *Wrapper:* Cameroon
Flavors of nuts and sweet spices domi-
nate this cigar. It has a bit of a tight
draw and a woody finish.
U.S.: $2.65 • U.K.: N/A

MONTESINO NO. 1 87
Dominican Republic
Ring Gauge: 43 • *Length:* 6¼"
Filler: Dom. Rep. • *Binder:* Dom.
Rep. • *Wrapper:* U.S.A./Conn.
Shade
A well-made cigar with a spicy attack
on the palate, but with a short finish.
U.S.: $1.70 • U.K.: N/A

RAMON ALLONES "B" 87
Dominican Republic
Ring Gauge: 42 • *Length:* 6½"
Filler: Dom. Rep., Mexico • *Binder:*
Mexico • *Wrapper:* Cameroon
A smooth brown wrapper leads to a
mild, medium-bodied spiciness with
cedar and coffee flavors.
U.S.: $3.00 • U.K.: N/A

SANCHO PANZA MOLINAS 87
Cuba
Ring Gauge: 42 • *Length:* 6½"
Filler: Cuba • *Binder:* Cuba •
Wrapper: Cuba

Some inconsistency in this otherwise
rich cigar, with spicy, nutty flavors
and a long finish.
U.S.: N/A • U.K.: £6.75

SOSA NO. 1 87
Dominican Republic
Ring Gauge: 43 • *Length:* 6½"
Filler: Dom. Rep., Brazil • *Binder:*
Honduras • *Wrapper:* Ecuador
A medium-bodied cigar with toasted
nut aromas, smooth, creamy, coffee
flavors and a sweet, spicy finish.
U.S.: $2.25 • U.K.: N/A

DON DIEGO LONSDALE 86
Dominican Republic
Ring Gauge: 42 • *Length:* 6⅝"
Filler: Dom. Rep. • *Binder:* Dom.
Rep. • *Wrapper:* U.S.A./Conn.
Shade
This cigar has a good draw with a mix
of coffee and toast flavors and a nice
spicy finish.
U.S.: $2.50 • U.K.: N/A

HOYO DE MONTERREY NO. 1 86
Honduras
Ring Gauge: 43 • *Length:* 6½"
Filler: Nica., Hon., Dom. Rep. •
Binder: U.S.A./Conn. Broadleaf •
Wrapper: Honduras
A medium-bodied cigar that has
earthy flavors with hints of coffee and
spice that fade quickly on the finish.
U.S.: $2.00 • U.K.: N/A

LEON JIMENES NO. 3 86
Dominican Republic
Ring Gauge: 42 • *Length:* 6½"
Filler: Dom. Rep. • *Binder:* Dom.
Rep. • *Wrapper:* Cameroon
This is a creamy, smooth cigar with
mild, floral-style aromas and flavors
and a touch of spiciness, but a short
finish.
U.S.: $3.85 • U.K.: N/A

MACANUDO VINTAGE II   86
Jamaica
Ring Gauge: 42 • *Length:* 6¼"
Filler: Mex., Jamaica, Dom. Rep. •
Binder: Mexico • *Wrapper:*
U.S.A./Conn. Shade
An easy, elegant smoke with light
tobacco and nut flavors and a creamy
smoothness on the palate.
U.S.: $6.50 • U.K.: N/A

NAT SHERMAN BUTTERFIELD   86
NO. 8
Dominican Republic
Ring Gauge: 42 • *Length:* 6½"
Filler: Dom. Rep. • *Binder:* Mexico
Wrapper: U.S.A./Conn. Shade
A mild cigar that offers flavors of
sweet spices like cinnamon and some
smooth creaminess.
U.S.: $4.45 • U.K.: N/A

PAUL GARMIRIAN LONSDALE   86
Dominican Republic
Ring Gauge: 42 • *Length:* 6½"
Filler: Dom. Rep. • *Binder:* Dom.
Rep. • *Wrapper:* U.S.A./ Conn. Shade
A cigar with a rough wrapper. A
slight, dried-out papery finish, but
with lots of spicy pepper flavors and a
solid tobacco aroma.
U.S.: $6.00 • U.K.: N/A

PETRUS NO. 2   86
Honduras
Ring Gauge: 43 • *Length:* 6¼"
Filler: Honduras • *Binder:*
Honduras • *Wrapper:* Honduras
A straightforward cigar with an
herbal character and creamy coffee
flavors on the palate and finish.
U.S.: $2.65 • U.K.: N/A

PUNCH NO. 1   86
Honduras
Ring Gauge: 43 • *Length:* 6¼"
Filler: Nica., Hon., Dom. Rep. •
Binder: Ecuador • *Wrapper:*

U.S.A./Conn. Shade
This easy-drawing cigar is well-balanced with an herbal spiciness, but it
has a fairly short finish.
U.S.: $2.00 • U.K.: N/A

ROMEO & JULIETA   86
VINTAGE NO. 1
Dominican Republic
Ring Gauge: 43 • *Length:* 6"
Filler: Dom. Rep. • *Binder:* Mexico
Wrapper: U.S.A./Conn. Shade
A solidly spicy cigar with a medium
body that finishes with a dried-wood
character.
U.S.: $4.50 • U.K.: N/A

SANTA ROSA CETROS   86
Honduras
Ring Gauge: 42 • *Length:* 6"
Filler: Honduras • *Binder:*
Honduras • *Wrapper:* Honduras
Mild nut and spice flavors dominate
this cigar that starts a bit slow, but
builds to a smooth, pleasant smoke.
U.S.: $2.00 • U.K.: N/A

TEMPLE HALL NO. 625   86
Jamaica
Ring Gauge: 42 • *Length:* 6¼"
Filler: Jamaica, Mexico, Dom. Rep. •
Binder: Mexico • *Wrapper:*
U.S.A./Conn. Shade
This is a pleasantly mild cigar with
smooth, creamy flavors, a spicy core,
and a cedary finish.
U.S.: $4.85 • U.K.: N/A

VERACRUZ RESERVE ESPECIAL   86
Mexico
Ring Gauge: 42 • *Length:* 6½"
Filler: Mexico • *Binder:* Mexico •
Wrapper: Mexico
A light-tasting cigar that smokes easi-
ly, with some spicy flavors.
U.S.: $5.00 • U.K.: N/A

AVO NO. 1   **85**
Dominican Republic
Ring Gauge: 42 • *Length:* 6¼"
Filler: Dom. Rep. • *Binder:* Dom.
Rep. • *Wrapper:* U.S.A./Conn.
Shade
A smooth, creamy smoke packed with
coffee flavors, a mild spiciness and a
pleasing, straight tobacco finish.
U.S.: $5.00 • U.K.: N/A

CANARIA D'ORO LONSDALE   **85**
Dominican Republic
Ring Gauge: 43 • *Length:* 5½"
Filler: Mexico, Dom. Rep. • *Binder:*
Mexico • *Wrapper:* Mexico
A medium-bodied cigar with a mild
spiciness. It has a slight vegetal quali-
ty on a short finish.
U.S.: $1.75 • U.K.: N/A

H. UPMANN LONSDALE   **85**
Dominican Republic
Ring Gauge: 42 • *Length:* 6⅝"
Filler: Dom. Rep. • *Binder:* Dom.
Rep. • *Wrapper:* Cameroon
This easy-drawing cigar has a base of
nutty flavors and finishes with a
strong pepper spice note.
U.S.: $2.50 • U.K.: N/A

LA GLORIA CUBANA   **85**
MEDAILLE D'OR NO. 2
Cuba
Ring Gauge: 43 • *Length:* 6 2/3"
Filler: Cuba • *Binder:* Cuba •
Wrapper: Cuba
A cigar that shows lots of promise,
with unusual sweetish flavors, but is a
bit short on the finish.
U.S.: N/A • U.K.: £7.15

MONTECRUZ NO. 210   **85**
Dominican Republic
Ring Gauge: 42 • *Length:* 6½"
Filler: Dom. Rep., Brazil • *Binder:*
Dom. Rep. • *Wrapper:*
U.S.A./Conn. Shade

A well-made cigar with rich flavors of
spice and coffee. It has an elegant finish with cedar-wood tones.
U.S.: $2.65 • U.K.: N/A

PARTAGAS NO. 1   **85**
Dominican Republic
Ring Gauge: 43 • *Length:* 6¾"
Filler: Mex., Dom. Rep., Jam. •
Binder: Mexico • *Wrapper:*
Cameroon
This is a straightforward cigar with a
good draw that delivers solid flavors
of spice and pepper.
U.S.: $3.30 • U.K.: N/A

SAINT LUIS REY LONSDALE   **85**
Cuba
Ring Gauge: 42 • *Length:* 6½"
Filler: Cuba • *Binder:* Cuba •
Wrapper: Cuba
An elegant, medium-bodied cigar with
smooth flavors of nutmeg and toffee
and a hint of cedar on the finish.
U.S.: N/A • U.K.: £6.95

SANTA DAMIANA NO. 700   **85**
Dominican Republic
Ring Gauge: 42 • *Length:* 6½"
Filler: Dom. Rep. • *Binder:* Dom.
Rep. • *Wrapper:* U.S.A./Conn.
Shade
A mild, medium-bodied cigar with
creamy, smooth flavors and an overall
cedary, dried-wood character on the
finish.
U.S.: $4.50 • U.K.: N/A

TE-AMO MEDITATION   **85**
Mexico
Ring Gauge: 42 • *Length:* 6"
Filler: Mexico • *Binder:* Mexico •
Wrapper: Mexico
A solid cigar with straight tobacco
flavors but a dry, woody finish.
U.S.: $2.10 • U.K.: N/A

THE GRIFFIN'S NO. 300   **85**
Dominican Republic
Ring Gauge: 44 • *Length:* 6¼"
Filler: Dom. Rep. • *Binder:* Dom.
Rep. • *Wrapper:* U.S.A./Conn.
Shade
A brown-wrappered cigar with a solid
core of spiciness and a smooth but
slightly dry finish.
U.S.: $4.10 • U.K.: N/A

ZINO TRADITION   **85**
Honduras
Ring Gauge: 44 • *Length:* 6¼"
Filler: Honduras • *Binder:*
Honduras • *Wrapper:* Ecuador
This cigar has a red-brown wrapper
that delivers a medium-bodied smoke
filled with spices.
U.S.: $5.40 • U.K.: N/A

EL REY DEL MUNDO LONSDALE   **84**
Honduras
Ring Gauge: 42 • *Length:* 6½"
Filler: Honduras • *Binder:*
Honduras • *Wrapper:* Nicaragua
A mild cigar with a tight fill that has
a sweet tobacco taste and mild spicy
finish.
U.S.: $3.00 • U.K.: N/A

JUAN CLEMENTE   **84**
GRAN CORONA
Dominican Republic
Ring Gauge: 42 • *Length:* 6"
Filler: Dom. Rep. • *Binder:* Dom.
Rep. • *Wrapper:* U.S.A./Conn.
Shade
This cigar has a woody aroma and fla-
vor and, as it gets going, takes on a
rustic, earthy character.
U.S.: $3.55 • U.K.: N/A

LA UNICA NO. 300   **84**
Dominican Republic
Ring Gauge: 43 • *Length:* 6¼"
Filler: Dom. Rep. • *Binder:* Dom.
Rep. • *Wrapper:* U.S.A./ Conn. Shade

This well-made cigar with a medium-
brown wrapper shows mild pepper
and nutmeg flavors with a dry finish.
U.S.: $1.50 • U.K.: N/A

NAT SHERMAN ALGONQUIN   **84**
Dominican Republic
Ring Gauge: 43 • *Length:* 6¼"
Filler: Dom. Rep. • *Binder:* Mexico
Wrapper: Cameroon
This is a pleasant, full-bodied cigar
that is a bit hot, but with a core of
spiciness.
U.S.: $4.75 • U.K.: N/A

ROMEO & JULIETA PALMA   **84**
Dominican Republic
Ring Gauge: 43 • *Length:* 6"
Filler: Dom. Rep., Brazil • *Binder:*
U.S.A./Conn. Broadleaf • *Wrapper:*
Cameroon
Mild pepper flavors show through this
medium-bodied cigar.
U.S.: $1.95 • U.K.: N/A

BACCARAT LUCHADORES   **83**
Honduras
Ring Gauge: 43 • *Length:* 6"
Filler: Honduras • *Binder:*
Honduras • *Wrapper:* Honduras
A cigar that uses sweet gum to secure
the wrapper. Not for everybody, but
it's well-made, with solid tobacco fla-
vors.
U.S.: $1.30 • U.K.: N/A

POR LARRAÑAGA CETROS   **81**
Dominican Republic
Ring Gauge: 42 • *Length:* 6⅞"
Filler: Dom. Rep. • *Binder:* Dom.
Rep. • *Wrapper:* U.S.A./Conn.
Shade
A light-bodied cigar that is a bit
green and grassy on the palate.
Finishes quickly.
U.S.: $3.50 • U.K.: N/A

BANCES CAZADORES　　**78**
Honduras
Ring Gauge: 43 • *Length:* 6¼"
Filler: Nicaragua • *Binder:* Mexico
Wrapper: Ecuador
Hints of coffee and cocoa, but this
cigar turns hot and has some slight
vegetal flavors.
U.S.: $ .85 • U.K.: N/A

CORONA

BOLIVAR CORONA　　**91**
Cuba
Ring Gauge: 42 • *Length:* 5½"
Filler: Cuba • *Binder:* Cuba •
Wrapper: Cuba
A rich, earthy cigar with a solid core
of nuts and spices with a very smooth
balance. A long spicy finish.
U.S.: N/A • U.K.: £6.80

EL REY DEL MUNDO CORONA　　**91**
Cuba
Ring Gauge: 42 • *Length:* 5½"
Filler: Cuba • *Binder:* Cuba •
Wrapper: Cuba
Although a little young, this cigar
exhibits great spice, including cinna-
mon, and a strong earthy finish that
lasts. Very well-made.
U.S.: N/A • U.K.: £6.65

H. UPMANN CORONA　　**91**
Cuba
Ring Gauge: 42 • *Length:* 5½"
Filler: Cuba • *Binder:* Cuba •
Wrapper: Cuba
This H. Upmann is bursting with
complex coffee, roasted nut and
tobacco flavors.
U.S.: N/A • U.K.: £5.85

LA FINCA CORONA　　**91**
Nicaragua
Ring Gauge: 42 • *Length:* 5½"
Filler: Nicaragua • *Binder:*
Nicaragua • *Wrapper:* Nicaragua
A rich tasting cigar with a lot of
depth. It has flavors of spice, raisins
and a cedary taste on the palate. It is
well-balanced and has a smooth finish.
U.S.: $1.40 • U.K.: N/A

MONTESINO DIPLOMATICOS　　**91**
Dominican Republic
Ring Gauge: 43 • *Length:* 5½"
Filler: Dom. Rep. • *Binder:* Dom.
Rep. • *Wrapper:* U.S.A./Conn.
Shade
A very well-made cigar. It has an
earthy depth, with delicious sweet
spice flavors of cinnamon, and strong
nut elements including walnuts. A
smooth, long-lasting finish.
U.S.: $1.90 • U.K.: N/A

PUROS INDIOS NO. 4 ESPECIAL　　**91**
Honduras
Ring Gauge: 44 • *Length:* 5½"
Filler: Brazil, Nicaragua, Dom. Rep.
Binder: Ecuador • *Wrapper:*
Ecuador
A rich, full-bodied cigar filled with
nutmeg and cinnamon spices, and a
great nutty character on the palate. It
has an long, earthy finish with a hint
of cocoa.
U.S.: $3.25 • U.K.: N/A

HOYO DE MONTERREY　　**90**
LE HOYO DU ROI
Cuba
Ring Gauge: 42 • *Length:* 5½"
Filler: Cuba • *Binder:* Cuba •
Wrapper: Cuba
A full-bodied, rich cigar with nutmeg
and earthy flavors. It is very well-bal-
anced and has a long, cedary finish.
U.S.: N/A • U.K.: £7.35

CASA BLANCA CORONA   **89**
Dominican Republic
Ring Gauge: 42 • *Length:* 5½"
Filler: Dom. Rep., Brazil • *Binder:*
Mexico • *Wrapper:* U.S.A./Conn.
Shade
A good tasting cigar with notes of
spice and cedar. It has excellent oils
in the wrapper, and a smooth, herb-
like character on the finish.
U.S.: $1.85 • U.K.: N/A

JOSÉ MARTI 1868 CORONA   **89**
Honduras
Ring Gauge: 45 • *Length:* 5⅝"
Filler: Dom. Rep., Honduras • *Binder:*
Honduras • *Wrapper:* Ecuador
A complex, medium-bodied cigar. It
has an earthy character, with notes of
leather, herbs and roasted nuts, and a
dark woody finish.
U.S.: $1.50 • U.K.: N/A

PUNCH CORONA   **89**
Cuba
Ring Gauge: 42 • *Length:* 5½"
Filler: Cuba • *Binder:* Cuba •
Wrapper: Cuba
This is a spicy cigar with some leather
notes. It finishes with a dry, woody
flavor.
U.S.: N/A • U.K.: £6.45

RAMON ALLONES CORONA   **89**
Cuba
Ring Gauge: 42 • *Length:* 5½"
Filler: Cuba • *Binder:* Cuba •
Wrapper: Cuba
A cigar with a firm draw. It has fancy
chocolate and almond flavors, but shows
its youth despite a solid tobacco core.
U.S.: N/A • U.K.: £6.65

ROMEO Y JULIETA CORONA   **89**
Cuba
Ring Gauge: 42 • *Length:* 5½"
Filler: Cuba • *Binder:* Cuba •
Wrapper: Cuba

A slightly rough, boxed cigar. It has
good spice, and a dose of nut flavors
with a smooth, leathery finish.
U.S.: N/A • U.K.: £6.80

SAVINELLI EXTRAORDINAIRE   **89**
Dominican Republic
Ring Gauge: 44 • *Length:* 5½"
Filler: Dom. Rep. • *Binder:* Dom.
Rep. • *Wrapper:* U.S.A./Conn.
Shade
This medium-bodied cigar has a
smooth, creamy nut element, and
solid tobacco flavors in an earthy
core. It has a long spicy finish with
wood notes.
U.S.: $5.75 • U.K.: N/A

CREDO ANTHANOR   **88**
Dominican Republic
Ring Gauge: 42 • *Length:* 5¼"
Filler: Dom. Rep. • *Binder:* Dom.
Rep. • *Wrapper:* U.S.A./Conn.
Shade
A good medium-bodied cigar. It has
flavors of dried orange peel with a
nutty, spicy component, and a well-
balanced finish.
U.S.: $4.80 • U.K.: N/A

DAVIDOFF GRAND CRU NO.2   **88**
Dominican Republic
Ring Gauge: 43 • *Length:* 5⅝"
Filler: Dom. Rep. • *Binder:* Dom.
Rep. • *Wrapper:* U.S.A./Conn.
Shade
A well-made, medium-bodied cigar
with excellent spice flavors including
nutmeg. There's a solid nutty core,
and a pleasant finish.
U.S.: $8.60 • U.K.: £7.96

HOYO DE MONTERREY NO. 55   **88**
Honduras
Ring Gauge: 43 • *Length:* 5¼"
Filler: Honduras, Nicaragua, Dom.
Rep. • *Binder:* Honduras •
Wrapper: Ecuador

There are hints of chocolate and nuts in this richly flavored, medium-bodied cigar and a sweet woody note on the finish.
U.S.: $1.10 • U.K.: N/A

LA GLORIA CUBANA GLORIAS 88
U.S.A.
Ring Gauge: 43 • Length: 5½"
Filler: Dom. Rep., Nicaragua • Binder: Nicaragua • Wrapper: Ecuador
A solid, medium-bodied cigar with strong spice and cedar notes, and flavors of chocolate. It has a strong spicy finish.
U.S.: $2.50 • U.K.: N/A

LEMPIRA CORONA 88
Honduras
Ring Gauge: 42 • Length: 5½"
Filler: Honduras, Nicaragua • Binder: Dom. Rep. • Wrapper: U.S.A./Conn. Shade
A rustic cigar with a pleasant cedary finish. It has flavors of nutmeg and cinnamon.
U.S.: $2.25 • U.K.: N/A

MONTECRISTO NO. 3 88
Cuba
Ring Gauge: 42 • Length: 5½"
Filler: Cuba • Binder: Cuba • Wrapper: Cuba
A smooth but full-bodied cigar with a solid core of exotic spices including cinnamon and nutmeg, and a pleasing cedary finish.
U.S.: N/A • U.K.: £7.80

OLOR MOMENTO 88
Dominican Republic
Ring Gauge: 43 • Length: 5½"
Filler: Dom. Rep. • Binder: Dom. Rep. • Wrapper: U.S.A./Conn. Shade
A sweet finish on a medium-bodied cigar. This cigar has a roasted chestnut flavor, and creamy, herbal character with mild spices.
U.S.: $2.35 • U.K.: N/A

PADRON ANIVERSARIO 88
CORONA
Honduras
Ring Gauge: 42 • Length: 6"
Filler: Nicaragua • Binder: Nicaragua • Wrapper: Nicaragua
Although it's slightly tight, this cigar is packed with good spices and a hint of chocolate. It's well-balanced with a medium-bodied smoke.
U.S.: $5.05 • U.K.: N/A

PUNCH CAFE ROYAL 88
Honduras
Ring Gauge: 44 • Length: 5⅝"
Filler: Honduras, Nicaragua, Dom.Rep. • Binder: Honduras • Wrapper: Ecuador
This cigar has good nut flavors including hints of chestnuts. It has a mild, spicy finish and is well-balanced overall.
U.S.: $2.65 • U.K.: N/A

ARTURO FUENTE 87
RESERVA NO. 3
Dominican Republic
Ring Gauge: 44 • Length: 5½"
Filler: Dom. Rep. • Binder: Dom. Rep. • Wrapper: Cameroon
An attractive dark brown wrapper. This cigar has an earthy quality with smooth flavors, but a dry wood finish.
U.S.: $6.75 • U.K.: N/A

AVO NO. 7 87
Dominican Republic
Ring Gauge: 44 • Length: 6"
Filler: Dom. Rep. • Binder: Dom. Rep. • Wrapper: U.S.A./Conn. Shade
This cigar, which is a medium-bodied smoke, offers some herbal notes followed by strong chestnut flavors and an overall toast-like character.
U.S.: $5.20 • U.K.: N/A

BELINDA BREVA CONSERVA **87**
Honduras
Ring Gauge: 43 • *Length:* 5½"
Filler: Dom. Rep., Honduras •
Binder: Honduras • *Wrapper:*
Ecuador
A cigar with a medium-bodied char-
acter. It has solid flavors of nuts, and
a core of spiciness. There is a good
toasty finish.
U.S.: $1.30 • U.K.: N/A

BERING CORONA ROYALE **87**
Honduras
Ring Gauge: 41 • *Length:* 6"
Filler: Honduras, Mexico, Dom. Rep,
Nicaragua • *Binder:* Honduras •
Wrapper: Mexico
This is medium-bodied cigar with a
solid spicy core of flavors. It has a
leathery aroma, and a pleasing tobac-
co character.
U.S.: $1.35 • U.K.: N/A

C.A.O. CORONA **87**
Honduras
Ring Gauge: 42 • *Length:* 6"
Filler: Nicaragua, Mexico • *Binder:*
Honduras • *Wrapper:*
U.S.A./Conn. Shade
This cigar has a firm draw, but a
pleasant toasty, creamy character.
There's a bit of dry straw in the flavor,
but it has a well-balanced finish.
U.S.: $4.25 • U.K.: N/A

CARRINGTON NO. 2 **87**
Dominican Republic
Ring Gauge: 42 • *Length:* 6"
Filler: Dom. Rep. • *Binder:* Dom.
Rep. • *Wrapper:* U.S.A./Conn.
Shade
This cigar has a light, spicy character,
with some earthy tones. It is smooth-
tasting.
U.S.: $3.65 • U.K.: N/A

CUESTA-REY DOMINICAN **87**
NO. 5
Dominican Republic
Ring Gauge: 43 • *Length:* 5½"
Filler: Dom. Rep. • *Binder:* Dom.
Rep. • *Wrapper:* U.S.A./Conn.
Shade
A well-balanced cigar that shows a
pleasing smooth, creamy texture with
hints of spice and leather and a solid
tobacco flavors.
U.S.: $2.75 • U.K.: £4.25

DON DIEGO CORONA **87**
MAJOR TUBE
Dominican Republic
Ring Gauge: 42 • *Length:* 5½"
Filler: Dom. Rep. • *Binder:* Dom.
Rep. • *Wrapper:* U.S.A./Conn.
Shade
A firm draw on a medium-bodied
cigar. It has a creamy tobacco charac-
ter and some hints of a toast-like
flavor.
U.S.: $2.95 • U.K.: N/A

DON LINO PETICETRO **87**
Honduras
Ring Gauge: 42 • *Length:* 5½"
Filler: Honduras • *Binder:*
Honduras • *Wrapper:* U.S.A.
A pleasing mild cigar with a flinty
character, and hints of toasted nuts. It
is a mild cigar overall, but with char-
acter.
U.S.: $2.30 • U.K.: N/A

DON TOMAS MATADOR **87**
Honduras
Ring Gauge: 42 • *Length:* 5½"
Filler: Honduras • *Binder:*
Honduras • *Wrapper:* Honduras
An interesting cigar with a spicy
quality that has an earthy hint, but it
ends with a sweet wood finish.
U.S.: $2.40 • U.K.: N/A

HOYO DE MONTERREY   **87**
CAFE ROYAL
Honduras
Ring Gauge: 43 • *Length:* 5⅝"
Filler: Honduras, Nicaragua, Dom.
Rep. • *Binder:* Honduras •
Wrapper: Ecuador
This is a well-made cigar with an oily
wrapper. It has a smooth herbal core
of flavors with a good woody finish.
U.S.: $2.65 • U.K.: N/A

MACANUDO VINTAGE No. 3   **87**
Jamaica
Ring Gauge: 43 • *Length:* 5⁹⁄₁₆"
Filler: Dom. Rep., Jam. • *Binder:*
Mexico • *Wrapper:* U.S.A./Conn.
Shade
Although some tightness was noted
in the draw, this cigar had a good
creamy texture with a strong nut fla-
vor of chestnuts and a pleasant toasty
finish.
U.S.: $8.00 • U.K.: N/A

MONTECRISTO No. 3   **87**
Dominican Republic
Ring Gauge: 44 • *Length:* 5½"
Filler: Dom. Rep. • *Binder:* Dom.
Rep. • *Wrapper:* U.S.A./Conn.
Shade
A well-made, medium-bodied cigar
with a solid nutty character. It has
some smooth herb and sweet spice
flavors including nutmeg.
U.S.: $4.50 • U.K.: N/A

MONTECRUZ No. 220   **87**
SUN GROWN
Dominican Republic
Ring Gauge: 42 • *Length:* 5½"
Filler: Dom. Rep., Brazil • *Binder:*
Dom. Rep. • *Wrapper:* Cameroon
This cigar delivers a creaminess with
a backbone of spicy flavors. It has a
medium-bodied character.
U.S.: $3.40 • U.K.: N/A

NAT SHERMAN LANDMARK   **87**
SELECTION HAMPSHIRE
Dominican Republic
Ring Gauge: 42 • *Length:* 5½"
Filler: Jam., Mex., Dom. Rep. •
Binder: Mexico • *Wrapper:*
Cameroon
This is a good-looking cigar with
solid tobacco flavors, and some notes
of chestnuts and chocolate with a
mild, peppery finish.
U.S.: $5.30 • U.K.: N/A

NAT SHERMAN METROPOLITAN   **87**
SELECTION ANGLERS
Dominican Republic
Ring Gauge: 43 • *Length:* 5½"
Filler: Dom. Rep. • *Binder:* Dom.
Rep. • *Wrapper:* U.S.A./Conn.
Shade
An earthiness dominates this cigar.
The medium-bodied smoke has good
rich flavors of leather and toast, and a
pleasant woody finish.
U.S.: $6.00 • U.K.: N/A

ROMEO & JULIETA   **87**
VINTAGE No. 1
Dominican Republic
Ring Gauge: 43 • *Length:* 6"
Filler: Dom. Rep. • *Binder:* Mexico
Wrapper: U.S.A./Conn. Shade
A cigar with a smooth, creamy tex-
ture. It has a touch of sweet spcies
and nutmeg, and a floral character.
U.S.: $5.75 • U.K.: N/A

SANTA CLARA 1830 No. 5   **87**
Mexico
Ring Gauge: 43 • *Length:* 6"
Filler: Mexico • *Binder:* Mexico •
Wrapper: Mexico
A well-made cigar packed with spices,
and a toasty herbal character, with
hints of nuts and coffee. A smooth
easy smoke.
U.S.: $2.00 • U.K.: £3.10

TROYA NO. 27   **87**
Dominican Republic
Ring Gauge: 42 • *Length:* 5½"
Filler: Dom. Rep. • *Binder:* Dom.
Rep. • *Wrapper:* U.S.A./Conn.
Shade
A good, solid medium-bodied cigar.
It has toasty flavors with hints of
nuts and flowers, and is smooth and
mellow.
U.S.: $3.25 • U.K.: N/A

ASHTON AGED MADURO   **86**
NO. 20
Dominican Republic
Ring Gauge: 44 • *Length:* 5½"
Filler: Dom. Rep. • *Binder:* Dom.
Rep. • *Wrapper:* U.S.A
This is a cigar with sweet herbal fla-
vors, and pleasant toasty flavor.
U.S.: $4.65 • U.K.: N/A

BANCES BREVAS   **86**
Honduras
Ring Gauge: 43 • *Length:* 5½"
Filler: Honduras, Nicaragua, Dom.
Rep. • *Binder:* Honduras •
Wrapper: Ecuador
A cigar with a flinty character on the
palate. There are some spicy pepper
flavors and a nice cedary finish.
U.S.: $1.10 • U.K.: N/A

CRUZ REAL NO. 2   **86**
Mexico
Ring Gauge: 42 • *Length:* 6"
Filler: Mexico • *Binder:* Mexico •
Wrapper: Mexico
A tart smoke with some slightly vege-
tal tones, but a spicy backbone that
includes hints of black pepper.
U.S.: $3.15 • U.K.: N/A

FELIPE GREGORIO SERENO   **86**
Honduras
Ring Gauge: 42 • *Length:* 5¾"
Filler: Honduras • *Binder:*
Honduras • *Wrapper:* Honduras

This is a medium-bodied cigar with
an earthy character. It has some nut
and herb flavors, with a smooth, well-
balanced finish.
U.S.: $4.70 • U.K.: N/A

FONSECA 8-9-8   **86**
Dominican Republic
Ring Gauge: 43 • *Length:* 6"
Filler: Dom. Rep. • *Binder:* Dom.
Rep. • *Wrapper:* U.S.A./Conn. Shade
This cigar has a nice nutty flavor with
hints of spice and dried orange peel,
and a strong woody finish.
U.S.: $3.50 • U.K.: N/A

H. UPMANN CORONA   **86**
Dominican Republic
Ring Gauge: 42 • *Length:* 5½"
Filler: Dom. Rep. • *Binder:* Dom.
Rep. • *Wrapper:* Indonesia
A medium-bodied cigar with a tangy
character, and a mild spice note on
the palate. A slightly earthy finish.
U.S.: $2.80 • U.K.: N/A

HABANA GOLD BLACK LABEL   **86**
CORONA
Honduras
Ring Gauge: 44 • *Length:* 6"
Filler: Nicaragua • *Binder:*
Nicaragua • *Wrapper:* Indonesia
A mild cigar with a creamy character.
It has some leather and toast notes
with a smooth herbal finish.
U.S.: $4.25 • U.K.: N/A

HOYO DE MONTERREY   **86**
SUPER HOYO
Honduras
Ring Gauge: 44 • *Length:* 5½"
Filler: Nica., Hon., Dom. Rep. •
Binder: Honduras • *Wrapper:*
Ecuador
A young-tasting cigar. It has a pun-
gent earthy aroma, with some vegetal
flavors and a slightly burnt taste.
U.S.: $1.60 • U.K.: N/A

JOSE BENITO PALMA   **86**
Dominican Republic
Ring Gauge: 43 • *Length:* 6"
Filler: Dom. Rep. • *Binder:*
Honduras • *Wrapper:* Cameroon
A corona with medium-bodied, fresh,
creamy tobacco aromas and flavors
and a light aftertaste.
U.S.: $1.90 • U.K.: N/A

JUAN CLEMENTE CLUB   **86**
SELECTION NO. 4
Dominican Republic
Ring Gauge: 42 • *Length:* 5¾"
Filler: Dom. Rep. • *Binder:* Dom.
Rep. • *Wrapper:* U.S.A./Conn. Shade
A good-looking medium-bodied cigar.
It has good spice and herb flavors,
and shows a solid construction.
U.S.: $7.05 • U.K.: N/A

LICENCIADOS NUMERO 4   **86**
Dominican Republic
Ring Gauge: 42 • *Length:* 5½"
Filler: Dom. Rep. • *Binder:* Dom.
Rep. • *Wrapper:* U.S.A./Conn. Shade
A mild- to medium-bodied cigar. It has
some rich creamy flavors, and a solid
core of nuttiness, with a woody finish.
U.S.: $2.10 • U.K.: N/A

MACABI MEDIA CORONA   **86**
U.S.A.
Ring Gauge: 43 • *Length:* 5½"
Filler: Dom. Rep., Nicaragua •
Binder: Mexico • *Wrapper:*
U.S.A./Conn. Shade
A well-balanced cigar with a good
floral character. It has nut and spice
flavors and a light woody finish.
U.S.: $2.65 • U.K.: N/A

MACANUDO DUKE OF DEVON   **86**
Jamaica
Ring Gauge: 42 • *Length:* 5½"
Filler: Dom. Rep., Jamaica • *Binder:*
Mexico • *Wrapper:* U.S.A./Conn.
Shade

A straightforward, mild- to medium-
bodied cigar with solid notes of nuts
and light coffee flavors, and a good
cedary finish.
U.S.: $3.85 • U.K.: N/A

PADRON LONDRES   **86**
Nicaragua
Ring Gauge: 42 • *Length:* 5½"
Filler: Nicaragua • *Binder:*
Nicaragua • *Wrapper:* Ecuador
A rich-tasting cigar with some dark
sweet flavors like chocolate. But a
very firm draw was noted.
U.S.: $1.85 • U.K.: N/A

PARTAGAS CORONA   **86**
Cuba
Ring Gauge: 42 • *Length:* 5½"
Filler: Cuba • *Binder:* Cuba •
Wrapper: Cuba
Another cigar that exhibits signs of
youthfulness. But it has a spicy core of
flavors and an interesting herbal and
woody finish.
U.S.: N/A • U.K.: £6.80

PARTAGAS SABROSOS   **86**
Dominican Republic
Ring Gauge: 43 • *Length:* 5⅛"
Filler: Mexico, Dom. Rep. • *Binder:*
Mexico • *Wrapper:* Cameroon
A rustic cigar that had a loose draw,
some strong grassy flavors, and a balsa
wood component.
U.S.: $4.15 • U.K.: N/A

PARTAGAS NO. 2   **86**
Dominican Republic
Ring Gauge: 44 • *Length:* 5⅛"
Filler: Dom. Rep., Mexico • *Binder:*
Mexico • *Wrapper:* Cameroon
This cigar has a rough-looking wrap-
per. But it has some nut and spice fla-
vors on the palate, and a dry woody
finish.
U.S.: $3.95 • U.K.: N/A

PAUL GARMIRIAN CORONA 86
Dominican Republic
Ring Gauge: 42 • *Length:* 5½"
Filler: Dom. Rep. • *Binder:* Dom.
Rep. • *Wrapper:* U.S.A./Conn.
Shade
Good-tasting, medium-bodied cigar
with baked bread flavors of cinnamon
and nutmeg. There is a sweet tobacco
character with a slightly leathery finish.
U.S.: $6.00 • U.K.: £5.60

RAMON ALLONES PRIVADA "D" 86
Dominican Republic
Ring Gauge: 42 • *Length:* 5"
Filler: Mexico, Dom. Rep. • *Binder:*
Mexico • *Wrapper:* Cameroon
With a dark-brown wrapper and a slow
draw, this cigar is medium-bodied with
a strong, spicy and savory style.
U.S.: $2.35 • U.K.: N/A

SANTA ROSA NO. 4 86
Honduras
Ring Gauge: 42 • *Length:* 5½"
Filler: Honduras • *Binder:*
Honduras • *Wrapper:* Ecuador
A good medium-bodied smoke. It has
a flinty character, but a core of nutti-
ness, and a smooth herbal texture.
U.S.: $2.40 • U.K.: N/A

THOMAS HINDS HONDURAN 86
SELECTION CORONA
Honduras
Ring Gauge: 42 • *Length:* 5½"
Filler: Honduras • *Binder:*
Honduras • *Wrapper:* Ecuador
Although it has a mild finish, this
cigar has some leather and floral
notes, with a hint of chocolate.
U.S.: $2.05 • Canada: $2.40

VUELTABAJO CORONA 86
Dominican Republic
Ring Gauge: 42 • *Length:* 5¼"
Filler: Dom. Rep. • *Binder:* Dom.
Rep. • *Wrapper:* U.S.A./Conn. Shade

A good draw leads into a medium-
bodied smoke with solid tobacco flavors. It has a peppery finish with a
good cedary character.
U.S.: $2.70 • U.K.: N/A

ZINO MOUTON-CADET NO. 1 86
Honduras
Ring Gauge: 44 • *Length:* 6½"
Filler: Honduras • *Binder:* Honduras
Wrapper: U.S.A./Conn. Shade
Well-made with a fine light-brown
wrapper, it shows lovely spicy, slightly
herbal aromas and flavors and a light
aftertaste.
U.S.: $5.50 • U.K.: N/A

BAUZA GRECOS 85
Dominican Republic
Ring Gauge: 42 • *Length:* 5½"
Filler: Dom. Rep., Nicaragua •
Binder: Mexico • *Wrapper:*
Cameroon
A spicy cigar with a light backbone of
flavors of nuts and mild chocolate. It
is still young.
U.S.: $2.50 • U.K.: N/A

BERING IMPERIAL 85
Honduras
Ring Gauge: 42 • *Length:* 5¼"
Filler: Honduras, Mexico, Dom. Rep.,
Nicaragua • *Binder:* Honduras •
Wrapper: Mexico
A bit rough. But it shows a nice
herbal complexity with an earthy
backbone and a toasty finish.
U.S.: $1.35 • U.K.: N/A

CAMACHO NACIONALES 85
Honduras
Ring Gauge: 44 • *Length:* 5½"
Filler: Honduras • *Binder:*
Honduras • *Wrapper:* Honduras
Tasters noted a sweet tobacco taste
with a floral character. There's a bit of
spice on a mild, earthy finish.
U.S.: $2.25 • U.K.: N/A

DON DIEGO CORONA **85**
Dominican Republic
Ring Gauge: 42 • *Length:* 5⅝"
Filler: Dom. Rep. • *Binder:* Dom.
Rep. • *Wrapper:* U.S.A./Conn. Shade
A smooth-tasting, mild cigar that has
some floral notes and a slight nutty fla-
vor, but an overall papery character.
U.S.: $2.85 • U.K.: N/A

DON MELO PETIT CORONA **85**
Honduras
Ring Gauge: 42 • *Length:* 5½"
Filler: Honduras, Nicaragua • *Binder:*
Honduras • *Wrapper:* Honduras
This cigar has a medium-bodied char-
acter. There are flavors of nuts, and a
hint of leather and coffee. A short
finish.
U.S.: $2.35 • U.K.: N/A

DUNHILL VALVERDES **85**
Dominican Republic
Ring Gauge: 42 • *Length:* 5½"
Filler: Dom. Rep., Brazil • *Binder:*
Dom. Rep. • *Wrapper:*
U.S.A./Conn. Shade
A creamy-tasting cigar. It is medium-
bodied with solid spice and herbal fla-
vors, and a light woody finish.
U.S.: $3.90 • U.K.: £5.70

DUNHILL TABARAS **85**
Dominican Republic
Ring Gauge: 42 • *Length:* 5½"
Filler: Dom. Rep., Brazil • *Binder:*
Dom. Rep. • *Wrapper:*
U.S.A./Conn. Shade
This is a mellow cigar with a smooth,
mild texture filled with creamy notes
and some light nutty flavors.
U.S.: $5.90 • U.K.: £6.30

EL RICO HABANO CORONA **85**
U.S.A.
Ring Gauge: 42 • *Length:* 5½"
Filler: Dom. Rep., Nicaragua • *Binder:*
Nicaragua • *Wrapper:* Ecuador

Oily with a rich-brown wrapper, this
cigar shows enticing aromas and flavors of coffee and cinnamon and a
rich long finish.
U.S.: $1.30 • U.K.: N/A

H. UPMANN CORONA MAJOR **85**
TUBE
Dominican Republic
Ring Gauge: 42 • *Length:* 5⅛"
Filler: Dom. Rep. • *Binder:* Dom.
Rep. • *Wrapper:* Indonesia
A solid, medium-bodied smoke.
Strong earthy notes dominate hints of
nut and sweet spices.
U.S.: $3.10 • U.K.: N/A

HOYO DE MONTERREY CORONA **85**
Cuba
Ring Gauge: 42 • *Length:* 5½"
Filler: Cuba • *Binder:* Cuba •
Wrapper: Cuba
A pleasant cigar that shows signs of
youth. It has spicy flavors, but overall a
woody, herbal character with some bite.
U.S.: N/A • U.K.: £6.80

HOYO DE MONTERREY **85**
EXCALIBUR NO. 5
Honduras
Ring Gauge: 43 • *Length:* 6¼"
Filler: Nica., Hon., Dom. Rep. •
Binder: Honduras • *Wrapper:*
Ecuador
Medium-brown-colored, this cigar is
firmly made with a sure and even
draw. Plenty of chocolate and spice
aromas and flavors.
U.S.: $2.30 • U.K.: N/A

LA AURORA NO. 4 **85**
Dominican Republic
Ring Gauge: 42 • *Length:* 5¼"
Filler: Dom. Rep. • *Binder:* Dom.
Rep. • *Wrapper:* Cameroon
A mild cigar with some pleasing
woody spiciness, and a hint of nuts.
U.S.: $1.85 • U.K.: N/A

LEON JIMENES NO. 4   85
Dominican Republic
Ring Gauge: 42 • *Length:* 5%6"
Filler: Dom. Rep. • *Binder:* Dom.
Rep. • *Wrapper:* U.S.A./Conn. Shade
A cigar with a medium-bodied smoke. It
has a light spiciness with a cedary aroma.
U.S.: $3.55 • U.K.: N/A

LOS LIBERTADORES   85
INSURRECTOS
Dominican Republic
Ring Gauge: 42 • *Length:* 5½"
Filler: Dom. Rep. • *Binder:* Dom.
Rep. • *Wrapper:* U.S.A./Conn. Shade
A mild cigar with solid tobacco fla-
vors and character. A bit of spice on
the finish.
U.S.: $3.98 • U.K.: N/A

MACANUDO HAMPTON COURT   85
Jamaica
Ring Gauge: 42 • *Length:* 5¾"
Filler: Dom. Rep., Jamaica • *Binder:*
Mexico • *Wrapper:* U.S.A./Conn.
Shade
A mild cigar with a nutty flavor and a
pleasant creamy texture. Smooth and
mellow.
U.S.: $4.00 • U.K.: N/A

MAYA PETIT CORONA   85
Honduras
Ring Gauge: 42 • *Length:* 5½"
Filler: Honduras, Nicaragua •
Binder: Honduras • *Wrapper:*
U.S.A./Conn. Shade
A medium-bodied cigar that offers hints
of the earth and herbs. It has a toasty
note in the aroma and on the palate.
U.S.: $2.00 • U.K.: N/A

MONTECRUZ SUN GROWN   85
TUBOS
Dominican Republic
Ring Gauge: 42 • *Length:* 6"
Filler: Dom. Rep., Brazil • *Binder:*
Dom. Rep. • *Wrapper:* Indonesia

Although tasters noted a pleasant,
nutty complexity, this cigar finished
with a metallic taste. Good earthy
spice and a touch of sweet tobacco
flavor.
U.S.: $3.75 • U.K.: N/A

TRESADO SELECCION NO. 500   85
Dominican Republic
Ring Gauge: 42 • *Length:* 5½"
Filler: Dom. Rep. • *Binder:*
Cameroon • *Wrapper:* Indonesia
A woody character dominates this
cigar. It has some hints of pepper, and
a fairly neutral finish.
U.S.: $1.60 • U.K.: N/A

ASHTON CORONA   84
Dominican Republic
Ring Gauge: 44 • *Length:* 5½"
Filler: Dom. Rep. • *Binder:* Dom.
Rep. • *Wrapper:* U.S.A./Conn. Shade
A nice mild cigar with some light
spicy flavors, and a pleasant herbal
character.
U.S.: $4.10 • U.K.: N/A

CANARIA D'ORO CORONA   84
Dominican Republic
Ring Gauge: 43 • *Length:* 5½"
Filler: Dom. Rep., Mexico • *Binder:*
Mexico • *Wrapper:* Mexico
A mild cigar with a decent draw. It is
rustic looking but provides some light
nuttiness, and dry, woody finish.
U.S.: $2.10 • U.K.: N/A

EL REY DEL MUNDO HABANA   84
CLUB
Honduras
Ring Gauge: 42 • *Length:* 5½"
Filler: Dom. Rep., Honduras •
Binder: Honduras • *Wrapper:*
Ecuador
A smooth-tasting cigar with a hint of
nuts, and a floral character. It ends up
with a dry finish.
U.S.: $3.50 • U.K.: N/A

EL SUBLIMADO CORONA **84**
Dominican Republic
Ring Gauge: 44 • *Length:* 6"
Filler: Dom. Rep. • *Binder:* Dom.
Rep. • *Wrapper:* U.S.A./Conn. Shade
A very yellow wrapper. This mild- to
medium-bodied cigar has straw-like,
herbal notes with a creamy coffee fla-
vor and a light woody finish.
U.S.: $3.00 • U.K.: £10.00

HENRY CLAY BREVAS **84**
Dominican Republic
Ring Gauge: 42 • *Length:* 5½"
Filler: Dom. Rep. • *Binder:* Dom.
Rep. • *Wrapper:* U.S.A./Conn. Shade
There is a some spice in this cigar, with
some coffee flavors. It has a slightly
earthy quality on the dry finish.
U.S.: $2.25 • U.K.: N/A

JOSÉ MARTI CORONA **84**
Dominican Republic
Ring Gauge: 42 • *Length:* 5½"
Filler: Dom. Rep. • *Binder:* Mexico
Wrapper: U.S.A./Conn. Shade
A smooth, mellow cigar with a
creamy texture, and a mild herbal
character.
U.S.: $2.25 • U.K.: N/A

KNOCKANDO NO. 3 **84**
Dominican Republic
Ring Gauge: 41 • *Length:* 5¼"
Filler: Dom. Rep. • *Binder:* Dom.
Rep. • *Wrapper:* U.S.A./Conn.
Shade
This cigar has an appealing nutty
character, and is well-made with a
surefire draw.
U.S.: $6.75 • U.K.: N/A

LA UNICA NO. 500 **84**
Dominican Republic
Ring Gauge: 42 • *Length:* 5½"
Filler: Dom. Rep. • *Binder:* Dom.
Rep. • *Wrapper:* U.S.A./Conn.
Shade

A greenish brown cigar with a slightly
rough construction. It has a weedy
character with some mild wood on
the finish.
U.S.: $2.35 • U.K.: N/A

LAS CABRILLAS MAGELLAN **84**
Honduras
Ring Gauge: 42 • *Length:* 6"
Filler: Nicaragua, Mexico • *Binder:*
Mexico • *Wrapper:* U.S.A./Conn.
Shade
A medium-bodied cigar with a balsa
wood tone, and a dry papery finish.
There's a touch of white pepper flavor.
U.S.: $1.65 • U.K.: N/A

LICENCIADOS SUPREME **84**
MADURO NO. 200
Dominican Republic
Ring Gauge: 42 • *Length:* 5"
Filler: Dom. Rep. • *Binder:* Dom.
Rep. • *Wrapper:* U.S.A./Conn. Shade
A good maduro cigar. It has flavors of
coffee and cola, with a solid spicy fin-
ish, and an overall mild character.
U.S.: $2.75 • U.K.: N/A

MI CUBANO NO. 542 **84**
Nicaragua
Ring Gauge: 42 • *Length:* 5"
Filler: Nicaragua • *Binder:*
Nicaragua • *Wrapper:* Nicaragua
All tasters noted a tight draw on this
otherwise medium-bodied cigar. It
had some smooth creamy flavors with
a hint of earthiness.
U.S.: $3.10 • U.K.: N/A

POR LARRAÑAGA NACIONALES **84**
Dominican Republic
Ring Gauge: 42 • *Length:* 5½"
Filler: Dom. Rep. • *Binder:* Dom.
Rep. • *Wrapper:* U.S.A./Conn. Shade
This is a well-balanced, medium-bod-
ied cigar. It has some good hints of
nuts with a creamy texture.
U.S.: $3.60 • U.K.: N/A

PRIMO DEL REY NO. 4   84
Dominican Republic
Ring Gauge: 42 • *Length:* 5½"
Filler: Dom. Rep. • *Binder:* Dom.
Rep. • *Wrapper:* Indonesia
This cigar has a light, salty character.
But it has some mild, light tobacco
flavors and an earthy finish.
U.S.: $1.65 • U.K.: N/A

PUNCH NO. 75   84
Honduras
Ring Gauge: 43 • *Length:* 5½"
Filler: Nica., Hon., Dom. Rep. •
Binder: Ecuador • *Wrapper:* Ecuador
Although there is a hint of a vegetal
quality, this cigar has a solid peppery
core. It needs time to age.
U.S.: $1.60 • U.K.: N/A

SOSA BREVAS   84
Dominican Republic
Ring Gauge: 43 • *Length:* 5½"
Filler: Dom. Rep. • *Binder:*
Honduras • *Wrapper:* Ecuador
A cigar with some vegetal notes on
the palate, but it finishes with a light
spiciness and earthiness.
U.S.: $2.50 • U.K.: N/A

THOMAS HINDS NICARAGUAN   84
SELECTION CORONA
Nicaragua
Ring Gauge: 42 • *Length:* 5½"
Filler: Nicaragua • *Binder:*
Nicaragua • *Wrapper:* Nicaragua
A cigar dominated by some woody
flavors with a creamy texture. There
is smoothness here with a light spicy
finish.
U.S.: $3.70 • Canada: $3.95

8-9-8 COLLECTION CORONA   83
Jamaica
Ring Gauge: 42 • *Length:* 5½"
Filler: Jamaica, Dom. Rep. • *Binder:*
Mexico • *Wrapper:* U.S.A./Conn.
Shade

A medium-bodied smoke with a
smooth texture and some spice, but
an overall dry, papery character.
U.S.: $5.50 • U.K.: N/A

CABALLEROS CORONA   83
Dominican Republic
Ring Gauge: 43 • *Length:* 5¾"
Filler: Dom. Rep. • *Binder:* Dom.
Rep. • *Wrapper:* U.S.A./Conn. Shade
A cigar with a creamy texture, and mild
character. It has an easy-smoking but-
tery flavor with a slight cedary finish.
U.S.: $2.80 • U.K.: N/A

JOYA DE NICARAGUA NO. 6   83
Nicaragua
Ring Gauge: 42 • *Length:* 6"
Filler: Nicaragua • *Binder:*
Nicaragua • *Wrapper:* Nicaragua
This cigar is rustic, with slightly sour
herbal flavors, although it has a touch
of spice on the finish.
U.S.: $2.20 • U.K.: N/A

LA HOJA SELECTA CETROS DE   83
ORO
U.S.A.
Ring Gauge: 43 • *Length:* 5¾"
Filler: Dom. Rep., Mexico, Brazil •
Binder: Dom. Rep. • *Wrapper:*
U.S.A./Conn. Shade
Straightforward corona with pleasing
herbal, tobacco character. Very hand-
some and well-constructed but one-
dimensional in flavor.
U.S.: $1.65 • U.K.: N/A

NAT SHERMAN CITY DESK   83
GAZETTE
Dominican Republic
Ring Gauge: 42 • *Length:* 6"
Filler: Dom. Rep. • *Binder:* Dom.
Rep. • *Wrapper:* Dom. Rep.
A maduro cigar. It has an earthy char-
acter with flavors of nuts and herbs,
and a solid tobacco core.
U.S.: $4.00 • U.K.: N/A

ONYX 642   83
Dominican Republic
Ring Gauge: 42 • *Length:* 6"
Filler: Dom. Rep., Mexico • *Binder:*
Indonesia • *Wrapper:* Mexico
A slightly rough maduro with a
smooth, round flavor, and a touch of
sweet spice on the palate.
U.S.: $2.50 • U.K.: N/A

PUNCH ROYAL CORONATION   83
Honduras
Ring Gauge: 44 • *Length:* 5¼"
Filler: Honduras, Nicaragua, Dom. Rep.
Binder: Honduras • *Wrapper:* Ecuador
This medium-bodied cigar has some
vegetal notes with a leathery flavor,
and some spice on a long finish.
Shows its youth.
U.S.: $2.35 • U.K.: N/A

ROMEO & JULIETA CORONA   83
Dominican Republic
Ring Gauge: 44 • *Length:* 5½"
Filler: Dom. Rep., U.S.A. • *Binder:*
U.S.A./Conn. Broadleaf • *Wrapper:*
Cameroon
The wrapper is a little rough and uneven
in color, but there's plenty of spicy nut-
meg and tobacco aromas and flavors.
U.S.: $1.80 • U.K.: N/A

V CENTENNIAL CORONA   83
Honduras
Ring Gauge: 42 • *Length:* 5½"
Filler: Honduras, Dom.Rep.,
Nicaragua • *Binder:* Mexico •
Wrapper: U.S.A./Conn. Shade
Some inconsistency noted. This cigar
showed some nutty flavors, and a bit
of spice, but a flat finish.
U.S.: $3.00 • U.K.: N/A

ZINO DIAMONDS   83
Honduras
Ring Gauge: 40 • *Length:* 5½"
Filler: Honduras • *Binder:* Honduras
Wrapper: U.S.A./Conneciteut Shade

A small cigar. It has a light, mild
character with some nutty flavors,
and a smooth woody finish.
U.S.: $4.20 • U.K.: N/A

PETERSON CORONA   82
Dominican Republic
Ring Gauge: 43 • *Length:* 5¼"
Filler: Dom. Rep. • *Binder:* Ecuador
Wrapper: U.S.A./Conn. Shade
A rather rustic, rough cigar. It has a
straw-like character, and a dry spice
finish.
U.S.: $6.00 • U.K.: N/A

BACCARAT PETIT CORONA   81
Honduras
Ring Gauge: 42 • *Length:* 5½"
Filler: Honduras • *Binder:* Mexico
Wrapper: Honduras
This cigar has a light sweet gum on
the wrapper. It has pleasing notes of
tobacco flavor, but has straw-like fla-
vors on the palate.
U.S.: $1.60 • U.K.: N/A

PLEIADES ORION   81
Dominican Republic
Ring Gauge: 42 • *Length:* 5¼"
Filler: Dom. Rep. • *Binder:* Dom.
Rep. • *Wrapper:* U.S.A./Conn.
Shade
This cigar has a dry, papery character
with some hints of grass in an other-
wise creamy texture.
U.S.: $5.48 • U.K.: N/A

DON JUAN CETRO   80
Nicaragua
Ring Gauge: 43 • *Length:* 6"
Filler: Nicaragua • *Binder:* Dom.
Rep. • *Wrapper:* U.S.A./Conn.
Shade
A mild cigar. It has some decent
tobacco components, but overall is a
little rough, and a vegetal character
dominates.
U.S.: $2.00 • U.K.: N/A

TE-AMO MEDITATION   80
Mexico
Ring Gauge: 42 • *Length:* 6"
Filler: Mexico • *Binder:* Mexico •
Wrapper: Mexico
A cigar with a tight draw. It also has a
salty character with flavors of straw
and paper. A hint of pepper on the
finish.
U.S.: $2.30 • U.K.: N/A

ROBUSTO

BOLIVAR ROYAL CORONAS   95
Cuba
Ring Gauge: 50 • *Length:* 5"
Filler: Cuba • *Binder:* Cuba •
Wrapper: Cuba
A powerful, spicy smoke with the
rich, earthy flavor of leather, sweet
spices like cinnamon and nutmeg,
and a dash of chocolate. It delivers a
smooth, nutty, long-lasting finish.
U.S.: N/A • U.K.: £6.08

HOYO DE MONTERREY EPICURE   94
NO. 2
Cuba
Ring Gauge: 50 • *Length:* 5"
Filler: Cuba • *Binder:* Cuba •
Wrapper: Cuba
A rich, full-bodied smoke filled with
solid spice, sweet coffee-bean and cocoa-
bean flavors and a long spicy finish.
U.S.: N/A • U.K.: £6.64

FLOR DE CANO SHORT   93
CHURCHILL
Cuba
Ring Gauge: 50 • *Length:* 5"
Filler: Cuba • *Binder:* Cuba •
Wrapper: Cuba
A rich, full-flavored smoke with lots
of spice and cinnamon, and mild
cocoa bean flavors.
U.S.: N/A • U.K.: £5.61

COHIBA ROBUSTO   92
Cuba
Ring Gauge: 50 • *Length:* 5"
Filler: Cuba • *Binder:* Cuba •
Wrapper: Cuba
This cigar's wrapper has a nice sheen.
It is a rich smoke that smooths out
quickly to full-bodied, earthy flavors
of nutmeg and cocoa with a long
spicy finish.
U.S.: N/A • U.K.: £10.12

OPUS X FUENTE FUENTE   90
ROBUSTO
Dominican Republic
Ring Gauge: 50 • *Length:* 5¼"
Filler: Dom. Rep. • *Binder:* Dom.
Rep. • *Wrapper:* Dom. Rep.
A strong, full-bodied smoke with rich
flavors of sweet spices and a leathery,
cedar box character.
U.S.: $8.00 • U.K.: N/A

RAMON ALLONES SPECIALLY   90
SELECTED
Cuba
Ring Gauge: 50 • *Length:* 5"
Filler: Cuba • *Binder:* Cuba •
Wrapper: Cuba
A rich, full-bodied cigar with spice
and coffee flavors, and a nice nut and
cedar finish.
U.S.: N/A • U.K.: £5.96

ARTURO FUENTE DON CARLOS   89
ROBUSTO
Dominican Republic
Ring Gauge: 50 • *Length:* 5"
Filler: Dom. Rep. • *Binder:* Dom.
Rep. • *Wrapper:* Cameroon
A nice oily wrapper. This is a full-
bodied cigar with rich, spicy flavors
and a long spicy finish.
U.S.: $7.00 • U.K.: N/A

Perfect Companion To A Great Cigar

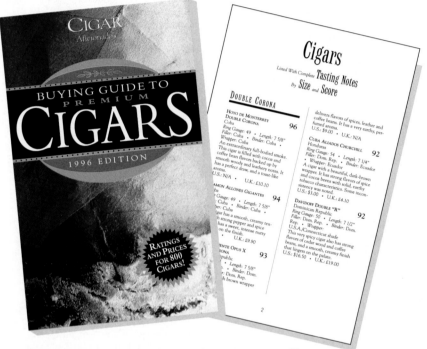

The 1996 edition to the *Buying Guide to Premium Cigars* is the ultimate resource for cigar lovers. It features over 800 ratings and tasting notes for every cigar ever reviewed in *Cigar Aficionado* magazine. Each cigar is listed with its price, country of origin, type of tobacco, and a description of its strength and flavor.

Find out if the robusto you're considering is a "classic" or if you shouldn't waste your money. Does it have a great draw? Is there a pleasing finish? Get the score from the cigar experts.

The 1996 edition also features a complete list of cigar-friendly restaurants as well as retailers in major cities across the country and around the world. For just $9.95, the *Buying Guide* will save you time and money and more importantly, enhance your enjoyment of a fine cigar. Buy a copy for yourself and a good friend!

CIGAR
Aficionado

FONSECA 5-50   **89**
Dominican Republic
Ring Gauge: 50 • *Length:* 5"
Filler: Dom. Rep. • *Binder:* Mexico
Wrapper: U.S.A./Conn. Shade
A well-balanced, medium-bodied
cigar that has mild spices and a soft,
mellow character that includes hints
of cocoa and caramel.
U.S.: $3.50 • U.K.: N/A

**ROMEO Y JULIETA EXHIBICION   89
NO. 4**
Cuba
Ring Gauge: 48 • *Length:* 5"
Filler: Cuba • *Binder:* Cuba •
Wrapper: Cuba
This cigar has a strong, earthy com-
ponent with leather and pepper fla-
vors, and a long, spicy finish.
U.S.: N/A • U.K.: £5.92

V CENTENNIAL ROBUSTO   89
Honduras
Ring Gauge: 50 • *Length:* 5"
Filler: Dom. Rep., Honduras,
Nicaragua • *Binder:* Mexico •
Wrapper: U.S.A./Conn. Shade
This cigar has mild coffee bean fla-
vors and a smooth spiciness on a solid
tobacco core.
U.S.: $3.75 • U.K.: N/A

ASHTON MAGNUM   88
Dominican Republic
Ring Gauge: 50 • *Length:* 5"
Filler: Dom. Rep. • *Binder:* Dom.
Rep. • *Wrapper:* U.S.A./Conn. Shade
A pleasant, medium-bodied cigar
with solid flavors of mild spices and
an earthy quality on the finish.
U.S.: $3.35 • U.K.: N/A

CANARIA D'ORO ROTHSCHILD   88
Dominican Republic
Ring Gauge: 50 • *Length:* 4½"
Filler: Mexico, Dom. Rep. • *Binder:*
Mexico • *Wrapper:* Mexico

A mild, fragrant cigar that has a light
creamy character with solid hints of
spice on the palate.
U.S.: $1.50 • U.K.: N/A

DUNHILL ALTAMIRA   88
Dominican Republic
Ring Gauge: 48 • *Length:* 5"
Filler: Dom. Rep. • *Binder:* Dom.
Rep. • *Wrapper:* U.S.A./Conn.
Shade
A pretty, medium-brown wrapper
leads into a well-balanced tobacco
character with mild spice and nut
flavors.
U.S.: $5.00 • U.K.: £5.65

ENCANTO ROTHSCHILD   88
Honduras
Ring Gauge: 50 • *Length:* 4½"
Filler: Honduras • *Binder:*
Honduras • *Wrapper:* Honduras
This cigar comes with an attractive
brown wrapper. It has rich spicy fla-
vors with notes of coffee beans, and a
long aftertaste.
U.S.: $2.00 • U.K.: N/A

LICENCIADOS WAVELL   88
Dominican Republic
Ring Gauge: 50 • *Length:* 5"
Filler: Dom. Rep. • *Binder:* Dom.
Rep. • *Wrapper:* U.S.A./Conn.
Shade
A well-balanced, well-made cigar
with light, creamy flavors, and a dried
sweet fruit and cedar character.
U.S.: $2.20 • U.K.: N/A

PARTAGAS SERIES D NO. 4   88
Cuba
Ring Gauge: 50 • *Length:* 5"
Filler: Cuba • *Binder:* Cuba •
Wrapper: Cuba
A solid, rich cigar with a mellow spici-
ness and coffee flavors. A good balance
on the finish. Can be slow to start.
U.S.: N/A • U.K.: £6.52

POR LARRAÑAGA ROBUSTO   88
Dominican Republic
Ring Gauge: 50 • *Length:* 5"
Filler: Dom. Rep. • *Binder:* Dom.
Rep. • *Wrapper:* U.S.A./Conn.
Shade
This is a well-made cigar with a firm draw. It has nice chestnut and sweet spice elements on the palate, and a smooth, mild finish.
U.S.: $3.60 • U.K.: N/A

ZINO MOUTON-CADET NO. 6   88
Honduras
Ring Gauge: 50 • *Length:* 5"
Filler: Honduras • *Binder:*
Honduras • *Wrapper:* Ecuador
There is a creamy smoothness to this mellow cigar, which has a long, mild spice finish and an elegant character.
U.S.: $6.00 • Switzerland: 6SF

AVO XO INTERMEZZO   87
Dominican Republic
Ring Gauge: 50 • *Length:* 5½"
Filler: Dom. Rep. • *Binder:* Dom.
Rep. • *Wrapper:* U.S.A./Conn.
Shade
A pretty wrapper with a nice sheen. The cigar has woody flavors and a pleasant spicy finish.
U.S.: $6.75 • U.K.: N/A

DAVIDOFF SPECIAL "R"   87
Dominican Republic
Ring Gauge: 50 • *Length:* 4⅞"
Filler: Dom. Rep. • *Binder:* Dom.
Rep. • *Wrapper:* U.S.A./Conn.
Shade
A cigar with some solid spice notes, but it has a bit of sourness on the finish and a dry wood character.
U.S.: $8.25 • U.K.: £11.12

DON TOMAS SPECIAL EDITION   87
NO. 300
Honduras
Ring Gauge: 50 • *Length:* 5"
Filler: Honduras • *Binder:*
Honduras • *Wrapper:* Honduras
A woody, earthy complexity highlights this medium-bodied cigar with a pretty brown wrapper.
U.S.: $3.45 • U.K.: N/A

MACANUDO HYDE PARK   87
Jamaica
Ring Gauge: 49 • *Length:* 5½"
Filler: Dom. Rep., Jamaica • *Binder:*
Mexico • *Wrapper:* U.S.A./Conn.
Shade
This is a mild, creamy smoke with a hint of nuttiness and a delicate cedar aroma.
U.S.: $3.20 • U.K.: N/A

PLEIADES PLUTON   87
Dominican Republic
Ring Gauge: 50 • *Length:* 5"
Filler: Dom. Rep. • *Binder:* Dom.
Rep. • *Wrapper:* U.S.A./Conn.
Shade
This cigar is a creamy smoke with solid spice notes. It burns very well and has a satisfying mild tobacco aftertaste.
U.S.: $5.35 • U.K.: N/A

ROYAL JAMAICA ROBUSTO   87
Dominican Republic
Ring Gauge: 49 • *Length:* 4½"
Filler: Jamaica • *Binder:* Java •
Wrapper: Cameroon
A nice brown wrapper. This is a medium-bodied cigar with well-balanced flavors of mild spices.
U.S.: $2.20 • U.K.: N/A

VUELTABAJO ROBUSTO — 87
Dominican Republic
Ring Gauge: 52 • *Length:* 4¼"
Filler: Dom. Rep. • *Binder:* Dom.
Rep. • *Wrapper:* U.S.A./Conn.
Shade
This is a solid mild cigar with some
hints of nuts and light spicy flavors
and a light creamy aftertaste.
U.S.: $2.10 • U.K.: N/A

H. UPMANN PEQUENOS 100 — 86
Dominican Republic
Ring Gauge: 50 • *Length:* 4½"
Filler: Dom. Rep., Brazil • *Binder:*
Dom. Rep. • *Wrapper:* Cameroon
This is a good, all-around robusto
with a dark brown wrapper. It is very
well-made and gives a good draw.
Attractive rich espresso flavors and a
medium finish.
U.S.: $1.50 • U.K.: N/A

H. UPMANN CABINET SELECTION No. 100 — 86
Dominican Republic
Ring Gauge: 50 • *Length:* 4¼"
Filler: Dom. Rep. • *Binder:* Dom.
Rep. • *Wrapper:* Cameroon
A dark-wrapped cigar with strong,
dark spice flavors, as well as hints of
chocolate. There is a bit of tartness
on the palate and the finish.
U.S.: $4.20 • U.K.: N/A

HOYO DE MONTERREY ROTHSCHILD — 86
Honduras
Ring Gauge: 50 • *Length:* 4½"
Filler: Honduras • *Binder:*
Honduras • *Wrapper:*
U.S.A./Conn. Shade
This full-bodied cigar has some solid
spice and pepper flavors with a woody
finish.
U.S.: $1.55 • U.K.: N/A

NAT SHERMAN ASTOR — 86
Dominican Republic
Ring Gauge: 50 • *Length:* 4½"
Filler: Dom. Rep. • *Binder:* Dom.
Rep. • *Wrapper:* U.S.A./Conn.
Shade
A light cigar with a smooth draw and
a mild spicy flavor that turns to a
dried wood character on the finish.
U.S.: $4.40 • U.K.: N/A

NAT SHERMAN HOBART — 86
Honduras
Ring Gauge: 50 • *Length:* 5"
Filler: Honduras • *Binder:* Mexico
Wrapper: U.S.A./Conn. Shade
A cigar with a few light grassy flavors
and a smooth, mild finish that con-
tains some medium spiciness.
U.S.: $3.40 • U.K.: N/A

PARTAGAS ROBUSTO — 86
Dominican Republic
Ring Gauge: 49 • *Length:* 4½"
Filler: Mexico, Dom. Rep. • *Binder:*
Mexico • *Wrapper:* Cameroon
A medium-bodied cigar with a strong
earthy component, and some mild
spicy flavors on a dry finish.
U.S.: $2.95 • U.K.: N/A

ROMEO & JULIETA VINTAGE No. 3 — 86
Dominican Republic
Ring Gauge: 50 • *Length:* 4½"
Filler: Dom. Rep. • *Binder:* Mexico
Wrapper: U.S.A./Conn. Shade
This cigar has a strong herbal compo-
nent, but soft spice flavors round out
the texture through a long finish.
U.S.: $5.00 • U.K.: N/A

SANTA DAMIANA NO. 500 **86**
Dominican Republic
Ring Gauge: 50 • *Length:* 5"
Filler: Dom. Rep. • *Binder:* Dom.
Rep. • *Wrapper:* U.S.A./Conn.
Shade
A medium-bodied cigar with a strong
cedary note on the palate, and a
smooth mellow finish.
U.S.: $5.50 • U.K.: N/A

THOMAS HINDS HONDURAN **86**
SELECTION ROBUSTO
Honduras
Ring Gauge: 50 • *Length:* 5"
Filler: Honduras • *Binder:*
Honduras • *Wrapper:* Ecuador
This is a medium-bodied cigar with
some solid earthy flavors, and a light
vegetal quality.
U.S.: $1.95 • Canada: $2.25

ARTURO FUENTE CHATEAU **85**
FUENTE
Dominican Republic
Ring Gauge: 50 • *Length:* 5"
Filler: Dom. Rep. • *Binder:* Dom.
Rep. • *Wrapper:* U.S.A./Conn.
Shade
Some inconsistency in this cigar.
Good spice flavors with several
woody notes.
U.S.: $1.90 • U.K.: N/A

ASHTON AGED MADURO **85**
NO. 10
Dominican Republic
Ring Gauge: 50 • *Length:* 5"
Filler: Dom. Rep. • *Binder:* Dom.
Rep. • *Wrapper:* Connecticut
Broadleaf
A solid cigar with a dark-brown wrap-
per. It has some good spicy flavors
and a nice tobacco finish.
U.S.: $3.75 • U.K.: N/A

CABALLEROS ROTHSCHILD **85**
Dominican Republic
Ring Gauge: 50 • *Length:* 5"
Filler: Dom. Rep. • *Binder:* Dom.
Rep. • *Wrapper:* U.S.A./Conn.
Shade
A cigar with some solid tobacco fla-
vors, also has a light spicy character
with medium-bodied smoke.
U.S.: $3.00 • U.K.: N/A

DON LINO COLORADO **85**
Honduras
Ring Gauge: 50 • *Length:* 5½"
Filler: Nicaragua, Honduras •
Binder: U.S.A./Conn. Broadleaf •
Wrapper: U.S.A./Conn. Shade
A firm, well-made cigar with solid
nutty flavors and a woody character,
with a hot, almost metallic finish.
U.S.: $5.20 • U.K.: N/A

DON TOMAS ROTHSCHILD **85**
Honduras
Ring Gauge: 50 • *Length:* 4½"
Filler: Honduras • *Binder:*
Honduras • *Wrapper:* Honduras
A cigar with some rough spots and a
tendency toward a loose fill. But it
has a solid spicy core with good
tobacco flavors.
U.S.: $1.65 • U.K.: N/A

EL SUBLIMADO REGARDETE **85**
Dominican Republic
Ring Gauge: 50 • *Length:* 4½"
Filler: Dom. Rep. • *Binder:* Dom.
Rep. • *Wrapper:* U.S.A./Conn.
Shade
Some inconsistencies in this cigar.
Overall, it has a mild character with
some spicy flavors and a decent,
smooth finish.
U.S.: $8.00 • France: 68FF

H. UPMANN CABINET   **85**
SELECTION ROBUSTO
Dominican Republic
Ring Gauge: 50 • *Length:* 4¾"
Filler: Dom. Rep. • *Binder:* Dom.
Rep. • *Wrapper:* Cameroon
A cigar with some earthy, herbaceous
flavors that come with an overlay of
light spices.
U.S.: $4.20 • U.K.: N/A

JUAN CLEMENTE ROTHSCHILD   **85**
Dominican Republic
Ring Gauge: 50 • *Length:* 4⅞"
Filler: Dom. Rep. • *Binder:* Dom.
Rep. • *Wrapper:* U.S.A./Conn. Shade
This cigar has strong, spicy flavors but
with a heavy, dry wood undertone
and a short finish.
U.S.: $4.70 • U.K.: N/A

LA GLORIA CUBANA WAVELL   **85**
U.S.A.
Ring Gauge: 50 • *Length:* 5"
Filler: Dom. Rep., Nicaragua •
Binder: Nicaragua • *Wrapper:*
Ecuador
A cigar with a clean finish, and a
mild spiciness and some exotic floral
flavors on the palate.
U.S.: $2.15 • U.K.: N/A

LEON JIMENES ROBUSTO   **85**
Dominican Republic
Ring Gauge: 50 • *Length:* 5½"
Filler: Dom. Rep. • *Binder:* Dom.
Rep. • *Wrapper:* U.S.A./Conn. Shade
This cigar shows some inconsistency
of construction, but it has a pleasant
cedary flavor tinged with spice.
U.S.: $4.35 • U.K.: N/A

MACANUDO VINTAGE No. V   **85**
Jamaica
Ring Gauge: 49 • *Length:* 5½"
Filler: Dom. Rep., Jamaica • *Binder:*
Mexico • *Wrapper:* U.S.A./Conn.
Shade

A light, easy-smoking cigar that tends
toward some grassy and straw flavors.
U.S.: $7.00 • U.K.: N/A

MONTECRISTO ROBUSTO   **85**
Dominican Republic
Ring Gauge: 50 • *Length:* 4¾"
Filler: Dom. Rep., Brazil • *Binder:*
Dom. Rep. • *Wrapper:* Cameroon
This cigar has some earthy, herbal
notes that blend at first into a slight
harshness, but the smoke ends with
nut and mild spice flavors.
U.S.: $6.00 • U.K.: N/A

PARTAGAS NATURAL   **85**
Dominican Republic
Ring Gauge: 49 • *Length:* 5½"
Filler: Mexico, Dom. Rep. • *Binder:*
Mexico • *Wrapper:* Cameroon
A well-made, medium-bodied cigar
that has some mild spice components
and a clean tobacco finish.
U.S.: $3.20 • U.K.: N/A

BACCARAT HAVANA   **84**
SELECTION ROBUSTO
Honduras
Ring Gauge: 50 • *Length:* 5"
Filler: Honduras • *Binder:* Mexico
Wrapper: Honduras
A cigar with sweet gum on the wrap-
per. It is mild with some light spicy
notes.
U.S.: $1.70 • U.K.: N/A

CUBA ALIADOS ROTHSCHILD   **84**
Honduras
Ring Gauge: 50 • *Length:* 5"
Filler: Dom. Rep. • *Binder:* Ecuador
Wrapper: Ecuador
This is a pretty, but simple, cigar. It
has slightly vegetal and earthy flavors
and a smooth, medium-bodied tex-
ture.
U.S.: $2.20 • U.K.: £2.20

DIANA SILVIUS ROBUSTO   **84**
Dominican Republic
Ring Gauge: 52 • *Length:* 4⅞"
Filler: Dom. Rep. • *Binder:* Dom.
Rep. • *Wrapper:* U.S.A./Conn.
Shade
This cigar had some nice pepper flavors, but it burned a little hot and several tasters noted a harsh aftertaste.
U.S.: $5.30 • U.K.: N/A

DON LINO ROBUSTO   **84**
Honduras
Ring Gauge: 50 • *Length:* 5½"
Filler: Sumatra • *Binder:* Sumatra
Wrapper: U.S.A./Conn. Shade
There is a tart, almost sour quality to this cigar. It has some dry, grassy flavors that turn to soft creamy notes on the finish.
U.S.: $2.10 • U.K.: N/A

DUNHILL ROMANAS VINTAGE   **84**
1987
Dominican Republic
Ring Gauge: 50 • *Length:* 4½"
Filler: Dom. Rep. • *Binder:* Dom.
Rep. • *Wrapper:* U.S.A./Conn. Shade
A cigar with medium-bodied flavors of spice and a toasty, almost burnt aroma.
U.S.: $4.45 • U.K.: £5.10

JOSE BENITO ROTHSCHILD   **84**
Dominican Republic
Ring Gauge: 50 • *Length:* 4¾"
Filler: Dom. Rep. • *Binder:*
Honduras • *Wrapper:* Cameroon
This cigar starts slowly, but offers pleasant spice flavors on a smooth texture.
U.S.: $2.15 • U.K.: N/A

JUAN CLEMENTE CLUB   **84**
SELECTION NO. 2
Dominican Republic
Ring Gauge: 46 • *Length:* 4½
Filler: Dom. Rep. • *Binder:* Dom.
Rep. • *Wrapper:* U.S.A./Conn.
Shade

Inconsistent. Some tasters noted strong spicy and cedar flavors. Others found the smoke harsh and sour.
U.S.: $5.75 • U.K.: N/A

LA UNICA NO. 400   **84**
Dominican Republic
Ring Gauge: 50 • *Length:* 4½"
Filler: Dom. Rep. • *Binder:* Dom.
Rep. • *Wrapper:* U.S.A./Conn.
Shade
This is a rough cigar that has a solid spicy flavor and a mild nuttiness.
U.S.: $1.65 • U.K.: N/A

NAT SHERMAN SUTTON   **84**
Dominican Republic
Ring Gauge: 49 • *Length:* 5½"
Filler: Dom. Rep. • *Binder:* Mexico
Wrapper: Mexico
An unattractive wrapper. The cigar has a toasty aroma but lacks some spice, and has a flat, almost bitter finish.
U.S.: $3.80 • U.K.: N/A

PAUL GARMIRIAN SERIES NO. 2 **84**
Dominican Republic
Ring Gauge: 48 • *Length:* 4¼"
Filler: Dom. Rep. • *Binder:* Dom.
Rep. • *Wrapper:* U.S.A./Conn. Shade
This cigar's wrapper has a gummy vegetal character that masks some complex spice flavors. It has a sharp, biting finish.
U.S.: $6.40 • U.K.: £6.35

ROMEO & JULIETA   **84**
ROTHSCHILD
Dominican Republic
Ring Gauge: 50 • *Length:* 5"
Filler: Dom. Rep., Brazil • *Binder:*
U.S.A./Conn. Broadleaf • *Wrapper:*
Cameroon
This is a very mild cigar with a dry, papery flavor, although there is a bit of spice.
U.S.: $2.10 • U.K.: N/A

SOSA WAVELL   84
Dominican Republic
Ring Gauge: 50 • *Length:* 4¾"
Filler: Dom. Rep., Brazil • *Binder:*
Honduras • *Wrapper:* Ecuador
A pleasant cigar with a slight vegetal
quality, but it also has a tangy and
spicy finish.
U.S.: $2.25 • U.K.: N/A

TEMPLE HALL NO. 550   84
Jamaica
Ring Gauge: 50 • *Length:* 5½"
Filler: Dom. Rep., Jamaica • *Binder:*
Mexico • *Wrapper:* U.S.A./Conn.
Shade
This is a light, creamy cigar with a
simple grassy element, and some
green, immature flavors.
U.S.: $5.20 • U.K.: N/A

AVO NO. 9   83
Dominican Republic
Ring Gauge: 48 • *Length:* 4¾"
Filler: Dom. Rep. • *Binder:* Dom.
Rep. • *Wrapper:* U.S.A./Conn. Shade
A cigar with earthy aromas, but with
slightly sour, acidic flavors.
U.S.: $4.75 • U.K.: N/A

BAUZA ROBUSTO   83
Dominican Republic
Ring Gauge: 50 • *Length:* 5½"
Filler: Dom. Rep., Nicaragua •
Binder: Mexico • *Wrapper:*
Cameroon
This cigar has a sour bite on the
palate, but some tasters noted a spicy
aftertaste.
U.S.: $2.25 • U.K.: N/A

DON LINO HABANA RESERVE   83
ROBUSTO
Honduras
Ring Gauge: 50 • *Length:* 5½"
Filler: Connecticut broadleaf •
Binder: Sumatra • *Wrapper:*
U.S.A./Conn. Shade

Grassy flavors dominate this mild
cigar with a firm draw.
U.S.: $3.95 • U.K.: N/A

EL REY DEL MUNDO ROBUSTO   83
Honduras
Ring Gauge: 54 • *Length:* 5"
Filler: Honduras • *Binder:*
Honduras • *Wrapper:* Honduras
A quite unattractive wrapper.
Inconsistencies in the draw were
noted, but otherwise the cigar has
some woody, spicy flavors.
U.S.: $2.50 • U.K.: N/A

LAS CABRILLAS CORTEZ   83
Honduras
Ring Gauge: 50 • *Length:* 4¾"
Filler: Dom. Rep., Mexico • *Binder:*
Mexico • *Wrapper:* U.S.A./Conn.
Shade
This mild cigar has some construction
flaws, but it shows off some light flo-
ral and dried fruit flavors.
U.S.: $1.20 • U.K.: N/A

MONTECRUZ SUN GROWN   83
ROBUSTO
Dominican Republic
Ring Gauge: 49 • *Length:* 4½"
Filler: Dom. Rep., Brazil • *Binder:*
Dom. Rep. • *Wrapper:* Cameroon
A medium-bodied cigar with earthy,
vegetal flavors that offer some hints
of spice on the finish.
U.S.: $2.20 • U.K.: N/A

PRIMO DEL REY NO. 100   83
Dominican Republic
Ring Gauge: 50 • *Length:* 4½"
Filler: Dom. Rep. • *Binder:* Dom.
Rep. • *Wrapper:* Brazil
A nice, well-balanced cigar with
some creamy flavors of mild coffee
and a hint of spice.
U.S.: $1.70 • U.K.: N/A

PUNCH ROTHSCHILD **83**
Honduras
Ring Gauge: 50 • *Length:* 4½"
Filler: Honduras, Nicaragua, Dom.
Rep. • *Binder:* Honduras •
Wrapper: U.S.A./ Connecticut Shade
A loose fill in this cigar creates a hot,
spicy draw that mellows a bit to some
nut and wood flavors.
U.S.: $1.55 • U.K.: N/A

PUNCH GRAND CRU ROBUSTO **83**
Honduras
Ring Gauge: 50 • *Length:* 5¼"
Filler: Honduras • *Binder:*
Honduras • *Wrapper:* Honduras
This is a straightforward robusto that
lacks a bit of depth, but it shows some
spice flavors and a good balance.
U.S.: $3.25 • U.K.: N/A

CRUZ REAL NO. 25 **82**
Mexico
Ring Gauge: 52 • *Length:* 5½"
Filler: Mexico • *Binder:* Mexico •
Wrapper: Sumatra
A rather rough wrapper leads into a
dry wood, almost cedar flavor that
lacks interest.
U.S.: $2.60 • U.K.: £3.50

EL REY DEL MUNDO ROBUSTO **82**
DE MANUEL
Honduras
Ring Gauge: 54 • *Length:* 5"
Filler: Honduras • *Binder:*
Honduras • *Wrapper:* Honduras
A solid cigar that lacks complexity. It
has dry, straw-like flavors with a few
woody notes and a short finish.
U.S.: $2.50 • U.K.: N/A

TE-AMO TORITO **82**
Mexico
Ring Gauge: 50 • *Length:* 4¾"
Filler: Mexico • *Binder:* Mexico •
Wrapper: Mexico

Irregular construction hurts this cigar.
It has a medium-bodied character
with spice and strong cedar components.
U.S.: $1.90 • U.K.: N/A

TROYA NO. 18 **82**
Dominican Republic
Ring Gauge: 50 • *Length:* 4¼"
Filler: Dom. Rep. • *Binder:* Dom.
Rep. • *Wrapper:* U.S.A./Conn.
Shade
A loose draw creates a grassy, papery
smoke with a bite.
U.S.: $2.80 • U.K.: N/A

DON RAMOS ROTHSCHILD **81**
Honduras
Ring Gauge: 50 • *Length:* 4½"
Filler: Hon., Dom. Rep., Ecu. •
Binder: U.S.A. • *Wrapper:* Ecuador
Attractive and pleasant, the Don
Ramos has light grassy aromas and
delicate, dusty, coffee flavors. It draws
well although a little quickly.
U.S.: N/A • U.K.: £2.71

JOYA DE NICARAGUA CONSUL **81**
Nicaragua
Ring Gauge: 52 • *Length:* 4½"
Filler: Nicaragua • *Binder:*
Nicaragua • *Wrapper:* Nicaragua
A rough, rustic smoke with creamy
notes but with straw-like flavors and a
sharp bite on the finish.
U.S.: $1.75 • U.K.: N/A

BELINDA MEDAGLIA D'ORO **80**
Honduras
Ring Gauge: 50 • *Length:* 4½"
Filler: Dom. Rep., Honduras •
Binder: Honduras • *Wrapper:*
Ecuador
This cigar shows rough construction
and an earthy flavor component, with
a hot, almost metallic finish.
U.S.: $1.80 • U.K.: N/A

LA INVICTA MAGNUM NO. 2 **79**
Honduras
Ring Gauge: 50 • *Length:* 4½"
Filler: Dom. Rep., Nica., Hon. •
Binder: Ecuador • *Wrapper:*
U.S.A./Conn. Shade
A very fast draw with nutty aromas,
this cigar is medium-bodied with
rather neutral flavors.
U.S.: N/A • U.K.: £2.81

PETRUS ROTHSCHILD **74**
Honduras
Ring Gauge: 50 • *Length:* 4¾"
Filler: Honduras • *Binder:*
Honduras • *Wrapper:* Honduras
A consistently underfilled cigar. It
burns hot with harsh, chemical fla-
vors and has a dry balsa wood, papery
character.
U.S.: $2.40 • U.K.: N/A

LA HOJA SELECTA PALAIS **72**
ROYAL
U.S.A.
Ring Gauge: 50 • *Length:* 4¼"
Filler: Dom. Rep., Bra., Mex. •
Binder: Dom. Rep. • *Wrapper:*
U.S.A./Conn. Shade
Inconsistency hurts this cigar. The
wrapper is uneven and the entire
cigar is loosely rolled. It smokes too
fast and gives very grassy, strawlike
flavors. Not a complete write-off, but
it could be better.
U.S.: $1.70 • U.K.: N/A

PETIT CORONA

COHIBA SIGLO I **93**
Cuba
Ring Gauge: 40 • *Length:* 4"
Filler: Cuba • *Binder:* Cuba •
Wrapper: Cuba
A lot of flavor in a small cigar.
Beautifully crafted with a rich choco-
late wrapper, it is soft-textured and
sumptuous to smoke, with dark choco-
late and spice aromas and flavors.
U.S.: N/A • U.K.: £6.00

EL RICO HABANO PETIT **89**
HABANO
U.S.A.
Ring Gauge: 40 • *Length:* 5"
Filler: Nicaragua, Dom. Rep. •
Binder: Ecuador • *Wrapper:*
Ecuador
This cigar has excellent flavors of tobac-
co, coffee and spicy pepper. The cigar
also has a sweet wood/cedary finish.
U.S.: $1.45 • U.K.: N/A

MONTECRISTO NO. 4 **89**
Cuba
Ring Gauge: 42 • *Length:* 5"
Filler: Cuba • *Binder:* Cuba •
Wrapper: Cuba
A perfumed aroma makes this an attrac-
tive cigar. It has smooth, round flavors
of herbs and spices, and is full-bodied.
U.S.: N/A • U.K.: £5.75

MONTESINO DIPLOMATICO **89**
Dominican Republic
Ring Gauge: 43 • *Length:* 5½ "
Filler: Dom. Rep. • *Binder:* Dom.
Rep. • *Wrapper:* U.S.A./Conn. Shade
A well-made cigar with a good draw
and a toasty aroma. There are earthy,
medium-bodied flavors mixed with
herbal and spice notes.
U.S.: $1.60 • U.K.: N/A

PARTAGAS PETIT CORONA 89
Cuba
Ring Gauge: 42 • *Length:* 5"
Filler: Cuba • *Binder:* Cuba •
Wrapper: Cuba
A beautiful, oily wrapper leads to a smoke with excellent leather and sweet spice flavors. It has a light, smooth finish.
U.S.: N/A • U.K.: £5.50

ROMEO Y JULIETA PETIT 89
CORONA
Cuba
Ring Gauge: 42 • *Length:* 5"
Filler: Cuba • *Binder:* Cuba •
Wrapper: Cuba
An elegant cigar with rich, spicy flavors. It is well-made and rich-looking, and has a long, full-bodied finish.
U.S.: N/A • U.K.: £5.20

8-9-8 COLLECTION CORONA 88
Jamaica
Ring Gauge: 42 • *Length:* 5½"
Filler: Jamaica, Dom. Rep. • *Binder:* Mexico • *Wrapper:* U.S.A./Conn. Shade
This cigar has very nice creamy flavors with touches of sweet spice like nutmeg and pepper. Well-made.
U.S.: $4.75 • U.K.: N/A

DAVIDOFF GRAN CRU NO. 4 88
Dominican Republic
Ring Gauge: 40 • *Length:* 5"
Filler: Dom. Rep. • *Binder:* Dom. Rep. • *Wrapper:* U.S.A./Conn. Shade
A cigar with a medium-bodied smoke. It has a smooth creamy texture, and good spicy flavors.
U.S.: $5.95 • U.K.: £7.00

DAVIDOFF GRAN CRU NO. 3 88
Dominican Republic
Ring Gauge: 42 • *Length:* 5"
Filler: Dom. Rep. • *Binder:* Dom. Rep. • *Wrapper:* U.S.A./Conn. Shade
This cigar showed some lack of maturity, with young tobacco characteristics. But it is some nice spice and sweet woody flavors.
U.S.: $6.85 • U.K.: N/A

HOYO DE MONTERREY 88
EXCALIBUR NO. 7
Honduras
Ring Gauge: 43 • *Length:* 5"
Filler: Honduras, Nicaragua, Dom. Rep. • *Binder:* Honduras • *Wrapper:* U.S.A./Conn. Shade
A pleasant cigar with an earthy complexity. At its core, there are smooth, creamy pepper flavors. It ends on a rich leathery note.
U.S.: $2.25 • U.K.: £2.13

MACANUDO LORD CLARIDGE 88
Jamaica
Ring Gauge: 38 • *Length:* 5½"
Filler: Dom. Rep., Jamaica, Mexico • *Binder:* Mexico • *Wrapper:* U.S.A./Conn. Shade
A nicely balanced cigar with a firm draw that has a smooth creamy texture, and a buttered toast component on the palate. The finish tastes like rich leather.
U.S.: $2.95 • U.K.: N/A

MACANUDO VINTAGE NO. 3 88
Jamaica
Ring Gauge: 42 • *Length:* 5"
Filler: Dom. Rep. • *Binder:* Mexico *Wrapper:* U.S.A./Conn. Shade
This rich cigar has a slightly rough construction, but it is filled with earthy, robust flavors and hints of coffee beans. It has a long, nutty finish.
U.S.: $7.00 • U.K.: N/A

AVO NO. 8   87
Dominican Republic
Ring Gauge: 40 • *Length:* 5½"
Filler: Dom. Rep. • *Binder:* Dom.
Rep. • *Wrapper:* U.S.A./Conn. Shade
This cigar has pleasant floral aromas.
There are sweet nutmeg flavors, and a
hint of coffee beans and creaminess
on the palate.
U.S.: $5.40 • U.K.: N/A

BACCARAT PETIT CORONA   87
Honduras
Ring Gauge: 42 • *Length:* 5½"
Filler: Honduras • *Binder:* Mexico
Wrapper: Honduras
Although it showed some inconsis-
tency, this cigar had a well-balanced,
smooth taste, and contained solid
notes of spice and coffee.
U.S.: $1.40 • U.K.: N/A

BOLIVAR PETIT CORONA   87
Cuba
Ring Gauge: 42 • *Length:* 5"
Filler: Cuba • *Binder:* Cuba •
Wrapper: Cuba
A well-made, medium-bodied cigar
with a good draw. It has some strong
elements of coffee and a hint of spice,
but it has a flat finish.
U.S.: N/A • U.K.: £5.50

EL REY DEL MUNDO HABANA   87
CLUB
Honduras
Ring Gauge: 42 • *Length:* 5½"
Filler: Dom. Rep., Honduras •
Binder: Honduras • *Wrapper:*
Honduras
Clean tobacco flavors dominate this
well-made cigar with a dark brown
wrapper. There is a solid, well-balanced
core of cedar and sweet spice notes.
U.S.: $3.00 • U.K.: N/A

HOYO DE MONTERREY SUPER   87
HOYOS
Honduras
Ring Gauge: 44 • *Length:* 5½"
Filler: Honduras, Nicaragua, Dom.
Rep. • *Binder:* Honduras •
Wrapper: Ecuador
Although it is a bit rustic-looking,
this is a pleasant cigar with some
spice and coffee flavors.
U.S.: $1.35 • U.K.: N/A

MACANUDO HAMPTON COURT   87
Jamaica
Ring Gauge: 43 • *Length:* 5¾"
Filler: Dom. Rep., Jamaica, Mexico •
Binder: Mexico • *Wrapper:*
U.S.A./Conn. Shade
A very well-made mild cigar. It has a
good draw and an even burn, and
solid flavors of tobacco and sweet
wood. A coffee bean character comes
out on the finish.
U.S.: $3.50 • U.K.: N/A

PLEIADES ANTARES   87
Dominican Republic
Ring Gauge: 40 • *Length:* 5½"
Filler: Dom. Rep. • *Binder:* Dom.
Rep. • *Wrapper:* U.S.A./Conn. Shade
A mellow cigar that has an interest-
ing aroma of roasting meat. There are
fruity flavors reminiscent of mango
and a smooth nutty finish.
U.S.: $4.15 • U.K.: N/A

PRIMO DEL REY NO. 4   87
Dominican Republic
Ring Gauge: 42 • *Length:* 5½"
Filler: Dom. Rep. • *Binder:* U.S.A.
Wrapper: Brazil
A full-bodied cigar with a rich, oily
smoke. There are strong sweet spice
flavors like nutmeg, and the finish
has a smooth, leathery tone.
U.S.: $1.40 • U.K.: N/A

THOMAS HINDS HONDURAN SELECTION CORONA · 87

Honduras
Ring Gauge: 42 · *Length:* 5½"
Filler: Honduras · *Binder:*
Honduras · *Wrapper:* Ecuador
A cigar with a generally loose draw, and a range of flavors that include dry wood and paper. There is a good level of spiciness on the finish.
U.S.: $2.05 · U.K.: N/A

ZINO MOUTON-CADET NO. 5 · 87

Honduras
Ring Gauge: 42 · *Length:* 5"
Filler: Honduras · *Binder:*
Honduras · *Wrapper:* Ecuador
A mild cigar with a slightly loose fill. The cigar had pronounced notes of cedar.
U.S.: $4.70 · U.K.: N/A

ARTURO FUENTE PETIT CORONA · 86

Dominican Republic
Ring Gauge: 38 · *Length:* 5"
Filler: Dom. Rep. · *Binder:* Dom.
Rep. · *Wrapper:* Cameroon
A well-made cigar with a firm draw. There is an oily texture to the smoke, and interesting sweetish tobacco flavors along with a solid cedary finish.
U.S.: $1.65 · U.K.: N/A

CUBA ALIADOS REMEDIOS · 86

Honduras
Ring Gauge: 42 · *Length:* 5½"
Filler: Dom. Rep., Brazil · *Binder:*
Ecuador · *Wrapper:* Ecuador
A cigar that needs more aging. It has some solid earthy tones with flavors of spice and coffee, and a nice light woody character.
U.S.: $2.00 · U.K.: N/A

CUESTA-REY DOMINICAN NO. 5 · 86

Dominican Republic
Ring Gauge: 42 · *Length:* 5½"
Filler: Dom. Rep. · *Binder:* Dom.
Rep. · *Wrapper:* U.S.A./Conn. Shade
A well-made cigar that lacks a bit of balance. It has some nice nutty and toasty flavors, and it ends with a mild spiciness.
U.S.: $2.30 · U.K.: £3.45

DON DIEGO PETIT CORONA · 86

Dominican Republic
Ring Gauge: 42 · *Length:* 5⅛"
Filler: Dom. Rep. · *Binder:* Dom.
Rep. · *Wrapper:* U.S.A./Conn. Shade
A nice, mild smoke. Although it lacks complexity, the cigar has a creamy texture with some fruit-like flavors that provide balance.
U.S.: $2.15 · U.K.: N/A

DON TOMAS BLUNT · 86

Honduras
Ring Gauge: 42 · *Length:* 5"
Filler: Honduras · *Binder:*
Honduras · *Wrapper:* Honduras
A pleasant, well-made cigar with a mild creaminesss, and a solid underlying core of spiciness.
U.S.: $1.45 · U.K.: N/A

H. UPMANN TUBOS · 86

Dominican Republic
Ring Gauge: 42 · *Length:* 5¹⁄₁₆"
Filler: Dom. Rep. · *Binder:* Dom.
Rep. · *Wrapper:* Cameroon
Although this cigar has a creamy texture, the flavors tend toward dry wood and paper. It has a loose draw.
U.S.: $2.70 · U.K.: N/A

H. UPMANN PETIT CORONA · 86

Dominican Republic
Ring Gauge: 42 · *Length:* 5¹⁄₁₆"
Filler: Dom. Rep. · *Binder:* Dom.
Rep. · *Wrapper:* Indonesia

A well-made cigar although it appears a bit rough. It has a cream and nut character, and is smooth and well-balanced.
U.S.: $2.25 • U.K.: N/A

HOYO DE MONTERREY LE HOYO DU PRINCE   86
Cuba
Ring Gauge: 40 • *Length:* 5"
Filler: Cuba • *Binder:* Cuba • *Wrapper:* Cuba
A decent cigar with some nice toasty aromas. The flavors tend toward cedar and sweet spices.
U.S.: N/A • U.K.: £5.55

NAT SHERMAN LANDMARK SELECTION HAMPSHIRE   86
Dominican Republic
Ring Gauge: 42 • *Length:* 5½"
Filler: Dom. Rep., Jamaica, Mexico • *Binder:* Mexico • *Wrapper:* Cameroon
A pretty, dark-brown wrapper produces nice earthy flavors that hint at spice and mushrooms. A dry balsa wood character is offset by some earthy qualities on the finish.
U.S.: $4.80 • U.K.: N/A

OLOR MOMENTOS   86
Dominican Republic
Ring Gauge: 43 • *Length:* 5½"
Filler: Dom. Rep. • *Binder:* Dom. Rep. • *Wrapper:* U.S.A./Conn. Shade
A cigar with an attractive oily wrapper. It is a bit dry on the palate with some woody flavors, but there are hints of herbs in the aroma and on the finish.
U.S.: $1.70 • U.K.: N/A

PAUL GARMIRIAN PETIT CORONA   86
Dominican Republic
Ring Gauge: 43 • *Length:* 5"
Filler: Dom. Rep. • *Binder:* Dom. Rep. • *Wrapper:* U.S.A./Conn. Shade

A medium-bodied smoke has creamy and mild spice qualities, and a mild woody finish.
U.S.: $5.30 • U.K.: £5.20

POR LARRAÑAGA PETIT CETROS EN CEDRO   86
Dominican Republic
Ring Gauge: 38 • *Length:* 5"
Filler: Dom. Rep. • *Binder:* Dom. Rep. • *Wrapper:* U.S.A./Conn. Shade
A well-balanced, medium-bodied cigar that has herb and pepper flavors and a toasty, almost leathery aroma.
U.S.: $3.00 • U.K.: N/A

PUNCH ROYAL SELECTION NO. 12   86
Cuba
Ring Gauge: 42 • *Length:* 5½"
Filler: Cuba • *Binder:* Cuba • *Wrapper:* Cuba
A cigar with a very sweet flavor profile that includes butterscotch and burnt caramel. It has a very woody component on the finish.
U.S.: N/A • U.K.: £5.20

ZINO DIAMONDS   86
Honduras
Ring Gauge: 40 • *Length:* 5½"
Filler: Honduras • *Binder:* Honduras • *Wrapper:* Ecuador
A light-wrapped cigar with a good spicy core of flavors, and some hints of herbs.
U.S.: $4.55 • U.K.: N/A

DAVIDOFF NO. 2000   85
Dominican Republic
Ring Gauge: 42 • *Length:* 5"
Filler: Dom. Rep. • *Binder:* Dom. Rep. • *Wrapper:* U.S.A./Conn. Shade
A medium-bodied cigar with a pleasant, mild nuttiness. It finishes with a nice dose of spice that is balanced by an overall creamy texture.
U.S.: $6.25 • U.K.: £8.00

DON LINO PETIT CETRO **85**
Honduras
Ring Gauge: 42 • *Length:* 5½"
Filler: Honduras • *Binder:*
Honduras • *Wrapper:*
U.S.A./Conn. Shade
A mild cigar with a nutty character. It
has a good draw and a creamy tex-
ture.
U.S.: $1.95 • U.K.: N/A

HOYO DE MONTERREY **85**
EXCALIBUR NO. 6
Honduras
Ring Gauge: 38 • *Length:* 5½"
Filler: Honduras, Nicaragua, Dom.
Rep. • *Binder:* Honduras •
Wrapper: U.S.A./Conn. Shade
Some inconsistency in this cigar. A
loose, hot draw was noted by several
tasters. But there are some earthy
tobacco flavors, and the cigar settles
down after a brief harshness.
U.S.: $2.40 • U.K.: £2.17

PADRON LONDRES **85**
Nicaragua
Ring Gauge: 42 • *Length:* 5½"
Filler: Nicaragua • *Binder:*
Nicaragua • *Wrapper:* Nicaragua
A pretty box-pressed cigar. A mild
smoke, it tastes of cocoa beans and
has some light woody notes.
U.S.: $1.60 • U.K.: N/A

PUNCH ELITE **85**
Honduras
Ring Gauge: 44 • *Length:* 5¼"
Filler: Honduras, Nicaragua, Dom.
Rep. • *Binder:* Honduras •
Wrapper: Ecuador
This cigar has a medium-bodied
smoke. There are nutmeg and burnt
spice flavors, and an overall woody
character.
U.S.: $.90 • U.K.: N/A

RAMON ALLONES SIZE "D" **85**
Dominican Republic
Ring Gauge: 42 • *Length:* 5"
Filler: Dom. Rep., Mexico • *Binder:*
Mexico • *Wrapper:* Cameroon
A cigar with an attractive dark-brown
wrapper. But it is dominated by woody
and very light, dry spice flavors.
U.S.: $3.00 • U.K.: N/A

SANCHO PANZA NON PLUS **85**
Cuba
Ring Gauge: 42 • *Length:* 5"
Filler: Cuba • *Binder:* Cuba •
Wrapper: Cuba
Although this cigar shows some nice
flavors of coffee and cream, it lacks
complexity and depth in its medium-
bodied smoke.
U.S.: N/A • U.K.: N/A

BAUZA GRECOS **84**
Dominican Republic
Ring Gauge: 42 • *Length:* 5½"
Filler: Dom. Rep., Nicaragua • *Binder:*
Mexico • *Wrapper:* Cameroon
A mild cigar with a short, dry finish.
It has some flowery aromas and fla-
vors, with a touch of spice.
U.S.: $1.80 • U.K.: N/A

BAUZA PETIT CORONA **84**
Dominican Republic
Ring Gauge: 38 • *Length:* 5"
Filler: Dom. Rep., Nicaragua •
Binder: Mexico • *Wrapper:*
Cameroon
A pleasant smoke that has a sweet
tobacco characteristic and some dry
spice flavors.
U.S.: $1.60 • U.K.: N/A

BERING IMPERIAL **84**
Honduras
Ring Gauge: 42 • *Length:* 5¼"
Filler: Mexico, Dom. Rep., Honduras
Binder: Honduras • *Wrapper:*
Mexico

This is a mild cigar. It has some light earthy flavors backed up by a hint of spice that ends with a somewhat dry finish.
U.S.: $1.15 • U.K.: N/A

JOSE BENITO PETITE 84
Dominican Republic
Ring Gauge: 38 • *Length:* 5½"
Filler: Dom. Rep. • *Binder:* Central America • *Wrapper:* Cameroon
A medium-bodied smoke with a decent construction and draw, a creamy texture, and wood and nut flavors.
U.S.: $2.10 • U.K.: N/A

LA FINCA CORONA 84
Nicaragua
Ring Gauge: 42 • *Length:* 5½"
Filler: Nicaragua • *Binder:* Nicaragua • *Wrapper:* Nicaragua
A medium-bodied cigar. It has hints of spice, leather and nuts, and a decent core of tobacco flavors.
U.S.: $1.40 • U.K.: N/A

LOS LIBERTADORES INSURRECTOS 84
Dominican Republic
Ring Gauge: 42 • *Length:* 5½"
Filler: Dom. Rep. • *Binder:* Dom. Rep. • *Wrapper:* U.S.A./Conn. Shade
A nice-looking, yellowish-brown Connecticut wrapper. The cigar has a good draw, but it also has dry, straw-like flavors and a mild, vegetal finish.
U.S.: $3.98 • U.K.: N/A

MACANUDO PETIT CORONA 84
Jamaica
Ring Gauge: 38 • *Length:* 5"
Filler: Dom. Rep., Jamaica, Mexico • *Binder:* Mexico • *Wrapper:* U.S.A./Conn. Shade
This is a mild, elegant cigar with a toasty aroma. Flavors of dry spice and wood dominate.
U.S.: $2.40 • U.K.: N/A

MONTECRUZ SUN GROWN NO. 230 84
Dominican Republic
Ring Gauge: 42 • *Length:* 5"
Filler: Dom. Rep., Brazil • *Binder:* Dom. Rep. • *Wrapper:* Cameroon
A nice cigar with medium body. Although it has some light spice and citrus flavors, it finishes a bit flat and dry.
U.S.: $2.45 • U.K.: N/A

PARTAGAS NO. 4 84
Dominican Republic
Ring Gauge: 38 • *Length:* 5"
Filler: Mexico, Dom. Rep., Jamaica • *Binder:* Mexico • *Wrapper:* Cameroon
This is a mild cigar with a good draw. There is dryness in the smoke, but there are some flavors of white pepper and flint, and an overall herbal character.
U.S.: $2.40 • U.K.: N/A

QUINTERO MEDIAS CORONAS 84
Cuba
Ring Gauge: 40 • *Length:* 5"
Filler: Cuba • *Binder:* Cuba • *Wrapper:* Cuba
This cigar showed some rough construction, but it has nice flavors of sweet spice and dry cedar wood.
U.S.: N/A • U.K.: N/A

TRESADO SELECCION NO. 500 84
Dominican Republic
Ring Gauge: 42 • *Length:* 5½"
Filler: Dom. Rep. • *Binder:* Cameroon • *Wrapper:* Indonesia
This cigar has a mild- to medium-bodied character. There are some spicy flavors, and it has a smooth round finish.
U.S.: $1.30 • U.K.: N/A

TROYA CLASICO **84**
Dominican Republic
Ring Gauge: 42 • *Length:* 5½"
Filler: Dom. Rep. • *Binder:* Dom.
Rep. • *Wrapper:* U.S.A./Conn.
Shade
A cigar with a flinty character, and a
toasty aroma with some nutty flavors.
A dry finish.
U.S.: $6.00 • U.K.: N/A

DON LINO NO. 4 **83**
Honduras
Ring Gauge: 42 • *Length:* 5"
Filler: Honduras • *Binder:* Honduras
Wrapper: U.S.A./Conn. Shade
A well-made cigar with a firm draw.
Mild sweet spice flavors support a
medium-bodied smoke.
U.S.: $1.75 • U.K.: N/A

H. UPMANN CORONA MAJOR **83**
Dominican Republic
Ring Gauge: 42 • *Length:* 5¹⁄₁₆"
Filler: Dom. Rep. • *Binder:* Dom.
Rep. • *Wrapper:* Cameroon
A rustic cigar with papery, vegetal fla-
vors. There is a touch of spice, but it
is dominated by a woodiness and a
green character.
U.S.: $2.70 • U.K.: N/A

HOYO DE MONTERREY NO. 55 **83**
Honduras
Ring Gauge: 43 • *Length:* 5¼"
Filler: Honduras, Nicaragua, Dom.
Rep. • *Binder:* Honduras •
Wrapper: Ecuador
A bit rustic, middle of the road smoke
that has some spicy flavors, and a bit
of dryness on the palate.
U.S.: $0.90 • U.K.: N/A

JOYA DE NICARAGUA PETITE **83**
Nicaragua
Ring Gauge: 38 • *Length:* 5½"
Filler: Nicaragua • *Binder:*
Nicaragua • *Wrapper:* Nicaragua

This cigar had some young tobacco.
As a result, there were some ammo-
nia-like aromas and tastes. It had an
overall dry paper characteristic.
U.S.: $1.65 • U.K.: N/A

MONTECRUZ SUN GROWN **83**
CEDAR AGED
Dominican Republic
Ring Gauge: 42 • *Length:* 5"
Filler: Dom. Rep., Brazil • *Binder:*
Dom. Rep. • *Wrapper:* Cameroon
A medium-bodied cigar with hints of
coffee bean flavors, but a rough,
earthy character.
U.S.: $2.80 • U.K.: N/A

ROYAL JAMAICA PETIT CORONA **83**
Dominican Republic
Ring Gauge: 40 • *Length:* 5"
Filler: Jamaica, Dom. Rep., Sumatra •
Binder: Java • *Wrapper:* Cameroon
A mild cigar with a tight draw. It has
some soft, creamy flavors with nutty
components.
U.S.: $2.40 • U.K.: N/A

TE-AMO NO. 4 **83**
Mexico
Ring Gauge: 42 • *Length:* 5"
Filler: Mexico • *Binder:* Mexico •
Wrapper: Mexico
This cigar showed some construction
flaws. It had a hot draw, and some
vegetal flavors that mar otherwise
pleasant spicy qualities.
U.S.: $1.80 • U.K.: N/A

VUELTABAJO CORONA **83**
Dominican Republic
Ring Gauge: 42 • *Length:* 5¼"
Filler: Dom. Rep. • *Binder:* Dom.
Rep. • *Wrapper:* U.S.A./Conn. Shade
This is a nice cigar with some solid
tobacco characteristics, but it has
some unusual flavors of strong hot
spices with a meaty aroma.
U.S.: $2.15 • U.K.: N/A

EL REY DEL MUNDO TINOS 82

Honduras
Ring Gauge: 38 • *Length:* 5½"
Filler: Dom. Rep., Honduras •
Binder: Honduras • *Wrapper:*
Honduras
This cigar had a loose fill and a poor, hot draw. It is spicy, but the hot smoke leaves a flat, dry taste in the mouth.
U.S.: $1.75 • U.K.: N/A

LICENCIADOS SUPREME 82
MADURO NO. 200

Dominican Republic
Ring Gauge: 42 • *Length:* 5½"
Filler: Dom. Rep. • *Binder:* Dom. Rep. • *Wrapper:* U.S.A./Conn. Broadleaf
A maduro-style cigar with an earthy aroma. It is well-balanced with a fruit, almost melon-like, flavor backed by cedar.
U.S.: $2.20 • U.K.: N/A

LICENCIADOS NO. 4 82

Dominican Republic
Ring Gauge: 42 • *Length:* 5½"
Filler: Dom. Rep. • *Binder:* Dom. Rep. • *Wrapper:* U.S.A./Conn. Shade
This cigar's roasted nut aroma is attractive. But it also had a stale spice flavor, and a very papery finish.
U.S.: $1.65 • U.K.: N/A

NAT SHERMAN VIP SELECTION 82
BARNUM GLASS TUBE

Dominican Republic
Ring Gauge: 42 • *Length:* 5½"
Filler: Dom. Rep. • *Binder:* Dom. Rep. • *Wrapper:* U.S.A./Conn. Shade
A light-bodied cigar with some slightly sour, acidic tones, and a vegetal character that is balanced on the finish with a touch of spice.
U.S.: $5.70 • U.K.: N/A

BANCES UNIQUE 81

Honduras
Ring Gauge: 38 • *Length:* 5½"
Filler: Honduras, Nicaragua, Dom. Rep. • *Binder:* Honduras •
Wrapper: Ecuador
A rustic cigar with a tight draw. Nuts and sweet spices dominate its flavors, but it suffered from uneven construction.
U.S.: $0.75 • U.K.: N/A

CASA BLANCA CORONA 81

Dominican Republic
Ring Gauge: 42 • *Length:* 5½"
Filler: Dom. Rep. • *Binder:* Mexico
Wrapper: U.S.A./Conn. Shade
This mild cigar has some interesting nutty aromas and spicy flavors, but with an overall dry wood character and finish.
U.S.: $1.90 • U.K.: £2.50

FONSECA COSACOS 81

Cuba
Ring Gauge: 42 • *Length:* 5 1/3"
Filler: Cuba • *Binder:* Cuba •
Wrapper: Cuba
Has a very rough, unattractive wrapper. The cigar is loosely filled, and has a grassy, sour flavor.
U.S.: N/A • U.K.: N/A

H. UPMANN PETIT CORONA 81

Cuba
Ring Gauge: 42 • *Length:* 5"
Filler: Cuba • *Binder:* Cuba •
Wrapper: Cuba
A cigar with a very tight draw. Although it has some nice citrus-style flavors, it ended up lacking complexity.
U.S.: N/A • U.K.: £5.50

CARRINGTON NO. 4 **80**
Dominican Republic
Ring Gauge: 40 • *Length:* 5½"
Filler: Dom. Rep. • *Binder:* Dom.
Rep. • *Wrapper:* U.S.A./Conn.
Shade
A rough wrapper on this mild cigar
gives a dried-out character to the fla-
vors. It tastes of paper, and some spice
on a hot finish.
U.S.: $3.40 • U.K.: £3.00

NAT SHERMAN HOST **80**
SELECTION HAMILTON
Honduras
Ring Gauge: 42 • *Length:* 5½"
Filler: Honduras • *Binder:* Mexico
Wrapper: U.S.A./Conn. Shade
A cigar with only slight tobacco char-
acter. There are flavors of orange peel
and some spice but with a dry finish.
U.S.: $2.85 • U.K.: N/A

HOYO DE MONTERREY **70**
SABROSAS
Honduras
Ring Gauge: 40 • *Length:* 5"
Filler: Honduras, Nicaragua, Dom.
Rep. • *Binder:* Ecuador •
Wrapper: Ecuador
This cigar has very little tobacco
taste, and it is dominated by dry paper
and burnt leaf flavors. The finish has
a sharp bite.
U.S.: $0.70 • U.K.: N/A

PANATELA

MONTECRISTO ESPECIAL NO. 2 **91**
Cuba
Ring Gauge: 38 • *Length:* 6"
Filler: Cuba • *Binder:* Cuba •
Wrapper: Cuba
A smooth, medium-bodied, mellow
smoke with flavors of nutmeg. A
dried-citrus/spice character builds as
the cigar burns.
U.S.: N/A • U.K.: £7.35

OPUS X PETIT LANCERO **91**
Dominican Republic
Ring Gauge: 38 • *Length:* 6"
Filler: Dom. Rep. • *Binder:* Dom.
Rep. • *Wrapper:* Dom. Rep.
A beautiful reddish-brown wrapper
and an easy elegant draw. Complex
flavors of robust spices with under-
tones of cedar and leather produce a
rich, full character.
U.S.: $8.50 • U.K.: N/A

COHIBA CORONA ESPECIAL **89**
Cuba
Ring Gauge: 38 • *Length:* 6"
Filler: Cuba • *Binder:* Cuba •
Wrapper: Cuba
A firm, well-made cigar that produces
well-rounded flavors of spices and
nuts. It has a solid tobacco character
with an earthy, chocolaty finish.
U.S.: N/A • U.K.: £11.35

PUNCH NINFAS **88**
Cuba
Ring Gauge: 38 • *Length:* 7"
Filler: Cuba • *Binder:* Cuba •
Wrapper: Cuba
This cigar has toasty aromas and
smooth, full-bodied flavors with
touches of cedar and spice.
U.S.: N/A • U.K.: £4.85

V CENTENNIAL NO. 1   88
Honduras
Ring Gauge: 38 • *Length:* 7½"
Filler: Dom. Rep., Honduras,
Nicaragua • *Binder:* Nicaragua •
Wrapper: U.S.A./Conn. Shade
A beautiful, oily brown wrapper
delivers a rich spiciness and a medium
body with a bit of tang.
U.S.: $4.50 • U.K.: N/A

AVO XO PRELUDIO   87
Dominican Republic
Ring Gauge: 40 • *Length:* 6"
Filler: Dom. Rep. • *Binder:* Dom.
Rep. • *Wrapper:* U.S.A./Conn. Shade
A smooth, brown wrapper. It has some
cedar-wood flavors and a spicy backbone.
U.S.: $7.00 • U.K.: N/A

BELINDA BELINDA   87
Honduras
Ring Gauge: 36 • *Length:* 6½"
Filler: Dom. Rep., Honduras • *Binder:*
Honduras • *Wrapper:* Ecuador
This dark-brown-wrapped cigar
with a rich spiciness is held back only
by a mild, short finish.
U.S.: $1.40 • U.K.: N/A

CUESTA-REY NO. 2 CABINET   87
Dominican Republic
Ring Gauge: 36 • *Length:* 7"
Filler: Dom. Rep. • *Binder:* Dom.
Rep. • *Wrapper:* Cameroon
A dark-brown wrapper produces a
nice, mild spiciness with a slightly
sweet, cocoa finish.
U.S.: $2.00 • U.K.: N/A

DAVIDOFF NO. 2   87
Dominican Republic
Ring Gauge: 38 • *Length:* 6"
Filler: Dom. Rep. • *Binder:* Dom.
Rep. • *Wrapper:* U.S.A./Conn. Shade
A rich, brown-red wrapper with a
slightly tight draw. Creamy, nutty fla-
vors are backed up by a mild spiciness.
U.S.: $8.25 • U.K.: £9.25

JUAN CLEMENTE PANATELA   87
Dominican Republic
Ring Gauge: 34 • *Length:* 6½"
Filler: Dom. Rep. • *Binder:* Dom.
Rep. • *Wrapper:* U.S.A./Conn. Shade
A well-made cigar with a full, rich
tobacco flavor, a good, spicy character
and a sweet, cocoa bean component.
U.S.: $2.95 • U.K.: £2.75

LA GLORIA CUBANA PANATELA DELUXE   87
U.S.A.
Ring Gauge: 37 • *Length:* 7"
Filler: Dom. Rep., Nicaragua •
Binder: Ecuador • *Wrapper:* Ecuador
This cigar has strong, delicious, spicy
notes, but it finishes a bit short and
flat.
U.S.: $1.75 • U.K.: N/A

PAUL GARMIRIAN PANATELA   87
Dominican Republic
Ring Gauge: 38 • *Length:* 7½"
Filler: Dom. Rep. • *Binder:* Dom.
Rep. • *Wrapper:* U.S.A./Conn.
Shade
A full-flavored smoke with some
spice and toasted-nut notes. It is ele-
gant and well-balanced, but has a
tight draw.
U.S.: $6.80 • U.K.: £6.75

TEMPLE HALL NO. 685   87
Jamaica
Ring Gauge: 34 • *Length:* 6⅛"
Filler: Dom. Rep., Mexico • *Binder:*
Mexico • *Wrapper:* U.S.A./Conn.
Shade
A light-wrapped cigar with a solid
draw leads to a smooth, creamy flavor
and some spice notes.
U.S.: $4.25 • U.K.: N/A

ASHTON PANATELA **86**
Dominican Republic
Ring Gauge: 36 • *Length:* 6"
Filler: Dom. Rep. • *Binder:* Dom.
Rep. • *Wrapper:* U.S.A./Conn.
Shade
This is a well-made cigar with a good
draw, spicy, pepper character and
solid tobacco flavors.
U.S.: $2.80 • U.K.: N/A

CUESTA-REY DOMINICAN NO. 3 **86**
Dominican Republic
Ring Gauge: 36 • *Length:* 7"
Filler: Dom. Rep. • *Binder:* Dom.
Rep. • *Wrapper:* U.S.A./
Connecticut Shade
A well-made cigar with a light-brown
wrapper. It has mild, spicy flavors and
a smooth, flinty aftertaste.
U.S.: $2.25 • U.K.: N/A

DON TOMAS SPECIAL EDITION **86**
NO. 400
Honduras
Ring Gauge: 36 • *Length:* 7"
Filler: Honduras • *Binder:*
Honduras • *Wrapper:* Honduras
A smooth-drawing cigar with a mel-
low tobacco character that is backed
by a mild spiciness.
U.S.: $2.00 • U.K.: N/A

HOYO DE MONTERREY LE **86**
HOYO DU DAUPHIN
Cuba
Ring Gauge: 38 • *Length:* 6"
Filler: Cuba • *Binder:* Cuba •
Wrapper: Cuba
A spicy, peppery cigar with an easy
elegance and a firm draw.
U.S.: N/A • U.K.: £6.75

LA FINCA FLORA **86**
Nicaragua
Ring Gauge: 36 • *Length:* 7"
Filler: Nicaragua • *Binder:*
Nicaragua • *Wrapper:* Nicaragua

A medium-bodied cigar with spicy
flavors and a well-balanced presence
in the mouth.
U.S.: $1.30 • U.K.: N/A

MAYA PALMA FINA **86**
Honduras
Ring Gauge: 36 • *Length:* 6⅛"
Filler: Honduras, Dom. Rep. •
Binder: Honduras • *Wrapper:*
U.S.A./Conn. Shade
This cigar has a good, solid draw and
mild flavors of spices and nuts.
U.S.: $1.50 • U.K.: N/A

MONTECRISTO ESPECIAL **86**
Cuba
Ring Gauge: 38 • *Length:* 7½"
Filler: Cuba • *Binder:* Cuba •
Wrapper: Cuba
This is a smooth-tasting cigar with
solid notes of pepper and spice and a
pleasant cedar finish.
U.S.: N/A • U.K.: £9.15

ARTURO FUENTE PANATELA **85**
FINA
Dominican Republic
Ring Gauge: 38 • *Length:* 7"
Filler: Dom. Rep. • *Binder:* Dom.
Rep. • *Wrapper:* Cameroon
A cigar with fine aromas and a flavor
that has notes of nuts and sweet
wood.
U.S.: $1.75 • U.K.: N/A

CARRINGTON NO. 3 **85**
Dominican Republic
Ring Gauge: 36 • *Length:* 7"
Filler: Dom. Rep. • *Binder:* Dom.
Rep. • *Wrapper:* U.S.A./Conn.
Shade
An elegant smoke with a smooth
mellowness. A good, firm draw pro-
duces some mild spice and toast flavors.
U.S.: $3.30 • U.K.: N/A

DON LINO HAVANA RESERVE PANATELA 85
Honduras
Ring Gauge: 36 • *Length:* 7"
Filler: Sumatra • *Binder:* Sumatra
Wrapper: U.S.A./Conn. Shade
The draw is a bit tight. There are some nutty traces, but the flavors tend toward a vegetal, dry paper finish.
U.S.: $3.65 • U.K.: N/A

DON TOMAS PANATELA LARGAS 85
Honduras
Ring Gauge: 38 • *Length:* 7"
Filler: Honduras • *Binder:* Honduras • *Wrapper:* Honduras
This cigar has a tight draw, but it has good nut and spice flavors and a solid tobacco core.
U.S.: $1.80 • U.K.: N/A

MACANUDO PORTOFINO 85
Jamaica
Ring Gauge: 34 • *Length:* 7"
Filler: Dom. Rep., Mex., Jam. • *Binder:* Mexico • *Wrapper:* U.S.A./Conn. Shade
A delicate, light-brown wrapper leads to a spicy and peppery flavor and a mild, cedary aftertaste.
U.S.: $3.20 • U.K.: N/A

ROMEO Y JULIETA SHAKESPEARE 85
Cuba
Ring Gauge: 28 • *Length:* 6½"
Filler: Cuba • *Binder:* Cuba • *Wrapper:* Cuba
This cigar has some solid, spicy notes, but draws a bit hot from a slightly loose fill.
U.S.: N/A • U.K.: £4.20

ZINO MOUTON-CADET NO. 2 85
Honduras
Ring Gauge: 35 • *Length:* 6"
Filler: Honduras • *Binder:* Honduras • *Wrapper:* Ecuador
A creamy, light cigar with some straightforward flavors although some tasters noted a vegetal, grassy note.
U.S.: $4.95 • U.K.: N/A

CASA BLANCA PANATELA 84
Dominican Republic
Ring Gauge: 36 • *Length:* 6"
Filler: Dom. Rep. • *Binder:* Mexico
Wrapper: U.S.A./Conn. Shade
A tight draw produces some hot, vegetal flavors although some spice comes through on the finish.
U.S.: $1.25 • U.K.: £2.50

DUNHILL PANATELA 84
Canary Islands
Ring Gauge: 30 • *Length:* 6"
Filler: Canary Is. • *Binder:* Canary Is. • *Wrapper:* Cameroon
A mild cigar with smooth, earthy flavors and a light, creamy finish.
U.S.: $2.90 • U.K.: N/A

MONTECRUZ TUBULARES SUN GROWN 84
Dominican Republic
Ring Gauge: 36 • *Length:* 6⅛"
Filler: Dom. Rep., Brazil • *Binder:* Dom. Rep. • *Wrapper:* Cameroon
A rustic, rough-looking cigar with some spice and coffee flavors, but a flat, dry, balsawood finish.
U.S.: $2.75 • U.K.: N/A

ROMEO Y JULIETA BELVEDERE 84
Cuba
Ring Gauge: 39 • *Length:* 5½"
Filler: Cuba • *Binder:* Cuba • *Wrapper:* Cuba
A pleasant cigar with some wood flavors and spicy notes. Tight on the draw.
U.S.: N/A • U.K.: £4.50

THE GRIFFIN'S NO. 400 **84**
Dominican Republic
Ring Gauge: 38 • *Length:* 6"
Filler: Dom. Rep. • *Binder:* Dom.
Rep. • *Wrapper:* U.S.A./Conn. Shade
A medium-brown wrapper. Slightly
vegetal, but with some backbone and
a tangy presence in the mouth.
U.S.: $3.95 • Switzerland: 6.60SF

COHIBA LANCERO **83**
Cuba
Ring Gauge: 38 • *Length:* 7½"
Filler: Cuba • *Binder:* Cuba •
Wrapper: Cuba
This cigar has great tobacco flavors,
but the tight draw makes it too hard
to smoke.
U.S.: N/A • U.K.: £14.10

DAVIDOFF NO. 1 **83**
Dominican Republic
Ring Gauge: 38 • *Length:* 7½"
Filler: Dom. Rep. • *Binder:* Dom.
Rep. • *Wrapper:* U.S.A./Conn. Shade
This mild, light wrapper delivers
some mild herbal flavors, but there
is an unpleasant, short, balsawood
finish.
U.S.: $9.30 • U.K.: £11.25

DUNHILL FANTINO **83**
Dominican Republic
Ring Gauge: 28 • *Length:* 7"
Filler: Dom. Rep. • *Binder:* Dom.
Rep. • *Wrapper:* U.S.A./Conn.
Shade
This smooth cigar has a medium-
length finish with some mild, peppery
notes.
U.S.: $3.30 • U.K.: £3.60

EL REY DEL MUNDO ELEGANTE **83**
Cuba
Ring Gauge: 28 • *Length:* 6¼"
Filler: Cuba • *Binder:* Cuba •
Wrapper: Cuba
Has a nice, oily brown wrapper that

holds a solid, spicy-nut core of flavors,
but otherwise this smoke is a bit
bland and one-dimensional.
U.S.: N/A • U.K.: £4.05

HOYO DE MONTERREY **83**
EXCALIBUR NO. VII
Honduras
Ring Gauge: 43 • *Length:* 5"
Filler: Honduras • *Binder:*
Honduras • *Wrapper:*
U.S.A./Conn. Shade
A dark, rough wrapper. This cigar has
some burnt spice flavors and a dryness
on the palate.
U.S.: $2.10 • U.K.: N/A

MACANUDO VINTAGE NO. VII **83**
Jamaica
Ring Gauge: 38 • *Length:* 7½"
Filler: Dom. Rep., Mex., Jam. •
Binder: Mexico • *Wrapper:*
U.S.A./Conn. Shade
This cigar has a tight draw and a
neutral, balsawood flavor.
U.S.: $7.00 • U.K.: N/A

NAT SHERMAN MURRAY HILL **83**
NO. 7
Dominican Republic
Ring Gauge: 38 • *Length:* 6"
Filler: Dom. Rep., Mex., Jam. •
Binder: Mexico • *Wrapper:*
U.S.A./Conn. Shade
This light-yellow-brown cigar has
mild, creamy flavors, but it is rolled
tight and has a tough draw.
U.S.: $4.90 • U.K.: N/A

ROYAL JAMAICA TUBE NO. 2 **83**
Dominican Republic
Ring Gauge: 34 • *Length:* 6½"
Filler: Jamaica • *Binder:* Java •
Wrapper: Cameroon
A well-made cigar with a brown
wrapper. A good, spicy component
overlays a simple tobacco core.
U.S.: $3.00 • U.K.: N/A

BAUZA FLORETE 82
Dominican Republic
Ring Gauge: 35 • *Length:* 6⅛"
Filler: Nicaragua, Dom. Rep. •
Binder: Mexico • *Wrapper:*
Cameroon
An overall tight draw with some solid spice flavors.
U.S.: $1.55 • U.K.: N/A

DON DIEGO ROYAL PALMA 82
Dominican Republic
Ring Gauge: 36 • *Length:* 6⅛"
Filler: Dom. Rep. • *Binder:* Dom. Rep. • *Wrapper:* U.S.A./Conn. Shade
A mild, easy smoke that burns a bit hot, but with some smooth nut and dry coffee bean flavors.
U.S.: $2.50 • U.K.: N/A

LICENCIADOS PANATELA LINDAS 82
Dominican Republic
Ring Gauge: 38 • *Length:* 7"
Filler: Dom. Rep. • *Binder:* Honduras • *Wrapper:* U.S.A./Conn. Shade
A very tight draw limits this cigar, but the mild, slightly dry finish has hints of herbs and nuts.
U.S.: $1.50 • U.K.: N/A

NAT SHERMAN METROPOLE 82
Dominican Republic
Ring Gauge: 34 • *Length:* 6"
Filler: Dom. Rep., Hon., Jam., Brazil
Binder: Mexico • *Wrapper:*
Cameroon
A mellow smoke with some perfumed aromas and mild flavors.
U.S.: $3.90 • U.K.: N/A

PARTAGAS TUBOS 82
Dominican Republic
Ring Gauge: 38 • *Length:* 7"
Filler: Dom. Rep., Mex., Jam. •
Binder: Mexico • *Wrapper:*
Cameroon
An unattractive wrapper with a good draw and a medium-bodied tobacco character. A short, spicy finish.
U.S.: $3.30 • U.K.: N/A

PLEIADES ANTARES 82
Dominican Republic
Ring Gauge: 40 • *Length:* 5½"
Filler: Dom. Rep. • *Binder:* Dom. Rep. • *Wrapper:* U.S.A./Conn. Shade
A tight draw on this mild cigar. There are some spicy notes, but it has a flat finish.
U.S.: $3.95 • France: 26FF

POR LARRAÑAGA DELICADOS 82
Dominican Republic
Ring Gauge: 36 • *Length:* 6½"
Filler: Dom. Rep. • *Binder:* Dom. Rep. • *Wrapper:* U.S.A./Conn. Shade
An inconsistent cigar. It has some smooth tobacco flavors and a light, dry finish.
U.S.: $2.55 • U.K.: N/A

AVO NO. 4 81
Dominican Republic
Ring Gauge: 38 • *Length:* 7"
Filler: Dom. Rep. • *Binder:* Dom. Rep. • *Wrapper:* U.S.A./Conn. Shade
This cigar appears well-made, but a tough draw leads into a parched, one-dimensional flavor. Some pepper notes, but with a bite.
U.S.: $4.80 • U.K.: N/A

BANCES UNIQUE 81
Honduras
Ring Gauge: 38 • *Length:* 5½"
Filler: Nicaragua • *Binder:* Mexico
Wrapper: Ecuador
This cigar has a firm, solid draw with decent spiciness. An unattractive wrapper.
U.S.: $.70 • U.K.: N/A

DUNHILL DOMINICAN 81
SAMANAS
Dominican Republic
Ring Gauge: 38 • *Length:* 6"
Filler: Dom. Rep. • *Binder:* Dom. Rep. • *Wrapper:* U.S.A./Conn. Shade
A yellow-brown wrapper on a light, mild cigar. It has some creamy spice, yet also grassy flavors and aromas.
U.S.: $3.30 • U.K.: £4.45

JOYA DE NICARAGUA NO. 5 81
Nicaragua
Ring Gauge: 38 • *Length:* 5½"
Filler: Nicaragua • *Binder:* Nicaragua • *Wrapper:* Nicaragua
This cigar has a sourness and an overall vegetal character, although some light spice comes through on the finish.
U.S.: $1.50 • U.K.: N/A

TE-AMO TORERO 81
Mexico
Ring Gauge: 35 • *Length:* 6⅜6"
Filler: Mexico • *Binder:* Mexico • *Wrapper:* Mexico
A nice-looking cigar, but with a very tight draw. Some dryness on the palate creates a mild smoothness, yet it lacks flavor.
U.S.: $1.80 • U.K.: N/A

EL REY DEL MUNDO TINO 80
Honduras
Ring Gauge: 38 • *Length:* 5½"
Filler: Dom. Rep., Honduras • *Binder:* Honduras • *Wrapper:* Honduras

A mild cigar with some vegetal and dry-metallic flavors. Not very well-made. Several tasters noted a hard draw.
U.S.: $1.75 • U.K.: N/A

EL RICO HABANO NO. 1 80
U.S.A.
Ring Gauge: 38 • *Length:* 7½"
Filler: Dom. Rep. • *Binder:* Nicaragua • *Wrapper:* Ecuador
A tight draw, with a spicy character and a dry, coffee bean flavor.
U.S.: $2.50 • U.K.: N/A

HOYO DE MONTERREY 80
DELIGHTS
Honduras
Ring Gauge: 37 • *Length:* 6¼"
Filler: Honduras • *Binder:* Honduras • *Wrapper:* U.S.A./Conn. Shade
This cigar smokes solidly with some straightforward, spice flavors, but with a hot aftertaste and finish.
U.S.: $.85 • U.K.: N/A

LA AURORA PALMAS EXTRA 80
Dominican Republic
Ring Gauge: 35 • *Length:* 6¼"
Filler: U.S.A./Conn. Broadleaf • *Binder:* Sumatra • *Wrapper:* U.S.A./Conn. Broadleaf
This rustic cigar has a burnt taste with some vegetal notes and very little spice.
U.S.: $1.65 • U.K.: N/A

DON LINO PANATELAS 79
Honduras
Ring Gauge: 36 • *Length:* 7"
Filler: Sumatra • *Binder:* Sumatra • *Wrapper:* U.S.A./Conn. Shade
A pretty wrapper doesn't deliver. The cigar has a tough draw with bitter flavors and a short, flat finish.
U.S.: $1.75 • U.K.: N/A

DON TOMAS INTERNATIONAL SELECTION NO. 4   **78**
Honduras
Ring Gauge: 36 • *Length:* 7"
Filler: Honduras • *Binder:*
Honduras • *Wrapper:* Honduras
A very tight draw with hot, harsh spices and a camphor element on the palate.
U.S.: $2.25 • U.K.: N/A

SOSA SANTE FE   **78**
Dominican Republic
Ring Gauge: 35 • *Length:* 6"
Filler: Dom. Rep., Brazil • *Binder:*
Honduras • *Wrapper:* Ecuador
Some inconsistency. A mild cigar with a smooth, medium body, but a sharp, vegetal finish.
U.S.: $1.80 • U.K.: N/A

DON JUAN LINDAS   **77**
Nicaragua
Ring Gauge: 38 • *Length:* 5½"
Filler: Nicaragua, Mexico • *Binder:*
Nicaragua • *Wrapper:* Nicaragua
An underfilled cigar that burns hot with a bitter, sour presence in the mouth and some dry, grassy flavors.
U.S.: $1.10 • U.K.: N/A

H. UPMANN NATURALES   **76**
Dominican Republic
Ring Gauge: 36 • *Length:* 6⅛"
Filler: Dom. Rep. • *Binder:* Dom.
Rep. • *Wrapper:* Cameroon
This cigar has a tart character and its loose fill produces hot, dry flavors of paper and balsa.
U.S.: $2.50 • U.K.: N/A

FIGURADO

ROMEO Y JULIETA FABULOSO   **96**
Cuba
Ring Gauge: 47 • *Length:* 9"
Filler: Cuba • *Binder:* Cuba •
Wrapper: Cuba
Superbly crafted, and it burns perfectly. Rich and teeming with tobacco character, the Fabuloso remains elegant and refined.
U.S.: N/A • U.K.: £15.00

MONTECRISTO "A"   **95**
Cuba
Ring Gauge: 47 • *Length:* 9½"
Filler: Cuba • *Binder:* Cuba •
Wrapper: Cuba
Wonderfully crafted, with a deep-colored, smooth wrapper. It burns perfectly and delivers rich yet mellow coffee and cedar flavors.
U.S.: N/A • U.K.: £18.00

MONTECRISTO NO. 2   **94**
Cuba
Ring Gauge: 52 • *Length:* 6⅛"
Filler: Cuba • *Binder:* Cuba •
Wrapper: Cuba
The benchmark torpedo. It is loaded with rich, complex flavors such as cinnamon, with strong full-bodied notes of chocolate and leather, and a long spicy finish.
U.S.: N/A • U.K.: £9.80

DIPLOMATICOS NO. 2   **92**
Cuba
Ring Gauge: 52 • *Length:* 6⅛"
Filler: Cuba • *Binder:* Cuba •
Wrapper: Cuba
A well-balanced cigar with a strong earthy characteristic and a complex core of spicy flavors that ends in a long finish.
U.S.: N/A • France: 62FF

Opus X No. 2   92
Dominican Republic
Ring Gauge: 52 • *Length:* 6¼"
Filler: Dom. Rep. • *Binder:* Dom.
Rep. • *Wrapper:* Dom. Rep.
A beautiful, oily wrapper. This cigar
has an excellent draw and is loaded
with spice and nut flavors with solid
notes of cedar. A long earthy finish.
U.S.: $12.00 • U.K.: N/A

Punch Diademas Extra   92
Cuba
Ring Gauge: 47 • *Length:* 9"
Filler: Cuba • *Binder:* Cuba •
Wrapper: Cuba
The Diademas Extra has a beautiful,
oily wrapper and is superbly made. It
smokes wonderfully and shows loads
of spicy, peppery and nutty character
yet remains very refined.
U.S.: N/A • U.K.: N/A

Puros Indios Piramide No. 1   92
Honduras
Ring Gauge: 60 • *Length:* 7½"
Filler: Brazil, Dom. Rep., Nicaragua
Binder: Ecuador • *Wrapper:*
Ecuador
A full-flavored cigar loaded with
sweet earthy flavors including cocoa
and leather with a coffee bean char-
acter on the palate.
U.S.: $6.50 • U.K.: N/A

Montecristo Especial No. 1   91
Cuba
Ring Gauge: 38 • *Length:* 7½"
Filler: Cuba • *Binder:* Cuba •
Wrapper: Cuba
The benchmark for this size. It's silky
and smooth with cedar, chocolate and
spice highlights and a long, flavorful
aftertaste.
U.S.: N/A • U.K.: £9.00

Bolivar Belicoso Fino   90
Cuba
Ring Gauge: 52 • *Length:* 5½"
Filler: Cuba • *Binder:* Cuba •
Wrapper: Cuba
A beautiful small torpedo. This full-
bodied smoke has a strong spiciness
and sweet earthy quality with a pleas-
ant tangy finish.
U.S.: N/A • U.K.: £8.25

Puros Indios Piramide No. 2   90
Honduras
Ring Gauge: 46 • *Length:* 6½"
Filler: Brazil, Dom. Rep., Nicaragua
Binder: Ecuador • *Wrapper:*
Ecuador
This is a rich-tasting pyramid with
lots of spice and nuts on the palate
and a long peppery finish. Well-made
with a smooth draw.
U.S.: $5.50 • U.K.: N/A

Romeo y Julieta Belicoso   90
Cuba
Ring Gauge: 52 • *Length:* 5½"
Filler: Cuba • *Binder:* Cuba •
Wrapper: Cuba
It draws well and is full-bodied, with
a rich, peppery, punchy character and
a long finish.
U.S.: N/A • U.K.: £7.00

Santiago Cabana Torpedo   90
U.S.A.
Ring Gauge: 54 • *Length:* 6¼"
Filler: Dom. Rep., Honduras,
Nicaragua • *Binder:* Ecuador
Wrapper: Ecuador
A very nice medium-bodied cigar.
Nutty flavors, including chestnuts,
dominate and there is a pleasant
sweet spice character with hints of
nutmeg. Medium length finish.
U.S.: $9.95 • U.K.: N/A

ARTURO FUENTE HEMINGWAY SIGNATURE 89
Dominican Republic
Ring Gauge: 46 • *Length:* 6"
Filler: Dom. Rep. • *Binder:* Dom.
Rep. • *Wrapper:* Cameroon
A beautiful dark wrapper. A smooth, rich cigar with an earthy combination of spice, pepper and leather flavors and a cedary finish.
U.S.: $3.85 • U.K.: N/A

ARTURO FUENTE HEMINGWAY SHORT STORY 89
Dominican Republic
Ring Gauge: 49 • *Length:* 4¼"
Filler: Dom. Rep. • *Binder:* Dom.
Rep. • *Wrapper:* Cameroon
This cigar's unique size makes blind tasting impossible. It is packed with flavors of pepper, spicy and espresso coffee. It has a long earthy finish.
U.S.: $2.85 • U.K.: N/A

ASHTON CABINET SELECTION No. 10 89
Dominican Republic
Ring Gauge: 52 • *Length:* 7½"
Filler: Dom. Rep. • *Binder:* Dom.
Rep. • *Wrapper:* U.S.A./Conn.
Shade
A mild- to medium-bodied cigar. It has a delicious combination of creaminess and a cocoa bean flavor with sweetish tobacco flavors. A slightly dry woody finish.
U.S.: $11.00 • U.K.: N/A

AVO XO PYRAMID 89
Dominican Republic
Ring Gauge: 50 • *Length:* 5½"
Filler: Dom. Rep. • *Binder:* Dom.
Rep. • *Wrapper:* U.S.A./Conn. Shade
A rich, spicy cigar. It has earthy flavors of leather and chocolate but with a smooth balance. A bit youthful, and should improve with age.
U.S.: $7.50 • U.K.: N/A

CUBA ALIADOS PIRAMIDE No. 2 89
Honduras
Ring Gauge: 46 • *Length:* 6½"
Filler: Honduras, Dom. Rep. •
Binder: Honduras, Dom. Rep. •
Wrapper: Ecuador
This full-bodied smoke has a rustic edge. There are well-balanced flavors of pepper and spice.
U.S.: $5.00 • U.K.: N/A

H. UPMANN No. 2 89
Cuba
Ring Gauge: 52 • *Length:* 6⅛"
Filler: Cuba • *Binder:* Cuba •
Wrapper: Cuba
A full-bodied smoke with flavors of cocoa bean and nutmeg, and a strong nutty core. A smooth, peppery finish. It is a little young.
U.S.: N/A • U.K.: £8.40

ASHTON CABINET SELECTION No. 3 88
Dominican Republic
Ring Gauge: 46 • *Length:* 6"
Filler: Dom. Rep. • *Binder:* Dom.
Rep. • *Wrapper:* U.S.A./Conn.
Shade
A medium-bodied cigar with a creamy texture and a solid core of nutty flavors that lead into a light spiciness.
U.S.: $7.00 • U.K.: N/A

EL REY DEL MUNDO GRANDES DE ESPAIGHT 88
Cuba
Ring Gauge: 38 • *Length:* 7½"
Filler: Cuba • *Binder:* Cuba •
Wrapper: Cuba
Extremely well-crafted and easy to draw. Medium-bodied with rich, nutty, coffee aromas and flavors and a lingering aftertaste.
U.S.: N/A • U.K.: N/A

EL RICO HABANO NO. 1   88
U.S.A.
Ring Gauge: 38 • *Length:* 7½"
Filler: Dom. Rep., Nicaragua •
Binder: Nicaragua • *Wrapper:*
Ecuador
A thin cigar packed with flavor. It
burns extremly well and fills the
mouth with rich, spicy flavors and
a soft, smooth texture.
U.S.: $1.75 • U.K.: N/A

MACABI BELICOSO FINO   88
U.S.A.
Ring Gauge: 52 • *Length:* 6¼"
Filler: Dom. Rep., Nicaragua •
Binder: Mexico • *Wrapper:*
U.S.A./Conn. Shade
A smooth tasting cigar with nice
flavors of nuts and cinnamon and a
creamy texture.
U.S.: $5.00 • U.K.: N/A

OSCAR NO. 700   88
Dominican Republic
Ring Gauge: 54 • *Length:* 7"
Filler: Dom. Rep. • *Binder:* Dom.
Rep. • *Wrapper:* U.S.A.
This cigar has a pleasant herbal
aroma, and offers up flavors of nuts
and spice on the palate. It finishes
with hints of dry spices.
U.S.: $9.70 • U.K.: N/A

PAUL GARMIRIAN BELICOSO   88
Dominican Republic
Ring Gauge: 52 • *Length:* 6¼"
Filler: Dom. Rep. • *Binder:* Dom.
Rep. • *Wrapper:* U.S.A./Conn.
Shade
A medium-bodied cigar with rich,
spicy flavors. It has a solid, earthy
tobacco backbone but lacks a bit of
intensity.
U.S.: $8.20 • U.K.: £8.10

PAUL GARMIRIAN   88
CELEBRATION
Dominican Republic
Ring Gauge: 50 • *Length:* 9"
Filler: Dom. Rep. • *Binder:* Dom.
Rep. • *Wrapper:* U.S.A./Conn.
Shade
A flavor-packed smoke that burns
extremely well. It has peppery aromas
and flavors and a rich finish.
U.S.: $12.80 • U.K.: £12.50

SOSA FAMILY SELECTION NO. 2   88
Dominican Republic
Ring Gauge: 54 • *Length:* 6¼"
Filler: Dom. Rep. • *Binder:* Dom.
Rep. • *Wrapper:* U.S.A./Conn.
Shade
A cigar with strong nut and toast fla-
vors. It has a medium-bodied smoke.
A well-made, attractive cigar.
U.S.: $6.00 • U.K.: N/A

TEMPLE HALL BELICOSO   88
Jamaica
Ring Gauge: 50 • *Length:* 6"
Filler: Jamaica, Dom. Rep., Mexico •
Binder: Mexico • *Wrapper:*
U.S.A./Conn. Shade
A well-balanced, medium-bodied
cigar with a light spiciness that
smooths out through a creamy and
nutty core. A woody finish.
U.S.: $5.75 • U.K.: N/A

ASHTON VINTAGE CABINET   87
NO. 1
Dominican Republic
Ring Gauge: 52 • *Length:* 9"
Filler: Dom. Rep. • *Binder:* Dom.
Rep. • *Wrapper:* U.S.A./Conn.
Shade
Another big cigar, yet it shows reserve.
It's mild and fresh with light coffee,
slightly herbal aromas and flavors.
U.S.: $10.50 • U.K.: N/A

ASHTON VINTAGE CABINET SELECTION NO. 2   87

Dominican Republic
Ring Gauge: 47 • *Length:* 7"
Filler: Dom. Rep. • *Binder:* Dom. Rep. • *Wrapper:* U.S.A./Conn. Shade
A medium-bodied cigar with a smooth creamy texture that rounds out to straightforward, nutty flavors with a touch of spice.
U.S.: $9.00 • U.K.: N/A

AVO BELICOSO   87

Dominican Republic
Ring Gauge: 50 • *Length:* 6"
Filler: Dom. Rep. • *Binder:* Dom. Rep. • *Wrapper:* U.S.A./Conn. Shade
This is mellow cigar with medium-bodied smoke. It has a floral aroma with solid flavors of toasted nuts and a creamy, sweetish character.
U.S.: $7.00 • U.K.: N/A

CARRINGTON NO. 8   87

Dominican Republic
Ring Gauge: 60 • *Length:* 6⅞"
Filler: Dom. Rep. • *Binder:* Dom. Rep. • *Wrapper:* U.S.A./Conn. Shade
A pleasant mild smoke with a creamy texture and a walnut-like flavor with an earthy finish.
U.S.: $6.00 • U.K.: N/A

COHIBA LANCERO   87

Cuba
Ring Gauge: 38 • *Length:* 7½"
Filler: Cuba • *Binder:* Cuba • *Wrapper:* Cuba
Our tasters found the Lancero too tightly rolled and difficult to draw, but it can be rich and harmonious with a coffee, nutty character.
U.S.: N/A • U.K.: £13.50

CUBA ALIADOS PIRAMIDE   87

Honduras
Ring Gauge: 60 • *Length:* 7½"
Filler: Honduras, Dom. Rep. • *Binder:* Honduras, Dom. Rep. • *Wrapper:* Ecuador
There are hints of cocoa bean in this big pyramid. It has solid flavors of toast and roasted nuts.
U.S.: $7.00 • U.K.: N/A

DAVIDOFF SPECIAL "T"   87

Dominican Republic
Ring Gauge: 52 • *Length:* 6"
Filler: Dom. Rep. • *Binder:* Dom. Rep. • *Wrapper:* U.S.A./Conn. Shade
This is a pleasant medium-bodied cigar that has a soft spicy character and a creamy texture with a dull finish.
U.S.: $10.30 • U.K.: £11.25

EL REY DEL MUNDO FLOR DE LLANEZA   87

Honduras
Ring Gauge: 54 • *Length:* 6½"
Filler: Honduras, Dom. Rep • *Binder:* Honduras • *Wrapper:* Ecuador
This is a full-flavored cigar showing good balance and notes of leather with an earthy quality. It has a slightly dry, flat finish.
U.S.: $4.50 • U.K.: N/A

FONSECA TRIANGULARE   87

Dominican Republic
Ring Gauge: 56 • *Length:* 5½"
Filler: Dom. Rep. • *Binder:* Mexico *Wrapper:* U.S.A./Conn. Shade
A cigar with a mellow quality and a medium body. It has a dry spiciness and a pleasant creamy texture with a long finish.
U.S.: $6.25 • U.K.: N/A

LA GLORIA CUBANA MEDAILLE 87 D'OR NO. 1
Cuba
Ring Gauge: 36 • *Length:* 7⅛"
Filler: Cuba • *Binder:* Cuba •
Wrapper: Cuba
Hard to draw, but it burns evenly and delivers light coffee and clove aromas and flavors.
U.S.: N/A • U.K.: N/A

LA GLORIA CUBANA 87 PIRAMIDES
U.S.A.
Ring Gauge: 56 • *Length:* 7¼"
Filler: Dom. Rep., Nicaragua •
Binder: Ecuador • *Wrapper:*
Ecuador
This is a medium-bodied style for this cigar. It has solid spicy flavors and a woody finish.
U.S.: $6.00 • U.K.: N/A

LOS LIBERTADORES FIGURADO 87
Dominican Republic
Ring Gauge: 52 • *Length:* 6½"
Filler: Dom. Rep. • *Binder:* Dom. Rep. • *Wrapper:* U.S.A./Conn. Shade
A well-balanced, medium-bodied cigar. It has flavors of sweet nuts and toast with a light finish.
U.S.: $7.50 • U.K.: N/A

MACANUDO DUKE OF 87 WINDSOR
Jamaica
Ring Gauge: 50 • *Length:* 6"
Filler: Jamaica, Dom. Rep., Mexico •
Binder: Mexico • *Wrapper:*
U.S.A./Conn. Shade
This is a mellow cigar with a mild to medium body. It has some delicate spice notes on otherwise woody flavors, and a bit of a tangy finish.
U.S.: $4.75 • U.K.: N/A

MONTECRISTO NO. 2 87
Dominican Republic
Ring Gauge: 50 • *Length:* 6"
Filler: Dom. Rep. • *Binder:* Dom. Rep. • *Wrapper:* U.S.A.
A mild- to medium-bodied cigar with a nice earthy quality, and flavors of spice and nuts with a light, well-balanced finish.
U.S.: $8.95 • U.K.: N/A

NAT SHERMAN METROPOLITAN 87
Dominican Republic
Ring Gauge: 52 • *Length:* 7"
Filler: Dom. Rep. • *Binder:* Dom. Rep. • *Wrapper:* U.S.A./Conn. Shade
A mellow cigar with plenty of nuttiness on the palate. It has a slightly balsa-like finish but a spiciness compensates for the dryness.
U.S.: $8.25 • U.K.: N/A

ROMEO Y JULIETA 87 CELESTIAL FINO
Cuba
Ring Gauge: 46 • *Length:* 5¾"
Filler: Cuba • *Binder:* Cuba •
Wrapper: Cuba
It looks a little coarse in its rough wrapper, but this pyramid smokes well, with an enticing rosemary and spice character and a smooth texture.
U.S.: N/A • U.K.: £7.00

TROYA TORPEDO NO. 81 87
Dominican Republic
Ring Gauge: 54 • *Length:* 7"
Filler: Dom. Rep. • *Binder:* Dom. Rep. • *Wrapper:* U.S.A./Conn. Shade
A well-made medium-bodied cigar with strong nut and solid tobacco flavors. It also has a spicy character with a ripe finish.
U.S.: $5.00 • U.K.: N/A

V CENTENNIAL TORPEDO 87
Honduras
Ring Gauge: 54 • *Length:* 7"
Filler: Dom. Rep., Nicaragua,
Honduras • *Binder:* Mexico •
Wrapper: U.S.A./Conn. Shade
A well-balanced cigar. It has some
spice and coffee flavors. Solid medi-
um-bodied smoke.
U.S.: $6.00 • U.K.: N/A

ARTURO FUENTE HEMINGWAY 86
CLASSIC
Dominican Republic
Ring Gauge: 48 • *Length:* 7"
Filler: Dom. Rep. • *Binder:* Dom.
Rep. • *Wrapper:* Cameroon
This cigar has a medium body with a dry
spice character. It has a slightly dry fin-
ish with a solid core of tobacco flavors.
U.S.: $4.75 • U.K.: N/A

ARTURO FUENTE HEMINGWAY 86
MASTERPIECE
Dominican Republic
Ring Gauge: 52 • *Length:* 9¼"
Filler: Dom. Rep. • *Binder:* Dom.
Rep. • *Wrapper:* Cameroon
A powerful and rich smoke. Good
draw; full-bodied with rich coffee
taste and spicy flavors.
U.S.: $7.00 • U.K.: N/A

AVO PYRAMIDE 86
Dominican Republic
Ring Gauge: 54 • *Length:* 7"
Filler: Dom. Rep. • *Binder:* Dom.
Rep. • *Wrapper:* U.S.A./Conn. Shade
This cigar has a sweet spice quality
with hints of leather and wood. There
is a tanginess on the finish.
U.S.: $7.00 • U.K.: N/A

AVO PETIT BELICOSO 86
Dominican Republic
Ring Gauge: 50 • *Length:* 4¼"
Filler: Dom. Rep. • *Binder:* Dom.
Rep. • *Wrapper:* U.S.A./Conn. Shade

A medium-bodied cigar with some
inconsistency; nuts and nutmeg flavors with notes of cocoa beans. A
slightly woody finish.
U.S.: $5.60 • U.K.: N/A

C.A.O. TRIANGULARES 86
Honduras
Ring Gauge: 54 • *Length:* 7"
Filler: Nicaragua, Mexico • *Binder:*
Honduras • *Wrapper:*
U.S.A./Conn. Shade
A nice mild cigar. It has a nutty qual-
ity with a good toast-like flavor.
U.S.: $6.75 • U.K.: N/A

EL SUBLIMADO TORPEDO 86
Dominican Republic
Ring Gauge: 54 • *Length:* 7"
Filler: Dom. Rep. • *Binder:* Dom.
Rep. • *Wrapper:* U.S.A.
This well-made cigar has some floral
aromas and a core of nutty flavors.
U.S.: $14.00 • U.K.: N/A

FELIPE GREGORIO BELICOSO 86
Honduras
Ring Gauge: 54 • *Length:* 6⅛"
Filler: Honduras • *Binder:*
Honduras • *Wrapper:* Honduras
A medium-bodied cigar with medi-
um-length finish. There are earthy
flavors with a mild spiciness.
U.S.: $7.10 • U.K.: £10.00

LA GLORIA CUBANA 86
TORPEDO NO. 1
U.S.A.
Ring Gauge: 54 • *Length:* 6½"
Filler: Dom. Rep., Nicaragua •
Binder: Nicaragua • *Wrapper:*
Ecuador
This cigar had strong toasty flavors
with an earthy leatherness. But a bit
of sourness was noted by several
tasters.
U.S.: $5.00 • U.K.: N/A

LOS LIBERTADORES FIGURADO **86**
RESERVA ESPECIAL
Dominican Republic
Ring Gauge: 52 • *Length:* 6½"
Filler: Dom. Rep. • *Binder:* Dom.
Rep. • *Wrapper:* U.S.A./Conn.
Shade
This is a mild to medium-bodied cigar
that has a creamy nut quality with a
light spicy finish.
U.S.: $7.50 • U.K.: N/A

MACANUDO DUKE OF **86**
WELLINGTON
Jamaica
Ring Gauge: 38 • *Length:* 8½"
Filler: Jam., Mex., Dom. Rep. •
Binder: Mexico • *Wrapper:*
U.S.A./Conn. Shade
A little difficult to draw, but it has a
very good, light coffee taste and a
spicy character with a fresh finish.
U.S.: $4.15 • U.K.: N/A

PAUL GARMIRIAN BELICOSO **86**
FINO
Dominican Republic
Ring Gauge: 52 • *Length:* 5½"
Filler: Dom. Rep. • *Binder:* Dom.
Rep. • *Wrapper:* U.S.A./Conn.
Shade
A cigar with rich spice flavors notes,
but with a slightly dry cedary finish.
U.S.: $7.80 • U.K.: N/A

PETRUS ANTONIUS **86**
Honduras
Ring Gauge: 54 • *Length:* 5"
Filler: Honduras, Nicaragua •
Binder: Honduras • *Wrapper:*
Ecuador
A mild-to-medium-bodied cigar that
has a salty nut and creamy flavor on
the palate and a well-balanced finish.
U.S.: $4.00 • U.K.: £7.00

POR LARRAÑAGA PYRAMID **86**
Dominican Republic
Ring Gauge: 50 • *Length:* 6"
Filler: Dom. Rep. • *Binder:* Dom.
Rep. • *Wrapper:* U.S.A.
This is a mild-to-medium-bodied
cigar with a light creaminess and
slightly dry woody finish.
U.S.: $5.95 • U.K.: N/A

SANCHO PANZA BELICOSO **86**
Cuba
Ring Gauge: 52 • *Length:* 5½"
Filler: Cuba • *Binder:* Cuba •
Wrapper: Cuba
A well-made cigar that has an herbal
aroma and leather and spice flavors,
but it finishes a little dry.
U.S.: N/A • U.K.: £8.25

THOMAS HINDS HONDURAN **86**
SELECTION TORPEDO
Honduras
Ring Gauge: 52 • *Length:* 6"
Filler: Honduras • *Binder:*
Honduras • *Wrapper:* Ecuador
A very pleasant, medium-bodied cigar
with a core of earthy tobacco flavors,
and a light finish.
U.S.: $3.90 • Canada: $4.45

ASTRAL PERFECCION **85**
Honduras
Ring Gauge: 48 • *Length:* 7"
Filler: Honduras, Nicaragua •
Binder: Honduras • *Wrapper:*
Honduras
A mild-tasting cigar with some dry
wood/paper notes that round out into
a mild spiciness and a woody finish.
U.S.: $6.40 • U.K.: N/A

CASA BLANCA JEROBOAM **85**
Dominican Republic
Ring Gauge: 66 • *Length:* 10"
Filler: Dom. Rep., Brazil • *Binder:*
Mexico • *Wrapper:* U.S.A./Conn.
Shade

The Jeroboam is so large it's a little overwhelming to smoke, yet it burns extremely well and the smoke is smooth, cool and rich in character.
U.S.: $5.00 • U.K.: N/A

DON LINO HABANA RESERVE TORPEDO CLASSICO **85**
Honduras
Ring Gauge: 48 • *Length:* 7"
Filler: Honduras • *Binder:*
Honduras • *Wrapper:*
U.S.A./Conn. Shade
A mild cigar with a nutty and creamy texture. It is well-made with a good draw.
U.S.: $5.25 • U.K.: N/A

EL REY DEL MUNDO FLOR DE LAVONDA **85**
Honduras
Ring Gauge: 52 • *Length:* 6½"
Filler: Honduras, Dom. Rep. •
Binder: Honduras • *Wrapper:*
Ecuador
This is a pleasant, mild smoke. It has light herb-like flavors.
U.S.: $3.25 • U.K.: N/A

HABANA GOLD TORPEDO **85**
Honduras
Ring Gauge: 52 • *Length:* 6"
Filler: Nicaragua, Honduras •
Binder: Nicaragua • *Wrapper:*
Indonesia
A medium-bodied cigar with nut and spice flavors that end on a slightly vegetal finish.
U.S.: $5.00 • U.K.: N/A

PUNCH GRAND CRU PRINCE CONSORT **85**
Honduras
Ring Gauge: 52 • *Length:* 8½"
Filler: Nica., Hon., Dom. Rep. •
Binder: U.S.A./Conn. Broadleaf •
Wrapper: Ecuador, Honduras

A little inconsistent, but it shows a medium-bodied, earthy, citrusy character and a smooth, soft texture.
U.S.: $4.40 • U.K.: N/A

ROMEO & JULIETA ROMEO **85**
Dominican Republic
Ring Gauge: 46 • *Length:* 6"
Filler: Dom. Rep., Brazil • *Binder:*
U.S.A. • *Wrapper:* Cameroon
Some hints of exotic spices and coffee bean flavors. It is a little rustic and rough.
U.S.: $3.25 • U.K.: N/A

ROYAL JAMAICA PARK LANE **85**
Dominican Republic
Ring Gauge: 47 • *Length:* 6"
Filler: Jamaica, Dom. Rep., Indonesia
Binder: Cameroon • *Wrapper:*
Indonesia
A good medium-bodied cigar. It has a pleasant spicy flavor with a tangy finish.
U.S.: $3.70 • U.K.: N/A

TE-AMO FIGURADO **85**
Mexico
Ring Gauge: 50 • *Length:* 6⅝"
Filler: Mexico • *Binder:* Mexico •
Wrapper: Mexico
This cigar has a deep earthiness and a strong pepper influence in the flavor, but with a bit of steeliness on the palate and a dry wood finish.
U.S.: $2.95 • U.K.: N/A

THE GRIFFIN'S DON BERNARDO **85**
Dominican Republic
Ring Gauge: 46 • *Length:* 9"
Filler: Dom. Rep. • *Binder:* Dom. Rep. • *Wrapper:* U.S.A./Conn. Shade
A large cigar that burns well and exhibits elegant, spicy flavors.
U.S.: $6.60 • U.K.: N/A

HOYO DE MONTERREY CULEBRA   84
Honduras
Ring Gauge: 35 • Length: 6¼"
Filler: Nica., Hon., Dom. Rep. •
Binder: U.S.A./Conn. Broadleaf •
Wrapper: Ecuador, Sumatra
Fun and quick to smoke, with an
even burn and light, fresh aromas and
flavors.
U.S.: $3.40 • U.K.: N/A

LAS CABRILLAS MAXIMILIAN   84
Honduras
Ring Gauge: 55 • Length: 7"
Filler: Nicaragua, Mexico • Binder:
Mexico • Wrapper: U.S.A./Conn.
Shade
A cigar with cedary and slightly
baked flavors including roasted cocoa.
A firm draw and a somewhat vegetal
finish.
U.S.: $2.60 • U.K.: N/A

PARTAGAS PRESIDENTE   84
Cuba
Ring Gauge: 47 • Length: 6⅛"
Filler: Cuba • Binder: Cuba •
Wrapper: Cuba
This cigar shows extreme youth and
some inconsistency in the draw. But
it has a rich, spicy core of flavors.
U.S.: N/A • France: 61FF

TE-AMO GRAN PYRAMIDE   84
Mexico
Ring Gauge: 54 • Length: 7¼"
Filler: Mexico • Binder: Mexico •
Wrapper: Mexico
A rough-looking cigar. Although it
has a slightly vegetal, grassy tone, it
also delivers some spicy pepper fla-
vors.
U.S.: $3.10 • U.K.: N/A

THE GRIFFIN'S NO. 100   84
Dominican Republic
Ring Gauge: 38 • Length: 7"
Filler: Dom. Rep. • Binder: Dom.
Rep. • Wrapper: U.S.A./Conn.
Shade
Slightly rough and coarse looking,
and it doesn't burn evenly, but it has
pleasant, creamy, spicy flavors and a
delicate texture.
U.S.: $4.40 • U.K.: N/A

VUELTABAJO PYRAMIDE   84
Dominican Republic
Ring Gauge: 50 • Length: 7"
Filler: Dom. Rep. • Binder: Dom.
Rep. • Wrapper: U.S.A./Conn.
Shade
A straightforward cigar. It has a mild,
creamy character with a touch of pep-
per. A slightly metallic aftertaste.
U.S.: $4.25 • U.K.: N/A

ASTRAL FAVORITO   83
Honduras
Ring Gauge: 48 • Length: 7"
Filler: Honduras, Nicaragua •
Binder: Honduras • Wrapper:
Honduras
This cigar had a firm draw. It has a
sweet woody quality, and a nice nutty
flavor, but a slight bitterness on the
finish.
U.S.: $6.40 • U.K.: N/A

AVO NO. 4   83
Dominican Republic
Ring Gauge: 38 • Length: 7"
Filler: Dom. Rep. • Binder: Dom.
Rep. • Wrapper: U.S.A./Conn.
Shade
Rather rough and unfinished looking,
but it has decent earthy aromas and
flavors. Some tasters noted an off-
putting grassy character.
U.S.: $4.75 • U.K.: N/A

DON LINO COLORADO   83
TORPEDO
Honduras
Ring Gauge: 48 • *Length:* 7"
Filler: Honduras, Nicaragua •
Binder: Honduras • *Wrapper:* U.S.A.
An attractive reddish-brown wrapper.
It has some spicy flavors, but an over-
all grassy, herbal quality and a woody
finish.
U.S.: $6.25 • U.K.: N/A

NAT SHERMAN VIP SELECTION 83
ZIGFIELD
Dominican Republic
Ring Gauge: 38 • *Length:* 6¾"
Filler: Dom. Rep. • *Binder:* Dom.
Rep. • *Wrapper:* U.S.A./Conn. Shade
An inconsistent draw. It had some
pleasant toast and spice notes on the
palate, and a dry, woody finish.
U.S.: $5.00 • U.K.: N/A

TE-AMO PIRAMIDE   83
Mexico
Ring Gauge: 50 • *Length:* 6¼"
Filler: Mexico • *Binder:* Mexico •
Wrapper: Mexico
A cigar with plenty of pepper taste. It
also has a flinty flavor, and some
inconsistency was noted in the draw.
U.S.: $2.30 • U.K.: N/A

DAVIDOFF ANIVERSARIO NO.1   82
Dominican Republic
Ring Gauge: 38 • *Length:* 7½"
Filler: Dom. Rep. • *Binder:* Dom.
Rep. • *Wrapper:* U.S.A./Conn. Shade
The No. 1 is very mild with grassy,
peppery flavors and a hot finish.
U.S.: $16.50 • U.K.: N/A

DAVIDOFF NO. 1   82
Dominican Republic
Ring Gauge: 38 • *Length:* 7½"
Filler: Dom. Rep. • *Binder:* Dom.
Rep. • *Wrapper:* U.S.A./Conn.
Shade

Very good draw for this sleek cigar,
and it's exceedingly mild and smooth
with a light, creamy character almost
verging on bland.
U.S.: $9.00 • U.K.: N/A

DUNHILL CENTENAS   82
Dominican Republic
Ring Gauge: 50 • *Length:* 6"
Filler: Dom. Rep., Brazil • *Binder:*
Dom. Rep. • *Wrapper:*
U.S.A./Conn. Shade
This cigar is smooth-tasting with
some vegetal flavors, and a touch of
spice on the finish.
U.S.: $8.00 • U.K.: £8.35

ORIENT EXPRESS EXPRESSO   82
Honduras
Ring Gauge: 48 • *Length:* 6"
Filler: Nicaragua, Mexico • *Binder:*
Dom. Rep. • *Wrapper:* Ecuador
A somewhat rustic and rough cigar
with a tartness on the palate. A
straightforward smoke.
U.S.: $10.50 • U.K.: N/A

PADRON PIRAMIDE   82
ANIVERSARIO
Honduras
Ring Gauge: 52 • *Length:* 6⅞"
Filler: Nicaragua • *Binder:*
Nicaragua • *Wrapper:* Nicaragua
A spicy cigar with plenty of pepper
notes. But it finishes a little short and
harsh.
U.S.: $8.00 • U.K.: N/A

SOSA PIRAMIDES   80
Dominican Republic
Ring Gauge: 64 • *Length:* 7"
Filler: Dom. Rep. • *Binder:*
Honduras • *Wrapper:* Ecuador
This is a mild, light cigar with a loose
draw that turned hot. It finished with
a fairly dry, burnt wood flavor.
U.S.: $5.00 • U.K.: N/A

Maduro

Nat Sherman Dispatch **92**
Dominican Republic
Ring Gauge: 46 • *Length:* 6½"
Filler: Dom. Rep. • *Binder:* Dom.
Rep. • *Wrapper:* Mexico
An oily wrapper delivers an opulent,
rich smoke. It is spicy with strong
tobacco and coffee flavors, and a long
aftertaste.
U.S.: $3.35 • U.K.: N/A

El Rey del Mundo Robusto **91**
Suprema
Honduras
Ring Gauge: 54 • *Length:* 7"
Filler: Dom. Rep., Honduras •
Binder: Honduras • *Wrapper:*
Honduras
This cigar has an oily, dark-brown
wrapper and a pleasant combination
of pungent-sweet flavors including
chocolate, roasted nuts and spice. A
long finish enhances this pleasant
cigar.
U.S.: $3.50 • U.K.: N/A

Don Lino Churchill **90**
Honduras
Ring Gauge: 50 • *Length:* 7"
Filler: Honduras • *Binder:*
Honduras • *Wrapper:*
U.S.A./Conn. Broadleaf
This cigar has a dark, smooth wrapper
and woody flavors that turn spicy on
the finish.
U.S.: $2.55 • U.K.: N/A

La Gloria Cubana Wavell **90**
U.S.A.
Ring Gauge: 50 • *Length:* 5"
Filler: Dom. Rep., Nica., Ecu. •
Binder: Ecuador • *Wrapper:*
U.S.A./Conn. Shade

A very dark, oily wrapper. This cigar
has a rich, creamy taste that is filled
with sweet, spicy flavors.
U.S.: $1.65 • U.K.: N/A

Bances President **89**
Honduras
Ring Gauge: 52 • *Length:* 8½"
Filler: Nicaragua, Honduras •
Binder: Mexico • *Wrapper:* Ecuador
A cool, big cigar with medium-bodied
smoke and flavors of chocolate, coffee
and sweet spices.
U.S.: $2.60 • U.K.: N/A

Henry Clay Brevas a La **89**
Conserva
Dominican Republic
Ring Gauge: 46 • *Length:* 5¾"
Filler: Dom. Rep. • *Binder:* Dom.
Rep. • *Wrapper:* U.S.A./Conn.
Broadleaf
This cigar fills the room with woody
aromas and has a pleasant, medium-
bodied, mild smoke with sweet spice
and coffee flavors.
U.S.: $1.80 • U.K.: N/A

Hoyo de Monterrey Sultans **89**
Honduras
Ring Gauge: 52 • *Length:* 7¼"
Filler: Dom. Rep., Nicaragua,
Honduras • *Binder:*
U.S.A./Connecticut • *Wrapper:*
U.S.A./Conn. Broadleaf
A cigar with an oily, brown-black
wrapper that has flavors of nutmeg,
spice and coffee. A complex finish
that has chocolate and coffee flavors.
U.S.: $2.60 • U.K.: N/A

La Gloria Cubana **89**
Churchill
U.S.A.
Ring Gauge: 50 • *Length:* 7"
Filler: Dom. Rep., Nicaragua •
Binder: Ecuador • *Wrapper:*
U.S.A./Conn. Broadleaf

A cigar with an oily, black-brown wrapper that delivers rich spicy flavors and smooth, round tobacco tastes on a short finish.
U.S.: $1.90 • U.K.: N/A

TRESADO NO. 200   89
Dominican Republic
Ring Gauge: 48 • *Length:* 7"
Filler: Dom. Rep. • *Binder:* Dom. Rep. • *Wrapper:* Indonesia
A very well-made cigar with a good draw, it has flavors of cloves and other sweet spices and a solid tobacco taste on the finish.
U.S.: $1.70 • U.K.: N/A

ALIADOS CHURCHILL DELUXE   88
Honduras
Ring Gauge: 54 • *Length:* 7¼"
Filler: Dom. Rep. • *Binder:* Ecuador
Wrapper: Ecuador
This cigar has great mouth-feel with a solid, pepper-and-spice flavor core and a smooth, mild finish.
U.S.: $3.00 • U.K.: N/A

ARTURO FUENTE CHATEAU FUENTE   88
Dominican Republic
Ring Gauge: 50 • *Length:* 4½"
Filler: Dom. Rep. • *Binder:* Dom. Rep. • *Wrapper:*
U.S.A./Connecticut Sun-Grown
This rich-tasting cigar has a smoky, coffee character with a medium body.
U.S.: $1.75 • U.K.: N/A

CUESTA-REY CABINET NO. 1884   88
Dominican Republic
Ring Gauge: 44 • *Length:* 6¼"
Filler: Dom. Rep. • *Binder:* Dom. Rep.
Wrapper: U.S.A./Conn. Broadleaf
This rustic-looking cigar has strong chocolate flavors and a smooth earthiness on the finish.
U.S.: $1.75 • U.K.: N/A

ONYX 750   88
Dominican Republic
Ring Gauge: 50 • *Length:* 7½"
Filler: Dom. Rep., Mexico • *Binder:* Indonesia • *Wrapper:* Mexico
A mild, light-bodied cigar with smooth, rich flavors on the palate and a light, pleasing finish.
U.S.: $2.50 • U.K.: N/A

PUNCH CHATEAU L   88
Honduras
Ring Gauge: 52 • *Length:* 7¼"
Filler: Hon., Nica., Dom. Rep. • *Binder:* Ecuador • *Wrapper:* Ecuador
A medium-bodied cigar with strong pepper flavors that add to a smooth, solid smoke despite a slightly rough construction.
U.S.: $2.60 • U.K.: N/A

SOSA ROTHSCHILD   88
Dominican Republic
Ring Gauge: 49 • *Length:* 4¼"
Filler: Dom. Rep., Brazil • *Binder:* Honduras • *Wrapper:*
U.S.A./Conn. Broadleaf
This cigar has a sharp, sweetish beginning on the palate and then shifts to flavors of pepper and spice.
U.S.: $1.90 • U.K.: N/A

ASHTON AGED MADURO NO. 30   87
Dominican Republic
Ring Gauge: 44 • *Length:* 6¼"
Filler: Dom. Rep. • *Binder:* Dom. Rep • *Wrapper:* U.S.A./Conn. Broadleaf
A lush, dark-brown wrapper helps deliver a dark chocolate aroma and a light, spicy flavor with a hint of sweetness. An enjoyable, pleasant finish.
U.S.: $3.75 • U.K.: N/A

BANCES CORONA INMENSA 87
Honduras
Ring Gauge: 48 • *Length:* 6¼"
Filler: Nicaragua, Honduras •
Binder: Mexico • *Wrapper:* Ecuador
A well-made maduro with a smooth, oily wrapper. It has rich coffee flavors and a light, almost-sweet taste on the palate.
U.S.: $2.10 • U.K.: N/A

CASA BLANCA DELUXE 87
Dominican Republic
Ring Gauge: 50 • *Length:* 6"
Filler: Dom. Rep. • *Binder:* Mexico
Wrapper: U.S.A./Conn. Broadleaf
A rustic cigar with some peppery flavors, but it is generally mild with simple, straightforward tobacco tastes.
U.S.: $2.25 • U.K.: £3.40

CASA BLANCA PRESIDENT 87
Dominican Republic
Ring Gauge: 50 • *Length:* 7½"
Filler: Dom. Rep. • *Binder:* Mexico
Wrapper: U.S.A./Conn. Broadleaf
A dark-brown, shiny-wrapped cigar that has good, spicy flavors and a finish that is earthy and slightly nutty.
U.S.: $2.55 • U.K.: £3.75

CUBA ALIADOS CORONA DELUXE 87
Honduras
Ring Gauge: 45 • *Length:* 6½"
Filler: Dom. Rep. • *Binder:* Ecuador
Wrapper: Ecuador
A smooth brown-black wrapper with good construction. A nice draw leads to mild spice flavors and smooth finish.
U.S.: $2.40 • U.K.: N/A

DON DIEGO PRIVADA NO. 1 87
Dominican Republic
Ring Gauge: 43 • *Length:* 6⅝"
Filler: Dom. Rep., Brazil • *Binder:* Dom. Rep. • *Wrapper:* U.S.A./Conn. Broadleaf

A medium-bodied smoke with good maduro characteristics and a mild chocolate taste on a smooth finish.
U.S.: $3.25 • U.K.: N/A

DON LINO ROTHSCHILD 87
Honduras
Ring Gauge: 50 • *Length:* 4½"
Filler: Honduras • *Binder:* Honduras • *Wrapper:* U.S.A./Conn. Broadleaf
A cigar with a black, oily wrapper loaded with classic maduro flavors of spice and pepper, with a dark-chocolate finish.
U.S.: $1.90 • U.K.: N/A

HOYO DE MONTERREY EXCALIBUR NO. 1 87
Honduras
Ring Gauge: 52 • *Length:* 7¼"
Filler: Hon., Nica., Dom. Rep. • *Binder:* Ecuador • *Wrapper:* U.S.A./Conn. Broadleaf
A cigar with floral characteristics, a mild, yet rich taste and a smooth finish.
U.S.: $2.95 • U.K.: N/A

PARTAGAS MADURO 87
Dominican Republic
Ring Gauge: 47 • *Length:* 6¼"
Filler: Mex., Jam., Dom. Rep. • *Binder:* U.S.A./Conn. Shade • *Wrapper:* Mexico
A well-made cigar with simple flavors that include hints of pepper and coffee. A pretty smoke.
U.S.: $3.05 • U.K.: N/A

PETRUS DOUBLE CORONA 87
Honduras
Ring Gauge: 50 • *Length:* 7¼"
Filler: Honduras • *Binder:* Honduras • *Wrapper:* Honduras
A well-balanced cigar with a smooth, creamy taste and flavors of citrus and nuts and a solid tobacco finish.
U.S.: $3.85 • U.K.: N/A

ROMEO & JULIETA **87**
ROTHSCHILD
Dominican Republic
Ring Gauge: 50 • *Length:* 5"
Filler: Dom. Rep. • *Binder:* Dom.
Rep. • *Wrapper:* U.S.A./Conn.
Broadleaf
A rich, black-brown cigar with hints
of coffee and spice on the palate. A
slightly woody finish comes through
the medium-bodied smoke.
U.S.: $2.10 • U.K.: N/A

ROYAL JAMAICA CORONA **87**
Dominican Republic
Ring Gauge: 40 • *Length:* 5½"
Filler: Jamaica • *Binder:* Indonesia
Wrapper: Mexico
A smooth-tasting cigar with a rich
black wrapper. It has rich coffee and
roasted nut flavors, but a mild finish.
U.S.: $2.30 • U.K.: N/A

SOSA CHURCHILL **87**
Dominican Republic
Ring Gauge: 49 • *Length:* 6⅞"
Filler: Dom. Rep., Brazil • *Binder:*
Honduras • *Wrapper:*
U.S.A./Conn. Broadleaf
A slightly rough wrapper produces a
spicy, floral flavor on the palate that
builds to a sweet tobacco taste. It has
a tangy, peatlike finish.
U.S.: $2.15 • U.K.: N/A

ARTURO FUENTE CORONA **86**
IMPERIAL
Dominican Republic
Ring Gauge: 46 • *Length:* 6½"
Filler: Dom. Rep. • *Binder:* Dom.
Rep. • *Wrapper:*
U.S.A./Connecticut Sun Grown
A black-wrapped cigar with mild
spiciness and nutty, coffee flavors. It
finishes a bit hot.
U.S.: $1.80 • U.K.: N/A

EL REY DEL MUNDO DELUXE **86**
Honduras
Ring Gauge: 48 • *Length:* 6⅛"
Filler: Dom. Rep., Honduras •
Binder: Honduras • *Wrapper:*
U.S.A./Conn. Broadleaf
A brownish-black-wrapped, well-
balanced cigar that delivers spicy and
burnt chocolate flavors on the palate.
U.S.: $3.50 • U.K.: N/A

FONSECA 5-50 **86**
Dominican Republic
Ring Gauge: 50 • *Length:* 5"
Filler: Dom. Rep. • *Binder:* Mexico
Wrapper: U.S.A./Conn. Broadleaf
A smooth, almost-black wrapper
gives this cigar a range of medium-
bodied, spicy flavors that finish with a
chocolaty, nutty taste.
U.S.: $3.00 • U.K.: N/A

HOYO DE MONTERREY **86**
ROTHSCHILD
Honduras
Ring Gauge: 50 • *Length:* 4½"
Filler: Nica., Hon., Dom. Rep. •
Binder: U.S.A./Conn. Broadleaf •
Wrapper: Ecuador
A well-made, medium-bodied maduro
with solid flavors of pepper and spice
and a long, flavorful finish.
U.S.: $1.45 • U.K.: N/A

MONTESINO DIPLOMATICO **86**
Dominican Republic
Ring Gauge: 42 • *Length:* 5½"
Filler: Dom. Rep. • *Binder:* Dom.
Rep. • *Wrapper:*
U.S.A./Connecticut Sun-Grown
A cigar with sweet flavors that range
from exotic floral notes to licorice.
An interesting smoke.
U.S.: $1.35 • U.K.: N/A

"Become a CHARTER Subscriber to CIGAR Insider"

Please send me *Marvin Shanken's CIGAR Insider*, the newsletter from the publisher of *CIGAR Aficionado*.

☐ 1 Year (12 issues) $60   ☐ 2 Years (24 issues) $110

Name: __(please print)__

Address: _____

City: _____ State: _____ Zip: _____

☐ Payment enclosed (check or money order payable to *CIGAR Insider*)

☐ Please bill me

☐ Charge to my: ☐ Visa ☐ MC ☐ AMEX

Acct #: _____ Exp.Date: _____

SignatureX _____

☐ Please also enter a subscription to Cigar Aficionado. One year $16.95 (4 issues)

Foreign: 1 year $85 U.S. Please allow 4-6 weeks for delivery of first issue.

46DZ0

Marvin Shanken's

CIGAR insider

FROM THE PUBLISHERS OF CIGAR AFICIONADO

"CIGAR Insider is *not* for everyone. But if you *really* love cigars, I can tell you that I have created this monthly newsletter especially for you."

BUSINESS REPLY MAIL

FIRST-CLASS MAIL   PERMIT NO 1302   BOULDER, CO

POSTAGE WILL BE PAID BY ADDRESSEE

CIGAR insider

P.O. Box 57602
Boulder, CO 80323-7602

NO POSTAGE
NECESSARY
IF MAILED
IN THE
UNITED STATES

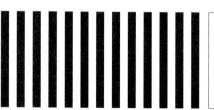

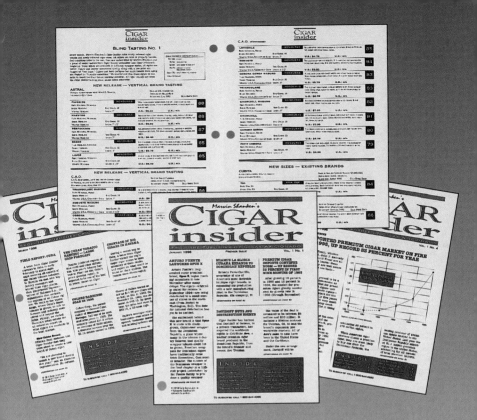

INSIDER INFORMATION

MONTESINO GRAN CORONA 86
Dominican Republic
Ring Gauge: 48 • *Length:* 6¾"
Filler: Dom. Rep. • *Binder:* Dom.
Rep. • *Wrapper:*
U.S.A./Connecticut Sun-Grown
This well-made corona draws well.
It has burnt sugar and spicy flavors
on the palate and a short but tangy
finish.
U.S.: $1.85 • U.K.: N/A

ONYX 650 86
Dominican Republic
Ring Gauge: 50 • *Length:* 6"
Filler: Dom. Rep., Mexico • *Binder:*
Indonesia • *Wrapper:* Mexico
A well-made cigar with a black wrap-
per. Rich, smooth-tasting flavors
with lots of tobacco character and an
earthy finish.
U.S.: $2.25 • U.K.: N/A

PUNCH CHATEAU M 86
Honduras
Ring Gauge: 46 • *Length:* 6¾"
Filler: Nica., Hon., Dom. Rep. •
Binder: Ecuador • *Wrapper:*
Ecuador
This rich-looking maduro delivers
spicy flavors with a sweetish, burnt
chocolate finish. A nice, well-
rounded cigar.
U.S.: $1.80 • U.K.: N/A

PUNCH DOUBLE CORONA 86
Honduras
Ring Gauge: 48 • *Length:* 6¾"
Filler: Nica., Hon., Dom. Rep. •
Binder: U.S.A./Conn Broadleaf •
Wrapper: U.S.A./Conn. Shade
A well-made cigar with a smooth
draw. It has clean tobacco flavors and
hints of sweet chocolate and spice on
a mild finish.
U.S.: $2.20 • U.K.: N/A

PUNCH ROTHSCHILD 86
Honduras
Ring Gauge: 50 • *Length:* 4½"
Filler: Nica., Hon., Dom. Rep. •
Binder: Ecuador • *Wrapper:* Ecuador
A medium-dark-brown wrapper. It is
an easy smoke with mild herbal fla-
vors to start, but it then offers some
sweet spice and coffee taste.
U.S.: $1.45 • U.K.: N/A

ROYAL JAMAICA CHURCHILL 86
Dominican Republic
Ring Gauge: 51 • *Length:* 8"
Filler: Jamaica • *Binder:* Indonesia
Wrapper: Mexico
A rough cigar with powerful spice and
pepper flavors, but a bit of an edge on
the finish.
U.S.: $4.10 • U.K.: N/A

TEMPLE HALL ESTATES 86
No. 450
Jamaica
Ring Gauge: 49 • *Length:* 4½"
Filler: Mex., Jam., Dom. Rep. • *Binder:*
U.S.A./Conn. Shade • *Wrapper:* Mexico
A dark-black wrapper with a slightly
tough draw. Rich flavors of coffee and
nuts.
U.S.: $4.50 • U.K.: N/A

ARTURO FUENTE CHURCHILL 85
Dominican Republic
Ring Gauge: 48 • *Length:* 7"
Filler: Dom. Rep. • *Binder:* Dom. Rep.
Wrapper: U.S.A./Conn. Sun Grown
This medium-bodied cigar has a slight
sweetness on the palate and strong
flavors of sweet nuts and spice.
U.S.: $2.15 • U.K.: N/A

ASHTON No. 40 85
Dominican Republic
Ring Gauge: 50 • *Length:* 6"
Filler: Dom. Rep. • *Binder:* Dom.
Rep. • *Wrapper:* U.S.A./Conn.
Broadleaf

Flavors of light chocolate, roasted nuts and a tinge of fruitiness dominate this cigar. But a tight draw and a short finish hold it back.
U.S.: $2.90 • U.K.: N/A

DON TOMAS PRESIDENTES   **85**
Honduras
Ring Gauge: 50 • *Length:* 7½"
Filler: Honduras • *Binder:*
Honduras • *Wrapper:* U.S.A./
Conn. Broadleaf
A good, smooth smoke with peppery spices and a light finish.
U.S.: $2.35 • U.K.: N/A

FONSECA 10-10   **85**
Dominican Republic
Ring Gauge: 49 • *Length:* 6¼"
Filler: Dom. Rep. • *Binder:* Mexico
Wrapper: U.S.A./Conn. Broadleaf
This cigar has an oily, black wrapper and a light body with slightly sweet flavors. A smooth smoke.
U.S.: $3.50 • U.K.: N/A

HOYO DE MONTERREY   **85**
GOVERNORS
Honduras
Ring Gauge: 50 • *Length:* 6"
Filler: Nica., Dom. Rep., Hon. •
Binder: U.S.A./Conn. Shade •
Wrapper: U.S.A./Conn. Broadleaf
This full-flavored cigar offers plenty of spice flavors and a sweetish cinnamon finish.
U.S.: $2.00 • U.K.: N/A

HOYO DE MONTERREY   **85**
EXCALIBUR NO. 2
Honduras
Ring Gauge: 46 • *Length:* 7"
Filler: Hon., Nica., Dom. Rep. •
Binder: Ecuador • *Wrapper:*
U.S.A./Conn. Broadleaf

A good, dark wrapper. The cigar has spicy, roasted coffee flavors, but some dry wood and vegetal notes on the finish.
U.S.: $2.75 • U.K.: N/A

MACANUDO PRINCE PHILIP   **85**
Jamaica
Ring Gauge: 49 • *Length:* 7½"
Filler: Mex., Jam., Dom. Rep. •
Binder: U.S.A./Conn. Shade •
Wrapper: Mexico
Rough construction hurts this cigar, but it has peppery flavors and a lightly spicy finish.
U.S.: $3.45 • U.K.: N/A

ONYX 642   **85**
Dominican Republic
Ring Gauge: 42 • *Length:* 6"
Filler: Dom. Rep., Mexico • *Binder:*
Indonesia • *Wrapper:* Mexico
A tight draw limits this cigar, but it has mild, earthy flavors with a sweetish taste.
U.S.: $1.85 • U.K.: N/A

PRIMO DEL REY NO. 4   **85**
Dominican Republic
Ring Gauge: 42 • *Length:* 5½"
Filler: Dom. Rep. • *Binder:*
U.S.A./Connecticut • *Wrapper:*
U.S.A./Conn. Broadleaf
A mild-flavored cigar with touches of spice and an earthy finish that make it a straightforward smoke.
U.S.: $1.25 • U.K.: N/A

ROYAL JAMAICA CORONA   **85**
GRANDE
Dominican Republic
Ring Gauge: 42 • *Length:* 6½"
Filler: Jamaica • *Binder:* Indonesia
Wrapper: Mexico
An easy-smoking cigar filled with a solid, rich taste and some sweet flavors. It has a smooth finish.
U.S.: $2.65 • U.K.: N/A

SANTA CLARA 1830 NO. 6   **85**
Mexico
Ring Gauge: 51 • *Length:* 6"
Filler: Mexico • *Binder:* Mexico •
Wrapper: Mexico
A pleasant but basic maduro with a
spicy, chocolate flavor and one of the
tasting's longest aftertastes.
U.S.: $1.55 • U.K.: N/A

ASHTON NO. 60   **84**
Dominican Republic
Ring Gauge: 52 • *Length:* 7½"
Filler: Dom. Rep. • *Binder:* Dom.
Rep. • *Wrapper:* U.S.A./Conn.
Broadleaf
A big cigar with a medium body and
loads of spice on the palate, but it fin-
ishes dry and sharp.
U.S.: $4.50 • U.K.: N/A

CABAÑAS CORONA   **84**
Dominican Republic
Ring Gauge: 42 • *Length:* 5½"
Filler: Dom. Rep. • *Binder:* Dom.
Rep. • *Wrapper:* Mexico
A tight draw limits this otherwise
well-balanced cigar. It has spice and
nut flavors and a medium finish.
U.S.: $1.80 • U.K.: N/A

CABAÑAS EXQUISITO MADURO **84**
Dominican Republic
Ring Gauge: 48 • *Length:* 6½"
Filler: Dom. Rep. • *Binder:* Dom.
Rep. • *Wrapper:* Mexico
This brownish-black-wrapped cigar
has slightly sweet, milk-chocolate fla-
vors and a long finish.
U.S.: $2.25 • U.K.: N/A

CUESTA-REY CABINET NO. 95 **84**
Dominican Republic
Ring Gauge: 42 • *Length:* 6¼"
Filler: Dom. Rep. • *Binder:* Dom.
Rep. • *Wrapper:* U.S.A./Conn.
Broadleaf

A firmly packed cigar that delivers
nuts and roasted-coffee flavors and
has a slightly sweet finish.
U.S.: $1.55 • U.K.: N/A

FLAMENCO BREVAS A LA   **84**
CONSERVA
Dominican Republic
Ring Gauge: 42 • *Length:* 5⁹⁄₁₆"
Filler: Dom. Rep. • *Binder:* Dom.
Rep. • *Wrapper:* U.S.A./Conn.
Broadleaf
A medium-bodied cigar that has rich
flavors of spice and pepper.
U.S.: $1.90 • U.K.: N/A

NAT SHERMAN TELEGRAPH   **84**
Dominican Republic
Ring Gauge: 50 • *Length:* 6"
Filler: Dom. Rep. • *Binder:* Dom.
Rep. • *Wrapper:* Mexico
A well-made classic maduro with dry,
woody flavors at first and a strong,
earthy tobacco finish.
U.S.: $3.60 • U.K.: N/A

PETRUS NO. 2   **84**
Honduras
Ring Gauge: 44 • *Length:* 6¼"
Filler: Honduras • *Binder:*
Honduras • *Wrapper:* Honduras
A rich-tasting cigar filled with spice
and an attractive, light, fruity after-
taste. However, showed inconsistency.
U.S.: $2.65 • U.K.: N/A

PETRUS ROTHSCHILD   **84**
Honduras
Ring Gauge: 50 • *Length:* 4¾"
Filler: Honduras • *Binder:*
Honduras • *Wrapper:* Honduras
This cigar has a medium-dark-brown
wrapper. Some inconsistency; at its
best, the smoke offers spice, light cof-
fee and tobacco flavors.
U.S.: $2.20 • U.K.: N/A

TROYA NO. 18 ROTHSCHILD 84
Dominican Republic
Ring Gauge: 50 • *Length:* 4¼"
Filler: Dom. Rep. • *Binder:* Dom.
Rep. • *Wrapper:* U.S.A./Conn.
Broadleaf
Some soft spots in this cigar, but it
has a very spicy, almost hot pepper
flavor with a medium body.
U.S.: $2.45 • U.K.: N/A

HOYO DE MONTERREY 83
EXCALIBUR NO. 3
Honduras
Ring Gauge: 48 • *Length:* 6½"
Filler: Hon., Nica., Dom. Rep. •
Binder: Ecuador • *Wrapper:*
U.S.A./Conn. Broadleaf
A cigar with herbal characteristics on
the palate, and woody, dry grass aro-
mas and flavors.
U.S.: $2.65 • U.K.: N/A

LICENCIADOS TOROS 83
Dominican Republic
Ring Gauge: 50 • *Length:* 6"
Filler: Dom. Rep. • *Binder:*
Honduras • *Wrapper:*
U.S.A./Conn. Broadleaf
A rough black wrapper delivers very
spicy flavors. Overall it is good cigar
with a light finish.
U.S.: $1.70 • U.K.: N/A

MACANUDO DUKE OF DEVON 83
Jamaica
Ring Gauge: 42 • *Length:* 5½"
Filler: Mex., Jam., Dom. Rep. •
Binder: U.S.A./Conn. Shade •
Wrapper: Mexico
A well-made cigar that offers mild
pepper and toasted nut flavors.
U.S.: $2.85 • U.K.: N/A

SANTA CLARA 1830 NO. 1 83
Mexico
Ring Gauge: 51 • *Length:* 7"
Filler: Mexico • *Binder:* Mexico •
Wrapper: Mexico
A rustic, medium-brown wrapper that
offers rich, spicy smoke with a cedary,
cinnamon note. A slightly hot finish.
U.S.: $1.85 • U.K.: N/A

TE-AMO TORO 83
Mexico
Ring Gauge: 50 • *Length:* 6"
Filler: Mexico • *Binder:* Mexico •
Wrapper: Mexico
This cigar showed some tendency
toward a tight draw, but it delivers a
rich smoke filled with toasted nut and
mild pepper flavors.
U.S.: $2.30 • U.K.: N/A

TE-AMO CHURCHILL 83
Mexico
Ring Gauge: 50 • *Length:* 7½"
Filler: Mexico • *Binder:* Mexico •
Wrapper: Mexico
A nice, dark wrapper delivers mild
coffee and spice flavors. A simple,
straightforward cigar.
U.S.: $2.85 • U.K.: N/A

TRESADO NO. 500 83
Dominican Republic
Ring Gauge: 42 • *Length:* 5½"
Filler: Dom. Rep. • *Binder:* Dom.
Rep. • *Wrapper:* Indonesia
This cigar has a light, delicate charac-
ter with a hint of spice on the palate.
U.S.: $1.20 • U.K.: N/A

TROYA NO. 45 CETRO   83
Dominican Republic
Ring Gauge: 44 • *Length:* 6"
Filler: Dom. Rep. • *Binder:* Dom. Rep.
Wrapper: U.S.A./Conn. Broadleaf
Inconsistent construction hurts this
cigar, but some tasters noted floral fla-
vors and a peppery finish.
U.S.: $1.45 • U.K.: N/A

CANARIA D'ORO ROTHSCHILD   81
Dominican Republic
Ring Gauge: 49 • *Length:* 4½"
Filler: Mexico, Dom. Rep. • *Binder:*
U.S.A./Conn. Shade • *Wrapper:*
Mexico
A cigar with mild, spicy flavors that
don't have much presence. A mild
finish.
U.S.: $1.50 • U.K.: N/A

LICENCIADOS NO. 4   80
Dominican Republic
Ring Gauge: 43 • *Length:* 5¾"
Filler: Dom. Rep. • *Binder:*
Honduras • *Wrapper:* U.S.A./
Conn. Broadleaf
Inconsistent construction. But it
delivers chocolate and tobacco flavors
even though it has a short, hot after-
taste.
U.S.: $1.30 • U.K.: N/A

LICENCIADOS PRESIDENTES   80
Dominican Republic
Ring Gauge: 50 • *Length:* 8"
Filler: Dom. Rep. • *Binder:*
Honduras • *Wrapper:*
U.S.A./Connnecticut Broadleaf
A tough cigar that either burns quick-
ly and hot or is too tight to draw. The
short finish has a bite.
U.S.: $1.95 • U.K.: N/A

CHAPTER 12

Cigars

Listed By Size *and* Country

RATING	BRAND	SIZE

DOUBLE CORONA

CUBA

96	Hoyo de Monterrey Double Corona	7⅝" x 49
94	Ramon Allones Gigantes	7⅝" x 49
92	Partagas Lusitania	7⅝" x 49
91	Punch Double Corona	7⅝" x 49

DOMINICAN REPUBLIC

93	Opus X Double Corona	7⅝" x 49
92	Davidoff Double "R"	7½" x 50
90	La Unica No. 100	8½" x 52
89	Paul Garmirian P.G. Reserve Gourmet	7⅝" x 50
89	Primo del Rey Soberano	7½" x 50
89	Romeo & Julieta Vintage No. 5	7½" x 50
88	Oscar Supreme	8" x 48
88	Paul Garmirian Gourmet Double Corona	7⅝" x 50
88	Por Larrañaga Fabuloso	7" x 50
88	Sosa Soberano	7½" x 52
87	Dunhill Peravias	7" x 50
87	Licenciados Presidente	8" x 50
87	Nat Sherman Dakota	7½" x 49
87	Royal Jamaica Churchill	8" x 51
86	Ashton Aged Maduro No. 60	7½" x 52
86	Bauza Fabuloso	7½" x 50

RATING	BRAND	SIZE
86	Nat Sherman Tribune	7½" x 50
86	Partagas No. 10	7½" x 49
85	Ashton Churchill	7½" x 50
85	Cuesta-Rey Dominican No. 2	7¼" x 48
85	El Sublimado Churchill	8" x 50
85	Jose Benito Presidente	7¾" x 50
85	Pleiades Aldebaran	8½" x 50
85	The Griffin's Prestige	8" x 48
84	Avo No. 3	7½" x 52
84	Casa Blanca Presidente	7½" x 50
83	Leon Jimenes No. 1	7½" x 50
83	Romeo & Julieta Churchill	7" x 50
83	Royal Jamaica Giant Corona	7½" x 49
83	Vueltabajo Gigante	8½" x 52
82	Troya Executive No. 72	7¾" x 50

HONDURAS

RATING	BRAND	SIZE
92	Cuba Aliados Churchill	7¼" x 54
91	Belinda Prime Minister	7½" x 50
89	Hoyo de Monterrey Excalibur No. 1	7¼" x 54
87	El Rey del Mundo Flor del Mundo	7½" x 54
87	Thomas Hinds Honduran Selection Presidente	8½" x 52
86	Don Lino Habano Reserve	7½" x 50
86	Petrus Double Corona Havana	7¾" x 50
86	Zino Veritas	7" x 50
85	Don Lino Churchill	8" x 50
85	Punch Diademas	7½" x 50
85	Punch Chateau L	7½" x 52
84	Don Lino Colorado	7½" x 50
83	La Fontana Michelangelo	7½" x 52
83	V Centennial Presidente	8" x 50
79	Baccarat Churchill	7" x 50

RATING	BRAND	SIZE

JAMAICA

90	Macanudo Vintage Cabinet Selection No. 1	7½" x 49
87	8-9-8 Collection Churchill	7½" x 49
85	Macanudo Prince Philip	7½" x 49

MEXICO

87	Cruz Real Churchill No.14	7½" x 50
87	Santa Clara 1830 No. 1	7½" x 52
82	Te-Amo Churchill	7½" x 50

NICARAGUA

88	Don Juan Presidente	8½" x 50
88	Joya de Nicaragua Viajante	8½" x 52
85	La Finca Bolivares	7½" x 50
83	Joya de Nicaragua Churchill	6⅞" x 49

U.S.A.

91	La Gloria Cubana Soberanos	8" x 52
88	La Gloria Cubana Churchill	7" x 50
85	El Rico Habano Gran Habanero	7¾" x 50
85	La Hoja Selecta Cosiac	7" x 49
80	El Rico Habano Gran Habanero Deluxe	7¾" x 50

CHURCHILL

CUBA

92	Romeo y Julieta Churchill	7" x 47
91	Punch Churchill	7" x 47
90	Bolivar Corona Gigantes	7" x 47
90	Quai d'Orsay Imperiales	7" x 47
89	Cohiba Esplendidos	7" x 47
89	Flor de Cano Diademas	7" x 47
89	Saint Luis Rey Churchill	7" x 47

RATING	BRAND	SIZE
88	Hoyo de Monterrey Churchill	7" x 47
87	El Rey del Mundo Tainos	7" x 47

DOMINICAN REPUBLIC

89	Arturo Fuente Double Chateau	6¾" x 50
89	Arturo Fuente Churchill	7¼" x 48
89	Montecristo Churchill	7" x 48
89	Partagas No. 10	7½" x 49
88	Diana Silvius Churchill	7" x 50
88	Juan Clemente Churchill	6⅞" x 46
88	La Unica No. 200	7" x 49
88	Los Libertadores Mambise	6⅞" x 48
88	Montecruz Sun Grown No. 200	7¼" x 46
88	Nat Sherman Exchange Selection Oxford No. 5	7" x 49
88	Olor Colossos	7½" x 48
88	Savinelli E.L.R. Churchill	7¼" x 48
88	Sosa Churchill	6¹⁵⁄₁₆" x 49
87	Avo No. 5	6¾" x 46
87	Carrington No. 5	6⅞" x 46
87	Nat Sherman Dakota	7½" x 49
87	Nat Sherman Gotham Selection No. 500	7" x 50
87	Por Larrañaga Fabuloso	7" x 50
86	Ashton Prime Minister	6⅞" x 48
86	Avo XO Maestoso	7" x 48
86	Cacique No. 7	6⅞" x 46
86	Cuesta-Rey Cabinet 8-9-8	7" x 49
86	Davidoff Aniversario No. 2	7" x 48
86	Don Diego Monarch	7¼" x 47
86	Dunhill Cabreras	7" x 48
86	Fonseca 10-10	7" x 50
86	José Marti Marti	7¼" x 50
86	Leon Jimenes No. 2	7" x 47

RATING	BRAND	SIZE
86	Montesino Gran Corona	6¾" x 48
86	Troya No. 63	6⅞" x 46
85	Caballeros Churchill	7" x 50
85	Los Libertadores Reserve Special Churchill	6⅞" x 49
85	Onyx 646	6⅝" x 46
85	Primo del Rey Aristocrat	6¾" x 48
85	Ramon Allones Redondos	7½" x 49
85	Romeo & Julieta Vintage No. 4	7" x 48
84	Ashton Churchill	7½" x 52
84	Ashton Prime Minister	7" x 48
84	Bauza Casa Grande	6¾" x 48
84	Credo Magnificat	6⅞" x 46
84	Cuesta-Rey Dominican No. 2	7¼" x 48
84	H. Upmann Monarch	7" x 47
84	Jose Benito Churchill	7" x 50
84	La Aurora Bristol Especial	6⅜" x 48
84	Santa Damiana Cabinet Selection No. 800	7" x 50
83	Primo del Rey Club Seleccion Regal	7" x 50
83	Royal Jamaica Giant Corona	7½" x 49
83	Santa Damiana Seleccion No. 100	6¾" x 48
83	Tresado Seleccion No. 200	7" x 48
83	Vueltabajo Churchill	7" x 48
82	Cubita 2000	7" x 50
82	Paul Garmirian Churchill	7" x 48
82	Primo Del Rey Soberanos	7½" x 50
81	Pleiades Sirius	6⅞" x 46
81	Primo del Rey Aristocrat	6¾" x 48

HONDURAS

89	Cuba Aliados Valentino No. 1	7" x 47
88	Thomas Hinds Honduran Churchill	7" x 49
87	Punch Gran Cru Monarch	6¾" x 48

RATING	BRAND	SIZE
87	Santa Rosa Churchill	7" x 49
87	V Centennial Churchill	7" x 48
86	El Rey del Mundo Double Corona	7" x 48
86	La Reserva No. 2	6½" x 48
86	Lempira Churchill	7" x 48
86	Punch Double Corona	6¾" x 48
86	Zino Veritas	7" x 50
85	Baccarat Churchill	7" x 50
85	Bances Corona Inmensa	6¾" x 48
85	Camacho Churchill	7" x 48
85	Maya Churchill	6⅞" x 49
85	Punch Chateau L	7¼" x 54
84	Baccarat Churchill	7" x 48
84	Cuba Aliados Churchill Extra	7¼" x 54
84	Habana Gold Churchill	7½" x 46
84	La Fontana Da Vinci	6⅞" x 48
83	Hoyo de Monterrey Double Corona	6¾" x 48
83	Las Cabrillas Desoto	6⅞" x 50
82	Hoyo de Monterrey Excalibur Banquet	6¾" x 48
82	Hoyo de Monterrey Sultan	7¼" x 54
82	Petrus Churchill	7" x 50
82	Punch Gran Cru Diademas	7¼" x 54
81	Punch Double Corona	6¾" x 48
80	Hoyo de Monterrey Excalibur No. 1	7¼" x 54

JAMAICA

88	8-9-8 Collection Churchill	7½" x 49
85	Macanudo Vintage No. 1	7½" x 49
84	Temple Hall 700	7½" x 49
83	Macanudo Prince Philip	7½" x 49

RATING	BRAND	SIZE
MEXICO		
84	Te-Amo Presidente	7" x 50
79	Ornelas Churchill	7" x 49
78	Santa Clara 1830 No. 2	6½" x 48
NICARAGUA		
90	Don Juan Churchill	7" x 49
85	Joya de Nicaragua Churchill	6⅛" x 49
84	Don Juan Churchill	7" x 46
U.S.A.		
85	El Rico Habano Double Corona	7" x 47

CORONA GORDA

CUBA		
92	Hoyo de Monterrey Epicure No. 1	5¾" x 46
91	Romeo y Julieta Exhibicion No. 3	5½" x 46
89	Cohiba Siglo IV	6" x 46
89	Punch Punch	5½" x 46
88	H. Upmann Magnum	5½" x 46
83	Bolivar Corona Extra	5¾" x 46
DOMINICAN REPUBLIC		
93	Licenciados Toro	6" x 50
89	Sosa Governor	6" x 50
88	Avo No. 2	6" x 50
88	Partagas Limited Reserve Regale	6¼" x 47
87	Casa Blanca Deluxe	6" x 50
87	Dunhill Condado	6" x 48
87	Onyx No. 650	6" x 50
87	Oscar No. 500	5½" x 50

RATING	BRAND	SIZE
87	Partagas Almirante	6¼" x 47
87	Romeo & Julieta Vintage No. 2	6" x 46
87	Royal Jamaica Director	6" x 45
86	Arturo Fuente 8-5-8	6" x 47
86	Nat Sherman Carnegie	6" x 48
86	Nat Sherman Gotham Selection No. 711	7" x 50
86	Primo del Rey Almirante	6" x 50
85	Canaria d'Oro Inmenso	5½" x 49
85	Davidoff 5000	5⅝" x 46
85	H. Upmann Churchill	5⅝" x 46
85	Juan Clemente Club Selection No. 1	6" x 50
85	Montecruz No. 201 Sun Grown	6¼" x 46
85	Paul Garmirian Epicure	5½" x 50
84	H. Upmann Corsario	5½" x 50
84	Nat Sherman Trafalgar No. 4	6" x 47
83	Cabañas Royale	5⅝" x 46
83	Don Diego Grande	6" x 50
81	Santa Damiana No. 300	5½" x 46
80	Nat Sherman Sutton	5½" x 49
78	Tresado No. 300	6" x 46

HONDURAS

89	Belinda Cabinet	5⅝" x 45
89	Hoyo de Monterrey Excalibur No. 3	6¼" x 50
87	Cuba Aliados No. 4	5½" x 46
87	Santa Rosa Toro	6" x 50
86	Don Tomas Corona	5½" x 50
86	Punch Super Rothschild	5¼" x 50
85	Bering Hispanos	6" x 50
85	Don Lino Havana Reserve Toro	5½" x 46
85	Petrus Corona Sublime	6" x 50

RATING	BRAND	SIZE
84	Hoyo de Monterrey Governors	6" x 48
83	Don Lino Oro Toro	5½" x 46
83	El Rey del Mundo Robusto Larga	6" x 50
83	Punch Superior	5½" x 48
82	El Rey del Mundo Choix Supreme	6" x 49

JAMAICA

88	Macanudo Hyde Park	5 ½" x 49
87	Macanudo Vintage No. 5	5½" x 49
85	Temple Hall No. 550	5½" x 50

MEXICO

| 85 | Santa Clara 1830 No. 1830 | 6" x 50 |
| 83 | Te-Amo Toro | 6" x 50 |

NICARAGUA

| 82 | La Finca Joyas | 6" x 50 |

U.S.A.

| 87 | La Gloria Cubana Extra | 6¼" x 46 |

LONSDALE

CUBA

96	Cohiba Siglo V	6¾" x 43
95	Cohiba Siglo III	6" x 42
92	Partagas No. 1	6½" x 42
92	Quintero Churchill	6½" x 42
91	El Rey del Mundo Lonsdale	6½" x 42
91	Rafael Gonzales Lonsdale	6½" x 42
90	Bolivar Gold Medal	6½" x 42
90	H. Upmann Lonsdale	6½" x 42
90	Montecristo No. 1	6½" x 42

RATING	BRAND	SIZE
89	Hoyo de Monterrey Le Hoyo des Dieux	6" x 42
87	Sancho Panza Molinas	6½" x 42
85	La Gloria Cubana Medaille d'Or No. 2	6⅔" x 43
85	Saint Luis Rey Lonsdale	6½" x 42

DOMINICAN REPUBLIC

RATING	BRAND	SIZE
91	Partagas Limited Reserve Royale	6¾" x 43
90	Troya Cetro	6¼" x 44
89	Davidoff Gran Cru No. 1	6" x 42
89	Davidoff 4000	6" x 42
89	Licenciados Excelentes	6¾" x 43
88	Arturo Fuente Reserva No. 1	6½" x 42
88	Arturo Fuente Spanish Lonsdale	6½" x 42
88	Ashton 8-9-8	6½" x 44
88	Bauza Jaguar	6½" x 42
88	Cuesta-Rey Dominican No. 4	6½" x 42
88	Cuesta-Rey No. 95	6¼" x 42
88	Dunhill Diamante	6⅝" x 42
88	Fonseca 8-9-8	6" x 43
88	Oscar No. 300	6¼" x 44
88	Primo del Rey No. 2	6¼" x 42
88	Royal Jamaica Corona Grande	6½" x 42
87	Casa Blanca Lonsdale	6½" x 42
87	Jose Benito Palma	6" x 43
87	Montecruz No. 210 Sun Grown	6½" x 42
87	Montesino No. 1	6¾" x 43
87	Ramon Allones "B"	6½" x 42
87	Sosa No. 1	6½" x 43
86	Don Diego Lonsdale	6⅝" x 42
86	Leon Jimenes No. 3	6½" x 42
86	Nat Sherman Butterfield No. 8	6½" x 42

RATING	BRAND	SIZE
86	Paul Garmirian Lonsdale	6½" x 42
86	Romeo & Julieta Vintage No. 1	6" x 43
85	Avo No. 1	6¾" x 42
85	Canaria d'Oro Lonsdale	5½" x 43
85	H. Upmann Lonsdale	6⅝" x 42
85	Montecruz No. 210	6½" x 42
85	Partagas No. 1	6¾" x 43
85	Santa Damiana No. 700	6½" x 42
85	The Griffin's No. 300	6¼" x 44
84	Juan Clemente Gran Corona	6" x 42
84	La Unica No. 300	6¾" x 43
84	Nat Sherman Algonquin	6¾" x 43
84	Romeo & Julieta Palma	6" x 43
81	Por Larrañaga Cetros	6⅞" x 42

HONDURAS

91	Cuba Aliados Lonsdale	6½" x 42
89	V Centennial Cetro	6½" x 44
88	Don Tomas Supremo	6¼" x 42
87	Bering Plaza	6" x 43
86	Hoyo de Monterrey No. 1	6½" x 43
86	Petrus No. 2	6¼" x 43
86	Punch No. 1	6½" x 43
86	Santa Rosa Cetros	6" x 42
85	Zino Tradition	6¼" x 44
84	El Rey del Mundo Lonsdale	6½" x 42
83	Baccarat Luchadores	6" x 43
78	Bances Cazadores	6¼" x 43

JAMAICA

89	Macanudo Amatista	6¼" x 42
86	Macanudo Vintage II	6¼" x 42
86	Temple Hall No. 625	6¼" x 42

RATING	BRAND	SIZE

MEXICO

| 86 | Veracruz Reserve Especial | 6½" x 42 |
| 85 | Te-Amo Meditation | 6" x 42 |

U.S.A.

| 88 | La Gloria Cubana Medaille d'Or No. 1 | 6¾" x 43 |

CORONA

CUBA

91	Bolivar Corona	5½" x 42
91	El Rey del Mundo Corona	5½" x 42
91	H. Upmann Corona	5½" x 42
90	Hoyo de Monterrey Le Hoyo du Roi	5½" x 42
89	Punch Corona	5½" x 42
89	Ramon Allones Corona	5½" x 42
89	Romeo y Julieta Corona	5½" x 42
88	Montecristo No. 3	5½" x 42
86	Partagas Corona	5½" x 42
85	Hoyo de Monterrey Corona	5½" x 42

DOMINICAN REPUBLIC

91	Montesino Diplomaticos	5½" x 43
89	Casa Blanca Corona	5½" x 42
89	Savinelli Extraordinaire	5½" x 44
88	Credo Anthanor	5¾" x 42
88	Davidoff Grand Cru No.2	5⅝" x 43
88	Olor Momento	5½" x 43
87	Arturo Fuente Reserva No. 3	5½" x 44
87	Avo No. 7	6" x 44
87	Carrington No. 2	6" x 42
87	Cuesta-Rey Dominican No. 5	5½" x 43

RATING	BRAND	SIZE
87	Don Diego Corona Major Tube	5½" x 42
87	Montecristo No. 3	5½" x 44
87	Montecruz No. 220 Sun Grown	5½" x 42
87	Nat Sherman Landmark Selection Hampshire	5½" x 42
87	Nat Sherman Metropolitan Selection Anglers	5½" x 43
87	Romeo & Julieta Vintage No. 1	6" x 43
87	Troya No. 27	5½" x 42
86	Ashton Aged Maduro No. 20	5½" x 44
86	Fonseca 8-9-8	6" x 43
86	H. Upmann Corona	5½" x 42
86	Jose Benito Palma	6" x 43
86	Juan Clemente Club Selection No. 4	5¾" x 42
86	Licenciados Numero 4	5½" x 42
86	Partagas Sabrosos	5⅞" x 43
86	Partagas No. 2	5⅞" x 44
86	Paul Garmirian Corona	5½" x 42
86	Ramon Allones Privada "D"	5" x 42
86	Vueltabajo Corona	5¾" x 42
85	Bauza Grecos	5½" x 42
85	Don Diego Corona	5⅝" x 42
85	Dunhill Valverdes	5½" x 42
85	Dunhill Tabaras	5½" x 42
85	H. Upmann Corona Major Tube	5⅛" x 42
85	La Aurora No. 4	5¼" x 42
85	Leon Jimenes No. 4	5⁹⁄₁₆" x 42
85	Los Libertadores Insurrectos	5½" x 42
85	Montecruz Sun Grown Tubos	6" x 42
85	Tresado Seleccion No. 500	5½" x 42
84	Ashton Corona	5½" x 44
84	Canaria d'Oro Corona	5½" x 43
84	El Sublimado Corona	6" x 44

RATING	BRAND	SIZE
84	Henry Clay Brevas	5½" x 42
84	José Marti Corona	5½" x 42
84	Knockando No. 3	5¾" x 41
84	La Unica No. 500	5½" x 42
84	Licenciados Supreme Maduro No. 200	5" x 42
84	Por Larrañaga Nacionales	5½" x 42
84	Primo del Rey No. 4	5½" x 42
84	Sosa Brevas	5½" x 43
83	Caballeros Corona	5¾" x 43
83	Nat Sherman City Desk Gazette	6" x 42
83	Onyx 642	6" x 42
83	Romeo & Julieta Corona	5½" x 44
82	Peterson Corona	5¾" x 43
81	Pleiades Orion	5¾" x 42

HONDURAS

RATING	BRAND	SIZE
91	Puros Indios No. 4 Especial	5½" x 44
89	José Marti 1868 Corona	5⅝" x 45
88	Hoyo de Monterrey No. 55	5¼" x 43
88	Lempira Corona	5½" x 42
88	Padron Aniversario Corona	6" x 42
88	Punch Cafe Royal	5⅝" x 44
87	Belinda Breva Conserva	5½" x 43
87	Bering Corona Royale	6" x 41
87	C.A.O. Corona	6" x 42
87	Don Lino Peticetro	5½" x 42
87	Don Tomas Matador	5½" x 42
87	Hoyo de Monterrey Cafe Royal	5⅝" x 43
86	Bances Brevas	5½" x 43
86	Felipe Gregorio Sereno	5¾" x 42
86	Habana Gold Black Label Corona	6" x 44

RATING	BRAND	SIZE
86	Hoyo de Monterrey Super Hoyo	5½" x 44
86	Santa Rosa No. 4	5½" x 42
86	Thomas Hinds Honduran Selection Corona	5½" x 42
86	Zino Mouton-Cadet No. 1	6½" x 44
85	Bering Imperial	5¼" x 42
85	Camacho Nacionales	5½" x 44
85	Don Melo Petit Corona	5½" x 42
85	Hoyo de Monterrey Excalibur No. 5	6¼" x 43
85	Maya Petit Corona	5½" x 42
84	El Rey del Mundo Habana Club	5½" x 42
84	Las Cabrillas Magellan	6" x 42
84	Punch No. 75	5½" x 43
83	Punch Royal Coronation	5¼" x 44
83	V Centennial Corona	5½" x 42
83	Zino Diamonds	5½" x 40
81	Baccarat Petit Corona	5½" x 42

JAMAICA

87	Macanudo Vintage No. 3	5⁹⁄₁₆" x 43
86	Macanudo Duke of Devon	5½" x 42
85	Macanudo Hampton Court	5¾" x 42

MEXICO

87	Santa Clara 1830 No. 5	6" x 43
86	Cruz Real No. 2	6" x 42
80	Te-Amo Meditation	6" x 42

NICARAGUA

91	La Finca Corona	5½" x 42
86	Padron Londres	5½" x 42
84	Mi Cubano No. 542	5" x 42
84	Thomas Hinds Nicaraguan Selection Corona	5½" x 42

RATING	BRAND	SIZE
83	Joya de Nicaragua No. 6	6" x 42
80	Don Juan Cetro	6" x 43

U.S.A.

88	La Gloria Cubana Glorias	5½" x 43
86	Macabi Media Corona	5½" x 43
85	El Rico Habano Corona	5½" x 42
83	La Hoja Selecta Cetros de Oro	5¾" x 43

ROBUSTO

CUBA

95	Bolivar Royal Coronas	5" x 50
94	Hoyo de Monterrey Epicure No. 2	5" x 50
93	Flor de Cano Short Churchill	5" x 50
92	Cohiba Robusto	5" x 50
90	Ramon Allones Specially Selected	5" x 50
89	Romeo y Julieta Exhibicion No. 4	5" x 48
88	Partagas Series D No. 4	5" x 50

DOMINICAN REPUBLIC

90	Opus X Fuente Fuente Robusto	5¼" x 50
89	Arturo Fuente Don Carlos Robusto	5" x 50
89	Fonseca 5-50	5" x 50
88	Ashton Magnum	5" x 50
88	Canaria d'Oro Rothschild	4½" x 50
88	Dunhill Altamira	5" x 48
88	Licenciados Wavell	5" x 50
88	Por Larrañaga Robusto	5" x 50
87	Avo XO Intermezzo	5½" x 50
87	Davidoff Special "R"	4⅞" x 50
87	Pleiades Pluton	5" x 50

RATING	BRAND	SIZE
87	Royal Jamaica Robusto	4½" x 49
87	Vueltabajo Robusto	4¾" x 52
86	H. Upmann Pequenos 100	4½" x 50
86	H. Upmann Cabinet Selection No. 100	4¾" x 50
86	Nat Sherman Astor	4½" x 50
86	Partagas Robusto	4½" x 49
86	Romeo & Julieta Vintage No. 3	4½" x 50
86	Santa Damiana No. 500	5" x 50
85	Arturo Fuente Chateau Fuente	5" x 50
85	Ashton Aged Maduro No. 10	5" x 50
85	Caballeros Rothschild	5" x 50
85	El Sublimado Regardete	4½" x 50
85	H. Upmann Cabinet Selection Robusto	4¾" x 50
85	Juan Clemente Rothschild	4⅞" x 50
85	Leon Jimenes Robusto	5½" x 50
85	Montecristo Robusto	4¾" x 50
85	Partagas Natural	5½" x 49
84	Diana Silvius Robusto	4⅞" x 52
84	Dunhill Romanas Vintage 1987	4½" x 50
84	Jose Benito Rothschild	4¾" x 50
84	Juan Clemente Club Selection No. 2	4½" x 46
84	La Unica No. 400	4½" x 50
84	Nat Sherman Sutton	5½" x 49
84	Paul Garmirian Series No. 2	4¾" x 48
84	Romeo & Julieta Rothschild	5" x 50
84	Sosa Wavell	4¾" x 50
83	Avo No. 9	4¾" x 48
83	Bauza Robusto	5½" x 50
83	Montecruz Sun Grown Robusto	4½" x 49
83	Primo del Rey No. 100	4½" x 50
82	Troya No. 18	4¼" x 50

RATING	BRAND	SIZE
HONDURAS		
89	V Centennial Robusto	5" x 50
88	Encanto Rothschild	4½" x 50
88	Zino Mouton-Cadet No. 6	5" x 50
87	Don Tomas Special Edition No. 300	5" x 50
86	Hoyo de Monterrey Rothschild	4½" x 50
86	Nat Sherman Hobart	5" x 50
86	Thomas Hinds Honduran Selection Robusto	5" x 50
85	Don Lino Colorado	5½" x 50
85	Don Tomas Rothschild	4½" x 50
84	Baccarat Havana Selection Robusto	5" x 50
84	Cuba Aliados Rothschild	5" x 50
84	Don Lino Robusto	5½" x 50
83	Don Lino Habana Reserve Robusto	5½" x 50
83	El Rey del Mundo Robusto	5" x 54
83	Las Cabrillas Cortez	4¾" x 50
83	Punch Rothschild	4½" x 50
83	Punch Grand Cru Robusto	5¼" x 50
82	El Rey del Mundo Robusto de Manuel	5" x 54
81	Don Ramos Rothschild	4½" x 50
80	Belinda Medaglia d'Oro	4½" x 50
79	La Invicta Magnum No. 2	4½" x 50
74	Petrus Rothschild	4¾" x 50
JAMAICA		
87	Macanudo Hyde Park	5½" x 49
85	Macanudo Vintage No. V	5½" x 49
84	Temple Hall No. 550	5½" x 50
MEXICO		
82	Cruz Real No. 25	5½" x 52
82	Te-Amo Torito	4¾" x 50

RATING	BRAND	SIZE
NICARAGUA		
81	Joya de Nicaragua Consul	4½" x 52
U.S.A.		
85	La Gloria Cubana Wavell	5" x 50
72	La Hoja Selecta Palais Royal	4¼" x 50

PETIT CORONA

RATING	BRAND	SIZE
CUBA		
93	Cohiba Siglo I	4" x 40
89	Montecristo No. 4	5" x 42
89	Partagas Petit Corona	5" x 42
89	Romeo y Julieta Petit Corona	5" x 42
87	Bolivar Petit Corona	5" x 42
86	Hoyo de Monterrey Le Hoyo du Prince	5" x 40
86	Punch Royal Selection No. 12	5½" x 42
85	Sancho Panza Non Plus	5" x 42
84	Quintero Medias Coronas	5" x 40
81	Fonseca Cosacos	5⅓" x 42
81	H. Upmann Petit Corona	5" x 42
DOMINICAN REPUBLIC		
89	Montesino Diplomatico	5½ " x 43
88	Davidoff Gran Cru No. 3	5" x 42
88	Davidoff Gran Cru No. 4	5" x 40
87	Avo No. 8	5½" x 40
87	Pleiades Antares	5½" x 40
87	Primo del Rey No. 4	5½" x 42
86	Arturo Fuente Petit Corona	5" x 38
86	Cuesta-Rey Dominican No. 5	5½" x 42
86	Don Diego Petit Corona	5⅛" x 42

RATING	BRAND	SIZE
86	H. Upmann Tubos	5¹⁄₁₆" x 42
86	H. Upmann Petit Corona	5¹⁄₁₆" x 42
86	Nat Sherman Landmark Selection Hampshire	5½" x 42
86	Olor Momentos	5½" x 43
86	Paul Garmirian Petit Corona	5" x 43
86	Por Larrañaga Petit Cetros en Cedro	5" x 38
85	Davidoff No. 2000	5" x 42
85	Ramon Allones Size "D"	5" x 42
84	Bauza Petit Corona	5" x 38
84	Bauza Grecos	5½" x 42
84	Jose Benito Petite	5½" x 38
84	Los Libertadores Insurrectos	5½" x 42
84	Montecruz Sun Grown No. 230	5" x 42
84	Partagas No. 4	5" x 38
84	Tresado Seleccion No. 500	5½" x 42
84	Troya Clasico	5½" x 42
83	H. Upmann Corona Major	5¹⁄₁₆" x 42
83	Montecruz Sun Grown Cedar Aged	5" x 42
83	Royal Jamaica Petit Corona	5" x 40
83	Vueltabajo Corona	5¾" x 42
82	Licenciados Supreme Maduro No. 200	5½" x 42
82	Licenciados No. 4	5½" x 42
82	Nat Sherman VIP Selection Barnum Glass Tube	5½" x 42
81	Casa Blanca Corona	5½" x 42
80	Carrington No. 4	5½" x 40

HONDURAS

88	Hoyo de Monterrey Excalibur No. 7	5" x 43
87	Baccarat Petit Corona	5½" x 42
87	El Rey del Mundo Habana Club	5½" x 42
87	Hoyo de Monterrey Super Hoyos	5½" x 44

RATING	BRAND	SIZE
87	Thomas Hinds Honduran Selection Corona	5½" x 42
87	Zino Mouton-Cadet No. 5	5" x 42
86	Cuba Aliados Remedios	5½" x 42
86	Don Tomas Blunt	5" x 42
86	Zino Diamonds	5½" x 40
85	Don Lino Petit Cetro	5½" x 42
85	Hoyo de Monterrey Excalibur No. 6	5½" x 38
85	Punch Elite	5¼" x 44
84	Bering Imperial	5¼" x 42
83	Don Lino No. 4	5" x 42
83	Hoyo de Monterrey No. 55	5¼" x 43
82	El Rey del Mundo Tinos	5½" x 38
81	Bances Unique	5½" x 38
80	Nat Sherman Host Selection Hamilton	5½" x 42
70	Hoyo de Monterrey Sabrosas	5" x 40

JAMAICA

88	8-9-8 Collection Corona	5½" x 42
88	Macanudo Lord Claridge	5½" x 38
88	Macanudo Vintage No. 3	5" x 42
87	Macanudo Hampton Court	5¾" x 43
84	Macanudo Petit Corona	5" x 38

MEXICO

83	Te-Amo No. 4	5" x 42

NICARAGUA

85	Padron Londres	5½" x 42
84	La Finca Corona	5½" x 42
83	Joya de Nicaragua Petite	5½" x 38

U.S.A.

89	El Rico Habano Petit Habano	5" x 40

RATING	BRAND	SIZE

PANATELA

CUBA

91	Montecristo Especial No. 2	6" x 38
89	Cohiba Corona Especial	6" x 38
88	Punch Ninfas	7" x 38
86	Hoyo de Monterrey Le Hoyo du Dauphin	6" x 38
86	Montecristo Especial	7½" x 38
85	Romeo y Julieta Shakespeare	6½" x 28
84	Romeo y Julieta Belvedere	5½" x 39
83	Cohiba Lancero	7½" x 38
83	El Rey del Mundo Elegante	6¾" x 28

DOMINICAN REPUBLIC

91	Opus X Petit Lancero	6" x 38
87	Avo XO Preludio	6" x 40
87	Cuesta-Rey No. 2 Cabinet	7" x 36
87	Davidoff No. 2	6" x 38
87	Juan Clemente Panatela	6½" x 34
87	Paul Garmirian Panatela	7½" x 38
86	Ashton Panatela	6" x 36
86	Cuesta-Rey Dominican No. 3	7" x 36
85	Arturo Fuente Panatela Fina	7" x 38
85	Carrington No. 3	7" x 36
84	Casa Blanca Panatela	6" x 36
84	Montecruz Tubulares Sun Grown	6⅛" x 36
84	The Griffin's No. 400	6" x 38
83	Davidoff No. 1	7½" x 38
83	Dunhill Fantino	7" x 28
83	Nat Sherman Murray Hill No. 7	6" x 38
83	Royal Jamaica Tube No. 2	6½" x 34

RATING	BRAND	SIZE
82	Bauza Florete	6⅞" x 35
82	Don Diego Royal Palma	6⅛" x 36
82	Licenciados Panatela Lindas	7" x 38
82	Nat Sherman Metropole	6" x 34
82	Partagas Tubos	7" x 38
82	Pleiades Antares	5½" x 40
82	Por Larrañaga Delicados	6½" x 36
81	Avo No. 4	7" x 38
81	Dunhill Dominican Samanas	6" x 38
80	La Aurora Palmas Extra	6¾" x 35
78	Sosa Sante Fe	6" x 35
76	H. Upmann Naturales	6⅛" x 36

HONDURAS

88	V Centennial No. 1	7½" x 38
87	Belinda Belinda	6½" x 36
86	Don Tomas Special Edition No. 400	7" x 36
86	Maya Palma Fina	6⅞" x 36
85	Don Lino Havana Reserve Panatela	7" x 36
85	Don Tomas Panatela Largas	7" x 38
85	Zino Mouton-Cadet No. 2	6" x 35
83	Hoyo de Monterrey Excalibur No. VII	5" x 43
81	Bances Unique	5½" x 38
80	El Rey del Mundo Tino	5½" x 38
80	Hoyo de Monterrey Delights	6¼" x 37
79	Don Lino Panatelas	7" x 36
78	Don Tomas International Selection No. 4	7" x 36

JAMAICA

87	Temple Hall No. 685	6⅞" x 34
85	Macanudo Portofino	7" x 34
83	Macanudo Vintage No. VII	7½" x 38

RATING	BRAND	SIZE
CANARY ISLANDS		
84	Dunhill Panatela	6" x 30
MEXICO		
81	Te-Amo Torero	6⁹⁄₁₆" x 35
NICARAGUA		
86	La Finca Flora	7" x 36
81	Joya de Nicaragua No. 5	5½" x 38
77	Don Juan Lindas	5½" x 38
U.S.A.		
87	La Gloria Cubana Panatela Deluxe	7" x 37
80	El Rico Habano No. 1	7½" x 38

FIGURADO

CUBA		
96	Romeo y Julieta Fabuloso	9" x 47
95	Montecristo "A"	9½" x 47
94	Montecristo No. 2	6⅛" x 52
92	Diplomaticos No. 2	6⅛" x 52
92	Punch Diademas Extra	9" x 47
91	Montecristo Especial No. 1	7½" x 38
90	Bolivar Belicoso Fino	5½" x 52
90	Romeo y Julieta Belicoso	5½" x 52
89	H. Upmann No. 2	6⅛" x 52
88	El Rey Del Mundo Grandes De España	7½" x 38
87	Cohiba Lancero	7½" x 38
87	La Gloria Cubana Medaille d'Or No. 1	7⅛" x 36
87	Romeo y Julieta Celestial Fino	5 ¾" x 46
86	Sancho Panza Belicoso	5½" x 52
84	Partagas Presidente	6⅛" x 47

RATING	BRAND	SIZE
DOMINICAN REPUBLIC		
92	Opus X No. 2	6¼" x 52
89	Arturo Fuente Hemingway Signature	6" x 46
89	Arturo Fuente Hemingway Short Story	4¼" x 49
89	Ashton Cabinet Selection No. 10	7½" x 52
89	Avo XO Pyramid	5½" x 50
88	Ashton Cabinet Selection No. 3	6" x 46
88	Oscar No. 700	7" x 54
88	Paul Garmirian Celebration	9" x 50
88	Paul Garmirian Belicoso	6¼" x 52
88	Sosa Family Selection No. 2	6¼" x 54
87	Ashton Vintage Cabinet No. 1	9" x 52
87	Ashton Vintage Cabinet Sel. No. 2	7" x 47
87	Avo Belicoso	6" x 50
87	Carrington No. 8	6⅞" x 60
87	Davidoff Special "T"	6" x 52
87	Fonseca Triangulare	5½" x 56
87	Los Libertadores Figurado	6½" x 52
87	Montecristo No. 2	6" x 50
87	Nat Sherman Metropolitan	7" x 52
87	Troya Torpedo No. 81	7" x 54
86	Arturo Fuente Hemingway Masterpiece	9¼" x 52
86	Arturo Fuente Hemingway Classic	7" x 48
86	Avo Pyramide	7" x 54
86	Avo Petit Belicoso	4¾" x 50
86	El Sublimado Torpedo	7" x 54
86	Los Libertadores Figurado Reserva Especial	6½" x 52
86	Paul Garmirian Belicoso Fino	5½" x 52
86	Por Larrañaga Pyramid	6" x 50
85	Casa Blanca Jeroboam	10" x 66
85	Romeo & Julieta Romeo	6" x 46

RATING	BRAND	SIZE
85	Royal Jamaica Park Lane	6" x 47
85	The Griffin's Don Bernardo	9" x 46
84	The Griffin's No. 100	7" x 38
84	Vueltabajo Pyramide	7" x 50
83	Avo No. 4	7" x 38
83	Nat Sherman VIP Selection Zigfield	6¾" x 38
82	Davidoff Aniversario No.1	7½" x 38
82	Davidoff No. 1	7½" x 38
82	Dunhill Centenas	6" x 50
80	Sosa Piramides	7" x 64

HONDURAS

92	Puros Indios Piramide No. 1	7½" x 60
90	Puros Indios Piramide No. 2	6½" x 46
89	Cuba Aliados Piramide No. 2	6½" x 46
87	Cuba Aliados Piramide	7½" x 60
87	El Rey del Mundo Flor de Llaneza	6½" x 54
87	V Centennial Torpedo	7" x 54
86	C.A.O. Triangulares	7" x 54
86	Felipe Gregorio Belicoso	6⅛" x 54
86	Petrus Antonius	5" x 54
86	Thomas Hinds Honduran Selection Torpedo	6" x 52
85	Astral Perfeccion	7" x 48
85	Don Lino Habana Reserve Torpedo Classico	7" x 48
85	El Rey del Mundo Flor de Lavonda	6½" x 52
85	Habana Gold Torpedo	6" x 52
85	Punch Grand Cru Prince Consort	8½" x 52
84	Hoyo de Monterrey Culebra	6¼" x 35
84	Las Cabrillas Maximilian	7" x 55
83	Astral Favorito	7" x 48
83	Don Lino Colorado Torpedo	7" x 48

RATING	BRAND	SIZE
82	Orient Express Expresso	6" x 48
82	Padron Piramide Aniversario	6⅞" x 52

JAMAICA

88	Temple Hall Belicoso	6" x 50
87	Macanudo Duke of Windsor	6" x 50
86	Macanudo Duke of Wellington	8½" x 38

MEXICO

85	Te-Amo Figurado	6⅝" x 50
84	Te-Amo Gran Pyramide	7¼" x 54
83	Te-Amo Piramide	6¼" x 50

U.S.A.

90	Santiago Cabana Torpedo	6¼" x 54
88	El Rico Habano No. 1	7½" x 38
88	Macabi Belicoso Fino	6¼" x 52
87	La Gloria Cubana Piramides	7¼" x 56
86	La Gloria Cubana Torpedo No. 1	6½" x 54

MADURO

DOMINICAN REPUBLIC

92	Nat Sherman Dispatch	6½" x 46
89	Henry Clay Brevas a La Conserva	5¾" x 46
89	Tresado No. 200	7" x 48
88	Arturo Fuente Chateau Fuente	4½" x 50
88	Cuesta-Rey Cabinet No. 1884	6¾" x 44
88	Onyx 750	7½" x 50
88	Sosa Rothschild	4¾" x 49
87	Ashton Aged Maduro No. 30	6¾" x 44
87	Casa Blanca President	7½" x 50
87	Casa Blanca Deluxe	6" x 50

RATING	BRAND	SIZE
87	Don Diego Privada No. 1	6⅝" x 43
87	Partagas Maduro	6¼" x 47
87	Romeo & Julieta Rothschild	5" x 50
87	Royal Jamaica Corona	5½" x 40
87	Sosa Churchill	6⅞" x 49
86	Arturo Fuente Corona Imperial	6½" x 46
86	Fonseca 5-50	5" x 50
86	Montesino Diplomatico	5½" x 42
86	Montesino Gran Corona	6¾" x 48
86	Onyx 650	6" x 50
86	Royal Jamaica Churchill	8" x 51
85	Arturo Fuente Churchill	7" x 48
85	Ashton No. 40	6" x 50
85	Fonseca 10-10	6¾" x 49
85	Onyx 642	6" x 42
85	Primo del Rey No. 4	5½" x 42
85	Royal Jamaica Corona Grande	6½" x 42
84	Ashton No. 60	7½" x 52
84	Cabañas Corona	5½" x 42
84	Cabañas Exquisito Maduro	6½" x 48
84	Cuesta-Rey Cabinet No. 95	6¼" x 42
84	Flamenco Brevas A La Conserva	5 9/16" x 42
84	Nat Sherman Telegraph	6" x 50
84	Troya No. 18 Rothschild	4¾" x 50
83	Licenciados Toros	6" x 50
83	Tresado No. 500	5½" x 42
83	Troya No. 45 Cetro	6" x 44
81	Canaria d'Oro Rothschild	4½" x 49
80	Licenciados No. 4	5¾" x 43
80	Licenciados Presidentes	8" x 50

RATING	BRAND	SIZE

H O N D U R A S

RATING	BRAND	SIZE
91	El Rey del Mundo Robusto Suprema	7" x 54
90	Don Lino Churchill	7" x 50
89	Bances President	8½" x 52
89	Hoyo de Monterrey Sultans	7¼" x 52
88	Aliados Churchill Deluxe	7¼" x 54
88	Punch Chateau L	7¼" x 52
87	Bances Corona Inmensa	6¾" x 48
87	Cuba Aliados Corona Deluxe	6½" x 45
87	Don Lino Rothschild	4½" x 50
87	Hoyo de Monterrey Excalibur No. 1	7¼" x 52
87	Petrus Double Corona	7¾" x 50
86	El Rey del Mundo Deluxe	6⅞" x 48
86	Hoyo de Monterrey Rothschild	4½" x 50
86	Punch Chateau M	6¾" x 46
86	Punch Double Corona	6¾" x 48
86	Punch Rothschild	4½" x 50
85	Don Tomas Presidentes	7½" x 50
85	Hoyo de Monterrey Governors	6" x 50
85	Hoyo de Monterrey Excalibur No. 2	7" x 46
84	Petrus No. 2	6¼" x 44
84	Petrus Rothschild	4¼ x 50
83	Hoyo de Monterrey Excalibur No. 3	6½" x 48

J A M A I C A

RATING	BRAND	SIZE
86	Temple Hall Estates No. 450	4½" x 49
85	Macanudo Prince Philip	7½" x 49
83	Macanudo Duke of Devon	5½" x 42

M E X I C O

RATING	BRAND	SIZE
85	Santa Clara 1830 No. 6	6" x 51
83	Santa Clara 1830 No. 1	7" x 51

RATING	BRAND	SIZE
83	Te-Amo Toro	6" x 50
83	Te-Amo Churchill	7½" x 50

U.S.A.

90	La Gloria Cubana Wavell	5" x 50
89	La Gloria Cubana Churchill	7" x 50

VINTAGE (PRE-CASTRO CUBAN CIGARS)

CUBA

98	Montecristo No. 1 Seleccion Suprema	6½" x 42
97	Cabañas No. 751 Alfred Dunhill	6½" x 42
97	Romeo y Julieta Seleccion Suprema Cedro	6½" x 42
95	H. Upmann No. 22 Seleccion Suprema	4½" x 55
95	H. Upmann No. 4 Alfred Dunhill	6½" x 46
93	La Corona Churchill	6½" x 46
93	Partagas No. 6 Seleccion Superba	4½" x 40
92	Belinda Belindas	5½" x 42
92	Flor de Farach Palmeras	5" x 38
92	Montecristo No. 4 Seleccion Suprema	5" x 42
89	Ramon Allones Ideales	6½" x 40
89	Romeo y Julieta Sun Grown Brevas	5½" x 44
87	Ramon Allones No. 66 (perfecto)	6" x N/A
86	Henry Clay Coronas	5½" x 42

CHAPTER 13

Cigars

Listed By Brand

CIGAR	CATEGORY	SIZE	RATING
8-9-8 COLLECTION (JAMAICA)			
Churchill	Double Corona	7½" x 49	87
Churchill	Churchill	7½" x 49	88
Corona	Corona	5½" x 42	83
Corona	Petit Corona	5½" x 42	88
ARTURO FUENTE (DOMINICAN REPUBLIC)			
8-5-8	Corona Gorda	6" x 47	86
Chateau Fuente	Maduro	4½" x 50	88
Chateau Fuente	Robusto	5" x 50	85
Churchill	Churchill	7¼" x 48	89
Churchill	Maduro	7" x 48	85
Corona Imperial	Maduro	6½" x 46	86
Don Carlos Robusto	Robusto	5" x 50	89
Double Chateau	Churchill	6¾" x 50	89
Hemingway Classic	Figurado	7" x 48	86
Hemingway Masterpiece	Figurado	9¼" x 52	86
Hemingway Short Story	Figurado	4¼" x 49	89
Hemingway Signature	Figurado	6" x 46	89
Panatela Fina	Panatela	7" x 38	85
Petit Corona	Petit Corona	5" x 38	86

CIGAR	CATEGORY	SIZE	RATING
ARTURO FUENTE (DOMINICAN REPUBLIC) *[continued]*			
Reserva No. 1	Lonsdale	6½" x 42	88
Reserva No. 3	Corona	5½" x 44	87
Spanish Lonsdale	Lonsdale	6½" x 42	88
ASHTON (DOMINICAN REPUBLIC)			
8-9-8	Lonsdale	6½" x 44	88
Aged Maduro No. 10	Robusto	5" x 50	85
Aged Maduro No. 20	Corona	5½" x 44	86
Aged Maduro No. 30	Maduro	6¾" x 44	87
Aged Maduro No. 60	Double Corona	7½" x 52	86
Cabinet Selection No. 10	Figurado	7½" x 52	89
Cabinet Selection No. 3	Figurado	6" x 46	88
Churchill	Double Corona	7½" x 50	85
Churchill	Churchill	7½" x 52	84
Corona	Corona	5½" x 44	84
Magnum	Robusto	5" x 50	88
No. 40	Maduro	6" x 50	85
No. 60	Maduro	7½" x 52	84
Panatela	Panatela	6" x 36	86
Prime Minister	Churchill	6⅞" x 48	86
Prime Minister	Churchill	7" x 48	84
Vintage Cabinet No. 1	Figurado	9" x 52	87
Vintage Cabinet Sel. No. 2	Figurado	7" x 47	87
ASTRAL (HONDURAS)			
Favorito	Figurado	7" x 48	83
Perfeccion	Figurado	7" x 48	85

CIGAR	CATEGORY	SIZE	RATING
AVO (DOMINICAN REPUBLIC)			
Belicoso	Figurado	6" x 50	87
No. 1	Lonsdale	6¾" x 42	85
No. 2	Corona Gorda	6" x 50	88
No. 3	Double Corona	7½" x 52	84
No. 4	Panatela	7" x 38	81
No. 4	Figurado	7" x 38	83
No. 5	Churchill	6¾" x 46	87
No. 7	Corona	6" x 44	87
No. 8	Petit Corona	5½" x 40	87
No. 9	Robusto	4¾" x 48	83
Petit Belicoso	Figurado	4¾" x 50	86
Pyramide	Figurado	7" x 54	86
AVO XO (DOMINICAN REPUBLIC)			
Intermezzo	Robusto	5½" x 50	87
Maestoso	Churchill	7" x 48	86
Preludio	Panatela	6" x 40	87
Pyramid	Figurado	5½" x 50	89
BACCARAT (HONDURAS)			
Churchill	Churchill	7" x 48	84
Churchill	Double Corona	7" x 50	79
Churchill	Churchill	7" x 50	85
Havana Selection Robusto	Robusto	5" x 50	84
Luchadores	Lonsdale	6" x 43	83
Petit Corona	Corona	5½" x 42	81
Petit Corona	Petit Corona	5½" x 42	87

CIGAR	CATEGORY	SIZE	RATING
BANCES (HONDURAS)			
Brevas	Corona	5½" x 43	86
Cazadores	Lonsdale	6¼" x 43	78
Corona Inmensa	Churchill	6¾" x 48	85
Corona Inmensa	Maduro	6¾" x 48	87
President	Maduro	8½" x 52	89
Unique	Panatela	5½" x 38	81
Unique	Petit Corona	5½" x 38	81
BAUZA (DOMINICAN REPUBLIC)			
Casa Grande	Churchill	6¾" x 48	84
Fabuloso	Double Corona	7½" x 50	86
Florete	Panatela	6⅞" x 35	82
Grecos	Corona	5½" x 42	85
Grecos	Petit Corona	5½" x 42	84
Jaguar	Lonsdale	6½" x 42	88
Petit Corona	Petit Corona	5" x 38	84
Robusto	Robusto	5½" x 50	83
BELINDA (CUBA)			
Belindas	Vintage	5½" x 42	92
BELINDA (HONDURAS)			
Belinda	Panatela	6½" x 36	87
Breva Conserva	Corona	5½" x 43	87
Cabinet	Corona Gorda	5⅝" x 45	89
Medaglia d'Oro	Robusto	4½" x 50	80
Prime Minister	Double Corona	7½" x 50	91

CIGAR	CATEGORY	SIZE	RATING
BERING (HONDURAS)			
Corona Royale	Corona	6" x 41	87
Hispanos	Corona Gorda	6" x 50	85
Imperial	Petit Corona	5¼" x 42	84
Imperial	Corona	5¼" x 42	85
Plaza	Lonsdale	6" x 43	87
BOLIVAR (CUBA)			
Belicoso Fino	Figurado	5½" x 52	90
Corona	Corona	5½" x 42	91
Corona Extra	Corona Gorda	5¾" x 46	83
Corona Gigantes	Churchill	7" x 47	90
Gold Medal	Lonsdale	6½" x 42	90
Petit Corona	Petit Corona	5" x 42	87
Royal Coronas	Robusto	5" x 50	95
C.A.O. (HONDURAS)			
Corona	Corona	6" x 42	87
Triangulares	Figurado	7" x 54	86
CABALLEROS (DOMINICAN REPUBLIC)			
Churchill	Churchill	7" x 50	85
Corona	Corona	5¾" x 43	83
Rothschild	Robusto	5" x 50	85
CABANAS (CUBA)			
No. 751 Alfred Dunhill	Vintage	6½" x 42	97

CIGAR	CATEGORY	SIZE	RATING
CABAÑAS (DOMINICAN REPUBLIC)			
Corona	Maduro	5½" x 42	84
Exquisito Maduro	Maduro	6½" x 48	84
Royale	Corona Gorda	5⅝" x 46	83
CACIQUE (DOMINICAN REPUBLIC)			
No. 7	Churchill	6⅞" x 46	86
CAMACHO (HONDURAS)			
Churchill	Churchill	7" x 48	85
Nacionales	Corona	5½" x 44	85
CANARIA D'ORO (DOMINICAN REPUBLIC)			
Corona	Corona	5½" x 43	84
Inmenso	Corona Gorda	5½" x 49	85
Lonsdale	Lonsdale	5½" x 43	85
Rothschild	Maduro	4½" x 49	81
Rothschild	Robusto	4½" x 50	88
CARRINGTON (DOMINICAN REPUBLIC)			
No. 2	Corona	6" x 42	87
No. 3	Panatela	7" x 36	85
No. 4	Petit Corona	5½" x 40	80
No. 5	Churchill	6⅞" x 46	87
No. 8	Figurado	6⅞" x 60	87
CASA BLANCA (DOMINICAN REPUBLIC)			
Corona	Corona	5½" x 42	89
Corona	Petit Corona	5½" x 42	81

CIGAR	CATEGORY	SIZE	RATING
Deluxe	Maduro	6" x 50	87
Deluxe	Corona Gorda	6" x 50	87
Jeroboam	Figurado	10" x 66	85
Lonsdale	Lonsdale	6½" x 42	87
Panatela	Panatela	6" x 36	84
President	Maduro	7½" x 50	87
Presidente	Double Corona	7½" x 50	84

COHIBA (CUBA)

Corona Especial	Panatela	6" x 38	89
Esplendidos	Churchill	7" x 47	89
Lancero	Panatela	7½" x 38	83
Lancero	Figurado	7½" x 38	87
Robusto	Robusto	5" x 50	92
Siglo I	Petit Corona	4" x 40	93
Siglo III	Lonsdale	6" x 42	95
Siglo IV	Corona Gorda	6" x 46	89
Siglo V	Lonsdale	6¾" x 43	96

CREDO (DOMINICAN REPUBLIC)

Anthanor	Corona	5¾" x 42	88
Magnificat	Churchill	6⅞" x 46	84

CRUZ REAL (MEXICO)

Churchill No.14	Double Corona	7½" x 50	87
No. 2	Corona	6" x 42	86
No. 25	Robusto	5½" x 52	82

CUBA ALIADOS (HONDURAS)

Churchill	Double Corona	7¼" x 54	92

CIGAR	CATEGORY	SIZE	RATING

CUBA ALIADOS (HONDURAS) [continued]

Churchill Deluxe	Maduro	7¼" x 54	88
Churchill Extra	Churchill	7¼" x 54	84
Corona Deluxe	Maduro	6½" x 45	87
Lonsdale	Lonsdale	6½" x 42	91
No. 4	Corona Gorda	5½" x 46	87
Piramide	Figurado	7½" x 60	87
Piramide No. 2	Figurado	6½" x 46	89
Remedios	Petit Corona	5½" x 42	86
Rothschild	Robusto	5" x 50	84
Valentino No. 1	Churchill	7" x 47	89

CUBITA (DOMINICAN REPUBLIC)

2000	Churchill	7" x 50	82

CUESTA-REY (DOMINICAN REPUBLIC)

Cabinet 8-9-8	Churchill	7" x 49	86
Cabinet No. 1884	Maduro	6¾" x 44	88
Cabinet No. 95	Maduro	6¼" x 42	84
Dominican No. 2	Churchill	7¼" x 48	84
Dominican No. 3	Panatela	7" x 36	86
Dominican No. 4	Lonsdale	6½" x 42	88
Dominican No. 5	Corona	5½" x 43	87
Dominican No. 5	Petit Corona	5½" x 42	86
No. 2	Double Corona	7¼" x 48	85
No. 2 Cabinet	Panatela	7" x 36	87
No. 95	Lonsdale	6¼" x 42	88

CIGAR	CATEGORY	SIZE	RATING
DAVIDOFF (DOMINICAN REPUBLIC)			
4000	Lonsdale	6" x 42	89
5000	Corona Gorda	5⅝" x 46	85
Aniversario No. 2	Churchill	7" x 48	86
Aniversario No.1	Figurado	7½" x 38	82
Double "R"	Double Corona	7½" x 50	92
Gran Cru No. 1	Lonsdale	6" x 42	89
Gran Cru No. 3	Petit Corona	5" x 42	88
Gran Cru No. 4	Petit Corona	5" x 40	88
Grand Cru No.2	Corona	5⅝" x 43	88
No. 1	Panatela	7½" x 38	83
No. 1	Figurado	7½" x 38	82
No. 2	Panatela	6" x 38	87
No. 2000	Petit Corona	5" x 42	85
Special "R"	Robusto	4⅞" x 50	87
Special "T"	Figurado	6" x 52	87
DIANA SILVIUS (DOMINICAN REPUBLIC)			
Churchill	Churchill	7" x 50	88
Robusto	Robusto	4⅞" x 52	84
DIPLOMATICOS (CUBA)			
No. 2	Figurado	6⅛" x 52	92
DON DIEGO (DOMINICAN REPUBLIC)			
Corona	Corona	5⅝" x 42	85
Corona Major Tube	Corona	5½" x 42	87
Grande	Corona Gorda	6" x 50	83
Lonsdale	Lonsdale	6⅝" x 42	86

CIGAR	CATEGORY	SIZE	RATING

DON DIEGO (DOMINICAN REPUBLIC) *[continued]*

CIGAR	CATEGORY	SIZE	RATING
Monarch	Churchill	7¼" x 47	86
Petit Corona	Petit Corona	5⅛" x 42	86
Privada No. 1	Maduro	6⅝" x 43	87
Royal Palma	Panatela	6⅛" x 36	82

DON JUAN (NICARAGUA)

CIGAR	CATEGORY	SIZE	RATING
Cetro	Corona	6" x 43	80
Churchill	Churchill	7" x 46	84
Churchill	Churchill	7" x 49	90
Lindas	Panatela	5½" x 38	77
Presidente	Double Corona	8½" x 50	88

DON LINO (HONDURAS)

CIGAR	CATEGORY	SIZE	RATING
Churchill	Maduro	7" x 50	90
Churchill	Double Corona	8" x 50	85
Colorado	Robusto	5½" x 50	85
Colorado	Double Corona	7½" x 50	84
Habana Reserve Robusto	Robusto	5½" x 50	83
Habano Reserve	Double Corona	7½" x 50	86
Havana Reserve Panatela	Panatela	7" x 36	85
Havana Reserve Toro	Corona Gorda	5½" x 46	85
No. 4	Petit Corona	5" x 42	83
Oro Toro	Corona Gorda	5½" x 46	83
Panatelas	Panatela	7" x 36	79
Peticetro	Corona	5½" x 42	87
Petit Cetro	Petit Corona	5½" x 42	85
Robusto	Robusto	5½" x 50	84
Rothschild	Maduro	4½" x 50	87

CIGAR	CATEGORY	SIZE	RATING

DON LINO COLORADO (HONDURAS)

Torpedo	Figurado	7" x 48	83

DON LINO HABANA RESERVE (HONDURAS)

Torpedo Classico	Figurado	7" x 48	85

DON MELO (HONDURAS)

Petit Corona	Corona	5½" x 42	85

DON RAMOS (HONDURAS)

Rothschild	Robusto	4½" x 50	81

DON TOMAS (HONDURAS)

Blunt	Petit Corona	5" x 42	86
Corona	Corona Gorda	5½" x 50	86
International Sel. No. 4	Panatela	7" x 36	78
Matador	Corona	5½" x 42	87
Panatela Largas	Panatela	7" x 38	85
Presidentes	Maduro	7½" x 50	85
Rothschild	Robusto	4½" x 50	85
Special Edition No. 300	Robusto	5" x 50	87
Special Edition No. 400	Panatela	7" x 36	86
Supremo	Lonsdale	6¼" x 42	88

DUNHILL (CANARY ISLANDS)

Panatela	Panatela	6" x 30	84

CIGAR	CATEGORY	SIZE	RATING
DUNHILL (DOMINICAN REPUBLIC)			
Altamira	Robusto	5" x 48	88
Cabreras	Churchill	7" x 48	86
Centenas	Figurado	6" x 50	82
Condado	Corona Gorda	6" x 48	87
Diamante	Lonsdale	6⅝" x 42	88
Dominican Samanas	Panatela	6" x 38	81
Fantino	Panatela	7" x 28	83
Peravias	Double Corona	7" x 50	87
Romanas Vintage 1987	Robusto	4½" x 50	84
Tabaras	Corona	5½" x 42	85
Valverdes	Corona	5½" x 42	85
EL REY DEL MUNDO (CUBA)			
Corona	Corona	5½" x 42	91
Elegante	Panatela	6¾" x 28	83
Grandes De Espaûa	Figurado	7½" x 38	88
Lonsdale	Lonsdale	6½" x 42	91
Tainos	Churchill	7" x 47	87
EL REY DEL MUNDO (HONDURAS)			
Choix Supreme	Corona Gorda	6" x 49	82
Deluxe	Maduro	6⅛" x 48	86
Double Corona	Churchill	7" x 48	86
Flor de Lavonda	Figurado	6½" x 52	85
Flor de Llaneza	Figurado	6½" x 54	87
Flor del Mundo	Double Corona	7½" x 54	87
Habana Club	Petit Corona	5½" x 42	87
Habana Club	Corona	5½" x 42	84
Lonsdale	Lonsdale	6½" x 42	84

CIGAR	CATEGORY	SIZE	RATING
Robusto	Robusto	5" x 54	83
Robusto Larga	Corona Gorda	6" x 50	83
Robusto Suprema	Maduro	7" x 54	91
Robusto de Manuel	Robusto	5" x 54	82
Tino	Panatela	5½" x 38	80
Tinos	Petit Corona	5½" x 38	82

EL RICO HABANO (U.S.A.)

Corona	Corona	5½" x 42	85
Double Corona	Churchill	7" x 47	85
Gran Habanero	Double Corona	7¾" x 50	85
Gran Habanero Deluxe	Double Corona	7¾" x 50	80
No. 1	Panatela	7½" x 38	80
No. 1	Figurado	7½" x 38	88
Petit Habano	Petit Corona	5" x 40	89

EL SUBLIMADO (DOMINICAN REPUBLIC)

Churchill	Double Corona	8" x 50	85
Corona	Corona	6" x 44	84
Regardete	Robusto	4½" x 50	85
Torpedo	Figurado	7" x 54	86

ENCANTO (HONDURAS)

Rothschild	Robusto	4½" x 50	88

FELIPE GREGORIO (HONDURAS)

Belicoso	Figurado	6⅛" x 54	86
Sereno	Corona	5¾" x 42	86

CIGAR	CATEGORY	SIZE	RATING
FLAMENCO (DOMINICAN REPUBLIC)			
Brevas A La Conserva	Maduro	5⁹⁄₁₆" x 42	84
FLOR DE CANO (CUBA)			
Diademas	Churchill	7" x 47	89
Short Churchill	Robusto	5" x 50	93
FLOR DE FARACH (CUBA)			
Palmeras	Vintage	5" x 38	92
FONSECA (CUBA)			
Cosacos	Petit Corona	5⅓" x 42	81
FONSECA (DOMINICAN REPUBLIC)			
10-10	Maduro	6¾" x 49	85
10-10	Churchill	7" x 50	86
5-50	Maduro	5" x 50	86
5-50	Robusto	5" x 50	89
8-9-8	Lonsdale	6" x 43	88
8-9-8	Corona	6" x 43	86
Triangulare	Figurado	5½" x 56	87
H. UPMANN (CUBA)			
Corona	Corona	5½" x 42	91
Lonsdale	Lonsdale	6½" x 42	90
Magnum	Corona Gorda	5½" x 46	88
No. 2	Figurado	6⅛" x 52	89
No. 22 Seleccion Suprema	Vintage	4½" x 55	95
No. 4 Alfred Dunhill	Vintage	6½" x 46	95

CIGAR	CATEGORY	SIZE	RATING
Petit Corona	Petit Corona	5" x 42	81

H. UPMANN (DOMINICAN REPUBLIC)

Cabinet Selection No. 100	Robusto	4¾" x 50	86
Cabinet Selection Robusto	Robusto	4¾" x 50	85
Churchill	Corona Gorda	5⅝" x 46	85
Corona	Corona	5½" x 42	86
Corona Major	Petit Corona	5¹⁄₁₆" x 42	83
Corona Major Tube	Corona	5⅛" x 42	85
Corsario	Corona Gorda	5½" x 50	84
Lonsdale	Lonsdale	6⅝" x 42	85
Monarch	Churchill	7" x 47	84
Naturales	Panatela	6⅛" x 36	76
Pequenos 100	Robusto	4½" x 50	86
Petit Corona	Petit Corona	5¹⁄₁₆" x 42	86
Tubos	Petit Corona	5¹⁄₁₆" x 42	86

HABANA GOLD (HONDURAS)

Black Label Corona	Corona	6" x 44	86
Churchill	Churchill	7½" x 46	84
Torpedo	Figurado	6" x 52	85

HENRY CLAY (CUBA)

Coronas	Vintage	5½" x 42	86

HENRY CLAY (DOMINICAN REPUBLIC)

Brevas	Corona	5½" x 42	84
Brevas a La Conserva	Maduro	5¾" x 46	89

CIGAR	CATEGORY	SIZE	RATING
HOYO DE MONTERREY (CUBA)			
Churchill	Churchill	7" x 47	88
Corona	Corona	5½" x 42	85
Double Corona	Double Corona	7⅝" x 49	96
Epicure No. 1	Corona Gorda	5¾" x 46	92
Epicure No. 2	Robusto	5" x 50	94
Le Hoyo des Dieux	Lonsdale	6" x 42	89
Le Hoyo du Dauphin	Panatela	6" x 38	86
Le Hoyo du Prince	Petit Corona	5" x 40	86
Le Hoyo du Roi	Corona	5½" x 42	90
HOYO DE MONTERREY (HONDURAS)			
Cafe Royal	Corona	5⅝" x 43	87
Culebra	Figurado	6¼" x 35	84
Delights	Panatela	6¼" x 37	80
Double Corona	Churchill	6¾" x 48	83
Excalibur Banquet	Churchill	6¾" x 48	82
Excalibur No. 1	Maduro	7¼" x 52	87
Excalibur No. 1	Double Corona	7¼" x 54	89
Excalibur No. 1	Churchill	7¼" x 54	80
Excalibur No. 2	Maduro	7" x 46	85
Excalibur No. 3	Maduro	6½" x 48	83
Excalibur No. 3	Corona Gorda	6¼" x 50	89
Excalibur No. 5	Corona	6¼" x 43	85
Excalibur No. 6	Petit Corona	5½" x 38	85
Excalibur No. 7	Petit Corona	5" x 43	88
Excalibur No. VII	Panatela	5" x 43	83
Governors	Maduro	6" x 50	85
Governors	Corona Gorda	6" x 48	84
No. 1	Lonsdale	6½" x 43	86

CIGAR	CATEGORY	SIZE	RATING
No. 55	Petit Corona	5¼" x 43	83
No. 55	Corona	5¼" x 43	88
Rothschild	Maduro	4½" x 50	86
Rothschild	Robusto	4½" x 50	86
Sabrosas	Petit Corona	5" x 40	70
Sultan	Churchill	7¼" x 54	82
Sultans	Maduro	7¼" x 52	89
Super Hoyo	Corona	5½" x 44	86
Super Hoyos	Petit Corona	5½" x 44	87

JOSE BENITO (DOMINICAN REPUBLIC)

Churchill	Churchill	7" x 50	84
Palma	Lonsdale	6" x 43	87
Palma	Corona	6" x 43	86
Petite	Petit Corona	5½" x 38	84
Presidente	Double Corona	7¾" x 50	85
Rothschild	Robusto	4¾" x 50	84

JOSÉ MARTI 1868 (HONDURAS)

Corona	Corona	5⅝" x 45	89

JOSÉ MARTI (DOMINICAN REPUBLIC)

Corona	Corona	5½" x 42	84
Marti	Churchill	7¼" x 50	86

JOYA DE NICARAGUA (NICARAGUA)

Churchill	Double Corona	6⅞" x 49	83
Churchill	Churchill	6⅞" x 49	85
Consul	Robusto	4½" x 52	81
No. 5	Panatela	5½" x 38	81

CIGAR	CATEGORY	SIZE	RATING
JOYA DE NICARAGUA (NICARAGUA) *[continued]*			
No. 6	Corona	6" x 42	83
Petite	Petit Corona	5½" x 38	83
Viajante	Double Corona	8½" x 52	88
JUAN CLEMENTE (DOMINICAN REPUBLIC)			
Churchill	Churchill	6⅞" x 46	88
Club Selection No. 1	Corona Gorda	6" x 50	85
Club Selection No. 2	Robusto	4½" x 46	84
Club Selection No. 4	Corona	5¾" x 42	86
Gran Corona	Lonsdale	6" x 42	84
Panatela	Panatela	6½" x 34	87
Rothschild	Robusto	4⅞" x 50	85
KNOCKANDO (DOMINICAN REPUBLIC)			
No. 3	Corona	5¾" x 41	84
LA AURORA (DOMINICAN REPUBLIC)			
Bristol Especial	Churchill	6⅜" x 48	84
No. 4	Corona	5¼" x 42	85
Palmas Extra	Panatela	6¾" x 35	80
LA CORONA (CUBA)			
Churchill	Vintage	6½" x 46	93
LA FINCA (NICARAGUA)			
Bolivares	Double Corona	7½" x 50	85
Corona	Petit Corona	5½" x 42	84
Corona	Corona	5½" x 42	91

CIGAR	CATEGORY	SIZE	RATING
Flora	Panatela	7" x 36	86
Joyas	Corona Gorda	6" x 50	82

LA FONTANA (HONDURAS)

Da Vinci	Churchill	6⅞" x 48	84
Michelangelo	Double Corona	7½" x 52	83

LA GLORIA CUBANA (CUBA)

Medaille d'Or No. 2	Lonsdale	6⅔" x 43	85
Medaille d'Or No. 1	Figurado	7⅛" x 36	87

LA GLORIA CUBANA (U.S.A.)

Churchill	Maduro	7" x 50	89
Churchill	Double Corona	7" x 50	88
Extra	Corona Gorda	6¼" x 46	87
Glorias	Corona	5½" x 43	88
Medaille d'Or No. 1	Lonsdale	6¾" x 43	88
Panatela Deluxe	Panatela	7" x 37	87
Piramides	Figurado	7¼" x 56	87
Soberanos	Double Corona	8" x 52	91
Torpedo No. 1	Figurado	6½" x 54	86
Wavell	Maduro	5" x 50	90
Wavell	Robusto	5" x 50	85

LA HOJA SELECTA (U.S.A.)

Cetros de Oro	Corona	5¾" x 43	83
Cosiac	Double Corona	7" x 49	85
Palais Royal	Robusto	4¼" x 50	72

CIGAR	CATEGORY	SIZE	RATING
LA INVICTA (HONDURAS)			
Magnum No. 2	Robusto	4½" x 50	79
LA RESERVA (HONDURAS)			
No. 2	Churchill	6½" x 48	86
LA UNICA (DOMINICAN REPUBLIC)			
No. 100	Double Corona	8½" x 52	90
No. 200	Churchill	7" x 49	88
No. 300	Lonsdale	6¾" x 43	84
No. 400	Robusto	4½" x 50	84
No. 500	Corona	5½" x 42	84
LAS CABRILLAS (HONDURAS)			
Cortez	Robusto	4¾" x 50	83
Desoto	Churchill	6⅞" x 50	83
Magellan	Corona	6" x 42	84
Maximilian	Figurado	7" x 55	84
LEMPIRA (HONDURAS)			
Churchill	Churchill	7" x 48	86
Corona	Corona	5½" x 42	88
LEON JIMENES (DOMINICAN REPUBLIC)			
No. 1	Double Corona	7½" x 50	83
No. 2	Churchill	7" x 47	86
No. 3	Lonsdale	6½" x 42	86
No. 4	Corona	5⁹⁄₁₆" x 42	85
Robusto	Robusto	5½" x 50	85

CIGAR	CATEGORY	SIZE	RATING
LICENCIADOS (DOMINICAN REPUBLIC)			
Excelentes	Lonsdale	6¾" x 43	89
No. 4	Maduro	5¾" x 43	80
No. 4	Petit Corona	5½" x 42	82
Numero 4	Corona	5½" x 42	86
Panatela Lindas	Panatela	7" x 38	82
Presidente	Double Corona	8" x 50	87
Presidentes	Maduro	8" x 50	80
Supreme Maduro No. 200	Petit Corona	5½" x 42	82
Supreme Maduro No. 200	Corona	5" x 42	84
Toro	Corona Gorda	6" x 50	93
Toros	Maduro	6" x 50	83
Wavell	Robusto	5" x 50	88
LOS LIBERTADORES (DOMINICAN REPUBLIC)			
Figurado	Figurado	6½" x 52	87
Figurado Reserva Especial	Figurado	6½" x 52	86
Insurrectos	Petit Corona	5½" x 42	84
Insurrectos	Corona	5½" x 42	85
Mambise	Churchill	6⅞" x 48	88
Reserve Special Churchill	Churchill	6⅞" x 49	85
MACABI (U.S.A.)			
Belicoso Fino	Figurado	6¼" x 52	88
Media Corona	Corona	5½" x 43	86
MACANUDO (JAMAICA)			
Amatista	Lonsdale	6¼" x 42	89
Duke of Devon	Maduro	5½" x 42	83

CIGAR	CATEGORY	SIZE	RATING
MACANUDO (JAMAICA) [continued]			
Duke of Devon	Corona	5½" x 42	86
Duke of Wellington	Figurado	8½" x 38	86
Duke of Windsor	Figurado	6" x 50	87
Hampton Court	Corona	5¾" x 42	85
Hampton Court	Petit Corona	5¾" x 43	87
Hyde Park	Corona Gorda	5½" x 49	88
Hyde Park	Robusto	5½" x 49	87
Lord Claridge	Petit Corona	5½" x 38	88
Petit Corona	Petit Corona	5" x 38	84
Portofino	Panatela	7" x 34	85
Prince Philip	Double Corona	7½" x 49	85
Prince Philip	Churchill	7½" x 49	83
Prince Philip	Maduro	7½" x 49	85
Vintage II	Lonsdale	6¼" x 42	86
Vintage No. 3	Corona	5⁹⁄₁₆" x 43	87
Vintage No. 5	Corona Gorda	5½" x 49	87
Vintage No. V	Robusto	5½" x 49	85
Vintage No. VII	Panatela	7½" x 38	83
MACANUDO VINTAGE (JAMAICA)			
Cabinet Selection No. 1	Double Corona	7½" x 49	90
No. 1	Churchill	7½" x 49	85
No. 3	Petit Corona	5" x 42	88
MAYA (HONDURAS)			
Churchill	Churchill	6⅞" x 49	85
Palma Fina	Panatela	6⅞" x 36	86
Petit Corona	Corona	5½" x 42	85

CIGAR	CATEGORY	SIZE	RATING
MI CUBANO (NICARAGUA)			
No. 542	Corona	5" x 42	84
MONTECRISTO (CUBA)			
"A"	Figurado	9½" x 47	95
Especial	Panatela	7½" x 38	86
Especial No. 1	Figurado	7½" x 38	91
Especial No. 2	Panatela	6" x 38	91
No. 1	Lonsdale	6½" x 42	90
No. 1 Seleccion Suprema	Vintage	6½" x 42	98
No. 2	Figurado	6⅛" x 52	94
No. 3	Corona	5½" x 42	88
No. 4	Petit Corona	5" x 42	89
No. 4 Seleccion Suprema	Vintage	5" x 42	92
MONTECRISTO (DOMINICAN REPUBLIC)			
Churchill	Churchill	7" x 48	89
No. 2	Figurado	6" x 50	87
No. 3	Corona	5½" x 44	87
Robusto	Robusto	4¾" x 50	85
MONTECRUZ (DOMINICAN REPUBLIC)			
No. 201 Sun Grown	Corona Gorda	6¼" x 46	85
No. 210	Lonsdale	6½" x 42	85
No. 210 Sun Grown	Lonsdale	6½" x 42	87
No. 220 Sun Grown	Corona	5½" x 42	87
Sun Grown Robusto	Robusto	4½" x 49	83
Sun Grown No. 230	Petit Corona	5" x 42	84
Sun Grown Cedar Aged	Petit Corona	5" x 42	83

CIGAR	CATEGORY	SIZE	RATING

MONTECRUZ (DOMINICAN REPUBLIC) [continued]

Sun Grown No. 200	Churchill	7¼" x 46	88
Sun Grown Tubos	Corona	6" x 42	85
Tubulares Sun Grown	Panatela	6⅛" x 36	84

MONTESINO (DOMINICAN REPUBLIC)

Diplomatico	Maduro	5½" x 42	86
Diplomatico	Petit Corona	5½ " x 43	89
Diplomaticos	Corona	5½" x 43	91
Gran Corona	Churchill	6¾" x 48	86
Gran Corona	Maduro	6¾" x 48	86
No. 1	Lonsdale	6¾" x 43	87

NAT SHERMAN (DOMINICAN REPUBLIC)

Algonquin	Lonsdale	6¾" x 43	84
Astor	Robusto	4½" x 50	86
Butterfield No. 8	Lonsdale	6½" x 42	86
Carnegie	Corona Gorda	6" x 48	86
City Desk Gazette	Corona	6" x 42	83
Dakota	Churchill	7½" x 49	87
Dakota	Double Corona	7½" x 49	87
Dispatch	Maduro	6½" x 46	92
Exchange Selection Oxford No. 5	Churchill	7" x 49	88
Gotham Selection No. 500	Churchill	7" x 50	87
Gotham Selection No. 711	Corona Gorda	7" x 50	86
Landmark Selection Hampshire	Corona	5½" x 42	87
Landmark Selection Hampshire	Petit Corona	5½" x 42	86
Metropole	Panatela	6" x 34	82
Metropolitan	Figurado	7" x 52	87
Metropolitan Selection Anglers	Corona	5½" x 43	87

CIGAR	CATEGORY	SIZE	RATING
Murray Hill No. 7	Panatela	6" x 38	83
Sutton	Robusto	5½" x 49	84
Sutton	Corona Gorda	5½" x 49	80
Telegraph	Maduro	6" x 50	84
Trafalgar No. 4	Corona Gorda	6" x 47	84
Tribune	Double Corona	7½" x 50	86
VIP Selection Barnum Glass Tube	Petit Corona	5½" x 42	82
VIP Selection Zigfield	Figurado	6¾" x 38	83

NAT SHERMAN (HONDURAS)

Hobart	Robusto	5" x 50	86
Host Selection Hamilton	Petit Corona	5½" x 42	80

OLOR (DOMINICAN REPUBLIC)

Colossos	Churchill	7½" x 48	88
Momento	Corona	5½" x 43	88
Momentos	Petit Corona	5½" x 43	86

ONYX (DOMINICAN REPUBLIC)

642	Maduro	6" x 42	85
642	Corona	6" x 42	83
646	Churchill	6⅜" x 46	85
650	Maduro	6" x 50	86
750	Maduro	7½" x 50	88
No. 650	Corona Gorda	6" x 50	87

OPUS X (DOMINICAN REPUBLIC)

Double Corona	Double Corona	7⅜" x 49	93
Fuente Fuente Robusto	Robusto	5¼" x 50	90
Petit Lancero	Panatela	6" x 38	91
No. 2	Figurado	6¼" x 52	92

CIGAR	CATEGORY	SIZE	RATING
ORIENT EXPRESS (HONDURAS)			
Expresso	Figurado	6" x 48	82
ORNELAS (MEXICO)			
Churchill	Churchill	7" x 49	79
OSCAR (DOMINICAN REPUBLIC)			
No. 300	Lonsdale	6¼" x 44	88
No. 500	Corona Gorda	5½" x 50	87
No. 700	Figurado	7" x 54	88
Supreme	Double Corona	8" x 48	88
PADRON (NICARAGUA)			
Londres	Petit Corona	5½" x 42	85
Londres	Corona	5½" x 42	86
PADRON ANIVERSARIO (HONDURAS)			
Corona	Corona	6" x 42	88
Piramide	Figurado	6⅛" x 52	82
PARTAGAS (CUBA)			
Corona	Corona	5½" x 42	86
Lusitania	Double Corona	7⅝" x 49	92
No. 1	Lonsdale	6½" x 42	92
No. 6 Seleccion Superba	Vintage	4½" x 40	93
Petit Corona	Petit Corona	5" x 42	89
Presidente	Figurado	6⅛" x 47	84
Series D No. 4	Robusto	5" x 50	88

CIGAR	CATEGORY	SIZE	RATING
PARTAGAS (DOMINICAN REPUBLIC)			
Almirante	Corona Gorda	6¼" x 47	87
Limited Reserve Regale	Corona Gorda	6¼" x 47	88
Limited Reserve Royale	Lonsdale	6¾" x 43	91
Maduro	Maduro	6¼" x 47	87
Natural	Robusto	5½" x 49	85
No. 1	Lonsdale	6¾" x 43	85
No. 10	Double Corona	7½" x 49	86
No. 10	Churchill	7½" x 49	89
No. 2	Corona	5⅞" x 44	86
No. 4	Petit Corona	5" x 38	84
Robusto	Robusto	4½" x 49	86
Sabrosos	Corona	5⅞" x 43	86
Tubos	Panatela	7" x 38	82
PAUL GARMIRIAN (DOMINICAN REPUBLIC)			
Belicoso	Figurado	6¼" x 52	88
Belicoso Fino	Figurado	5½" x 52	86
Celebration	Figurado	9" x 50	88
Churchill	Churchill	7" x 48	82
Corona	Corona	5½" x 42	86
Epicure	Corona Gorda	5½" x 50	85
Gourmet Double Corona	Double Corona	7⅝" x 50	88
Lonsdale	Lonsdale	6½" x 42	86
P.G. Reserve Gourmet	Double Corona	7⅝" x 50	89
Panatela	Panatela	7½" x 38	87
Petit Corona	Petit Corona	5" x 43	86
Series No. 2	Robusto	4¾" x 48	84

CIGAR	CATEGORY	SIZE	RATING
PETERSON (DOMINICAN REPUBLIC)			
Corona	Corona	5¾" x 43	82
PETRUS (HONDURAS)			
Antonius	Figurado	5" x 54	86
Churchill	Churchill	7" x 50	82
Corona Sublime	Corona Gorda	6" x 50	85
DC Havana	Double Corona	7¾" x 50	86
Double Corona	Maduro	7¾" x 50	87
No. 2	Lonsdale	6¼" x 43	86
No. 2	Maduro	6¼" x 44	84
Rothschild	Maduro	4¾" x 50	84
Rothschild	Robusto	4¾" x 50	74
PLEIADES (DOMINICAN REPUBLIC)			
Aldebaran	Double Corona	8½" x 50	85
Antares	Panatela	5½" x 40	82
Antares	Petit Corona	5½" x 40	87
Orion	Corona	5¾" x 42	81
Pluton	Robusto	5" x 50	87
Sirius	Churchill	6⅞" x 46	81
POR LARRAÑAGA (DOMINICAN REPUBLIC)			
Cetros	Lonsdale	6⅞" x 42	81
Delicados	Panatela	6½" x 36	82
Fabuloso	Double Corona	7" x 50	88
Fabuloso	Churchill	7" x 50	87
Nacionales	Corona	5½" x 42	84
Petit Cetros en Cedro	Petit Corona	5" x 38	86
Pyramid	Figurado	6" x 50	86

CIGAR	CATEGORY	SIZE	RATING
Robusto	Robusto	5" x 50	88

PRIMO DEL REY (DOMINICAN REPUBLIC)

Almirante	Corona Gorda	6" x 50	86
Aristocrat	Churchill	6¾" x 48	85
Aristocrat	Churchill	6¾" x 48	81
Club Seleccion Regals	Churchill	7" x 50	83
No. 100	Robusto	4½" x 50	83
No. 2	Lonsdale	6¼" x 42	88
No. 4	Maduro	5½" x 42	85
No. 4	Petit Corona	5½" x 42	87
No. 4	Corona	5½" x 42	84
Soberano	Double Corona	7½" x 50	89
Soberanos	Churchill	7½" x 50	82

PUNCH (CUBA)

Churchill	Churchill	7" x 47	91
Corona	Corona	5½" x 42	89
Diademas Extra	Figurado	9" x 47	92
Double Corona	Double Corona	7⅝" x 49	91
Ninfas	Panatela	7" x 38	88
Punch	Corona Gorda	5½" x 46	89
Royal Selection No. 12	Petit Corona	5½" x 42	86

PUNCH (HONDURAS)

Cafe Royal	Corona	5⅝" x 44	88
Chateau L	Maduro	7¼" x 52	88
Chateau L	Double Corona	7½" x 52	85
Chateau L	Churchill	7¼" x 54	85
Chateau M	Maduro	6¾" x 46	86
Diademas	Double Corona	7½" x 50	85

CIGAR	CATEGORY	SIZE	RATING
PUNCH (HONDURAS) *[continued]*			
Double Corona	Churchill	6¾" x 48	86
Double Corona	Maduro	6¾" x 48	86
Double Corona	Churchill	6¾" x 48	81
Elite	Petit Corona	5¼" x 44	85
Gran Cru Diademas	Churchill	7¼" x 54	82
Grand Cru Prince Consort	Figurado	8½" x 52	85
Grand Cru Robusto	Robusto	5¼" x 50	83
No. 1	Lonsdale	6½" x 43	86
No. 75	Corona	5½" x 43	84
Rothschild	Maduro	4½" x 50	86
Rothschild	Robusto	4½" x 50	83
Royal Coronation	Corona	5¼" x 44	83
Super Rothschild	Corona Gorda	5¼" x 50	86
Superior	Corona Gorda	5½" x 48	83
PUNCH GRAN CRU (HONDURAS)			
Monarch	Churchill	6¾" x 48	87
PUROS INDIOS (HONDURAS)			
No. 4 Especial	Corona	5½" x 44	91
Piramide No. 1	Figurado	7½" x 60	92
Piramide No. 2	Figurado	6½" x 46	90
QUAI D'ORSAY (CUBA)			
Imperiales	Churchill	7" x 47	90

CIGAR	CATEGORY	SIZE	RATING
QUINTERO (CUBA)			
Churchill	Lonsdale	6½" x 42	92
Medias Coronas	Petit Corona	5" x 40	84
RAFAEL GONZALES (CUBA)			
Lonsdale	Lonsdale	6½" x 42	91
RAMON ALLONES (CUBA)			
Corona	Corona	5½" x 42	89
Gigantes	Double Corona	7⅜" x 49	94
Ideales	Vintage	6½" x 40	89
No. 66 (perfecto)	Vintage	6" x N/A	87
Specially Selected	Robusto	5" x 50	90
RAMON ALLONES (DOMINICAN REPUBLIC)			
"B"	Lonsdale	6½" x 42	87
Privada "D"	Corona	5" x 42	86
Redondos	Churchill	7½" x 49	85
Size "D"	Petit Corona	5" x 42	85
ROMEO & JULIETA (DOMINICAN REPUBLIC)			
Churchill	Double Corona	7" x 50	83
Corona	Corona	5½" x 44	83
Palma	Lonsdale	6" x 43	84
Romeo	Figurado	6" x 46	85
Rothschild	Maduro	5" x 50	87
Rothschild	Robusto	5" x 50	84

CIGAR	CATEGORY	SIZE	RATING

ROMEO & JULIETA VINTAGE (DOMINICAN REPUBLIC)

CIGAR	CATEGORY	SIZE	RATING
No. 1	Lonsdale	6" x 43	86
No. 1	Corona	6" x 43	87
No. 2	Corona Gorda	6" x 46	87
No. 3	Robusto	4½" x 50	86
No. 4	Churchill	7" x 48	85
No. 5	Double Corona	7½" x 50	89

ROMEO Y JULIETA (CUBA)

CIGAR	CATEGORY	SIZE	RATING
Belicoso	Figurado	5½" x 52	90
Belvedere	Panatela	5½" x 39	84
Celestial Fino	Figurado	5¾" x 46	87
Churchill	Churchill	7" x 47	92
Corona	Corona	5½" x 42	89
Exhibicion No. 3	Corona Gorda	5½" x 46	91
Exhibicion No. 4	Robusto	5" x 48	89
Fabuloso	Figurado	9" x 47	96
Petit Corona	Petit Corona	5" x 42	89
Seleccion Suprema Cedro	Vintage	6½" x 42	97
Shakespeare	Panatela	6½" x 28	85
Sun-Grown Brevas	Vintage	5½" x 44	89

ROYAL JAMAICA (DOMINICAN REPUBLIC)

CIGAR	CATEGORY	SIZE	RATING
Churchill	Maduro	8" x 51	86
Churchill	Double Corona	8" x 51	87
Corona	Maduro	5½" x 40	87
Corona Grande	Lonsdale	6½" x 42	88
Corona Grande	Maduro	6½" x 42	85
Director	Corona Gorda	6" x 45	87
Giant Corona	Double Corona	7½" x 49	83

CIGAR	CATEGORY	SIZE	RATING
Giant Corona	Churchill	7½" x 49	83
Park Lane	Figurado	6" x 47	85
Petit Corona	Petit Corona	5" x 40	83
Robusto	Robusto	4½" x 49	87
Tube No. 2	Panatela	6½" x 34	83

SAINT LUIS REY (CUBA)

Churchill	Churchill	7" x 47	89
Lonsdale	Lonsdale	6½" x 42	85

SANCHO PANZA (CUBA)

Belicoso	Figurado	5½" x 52	86
Molinas	Lonsdale	6½" x 42	87
Non Plus	Petit Corona	5" x 42	85

SANTA CLARA 1830 (MEXICO)

No. 1	Maduro	7" x 51	83
No. 1	Double Corona	7½" x 52	87
No. 2	Churchill	6½" x 48	78
No. 5	Corona	6" x 43	87
No. 6	Maduro	6" x 51	85
No. 1830	Corona Gorda	6" x 50	85

SANTA DAMIANA (DOMINICAN REPUBLIC)

Cabinet Selection No. 800	Churchill	7" x 50	84
No. 300	Corona Gorda	5½" x 46	81
No. 500	Robusto	5" x 50	86
No. 700	Lonsdale	6½" x 42	85
Seleccion No. 100	Churchill	6¾" x 48	83

CIGAR	CATEGORY	SIZE	RATING
SANTA ROSA (HONDURAS)			
Cetros	Lonsdale	6" x 42	86
Churchill	Churchill	7" x 49	87
No. 4	Corona	5½" x 42	86
Toro	Corona Gorda	6" x 50	87
SANTIAGO CABANA (U.S.A.)			
Torpedo	Figurado	6¼" x 54	90
SAVINELLI (DOMINICAN REPUBLIC)			
E.L.R. Churchill	Churchill	7¼" x 48	88
Extraordinaire	Corona	5½" x 44	89
SOSA (DOMINICAN REPUBLIC)			
Brevas	Corona	5½" x 43	84
Churchill	Maduro	6⅞" x 49	87
Churchill	Churchill	6¹⁵⁄₁₆" x 49	88
Family Selection No. 2	Figurado	6¼" x 54	88
Governor	Corona Gorda	6" x 50	89
No. 1	Lonsdale	6½" x 43	87
Piramides	Figurado	7" x 64	80
Rothschild	Maduro	4¾" x 49	88
Sante Fe	Panatela	6" x 35	78
Soberano	Double Corona	7½" x 52	88
Wavell	Robusto	4¾" x 50	84
TE-AMO (MEXICO)			
Churchill	Maduro	7½" x 50	83
Churchill	Double Corona	7½" x 50	82

CIGAR	CATEGORY	SIZE	RATING
Figurado	Figurado	6⅝" x 50	85
Gran Pyramide	Figurado	7¼" x 54	84
Meditation	Lonsdale	6" x 42	85
Meditation	Corona	6" x 42	80
No. 4	Petit Corona	5" x 42	83
Piramide	Figurado	6¼" x 50	83
Presidente	Churchill	7" x 50	84
Torero	Panatela	6⁹⁄₁₆" x 35	81
Torito	Robusto	4¾" x 50	82
Toro	Maduro	6" x 50	83
Toro	Corona Gorda	6" x 50	83

TEMPLE HALL (JAMAICA)

700	Churchill	7½" x 49	84
Belicoso	Figurado	6" x 50	88
Estates No. 450	Maduro	4½" x 49	86
No. 550	Corona Gorda	5½" x 50	85
No. 550	Robusto	5½" x 50	84
No. 625	Lonsdale	6¼" x 42	86
No. 685	Panatela	6⅞" x 34	87

THE GRIFFIN'S (DOMINICAN REPUBLIC)

Don Bernardo	Figurado	9" x 46	85
No. 100	Figurado	7" x 38	84
No. 300	Lonsdale	6¼" x 44	85
No. 400	Panatela	6" x 38	84
Prestige	Double Corona	8" x 48	85

CIGAR	CATEGORY	SIZE	RATING
THOMAS HINDS (HONDURAS)			
Honduran Churchill	Churchill	7" x 49	88
Honduran Selection Corona	Corona	5½" x 42	86
Honduran Selection Corona	Petit Corona	5½" x 42	87
Honduran Selection Presidente	Double Corona	8½" x 52	87
Honduran Selection Robusto	Robusto	5" x 50	86
Honduran Selection Torpedo	Figurado	6" x 52	86
THOMAS HINDS (NICARAGUA)			
Nicaraguan Selection Corona	Corona	5½" x 42	84
TRESADO (DOMINICAN REPUBLIC)			
No. 200	Maduro	7" x 48	89
No. 300	Corona Gorda	6" x 46	78
No. 500	Maduro	5½" x 42	83
Seleccion No. 200	Churchill	7" x 48	83
Seleccion No. 500	Petit Corona	5½" x 42	84
Seleccion No. 500	Corona	5½" x 42	85
TROYA (DOMINICAN REPUBLIC)			
Cetro	Lonsdale	6¼" x 44	90
Clasico	Petit Corona	5½" x 42	84
Executive No. 72	Double Corona	7¾" x 50	82
No. 18	Robusto	4¼" x 50	82
No. 18 Rothschild	Maduro	4¾" x 50	84
No. 27	Corona	5½" x 42	87
No. 45 Cetro	Maduro	6" x 44	83
No. 63	Churchill	6⅞" x 46	86
Torpedo No. 81	Figurado	7" x 54	87

CIGAR	CATEGORY	SIZE	RATING

V CENTENNIAL (HONDURAS)

CIGAR	CATEGORY	SIZE	RATING
Cetro	Lonsdale	6½" x 44	89
Churchill	Churchill	7" x 48	87
Corona	Corona	5½" x 42	83
No. 1	Panatela	7½" x 38	88
Presidente	Double Corona	8" x 50	83
Robusto	Robusto	5" x 50	89
Torpedo	Figurado	7" x 54	87

VERACRUZ (MEXICO)

CIGAR	CATEGORY	SIZE	RATING
Reserve Especial	Lonsdale	6½" x 42	86

VUELTABAJO (DOMINICAN REPUBLIC)

CIGAR	CATEGORY	SIZE	RATING
Churchill	Churchill	7" x 48	83
Corona	Petit Corona	5¾" x 42	83
Corona	Corona	5¾" x 42	86
Gigante	Double Corona	8½" x 52	83
Pyramide	Figurado	7" x 50	84
Robusto	Robusto	4¾" x 52	87

ZINO (HONDURAS)

CIGAR	CATEGORY	SIZE	RATING
Diamonds	Petit Corona	5½" x 40	86
Diamonds	Corona	5½" x 40	83
Mouton-Cadet No. 1	Corona	6½" x 44	86
Mouton-Cadet No. 2	Panatela	6" x 35	85
Mouton-Cadet No. 5	Petit Corona	5" x 42	87
Mouton-Cadet No. 6	Robusto	5" x 50	88
Tradition	Lonsdale	6¼" x 44	85
Veritas	Double Corona	7" x 50	86
Veritas	Churchill	7" x 50	86

CHAPTER 14

Cigar Retailers

*The cigar stores that follow are divided into two sections: United States and International.
The stores in the United States are listed by state, and then alphabetically by city.
International stores are listed by country, and then alphabetically by city.*

UNITED STATES

ALABAMA

BIRMINGHAM

The Briary
Brookwood Village, 741-B
Birmingham 35209
(205) 871-2839

Dee's Package Store
2398 Green Springs Hwy.
Birmingham 35205
(205) 322-3333

J. Blackburn & Co
2000 Galleria Pkwy., 226
Birmingham 35244
(205) 985-0409

Overton & Vine
3150 Overton Rd., Ste. 5
Birmingham 35223
(205) 967-1409

Puff & Browse
1901 6th Ave., #175, Ste. 190
Birmingham 35203
(205) 251-9251

Tobacco Express
1813 Center Point Pkwy.
Birmingham 35215
(205) 856-1155

Tobacco Road
219-A 2nd Ave. SE
Decatur 35601
(205) 355-8065

Tinder Box
10-C S. Church St.
Fairhope 36532
(334) 473-1221

Tobacco Shack
Eastern Shore Plaza
Hwy. 98
Fairhope 36532
(334) 928-9974

Tobacco Express
3290 Florence Blvd.
Florence 35630
(205) 764-7641

Antonelli's
525 Broad St.
Gadsden 35901
(205) 543-7473

Humidor Pipe Shop
2502 S. Memorial Pkwy.
Huntsville 35801
(205) 539-6431

Tobacco Junction
8890 Hwy. 72 W.
Madison 35758
(205) 890-0557

Tinder Box
3484 Bel Air Mall
Mobile 36606
(205) 473-1221

Tobacco Shack
5441 Hwy. 90 W.
Mobile 36619
(334) 666-8116

Tobacco Leaf
6150 Atlanta Hwy.
Montgomery 36117
(205) 277-3880

Tobacco Road
25405 Perdido Beach Blvd., Ste. 14
Orange Beach 36561
(205) 981-6105

ALASKA

ANCHORAGE

Brown Jug Inc.
4140 Old Seward Hwy.
Anchorage 99503
(907) 563-3286

Pete's Tobacco Shop
3930 Mountain View
Anchorage 99508
(907) 274-7473

Sourdough News & Tobacco
735 W. 4th Ave.
Anchorage 99501
(907) 274-6397

Tobacco Cash
601 E. Northern Lights Blvd., Ste. L
Anchorage 99503
(907) 279-9411

Percy's
214 Front St.
Juneau 99801
(907) 463-3100

Island Spirits
3420 Rezanof Dr. E.
Kodiak 99615
(907) 486-4884

ARIZONA

Stag Tobacconist
Arrowhead Towne Center
Glendale 85308
(602) 979-7500

Stag Tobacconist
Superstition Springs Center
Mesa 85206
(602) 830-4134

Tinder Box Internationale
1312 W. Southern Ave., Ste. 1
Mesa 85202
(602) 644-9300

Welcome Smokers
9210 W. Peoria Ave., #7
Peoria 85029
(602) 878-3834

PHOENIX

Christopher's
2398 E. Camelback Rd., Ste. 290
Phoenix 85016
(602) 957-3214

Churchill's Fine Cigars
5021 N. 44th St.
Phoenix 85018
(602) 840-9080

Fine Wine & Spirits
3205 E. Camelback Rd.
Phoenix 85018
(602) 955-7730

Smoker's Knight Gallery
Paradise Valley Mall
4550 E. Cactus Rd., #40
Phoenix 85032
(602) 996-6610

Stag Tobacconist
9627-A Metro Pkwy. W.
Phoenix 85051
(602) 943-7517

Stag Tobacconist
132 Park Central Mall
Phoenix 85013
(602) 265-2748

Welcome Smokers
70-15 N. 19th Ave.
Phoenix 85021
(602) 995-7176

Welcome Smokers
717 W. Union Hills
Phoenix 85027
(602) 548-3370

Welcome Smokers
23-10 W. Bell Rd., Ste. 6
Phoenix 85023
(602) 504-9299

Welcome Smokers
11801 N. 19th Ave., Ste. 3
Phoenix 85029
(602) 331-6051

Welcome Smokers
12038 N. 35th Ave., Ste. 3
Phoenix 85029
(602) 938-9288

Ye Old Pipe Shoppe
2115 E. Camelback Rd.
Phoenix 85016
(602) 955-7740

SCOTTSDALE

Ford & Haig Tobacconist
7076 5th Ave.
Scottsdale 85251
(602) 946-0608

Hiland Trading Co.
6917 E. Thomas Rd.
Scottsdale 85251
(602) 945-7050

Lonsdales
23535 N. Scottsdale Rd.
Scottsdale 85255
(602) 585-8330

Stag Tobacconist
Scottsdale Fashion Square
Scottsdale 85251
(602) 994-4282

The Village Smoke Shop
8989 E. Vialinda Ste., #111
Scottsdale 85258
(602) 314-9898

Rural Road Liquor
7420 S. Rural Rd., B-1
Tempe 85283
(602) 345-9110

Tempe Tobacco
7 W. Baseline
Tempe 85283
(602) 777-7710

TUCSON

The Moon Smoke Shop
120 W. Grant Rd.
Tucson 85705
(520) 622-7261

Smoker's Haven
Park Mall
5870 E. Broadway
Tucson 85711
(520) 747-8989

Tinder Box
3601 E. Broadway
Tucson 85716
(520) 326-7198

The Wooden Indian Tobacco
224 Main, #114
Yuma 85364
(520) 343-1315

ARKANSAS

Tobacco Mart
309 Watson St.
Benton 72015
(501) 776-1888

Ric's Fine Cigars
50½ Spring St.
Eureka Springs 72632
(501) 253-4079

The Southern Gentleman
21 W. Mountain
Fayetteville 72701
(501) 521-1422

The Tobacco Shop
121 W. Township, #21
Fayetteville 72703
(501) 444-8311

Hot Off the Press
5220 Townson Ave.
Fort Smith 72902
(501) 646-3200

Taylor Pipe & Tobacco
5304 Rogers Ave.
Fort Smith 72903
(501) 542-1449

Tobacco Box Limited
Indian Mall
Jonesboro 72401
(501) 972-6420

Gatsby's Fine Cigars
425 W. Capital Ste. 3565
Little Rock 72201
(501) 399-9900

The Pipe & Tobacco
2908 S. University
Little Rock 72204
(501) 562-7473

Smoke Shoppe
7420 N. Hills Blvd.
N. Little Rock 72116
(501) 835-6067

**Stogie's Fine Cigars, Tobaccos
And Much More!**
224 S. 2nd St., Ste. J
Rogers 72756
(501) 621-6610

Davis Smoke Shop
2 Davis Bldg., E. Gate Plaza
Russellville 72801
(501) 968-6760

CALIFORNIA

Agoura Liquor & Deli
5003 Kanan Rd.
Agoura Hills 91301
(818) 991-3946

Cigarette's Cheaper!
Shore Shopping Center, 2220-C S.
Alameda 94501
(510) 337-1879

Mel's Land Mark
1240 High St.
Alameda 94501
(510) 865-2646

Beverages & More!
836 San Pablo Ave.
Albany 94706
(510) 525-9582

Cigarette's Cheaper!
9620 Baseline Rd.
Alta Loma 91701
(909) 484-9147

Cigarette's Cheaper!
Angels Towne Shopping Center
274 S. Main St.
Angels Camp 95222
(209) 736-6735

Cigarette's Cheaper!
Terrace Shopping Center
2767 Lone Tree Way
Antioch 94509
(510) 777-9795

Dave's Liquors
1008 Fitzuren Rd.
Antioch 94509
(510) 754-8490

Deer Park Wine & Spirits
783 Rio Del Mar Blvd., #27
Aptos 95003
(408) 688-1228

Vons Company
618 Michillinda Ave.
Arcadia 91007-6300
(310) 821-7208

Cigarette's Cheaper!
Woodman-Van Nuys Shopping
  Center
9700 Woodman Ave., A-1
Arleta 91331
(818) 894-4998

Cigarette's Cheaper!
Arroyo Town & Country Square
1466 Grand Ave.
Arroyo Grande 93420
(805) 473-0992

Cigarette's Cheaper!
Food 4 Less Center
3810-B El Camino Real
Atascadero 93422
(805) 466-4494

Cigarette's Cheaper!
Lucky Center
1880 Bellevue Rd.
Atwater 95301
(209) 358-4744

Cigarette's Cheaper!
Auburn Town Center
350 Elm Ave.
Auburn 95603
(916) 885-9754

Cigarette's Cheaper!
Rock Creek Plaza
2535 Bell Rd.
Auburn 95603
(916) 889-8752

BAKERSFIELD

Cigarette's Cheaper!
Ming Plaza
3829 Ming Ave.
Bakersfield 93309
(805) 837-0603

Cigarette's Cheaper!
1656 Oak St.
Bakersfield 93301
(805) 325-9368

Cigarette's Cheaper!
Chester Loop Shopping Center
2431 N. Chester Ave.
Bakersfield 93308
(805) 399-7137

Cigarette's Cheaper!
2781 Calloway Dr., #500
Bakersfield 93312
(805) 587-0602

Cigarette's Cheaper!
2631 Fashion Place, Ste. B
Bakersfield 93301
(805) 871-5874

Cigarette's Cheaper!
Niles Center
6221-A Niles St.
Bakersfield 93305
(209) 363-5448

Gerry's Fine Cigars
2324 Brundage Lane
Bakersfield 93304
(805) 633-1440

Hiland Gift & Tobacco
East Hill Mall
3000 Mall View Rd., #1051
Bakersfield 93306
(805) 872-7890

John T's
84 Valley Plaza
Bakersfield 93304
(805) 832-7002

The Wine Sellar
1920 Eye St.
Bakersfield 93301
(805) 327-1978

Cigarette's Cheaper!
4457 Park Rd.
Benicia 94510
(707) 745-6691

BERKELEY

Dave's Smoke Shop
2444 Durant Ave.
Berkeley 94704
(510) 883-0325

Juicy News
1849 Shattuck Ave.
Berkeley 94709
(510) 548-8268

Juicy News II
3167 College Ave., 1st Floor
Berkeley 94705
(510) 548-8268

BEVERLY HILLS

Al's Newsstand
216 S. Beverly Dr.
Beverly Hills 90212
(310) 278-6397

Alfred Dunhill of London
201 N. Rodeo Dr.
Beverly Hills 90210
(310) 274-5351

**Beverly Hills Hotel Gift
Shop & Logo Shop**
9641 Sunset Blvd.
Beverly Hills 90210
(310) 276-2251

Davidoff of Geneva
232 N. Rodeo Dr.
Beverly Hills 90210
(310) 278-8884

Grand Havana Room
301 N. Canon Dr.
Beverly Hills 90210
(310) 274-8100

Nazareths
350 N. Canon Dr.
Beverly Hills 90210
(310) 271-5863

Philip Dane's Cigar Lounge
9669 Little Santa Monica
Beverly Hills 90210
(310) 285-9945

Thomas Hinds Tobacconist
9632 S. Santa Monica Blvd.
Beverly Hills 90210
(310) 275-9702

John's Pipe Shop
563 Pineknot Ave.
Big Bear Lake 92315
(909) 866-1755

Maxwell's Tobacco Shop
2500 E. Imperial Hwy., Ste. 199
Brea 92621
(714) 256-2344

Burlingame Smoke Shop
1400 Burlingame Dr.
Burlingame 94010
(415) 343-3363

Cigarette's Cheaper!
Central Plaza Shopping Center
740 Arneill Rd.
Camarillo 93010
(805) 383-0335

Bob & Jon's Bottle Shop
2292 Main St.
Cambria 93428
(805) 927-4909

Cambria Cargo Co.
4044 Burton Dr.
Cambria 93428
(805) 927-2400

Duke of Bourbon
20908 Roscoe Blvd.
Canoga Park 91304
(818) 341-1234

Ugly Al's Fine Cigars
7239 Corbin Ave.
Canoga Park 91306
(818) 709-1525

Cardiff Seaside Market
2087 San Elijo Ave.
Cardiff By The Sea 92007
(619) 753-5445

Hiland Gift & Tobacco
Plaza Camino Real
2525 El Camino Real, #206
Carlsbad 92008
(619) 434-2788

Carmel Pipe Shop
Lincoln (South of Ocean)
Carmel By The Sea 93921
(408) 624-9737

Cigarette's Cheaper!
4949 Marconi, Ste. G
Carmichael 95608
(916) 481-9501

Briar Rose
Carson Mall, #560
20700 S. Avalon Blvd.
Carson 90746
(310) 538-1018

Cigarette's Cheaper!
Date Palm Shopping Center
35790 Date Palm Dr.
Cathedral City 92234
(619) 324-5018

The Pipe Rack
2020 Ave. of the Stars, Level 2
Century City 90067
(310) 552-9842

M.K.'s Cigar Box
19116 Pioneer Blvd.
Cerritos 90703
(310) 865-5111

Cigarette's Cheaper!
10216½ Mason Avenue
Chatsworth 91311
(818) 886-3379

Club Cohiba
21638 Lassen St.
Chatsworth 91311
(818) 718-8816

Radbogliattis
802 W. 5th St.
Chico 95928
N/A

Cigarette's Cheaper!
County Fair Shopping Center
12079 Central Ave.
Chino 91710
(909) 590-1325

Tinder Box
6144 Sunrise Mall
Citrus Heights 95610
(916) 725-3231

Claremont Tobacco House
272 W. 2nd St.
Claremont 91711
(714) 625-6321

Cigarette's Cheaper!
1820 Shaw Ave., #104
Clovis 93611
(209) 207-7455

Cigarette's Cheaper!
Coalinga Shopping Center
139 W. Polk St.
Coalinga 93210
(209) 934-1196

Cigarette's Cheaper!
Olive Tree Plaza
632 Edith Ave.
Corning 96021
(916) 824-6384

Arnett's Smoke Shop
1185 Magnolia Ave., Ste. F
Corona 91719
(909) 340-2739

COSTA MESA

Alfred Dunhill of London
South Coast Plaza
3333 Bristol St.
Costa Mesa 92626
(714) 641-0521

Cheers's Tobacco
1525 Mesa Verde Dr., #127
Costa Mesa 92626
(714) 662-2880

Smoke Shack
250 Ogle St.
Costa Mesa 92627
(714) 650-8463

Tinder Box
3333 Bear St., #136
Costa Mesa 92626
(714) 540-8262

Cigarette's Cheaper!
10555 De Anza Blvd.
Cupertino 95014
(408) 252-9655

Cigarette's Cheaper!
Westlake Shopping Center
19 Westlake Mall
Daly City 94015
(415) 757-9957

Tinder Box
107 Serramante Center
Daly City 94015
(415) 756-1771

Danville Cigar & Fine Gifts
28 Ceder Hollow Dr.
Danville 94526
(510) 820-6556

Del Mar Hills Liquors
2654 Del Mar Heights Rd.
Del Mar 92014
(619) 481-8148

Primo Cigar
2670 De La Bia Valley, Ste. A-170
Del Mar 92014
(619) 259-0855

Cigarette's Cheaper!
Desert Hot Springs Town Center
14208 Palm Dr.
Desert Hot Springs 92240
(619) 251-8853

Cigarette's Cheaper!
Mercantile Row Shopping Center
2190 E. El Monte Way
Dinuba 93618
(209) 591-1551

The Cigarette Store
6942 Village Pkwy.
Dublin 94568
(510) 829-9615

Smokers Depot
145 Jamacha Rd.
El Cajon 92019
(619) 440-3400

Tinder Box
329 Parkway Plaza
El Cajon 92020
(619) 440-1121

Cigarette's Cheaper!
8557 Elk Grove Blvd.
Elk Grove 95624
(916) 686-2173

Cigarette's Cheaper!
Camden Shopping Center
9170 Elk Grove-Florin Rd.
Elk Grove 95624
(916) 685-8720

Puff and Stuff
335 1st St.
Encinitus 92024
(619) 753-3839

ENCINO

Cigar Den
17933 Ventura Blvd.
Encino 91316
(818) 343-5768

Cigarette's Cheaper!
16060 Ventura Blvd., #110
Encino 91436
(818) 789-6651

Cigarette's Cheaper!
Encino Oaks Shopping Center
17330 Ventura Blvd.
Encino 91316
(818) 981-7059

Holiday Wine Cellars
302 W. Mission
Escondido 92025
(619) 745-1200

Tinder Box
North County Fair, Ste. 157
200 E. Via Rancho Pkwy.
Escondido 92025
(619) 745-9230

**Enchanted Victorian Tobacco
& Gift Shop**
317 E. St.
Eureka 95501
(707) 441-1888

John's Cigars
2211 Myrtle Ave.
Eureka 95501
(701) 444-8869

John T's
1419-B Solano Mall
Fairfield 94533
(707) 426-5566

D R Cigars
657 E. Bidwell St.
Folsom 95630
(916) 983-4278

Cigarette's Cheaper!
Fontana Square Shopping Center
17151 Foothill Blvd.
Fontana 92335
(909) 427-9098

Cigarette's Cheaper!
Palm Court @ Empire Center
17122 Stover Ave.
Fontana 92331
(909) 428-7097

Cigarette's Cheaper!
Westhaven Plaza, Ste. J
16027 Brookhurst St.
Fountain Valley 92728
(714) 531-2474

H & H Tobacco
18225 S. Brookhurst, #6
Fountain Valley 92708
(714) 962-2927

Cigarette's Cheaper!
Crossroads Shopping Center
39471 Fremont Blvd.
Fremont 94538
(510) 651-0441

FRESNO

Cigarette's Cheaper!
Hoover Market Place
5730 N. 1st St., #113
Fresno 93710
(209) 448-0871

Cigarette's Cheaper!
The Canyons Shopping Center
4910 E. Kings Canyon Rd.
Fresno 93727
(209) 251-2033

Cigarette's Cheaper!
C & O Shopping Center
4849 E. Olive Ave.
Fresno 93727
(209) 252-6705

Cigars Ltd.
5132 N. Palm
Fresno 93704
(209) 221-0161

Hardwick's Briar Shoppe
3402 N. Blackstone Ave., #124
Fresno 93726
(209) 228-1389

Havana's
2051 W. Bullard
Fresno 93711
(209) 439-4642

John T's
581 E. Shaw Ave.
Fresno 93710
(209) 229-4253

Wine Barrel
1105 E. Champlain Dr.
Fresno 93720
(209) 434-1057

GARDEN GROVE

Cigarette's Cheaper!
Town & Country Shopping Center
12841 Harbor Blvd.
Garden Grove 92640
(714) 530-4967

J & H Tobacco
11912 Valley View
Garden Grove 92645
(714) 895-6209

Meercher King
11111 Palmwood Dr.
Garden Grove 92640
(714) 530-1521

Cigarette's Cheaper!
340 E. 10th St., Space C
Gilroy 95020
(408) 847-2060

Red Carpet Wines & Spirits
400 E. Glen Oaks Blvd.
Glendale 91207
(818) 247-5544

Marty's Cigar and Divan
109 W. Foothill Blvd.
Glendora 91741
(818) 852-9337

GRANADA HILLS

Cigarette's Cheaper!
16287 San Fernando Mission Blvd.
Granada Hills 91344
(818) 368-8635

Cigarette's Cheaper!
16925 Devonshire St.
Granada Hills 91344
(818) 363-1855

Ugly Al's Fine Cigars
11027 Balboa Blvd.
Granada Hills 91344
(818) 363-0021

Cigarette's Cheaper!
Gold Country Center
12031 Sutton Way
Grass Valley 95945
(916) 272-5569

Cigarette's Cheaper!
Heritage Oak Shopping Center
1562 State Hwy. 99
Gridley 95948
(916) 846-3067

Cigarette's Cheaper!
Centennial Plaza Shopping Center
1868 W. Lacey Blvd.
Hanford 93230
(209) 584-6793

Cigarette's Cheaper!
20930 Mission Blvd.
Hayward 94541
(510) 481-8037

Cigarette's Cheaper!
24703 Amador St., #8
Hayward 94544
(510) 732-5579

Cigarette's Cheaper!
Vineyard Plaza Shopping Center
1087 Vine St.
Healdsburg 95448
(707) 431-2446

Root & Eastwood Wine & Spirits
1123 Vine St.
Healdsburg 95448
(707) 433-8311

Holy Smoke Tobacco
3220 W. Florida
Hemet 92545
(909) 925-1945

Liquor Plus
347 S. State St.
Hemet 92543
(909) 652-6575

Ben's Smoke Shop
6423 Hollywood Blvd.
Hollywood 90028
(213) 467-5000

Chalet Gourmet & Wine
7880 Sunset Blvd.
Hollywood 90046
(213) 874-6301

Cigarette's Cheaper!
Margarita Plaza
7004 S. Santa Fe Ave.
Huntington Park 90255
(213) 581-7091

Cigarette's Cheaper!
Pacific Center
5942 Pacific Blvd.
Huntington Park 90255
(213) 582-9559

Hiland Gift & Tobacco
15931 Golden West St.
Huntington Beach 92647
(714) 897-1172

Huntington Beach Smoke Shop
7194 Edinger Ave.
Huntington Beach 92647
(714) 841-9929

K & B Cigars
17555 Cameron St.
Huntington Beach 92647
(714) 842-2637

Tobacco Road
54200 N. Circle Dr., Vlg. Lane
Idyllwild 92549
(909) 659-3930

Tinder Box
333 Puente Hills Mall
Industry 91748
(818) 965-7215

Dierich Coffee
2144 Michaelson
Irvine 92715
(714) 260-1600

Staffords Fine Wine
17801 N. Main St., Ste. F
Irvine 92714
(714) 474-4416

Cigarette's Cheaper!
11960 W. Hwy. 88
Jackson 95642
(209) 223-9564

Cigarette's Cheaper!
Jackson Creek Plaza
525-4 Hwy. 49
Jackson 95642
(916) 223-9570

Cigarette's Cheaper!
King City Shopping Center
510-Q Canal St.
King City 93930
(408) 385-9297

The Cigar Cellar
1261 Prospect St., Ste. 2
La Jolla 92037
(619) 459-3255

Spirits of St. Germain
3251 Holiday Court, Ste. 101
La Jolla 92037
(619) 455-1414

Boley's Tobacco Shop
12234 La Mirada Blvd.
La Mirada 90638
(310) 943-6546

La Quinta Hotel Wine Shop
49-499 Eisenhower Dr.
La Quinta 92253
(619) 564-5705

Cigarette's Cheaper!
La Verne Town Center
2320 Foothill Blvd.
La Verne 91750
(909) 596-6399

Jackson Wine & Spirits
3524 Mount Diablo Blvd.
Lafayette 94549
(510) 376-6000

Laguna Hill Smoke Shop
25614 Alicia Pkwy.
Laguna Hill 92653
(714) 699-2651

Tobacco Barn Pipe Shop
23532 El Toro Rd., #14
Lake Forest 92630
(714) 830-7110

London Pipe & Gift Shop
1120 W. Ave. K
Lancaster 93534
(805) 948-5352

Discount Cigarette Outlets
16129 Hawthorne Blvd.
Lawndale 90260
(310) 542-5884

Cigarette's Cheaper!
Pepper Tree Plaza
863 E. Stanley Blvd.
Livermore 94550
(510) 449-3327

Cigarette's Cheaper!
Nob Hill Shopping Center
3024 Pacific Ave.
Livermore 95242
(510) 606-7298

Cigarette's Cheaper!
Cherokee Retail Center
550-G S. Cherokee Lane
Lodi 95240
(209) 333-2568

Fred's Puff n' Stuff
228 W. Pine St.
Lodi 95240
(209) 334-1088

Cigarette's Cheaper!
Lompoc Mission Plaza
1412 N. H St., Ste. A
Lompoc 93436
(805) 737-9698

LONG BEACH

Churchill's
Maples Island
5844 E. 2nd St.
Long Beach 90803
(310) 433-2034

Havana Cigar Club
3939 E. Broadway
Long Beach 90803
(310) 433-8053

Hiland Gift & Tobacco
Von's Pavillion Center
5937 Spring St.
Long Beach 90808
(213) 425-3258

Morry's of Naples
5764 E. 2nd St.
Long Beach 90803
(310) 433-0405

Naples Pipe Shop
5662 E. 2nd St.
Long Beach 90803
(310) 439-8515

Edward's Pipe & Tobacco
4546 El Camino Real
Los Altos 94022
(510) 796-7779

LOS ANGELES

Al's Newsstand
370 N. Fairfax Ave.
Los Angeles 90036
(213) 935-8525

Al's Newsstand - Larchmont
226 N. Larchmont Blvd.
Los Angeles 90004
(213) 464-6397

Beverage Warehouse
4935 McConnell Ave., Unit #21
Los Angeles 90066
(310) 306-2822

Brentwood Cigar Club
150 S. Barrington Ave., #9
Los Angeles 90049
(310) 440-4213

Century City Tobacco
10250 Santa Monica Blvd., #27
Los Angeles 90067
(310) 277-0760

Cigar Joint
7153 Beverly Blvd.
Los Angeles 90036
(213) 930-2341

Kenny's Cellar
11151 W. Olympic Blvd.
Los Angeles 90064
(310) 478-9463

La Plata Cigar Manufacturer
1026 S. Grand Ave.
Los Angeles 90015
(213) 747-8561

Larchmont Village Wine & Spirits
223 N. Larchmont Blvd.
Los Angeles 90004
(213) 856-8799

Smoke n' Stuff
750 W. 7th St.
Los Angeles 90017
(213) 627-0334

The Smoking Section
7801 Melrose Ave., Unit #4
Los Angeles 90046
(213) 653-0328

Cigarette's Cheaper!
Canal Farm Shopping Center
1341-H Pacheco Blvd.
Los Banos 93635
(209) 827-1632

Cigarette's Cheaper!
Madera Marketplace Shopping
   Center
2295-B W. Cleveland
Madera 93637
(209) 662-0442

Manhattan Liquors
1157-A Artesua Blvd.
Manhattan Beach 90266-6903
(310) 374-3454

Royal Cigar Society
1145 N. Sepulveda Blvd.
Manhattan Beach 90266
(310) 796-5577

Cigarette's Cheaper!
Raley's Union Square Shopping
   Center
1252 Lathrop Rd.
Manteca 95336
(209) 823-0169

Cigarette's Cheaper!
Seacrest Plaza, Ste. B
266 Reservation Rd.
Marina 93933
(408) 384-3432

Tobacco Trader
4722¼ Admiralty Way
Marina Del Ray 90292
(310) 823-5831

The Cigar Post
5202 Cole Rd.
Mariposa 95338
(209) 742-6409

Cigar Box
311 D St.
Marysville 95901
(916) 742-4354

Draeger's Market
1010 University Dr.
Menlo Park 94026
(415) 688-0682

Cigarette's Cheaper!
Raley's Yosemite North Shopping
 Center
3528 G St.
Merced 95340
(209) 384-3965

Sherlock Holmes Tobacconist
1712 Canal St.
Merced 95340
(209) 723-9071

Telfords Pipe Shop
119 Strawberry Village
Mill Valley 94941
(415) 388-0440

Hiland Gift & Tobacco
27000 Crown Valley Pkwy., Ste. 638
Mission Viejo 92691
(714) 347-8665

Southwest Gift & Tobacco
2700 Craus Valley Pkwy., Ste. 726
Mission Viejo 92691
(714) 347-1442

MODESTO

Cigarette's Cheaper!
Lakes Shopping Center
2601 N. Oakdale Rd.
Modesto 95355
(209) 523-7733

Cigarette's Cheaper!
1221 E. Orangeburg Ave., #6
Modesto 95350
(209) 577-4147

Cigarette's Cheaper!
901 N. Carpenter Rd., Ste. 8
Modesto 95351
(209) 579-1503

Cigarette's Cheaper!
1801 H St., Ste. A-2
Modesto 95354
(209) 526-0756

Cigarette's Cheaper!
2225 Plaza Pkwy., C-6
Modesto 95359
(209) 544-6824

Cigarette's Cheaper!
3848 McHenry Ave., #175
Modesto 95350
(209) 571-1284

The Wine Bistro
1280 Coast Village Rd.
Montecito 93108
(805) 969-3955

Cigarette's Cheaper!
541 Tyler St.
Monterey 93942
(408) 646-9248

Hellam's Tobacco Shop
423 Alvarado St.
Monterey 93940
(408) 373-2816

Country Home Tobacco
2240 S. Atlantic Blvd.
Monterey Park 91754
(213) 721-1192

Cigarette's Cheaper!
Moorpark Town Center
231 W. Los Angeles Ave.
Moorpark 93021
(805) 529-8390

Cigarette's Cheaper!
Cypress Plaza Shopping Center
640 Quintana Way
Morro Bay 93442
(805) 772-1769

NAPA

Baker St. Tobacconist
3053 Jefferson St.
Napa 94558
(707) 252-2766

Cigarette's Cheaper!
River Park Shopping Center
1441 Imola Ave. W.
Napa 94559
(707) 253-9565

The Hess Collection
4441 Redwood Rd.
Napa 94558
(707) 255-1144

Cigarette's Cheaper!
5841 Jarvis Ave.
Newark 94560
(510) 793-2910

Stagecoach Liquors Inc.
1536 Newbury Rd.
Newbury Park 91320
(805) 498-4343

Accents on Newport Beach
690 Newport Center Dr.
Newport Beach 92660
(714) 640-2394

Newport Tobacco
Fashion Island
533 Newport Center Dr.
Newport Beach 92660
(714) 644-5153

McGrueder's
1943 River Rd.
Norco 91760
(909) 737-5230

Cigarette's Cheaper!
Lucky Center
15439 Parthenia St.
North Hills 91343
(818) 894-4998

Cigarette's Cheaper!
16154 Nordhoff St., #103
North Hills 91343
(818) 894-8038

Cigarette's Cheaper!
College Block Shopping Center
9420 Reseda Blvd.
Northridge 91324
(818) 772-2051

Cigarette's Cheaper!
Paddison Square
12407 S. Norwalk Blvd.
Norwalk 90650
(310) 863-3913

Cigarette's Cheaper!
Foothill Oaks Shopping Center
156 S. Maag Ave.
Oakdale 95361
(209) 848-8310

Cigarette City
40015 Hwy. 49
Oakhurst 93644
(209) 683-6055

OAKLAND

Beverages & More!
525 Embarcadero
Oakland 94607
(510) 208-5126

Grand Lake Smoke Shop
3206 Grand Ave.
Oakland 94610
(510) 268-4070

The Piedmont Tobbaconist
17 Glen Ave.
Oakland 94611
(501) 652-PIPE

Cigarette's Cheaper!
Vineyard Ontario Plaza
1955 E. 4th St.
Ontario 91764
(909) 484-4386

Tinder Box
2483 The Mall of Orange
Orange 92665
(714) 998-0792

Wine Exchange
2368 N. Orange Mall
Orange 92665
(714) 974-1454

Cigarette's Cheaper!
Cable Park Shopping Center
8811 Greenback Lane
Orangeville 95662
(916) 987-9748

OXNARD

Cigarette's Cheaper!
Island Plaza
2506 S. Saviers Rd.
Oxnard 93030
(805) 487-7936

Cigarette's Cheaper!
Fremont Square
800 N. Ventura Rd., Unit B
Oxnard 93030
(805) 278-9706

Pipe & Stein
2540 Vineyard Ave.
Oxnard 93030
(805) 485-6974

The Humidor
73405 El Paseo, Ste. 31-A
Palm Desert 92260
(619) 568-1892

Palm Desert Tobacco & Gift
72-840 Hwy. 111, G-235
Palm Desert 92260
(619) 340-3364

Cigarette's Cheaper!
1775 E. Palm Canyon Dr., RA-C
Palm Springs 93364
(619) 223-9570

Tinder Box
123 N. Palm Canyon Dr., Ste. 183
Palm Springs 92262
(619) 325-4041

Hiland Gift & Tobacco
Antelope Valley Mall
1233 W. Ave. P, #305
Palmdale 93551
(805) 538-9620

Mac's Smoke Shop
534 Emerson St.
Palo Alto 94301
(415) 323-3724

PASADENA

The Cigar Co.
380 S. Lake Ave.
Pasadena 91101
(818) 792-2112

Cigarette's Cheaper!
Orangewood Plaza
137 W. California Blvd.
Pasadena 91105
(818) 795-8743

Mr. S. Liquor Mart #5
2044 E. Colorado St.
Pasadena 91107
(818) 795-5700

Tinder Box
165 Plaza Pasadena
Pasadena 91101
(818) 449-6479

Cigarette's Cheaper!
Woodland Plaza
181 Niblick Rd.
Paso Robles 93446
(805) 238-6988

PETALUMA

A Man's World
40 Kentucky St.
Petaluma 94952
(707) 778-9100

Cigarette's Cheaper!
Petaluma Gateway
911 Lakeville Hwy.
Petaluma 94954
(707) 766-8131

Cigarette's Cheaper!
Plaza North Shopping Center
249 N. McDowell Blvd.
Petaluma 94954
(707) 776-4847

Cigarette's Cheaper!
Pacific Coast Plaza
891 Oak Park Blvd.
Pismo Beach 93449
(805) 473-1130

Cigarette's Cheaper!
Save Mart Center
2951-B Harbor St.
Pittsburg 94565
(510) 432-4466

Cigarette's Cheaper!
Carriage Trade Shopping Center
1438 Broadway
Placerville 95667
(916) 621-0386

Tobacco Loft
1920 Contra Costa Blvd.
Pleasant Hill 94523
(510) 686-3440

Express Liquors
4363 1st. St.
Pleasanton 94566
(510) 846-5511

Tobacco Loft
Rose Pavilion
4001-4 Santa Rita Rd.
Pleasanton 94588
(510) 463-0100

Express West
1120 Price Ave.
Pomona 91767
(909) 988-3126

Cigarette's Cheaper!
Eastridge Plaza Shopping Center
313 E. Olive Ave.
Porterville 93257
(209) 783-8390

Cigarette's Cheaper!
Porterville Marketplace
1283 W. Henderson
Porterville 93257
(209) 781-1461

John's Liquors
290 Ladera Shoping Center
Alpine Rd.
Portola Valley 94028
(415) 854-6816

Cigarette's Cheaper!
Westwood Village
6478-F Westside Rd.
Redding 96001
(916) 241-4838

Arnett's Smoke Shop
446 N. Orange St.
Redland 92374
(909) 792-6161

Bombay Cigar Society
209 Ave. I
Redondo Beach 90277
(310) 798-6568

Tinder Box
1283 Galleria at Tyler
Riverside 92503
(909) 689-4401

Duffy's Liquor & Cigar
329 Vernon St.
Roosevelt 95678
(916) 783-3258

SACRAMENTO
Berkley Fine Wines
515 Pavillions Lane
Sacramento 95825
(916) 929-4422

Briar Patch Smoke Shop
Arden Fair
1689 Arden Way, Ste. 2006
Sacramento 95815
(916) 929-8965

Chuck's Quality Cigars Etc...
1328 Fulton Ave.
Sacramento 95825
N/A

Cigarette's Cheaper!
Norwood Center
4201 Norwood Ave.
Sacramento 95953
(916) 924-0816

Cigarette's Cheaper!
3643 Bradshaw Rd., Ste. F
Sacramento 95827
(916) 366-0253

Garcia y Vega Smoke Shop
725 K St.
Sacramento 95814
(916) 447-0804

Select Wine & Spirits
7485 Rush River Dr., Ste. 730
Sacramento 95831
(916) 393-3132

Tower Pipe & Cigars
2518 Land Park Dr.
Sacramento 95818
(916) 443-8466

ST. HELENA
St. Helena Grocery Co.
607 S. St. Helena Hwy.
St. Helena 94574
(707) 963-2662

St. Helena Wine Center
1321 Main St.
St. Helena 94574
(707) 963-1313

St. Helena Wine Merchants
699 St. Helena Hwy.
St. Helena 94574
(707) 963-7888

Cigarette's Cheaper!
Santa Rita Plaza
1980 N. Main St.
Salinas 93906
(408) 449-3648

Cigarette's Cheaper!
Main Steet Plaza
1168 S. Main St.
Salinas 93901
(408) 758-5882

Grapes & Grains
385 Salinas
Salinas 93901
(408) 424-3482

Ludwig's Smoke Shop
431 San Anselmo Ave.
San Anselmo 94960
(415) 456-1820

Hiland Gift & Tobacco
212 Inland Center
San Bernardino 92408
(714) 885-8282

Poor Richards Pipe Shop
364 W. Highland Ave.
San Bernardino 92405
(714) 883-7031

Eds Smoke Shop
1221 San Carlos Ave.
San Carlos 94070
(415) 591-6266

Bob's Fine Wines
470 Camine De Estrella
San Clemente 52672
(714) 496-3313

Jeff's Fine Tobacco
157 Del Mar Ave.
San Clemente 92672
(714) 492-6311

SAN DIEGO

Bad Habits
3850 5th Ave.
San Diego 92103
(619) 298-6340

Captain Hunt Tobacconist
851-D W. Harbor Dr.
San Diego 92101
(619) 232-2938

Cuban Cigar Factory
551 5th Ave.
San Diego 92101
(619) 238-2429

Fumar Cigar
1165-A Garnet
San Diego 92105
(619) 270-9227

Gaslamp Tobacco Shoppe
428 G St.
San Diego 92101
(619) 239-5272

Liberty Tobacco
7341 Clairemont Mesa Blvd.,
  Ste. 110
San Diego 92111
(619) 292-1772

Smoker's Land
13295 Black Mountain Rd.
San Diego 92129
(619) 484-7373

Tinder Box
Fashion Valley Mall
642 Fashion Valley Rd.
San Diego 92108
(819) 291-7337

The Village Spirit Shop
11936 Bernardo Plaza Dr.
San Diego 92128
(619) 487-4949

The Wine Bank
363 5th Ave., Ste. 100
San Diego 92101
(619) 234-7487

SAN FRANCISCO

Alfred Dunhill of London
250 Post St.
San Francisco 94108
(415) 781-3368

Another Hennessy's
199 Brannan St.
San Francisco 94107
(415) 777-9403

Ashbury Tobacco
1524 Haight St.
San Francisco 94117
(415) 552-5556

Beverages & More!
201 Bayshore Blvd.
San Francisco 94124
(415) 648-1233

California Tobacco Center
1501 Polk St.
San Francisco 94109
(415) 885-5479

Cigarette's Cheaper!
17 Kearny St.
San Francisco 94108
(415) 986-8568

Cigarette's Cheaper!
2304 Mission St.
San Francisco 94110
(415) 285-1193

Cigarette's Cheaper!
123 Powell St.
San Francisco 94102
(415) 732-7746

D & M Liquors
2200 Fillmore
San Francisco 94115
(415) 346-1325

Grant's Pipe Shop
562 Market St.
San Francisco 94104
(415) 981-1000

Jim Mate Pipe Shop
575 Geary St.
San Francisco 94102
(415) 775-6634

The Jug Shop Inc.
1567 Pacific Ave.
San Francisco 94109
(415) 885-2922

Juicy News
2453 Fillmore St.
San Francisco 94115
(415) 441-3051

Michael's Liquors
2198 Union St.
San Francisco 94123
(415) 921-5700

Mr. Liquor
250 Taraval Ave.
San Francisco 94116
(415) 731-6222

N. A. Tobacco
1343 Polk St.
San Francisco 94102
(415) 776-5650

Plump Jack Wines
3201 Fillmore St.
San Francisco 94123
(415) 346-9870

Sherlocks Haven
1 Embarcadero Center
San Francisco 94111
(415) 362-1405

Smoke Signals
2223 Polk St.
San Francisco 94109
(415) 292-6025

Vendetta
12 Tillman Place
San Francisco 94108
(415) 397-7755

The Wine Club
953 Harrison St.
San Francisco 94107
(415) 512-1196

SAN JOSE

Beverages & More!
14800 Camden Ave.
San Jose 95124
(408) 369-0990

Cigarette's Cheaper!
Almaden Oaks Plaza
6113 Meridian Ave.
San Jose 95120
(408) 927-6939

Cigarette's Cheaper!
7110 Santa Teresa Blvd.
San Jose 95139
(408) 629-1287

Cigarette's Cheaper!
Berryessa Hills Shopping Center
1190 N. Capitol Ave.
San Jose 95132
(408) 926-9618

Cigarette's Cheaper!
Park Almaden Shopping Center
950 Branham Lane
San Jose 91536
(408) 448-8266

Cigarette's Cheaper!
Winchester Pavillion
700 S. Winchester Blvd.
San Jose 95128
(408) 260-1212

Mission Pipe Shop
812 Town & Country Dr.
San Jose 95128
(408) 241-8868

Smokers Paradise
3617 Union Ave.
San Jose 95124
(408) 377-1335

Willow Glen Cigars & Tobacco
1068 Lincoln Ave.
San Jose 95125
(408) 283-9323

Prestige Cigar
32281 Camino Capistrano, C-103
San Juan Capistrano 92675
(714) 496-1199

Cigarette's Cheaper!
793 Foothill Blvd., Ste. E
San Luis Obispo 93405
(805) 594-1850

Sanctuary Tobacco Shop
1111 Chorro St.
San Luis Obispo 93401
(805) 543-1958

Third Ave. News & Tobacco
36 E. 3rd
San Mateo 94401
(415) 579-5719

Tinder Box
139 Hillsdale Mall
San Mateo 94403
(415) 341-4945

Cigarette's Cheaper!
298-A El Portal Center
San Pablo 94806
(510) 236-8568

Cigarette's Cheaper!
402 San Pablo Towne Center
San Pablo 94806
(510) 235-1866

Beverages & More!
760 Francisco Blvd. W.
San Rafael 94901
(415) 456-8367

Teri Cigar Co.
310 E. 1st St.
Santa Ana 92701
(714) 541-9142

The Wine Club
2110 McFadden, Ste. E
Santa Ana 92705
(714) 835-0163

SANTA BARBARA

Accents at the Biltmore
Four Seasons Hotel
1260 Channel Dr.
Santa Barbara 93108
(805) 969-2240

The Bottle Shop Liquor
1200 Coast Village Rd.
Santa Barbara 93108
(805) 969-4466

The Cigar Co.
1005 Santa Barbara St.
Santa Barbara 93101
(805) 962-4427

Cigar Trader
29 E. Canon Perdido
Santa Barbara 93101
(805) 730-7500

Santa Barbara Cigar & Tobacco
10 W. Figueroa St.
Santa Barbara 93101
(805) 963-1979

Tinder Box
1307 State St.
Santa Barbara 93101
(805) 963-8464

Beverages & More!
4175 Stevens Creek Blvd.
Santa Clara 95051
(408) 248-2776

The Wine Club
1200 Coleman Ave.
Santa Clara 95050
(408) 567-0490

Cigarette's Cheaper!
922 Soquel Ave.
Santa Cruz 95062
(408) 458-2744

Pipe Line
818 Pacific Ave.
Santa Cruz 95060
(408) 425-7473

Cigarette's Cheaper!
Acorn Plaza
4869 S. Bradley Rd., Ste. B-32
Santa Maria 93455
(805) 934-8158

Cigarette's Cheaper!
Broadway Pavilion
2530-D S. Broadway
Santa Maria 93455
(805) 922-8942

SANTA MONICA

**Al's Newsstand - Santa Monica
Promenade**
3rd St. Promenade at Arizona
Santa Monica 90401
(310) 393-2690

Hiland Gifts & Collectibles
265 Santa Monica
Santa Monica 90401
(310) 394-1580

Tinder Box
2729 Wilshire Blvd.
Santa Monica 90403
(310) 828-2313

SANTA ROSA

Beverages & More!
2090 Santa Rosa Ave.
Santa Rosa 95404
(707) 573-1544

Cigarette's Cheaper!
711 Stony Point Rd., 8-B
Santa Rosa 94544
(707) 573-4748

The Squire
346 Coddington Center
Santa Rosa 95401
(707) 573-8544

Tinder Box
2048 Santa Rosa Plaza
Santa Rosa 95401
(707) 579-4442

Cigarette's Cheaper!
Scotts Village Shopping Center
235-C Mt. Herman Rd.
Scotts Valley 95066
(408) 461-9361

Romeo et Juliet
1198 Pacific Coast Hwy., Ste. E
Seal Beach 90740
(310) 430-2331

Cigarette's Cheaper!
Laguna Plaza Shopping Center
1130 N. Fremont, Ste. 203
Seaside 93955
(408) 899-1861

Gus' Smoke Shop
13420 Ventura Blvd.
Sherman Oaks 91423
(818) 789-1401

Happy's Wine & Spirits
12 W. Sierra Madre Blvd.
Sierra Madre 91024
(818) 355-9444

Cigarette's Cheaper!
5197 E. Los Angeles Ave., C-3
Simi Valley 93063
(805) 520-4922

Cigarette's Cheaper!
150 W. Stockton Rd.
Sonora 95370
(209) 533-0671

Cigarette's Cheaper!
Sonora Crossroads Shopping Center
1245 Sanguinetti Rd.
Sonora 95370
(209) 533-2305

Bay Briar Shoppe
2910 Danbenbeis Ave.
Soquel 95073
(408) 462-1965

Cigarette's Cheaper!
Stanton Lucky Center
7034 Katella Ave.
Stanton 91436
(714) 373-9394

Prissy's Smoke Shop
12136 Beach Blvd.
Stanton 90680
(714) 893-0066

STOCKTON
Cigarette's Cheaper!
1540 E. March Lane, Ste. B-8
Stockton 95210
(209) 476-8097

Cigarette's Cheaper!
Eastland Plaza Center
768 Wilson Way
Stockton 95205
(209) 460-0925

Tobacco Leaf
123 Lincoln Center
Stockton 95207
(209) 474-8216

The Big Easy
12604 Ventura Blvd.
Studio City 91604
(818) 762-3279

American Rag
9175 San Fernando Rd.
Sun Valley 91352
(818) 768-2020

Murphy Avenue Smoke Shop
114 S. Murphy St.
Sunnyvale 94086
(408) 735-9127

Cigarette's Cheaper!
Taft Hills Plaza
1068 W. Kern
Taft 93268
(805) 763-0171

Cigarette's Cheaper!
Tarzana Plaza
19001½ Ventura Blvd.
Tarzana 91356
(818) 705-4802

Party House
18839 Ventura Blvd.
Tarzana 91356
(818) 342-0355

Cigarette's Cheaper!
Red Apple Plaza
785-K Tucker Rd.
Tehachapi 93561
(805) 823-0452

Old Town Smokers Shop
34189 Business Park Dr.
Temecula 92590
(909) 699-1831

Liberson's Gourmet International Tobaccos
10143 Riverside Dr.
Toluca Lake 91602
(818) 985-4310

Tinder Box
71 Del Amo Fashion Square
Torrance 90503
(310) 542-7975

Cigarette's Cheaper!
Madera Marketplace Shopping
  Center
3161 N. Tracy Blvd.
Tracy 95376
(209) 836-5806

Tourist Liquor
10092 Donner Pass Rd.
Truckee 96161
(916) 582-3521

Cigarette's Cheaper!
Heritage Place Shopping Center
238 E. Cross St.
Tulare 93274
(209) 684-9084

Cigarette's Cheaper!
Turlock Town Center
529 N. Golden State Blvd.
Turlock 95380
(209) 667-1409

Cigarette's Cheaper!
1805 Countryside Dr.
Turlock 95382
(209) 664-1736

Kelly's Mens Store
330 El Camino Real
Tustin 92680
(714) 731-1385

Cigarette's Cheaper!
31834 Alvarado Blvd.
Union City 94587
(510) 487-1432

Cigar Exchange International
134 N. 2nd Ave., Ste. G
Upland 91786
(909) 946-6782

Cigarette's Cheaper!
Golden Hills Shopping Center
973 Alamo Dr.
Vacaville 95687
(707) 449-9094

Lil' Havana
1011 Mason St., Ste. 1
Vacaville 95688
(707) 447-8678

VENTURA

Cigarette's Cheaper!
Mission Plaza Shopping Center
51-H W. Main St.
Ventura 93001
(805) 653-5134

Cigarette's Cheaper!
Victoria Plaza
6108 Telegraph Rd.
Ventura 93003
(805) 658-6832

John T's
Buena Ventura Mall
363 S. Mills Rd., Ste. 1610
Ventura 93003
(805) 654-1570

Salzers
5777 Valentine Rd.
Ventura 93003
(805) 639-2161

VICTORVILLE

Cigarette's Cheaper!
Liberty Village
13790 Bear Valley Rd., E-2
Victorville 92392
(619) 241-5629

Cigarette's Cheaper!
Payless Shopping Center
14592 Palmdale Rd., D-8
Victorville 92392
(619) 241-4389

Highland Gift & Tobacco
Mall of Victor Valley
14400 Bear Valley Rd., 11
Victorville 92392
(619) 241-5821

VISALIA

Cigarette's Cheaper!
Visalia Village
2615 S. Mooney
Visalia 93277
(209) 741-9826

John T's
2183 S. Mooney Blvd.
Visalia 93277
(209) 627-9252

Urban Gourmet
1679 E. Noble Ave.
Visalia 93292
(209) 635-0245

- -

Pipes & Tobacco
512 E. Vista Way
Vista 92084
(619) 758-9881

Cigarette's Cheaper!
Walnut Hills Village
20633-2 Amar Rd.
Walnut 91789
(909) 444-9196

WALNUT CREEK

Beverages & More!
2900 N. Main St.
Walnut Creek 94596
(510) 472-0130

Cigarette's Cheaper!
1546 Palos Verdes Mall
Walnut Creek 94596
(510) 935-9038

Cigarette's Cheaper!
Newell Center
1485 Newell Ave.
Walnut Creek 94596
(510) 944-0675

- -

Cigarette's Cheaper!
Barker Square
2351 Hwy. 46
Wasco 93280
(805) 758-4626

Tinder Box
394 Fashion Plaza Lane
West Corina 91790
(818) 338-2025

Cigarette's Cheaper!
Platt Village
6434 Platt Ave.
West Hill 91307
(818) 716-7097

Up in Smoke
8278 Santa Monica Blvd.
West Hollywood 90046
(213) 654-8173

WEST LOS ANGELES

Cigarette's Cheaper!
11221 National Blvd.
West Los Angeles 90064
(310) 479-8779

**Politically Incorrect Cigar
  Shop & Lounge**
10850 W. Pico Blvd., #505
West Los Angeles 90064
(310) 446-9979

The Wine House
2311 Cotner Ave.
West Los Angeles 90064
(310) 479-3731

The Cigar Co.
3845-A E. Thousand Oaks Blvd.
Westlake Village 91362
(805) 494-1886

Intermezzo's of Uptown
6740 Green Leaf Ave.
Whittier 90601
(310) 945-1349

WOODLAND HILLS

The Cigar Company
21744 Ventura Blvd.
Woodland Hills 91364
(818) 346-1505

Discount Cigarette Outlets
21849 Ventura Blvd.
Woodland Hills 91364
(818) 883-2307

Green Jug Liquor
6307 Platt Ave.
Woodland Hills 91367
(818) 887-9463

Vendome Liquors
6041 Topanga Canyon Blvd.
Woodland Hills 91367
(818) 346-4400

Roberts of Woodside
3015 Woodside Rd.
Woodside 94062
(415) 851-2640

COLORADO

Aspen's Pen Perfecto
645 E. Durant St. (at the Little
  Nell Hotel)
Aspen 81611
(800) 250-5089, (970) 544-9777

The Baggage Claim
307 S. Galena St.
Aspen 81611
(800) 845-6291

Avon Liquor
100 W. Beaver Creek Blvd.
Avon 81620
(970) 949-4384

The Cigarette Store
1750 15th St.
Boulder 80302
(303) 449-7087

Harvest Wine & Spirits
3075 Arapahoe Ave.
Boulder 80303
(303) 447-9832

COLORADO SPRINGS

Cheer's Liquor Mart
1105 N. Circle Dr.
Colorado Springs 80909
(719) 574-2244

Coaltrain Wine & Liquor
330 W. Vintah
Colorado Springs 80905
(719) 475-9700

Hathaway's Mag & Smoke
216 N. Tejon
Colorado Springs 80903
(719) 632-1441

Sherlock's Pipes & Tobacco
3650 Austin Bluffs Pkwy.
Colorado Springs 80918
(719) 598-4444

Southwest Wine & Spirits
1785 S. 8th St.
Colorado Springs 80906
(719) 389-0906

Stag Tobacconist
750 Citadel Dr. E., Ste. 2214
Colorado Springs 80909
(719) 596-5363

Welcome Smokers
815 S. Sierra Madre St.
Colorado Springs 80903
(719) 471-0854

Welcome Smokers
1730 W. Colorado Ave.
Colorado Springs 80904
(719) 444-8805

Welcome Smokers
1150 E. Fillmore St.
Colorado Springs 80907
(719) 471-1074

Welcome Smokers
2355 E. Platte Place
Colorado Springs 80909
(719) 471-7448

Welcome Smokers
5219 Galley Rd.
Colorado Springs 80915
(719) 591-6883

Welcome Smokers
3111 S. Academy Blvd.
Colorado Springs 80916
(719) 390-5343

Welcome Smokers
4337 N. Academy Blvd., Ste. B
Colorado Springs 80918
(719) 532-1747

The Tobacconist
218 Maroon Ave.
Crested Butte 81224
(970) 349-7174

DENVER

Argonaut Wine & Liquor Co.
700 E. Colfax Ave.
Denver 80203
(303) 831-7788

Cigar & Tobacco World
5227 Leetsdale Dr.
Denver 80222
(303) 321-7308

The Cigarette Store
2120 S. Broadway, Ste. 16
Denver 80210
(303) 442-2520

Havana's Fine Cigars
2727 E. 2nd Ave.
Denver 80206
(303) 355-2003

Highlands Cellars
3245 Osage St.
Denver 80211
(303) 477-9463

Jerri's Tobacco Shops
1616 Glenarm
Denver 80202
(303) 825-3522

Prince Philips
Tamarac Square
7777 E. Hampden
Denver 80231
(303) 695-1959

Smokers Inn
1685 S. Colorado Blvd., Unit K
Denver 80222
(303) 758-5030

The Tobacco Leaf
7111 W. Alameda, Unit N
Denver 80226
(303) 935-8188

The Vineyard
261 Fillmore St.
Denver 80206
(303) 355-8324

Durango Smoke Shop
113 W. Collage Dr.
Durango 81301
(303) 247-9115

Edward Pipe & Tobacco Shop
3439 S. Broadway
Englewood 80110
(303) 781-7662

Heritage Wine & Liquor
7475 E. Arapahoe Rd.
Englewood 80112
(303) 770-8212

Edwards Tobacco & Darts
3307 S. College, Unit 102-B
Fort Collins 80525
(303) 226-5311

West Lake Wine & Spirits
2024 35th Ave.
Greeley 80634
(303) 330-8466

Welcome Smokers
401 Colorado Ave.
La Junta 81050
(719) 384-8533

Cigarette Express
6630 W. Colfax
Lakewood 80214
(303) 235-2755

County Line Liquor
181 W. County Line Rd.
Littleton 80126
(303) 730-8211

Village West Liquors
8555 W. Belleview, A-03
Littleton 80123
(303) 978-9418

Tobacco Haven
10572-B Melody Dr.
North Glenns 80234
(303) 450-0953

PUEBLO
Cigar Ltd.
307 S. Union
Pueblo 81003
(719) 542-4300

Welcome Smokers
401 N. Greenwood., Ste. H
Pueblo 81003
(719) 543-6846

Welcome Smokers
1326 U.S. Hwy. 50 Bypass
Pueblo 81001
(719) 583-0271

Welcome Smokers
2211 W. Northern Ave.
Pueblo 81005
(719) 566-1760

Welcome Smokers
2514 Santa Fe Dr.
Pueblo 81006
(719) 543-7751

Welcome Smokers
951 U.S. Hwy. 50 W.
Pueblo 81008
(719) 545-3646

Welcome Smokers
249 W. Rainbow Blvd.
Salida 81201
(719) 539-5476

Welcome Smokers
362 Security Shopping Center
182 Main St.
Security 80911
(719) 390-5996

The Santa Fe Cigar Co.
123 E. Colorado Ave.
Telluride 81435
(970) 728-9011

The Baggage Cheque
244 Wall St.
Vail 81657
(970) 476-1747

Welcome Smokers
110 W. Midland
Woodland Park 80863
(719) 687-9890

CONNECTICUT

The Aperitif
50 Albany Tpke., Bldg. 4, Unit C
Canton 06019
(203) 693-9373

Timberline Humidors
265 Highland Ave.
Cheshire 06410
(203) 272-2088

Post Wines & Spirits
230 Post Rd.
Cos Cob 06807
(203) 661-0201

Cigar Box
279 Main St.
Danbury 06810
(203) 748-5718

Street Corner News
Danbury Fair Mall
7 Backus Ave., Ste. 395
Danbury 06810
(203) 790-9595

Olive Oyls
77 Main St.
Essex 06426
(203) 767-4909

Arcade Cigars
1636 Post Rd.
Fairfield 06430
(203) 259-1994

Wright's Wine & Spirits
771 Farmington Ave.
Farmington 06034
(203) 677-1901

Greenwich Cigar Store
91 Railroad Ave.
Greenwich 06830
(203) 622-9831

Tobacconist of Greenwich
8 Havemeyer Pl.
Greenwich 06830
(203) 869-5401

Guilford News & Tobacco
1016 Boston Post Rd.
Guilford 06437
(203) 453-1349

The Calabash Shoppe
2450 Whitney Ave.
Hamden 06518
(203) 248-6185

**De La Concha Tobacconist
of Hartford**
1 Civic Center Plaza
Hartford 06103
(203) 527-4291

The Tobacco Shop
Old Bank Lane
Hartford 06103
(860) 524-8577

Tobacco Road Ltd.
1201 Connecticut Post Mall
Milford 06460
(203) 877-1957

MacKenzie's
7 South Ave.
New Caanan 06840
(203) 972-1277

Owl Shop
268 College St.
New Haven 06510
(203) 624-3250

Archway News
64 Bank St.
New Milford 06776
(203) 355-1557

J & J Tobacco
3273 Berlin Tpke.
Newington 06111
(203) 666-0439

Tobbaco Plaza
1393 Boston Post Rd.
Old Saybrook 06475
(860) 388-4811

Wine & Liquor Outlet
528 Boston Post Rd.
Orange 06477
(203) 795-8302

Sam's Smoke Junction
71 Oxford Rd.
Oxford 06478
(203) 888-4995

Torpedoes Smoke Shop
922 Hopmeadow St.
Simsbury 06070
(203) 658-7502

Have a Cigar
980 Sullivan Ave.
South Windsor 06074
(203) 644-5800

The Smoke Shop
Harrison Inn Arcade
Heritage Village
Southbury 06488
(203) 264-5075

Bull's Head News/Variety
51 High Ridge Rd.
Stamford 06905
(203) 359-0740

Smokin Sounds
1026 High Ridge Rd.
Stamford 06405
(203) 329-2808

Denby's Tobacco & Collectibles
908 White Plains Rd.
Trumbull 06611
(203) 261-8114

Best Cigar Co.
58 Clifford Dr.
West Hartford 06107
(860) 231-7224

The Cigar Shop
52 LaSalle Rd.
West Hartford 06107
(203) 236-5041

Cigar Port
7 Riverside Ave.
Westport 06880
(203) 227-6800

DELAWARE

Books & Tobacco
214 Lantana Dr.
Hockessin 19707
(302) 239-4224

Tobacco Outlet
Town Square Shopping Center
Rte. 113
Millsboro 19966
(302) 934-8045

Three Sons Smoke Shop
Farmers Market
110 N. Dupont Hwy.
New Castle 19720
(302) 322-2116

Greybeards of London
211 Rehoboth Ave.
Rehoboth Beach 19971
(302) 227-4972

**Rehoboth Cigarette Outlet
& Newsstand**
2 The Marketplace
Rehoboth Beach 19971
(302) 226-3151

WILMINGTON

Books & Tobacco
4555 Kirkwood Hwy.
Wilmington 19808
(302) 994-3156

**Brandywine Cigarette and
Tobacco Outlet**
3101 Concord Pike
Wilmington 19803
(302) 478-3362

Frank's Union Liquors
1902 W. 13th St.
Wilmington 19806
(302) 429-1978

Kirkwood News & Tobacco
5998 Kirkwood Hwy.
Wilmington 19808
(302) 995-2881

Kirkwood Tobacco
3606 Kirkwood Hwy.
Wilmington 19808
(302) 995-6680

Peco's Liquors
522 Philadelphia Pike
Wilmington 19809
(302) 764-0377

Steve's Emporium
508 Green Hill Ave.
Wilmington 19805
(302) 654-8794

Tobacco Village
4011-B Concord Pike
Wilmington 19803
(302) 478-5075

DISTRICT OF
COLUMBIA

Calvert Woodley Wines & Liquors
4339 Connecticut Ave.
Washington, D.C. 20008
(202) 966-4400

Central Liquors
726 9 St. NW
Washington, D.C. 20001
(202) 737-2800

Eagle Wine & Cheese
3345 M St. NW
Washington, D.C. 20007
(202) 333-5500

Georgetown Tobacco
3144 M St. NW
Washington, D.C. 20007
(800) 345-1459, (202) 338-5100

Heart of Town News
1301 Pennsylvania Ave. NW
Washington, D.C. 20004
(202) 347-4640

J.R. Tobacco
1667 K St. NW
Washington, D.C. 20006
(202) 296-3872

Paul's Liquor & Wines
5205 Wisconsin Ave. NW
Washington, D.C. 20015
(202) 537-1900

W. Curtis Draper
640 14th NW
Washington, D.C. 20005
(202) 638-2555

Wide World of Wines
2201 Wisconsin Ave. NW
Washington, D.C. 20007
(202) 333-7500

FLORIDA

Amelia Liquors South
4924 First Coast Hwy.
Amelia Island 32035
(904) 261-7701

The Wharf
973 Atlantic
Atlantic Beach 32233
(904) 246-8616

Mike's Cigars
1030 Kane Concourse
Bay Harbor (near Miami Beach) 33154
(305) 866-2277

BOCA RATON

Bennington Tobacconist
Royal Palm Plaza, #80
501 SE Mizner Blvd.
Boca Raton 33432
(407) 391-1372

Carmody Fine Wine & Liquor
6060 SW 18th St.
Boca Raton 33433
(407) 394-3766

Crown Liquors & Wine Merchants
4131 N. Federal Hwy.
Boca Raton 33432
(407) 392-6366

Crown Liquors & Wine Merchants
7154 Beracasa Way
Boca Raton 33433
(407) 391-6009

Crown Liquors & Wine Merchants
757 S. Federal Hwy.
Boca Raton 33433
(407) 394-3828

Garden Shop Liquors
7050 W. Palmetto Park Rd.
Boca Raton 33433
(407) 368-7032

Hamptons Tobacco
Mizner Park
Boca Raton
N/A

Bonita Smoke Shop
3300 Bonita Beach Blvd.
Bonita Springs 33923
(813) 495-9296

Crown Liquors & Wine Merchants
564 SE 15th Ave.
Boynton Beach 33435
(407) 734-9463

Smoker's Gallery
Boynton Beach Mall
801 N. Congress Ave.
Boynton Beach 33426
(407) 736-5533

Smoke n' Snuff
205 S. DeSoto Square Mall
Bradenton 34205
(941) 747-9700

Smoke n' Snuff
666 Brandon Town Center
Brandon 33511
(813) 654-2566

Cape Smoke Shop
3512 Del Prado Blvd.
Cape Coral 33904
(914) 549-2667

CLEARWATER
Mr. D's Pipe & Tobacco
Countryside Mall
27001 U.S. 19 N.
Clearwater 34621
(813) 796-1220

Smoke n' Snuff
14077 63rd Way N.
Clearwater 34620
(813) 573-5601

Smoke n' Snuff
104 Clearwater Mall
Clearwater 34624
(813) 796-1668

Havana Ray's
Mayfair Shops
3399 Virginia St.
Coconut Grove 33133
(305) 446-4003

Bill's Pipe & Tobacco Shop
2309 Ponce De Leon Blvd.
Coral Gables 33134
(305) 444-1764

Crown Liquors & Wine Merchants
6731-51 Red Rd.
Coral Gables 33143
(305) 669-0225

Tinder Box
2455 W. International Speedway   Blvd.
Daytona Beach 32114
(904) 253-0708

Tobacco Exotica
749 W. International Speedway Blvd.
Daytona Beach 32114
(904) 255-3782

Tobacco Exotica
3404 S. Atlantic Ave.
Daytona Beach Shores 32118
(904) 761-2400

Crown Liquors & Wine Merchants
300 S. Federal Hwy.
Deerfield Beach 33441
(305) 427-5274

Delray News & Tobacco
429 E. Atlantic
Delray Beach 33483
(407) 278-3399

FORT LAUDERDALE
Chester's Tobacco
7770 NW 44th
Fort Lauderdale 33351
(954) 741-4888

Churchill's Inc.
8348 State Rd. 84
Fort Lauderdale 33324
(954) 475-9431

Crown Liquors & Wine Merchants
2850 N. Federal Hwy.
Fort Lauderdale 33306
(954) 566-5322

Crown Liquors & Wine Merchants
3518 N. Ocean Blvd.
Fort Lauderdale 33308
(954) 566-2337

Mushroom Plus
903 Sunrise Lane
Fort Lauderdale 33304
(954) 630-0615

The 67 Liquor Shop
5479 N. Federal Hwy.
Fort Lauderdale 33308
(954) 771-9000

Smoke & Beanery
1225 E. Las Olas Blvd.
Fort Lauderdale 33301
(954) 764-8566

Smoker's Gallery
The Galleria
2356 E. Sunrise Blvd.
Fort Lauderdale 33304
(954) 561-0002

Sir Richard's
2320 McGregor Blvd.
Fort Myers 33901
(941) 332-7722

Beach Tobacco Candy & Nut
19041 San Carlos Blvd., Unit 7
Fort Myers Beach 33931
(813) 463-5177

The Brass Pipe
2573 S. U.S. 1
Fort Pierce 34982
(407) 461-7451

Smoke n' Snuff
6451 W. Newberry Rd.
The Oaks Mall, C-4
Gainesville 32605
(904) 331-3696

The Essence of Smoke
1946 Hollywood Blvd.
Hollywood 33020
(954) 923-2877

Vlass's Curiosity Shop
974 Pine Tree Drive
Indian Harbor Beach 32937
(407) 777-9460

JACKSONVILLE

Broudy's Liquors
353 Marsh Landing Pkwy.
Jacksonville 32250
(904) 273-6119

Edward's of San Marco
2016 San Marco Blvd.
Jacksonville 32207
(904) 396-7990

Edwards Pipe & Tobacco
5566-23 Ft. Caroline Rd.
Jacksonville 32277
(904) 745-6368

Fast Eddy's
4940 Blanding Blvd.
Jacksonville 32210
(404) 771-3200

Gourmet's Delight
12401 Beit Blvd., Ste. 7
Jacksonville 32246
(904) 641-1833

Smoke n' Snuff
2540 The Avenues Mall
Jacksonville 32258
(904) 363-2161

Tobacco Cove
3849 Bay Meadows Rd.
Jacksonville 32217
(904) 731-2890

The Tobacco Shop
17 N. Ocean St.
Jacksonville 32202
(904) 355-9319

Caribbean Cigar Factory
103400 Overseas Hwy.
Key Largo 33037
(305) 453-4014

KEY WEST

Caribbean Cigar Factory
112 Fitzpatrick
Key West 33040
(305) 292-9595

Conch Republic Cigar Factory
512 Green St.
Key West 33040
(800) 317-2167

Key West Havana Cigar
1117 Duval St.
Key West 33040
(305) 296-2680

La Tobacoria
326 Duval St.
Key West 33040
(305) 294-3200

King's Liquor & Tobacco
7099 Lake Worth Rd.
Lake Worth 33467
(407) 964-4440

Edwards Pipe & Tobacco
2118 S. Florida Ave.
Lakeland 33803
(813) 687-4168

City Newsstand
4400 Bougainvilla Dr.
Lauderdale By The Sea 33308
(305) 776-0940

Crown Liquors & Wine Merchants
5000 N. University Dr.
Lauderhill 33351
(305) 741-7070

Smoke n' Snuff
311 Lake Square Mall
10401 S. Hwy. 441
Leesburg 34788
(904) 326-8055

The 67 Liquor Shop
5360 N. Federal Hwy.
Lighthouse Point 33064
(305) 428-6255

Tobacco Depot
23038 State Rd. 54
Lutz 33549
(813) 948-3844

Margate Newstand
5430 W. Atlantic
Margate 33063
(305) 968-7563

Tobacerie
1700 W. New Haven Ave.
Melbourne 32904
(407) 768-0170

MIAMI

Caribbean Cigar Factory
6265 SW 8th St.
Miami 33144
(305) 267-3911

Cigar Box
19501 Biscayne Blvd.
Miami 33180
(305) 936-8808

Crossings Liquor
12993 SW 112th St.
Miami 33186
(305) 387-3675

Cuban Aliados
114 NW 22nd Ave.
Miami 33125
(305) 856-8138

Gulf Liquors & Wine Merchant
15728 SW 72nd St.
Miami 33193
(305) 388-WINE

Harriel Tobacco Shoppe
11401 S. Dixie Hwy.
Miami 33156
(305) 252-9010

King's Treasure Tobacco
401 Biscayne Blvd., S-144
Miami 33132
(305) 374-5593

La Tradicion Cubana
172-B W. Flagler St.
Miami 33130
(305) 374-2339

Smoke Shop
1601 Biscayne Blvd.
Miami 33132
(305) 358-1886

Tio Pepe Liquors
9800 SW 8th St.
Miami 33174
(305) 227-7090

Tobacco News
255 E. Flager St., Ste. 84-85
Miami 33131
(305) 358-6865

MIAMI BEACH

The Cuba Club
432 41st St.
Miami Beach 33140
(305) 604-9798

Cy's at Sobe
1504 Alton Rd.
Miami Beach 33139
(305) 532-5301

South Beach News & Tobacco
710 Washington Ave., #9
Miami Beach 33139
(305) 673-3002

Zelick's Tobacco Corp.
326 Lincoln Rd.
Miami Beach 33139
(305) 538-1544

NAPLES

Heaven
2950 N. Tamiami Trail
Naples 33940
(941) 649-6373

Rick's Discount Cigarettes & Cigar
8793 E. Tamiami Trail
Naples 33962
(813) 774-2888

Smoke n' Snuff
Square Mall
820 Tamiami Trail
Naples 34238
(941) 921-6147

Smoke n' Snuff
Coastland Center, B-13
1946 N. Tamiami Trail
Naples 33940
(941) 649-5599

Tobacco Road
Waterloo Station Plaza
200 Goodlette Rd. S.
Naples 33940
(813) 262-2098

Pipe & Pouch Smoke Shop
8090-B Navarre Pkwy.
Navarre 32566
(904) 939-9769

Eight 'til Late
241 3rd St.
Neptune Beach 32266
(904) 241-1127

Tobacco Hut
Elfers Square
4036 S. Madison St.
New Port Richey 34652
(813) 842-2139

La Havana Cavana
324-B Flagler Ave.
New Smyrna Beach 32164
(904) 426-5400

Crown Liquors & Wine Merchants
12555 Biscayne Blvd.
North Miami 33181
(305) 892-9463

NORTH MIAMI BEACH

Laurenzo's
16385 W. Dixie Hwy.
North Miami Beach 33160
(305) 945-6381

Phil's Cigar Shop
1100 NE 196th St.
North Miami Beach 33162
(305) 651-9505

Smokers World
20097 Biscayne Blvd.
North Miami Beach 33180
(305) 931-1117

Smoke Shop
4625 N. Tamiami Trail
North Naples 33940
(813) 435-1862

Smoke n' Snuff
Paddock Mall, Room 520
Ocala 34474
(904) 237-2883

Mike's Tobacco & Gifts
226 S. Volusia Ave.
Orange City 32763
(904) 775-3707

ORLANDO

Art's Fine Cigars
1235 N. Orange Ave.
Orlando 32804
(407) 239-3702

Cigars on the Avenue
515 Lake Ave.
Orlando 32801
(407) 841-9689

Heart's Liquors & Brewing Supplies
5824 N. Orange Blossom Trail
Orlando 32810
(407) 298-4103

Lee's Liquor
4100 Town Center Blvd.
Orlando 32827
(407) 850-2435

Prestige Cigar
3519 Gatlin Ave.
Orlando 32812
(407) 857-1160

Pipe & Pouch Smoke Shop
53 N. Orange Ave.
Orlando 32801
(407) 841-7980

Smoke n' Snuff
244 The Florida Mall
Orlando 32809
(407) 826-5053

The Breakers
1 S. County Rd.
Palm Beach 33480
(407) 653-6624

Hamptons Tobacco
247 Worth Ave.
Palm Beach 33480
(407) 835-0060

Smoker's Gallery
The Gardens
3101 PGA Blvd.
Palm Beach Gardens 33410
(407) 694-9440

Briar & Burley
425 Grace Ave.
Panama City 32401
(904) 785-8969

Jim's Pipe & Tobacco Shop
2812-C W. 23rd St.
Panama City 32405
(904) 785-1022

Florida Tobacco Book & Novelty
7948 Pines Blvd.
Pembroke Pines 33024
(305) 963-4358

PENSACOLA

Tinder Box
Cordova Mall
5100 N. 9th Ave.
Pensacola 32504
(904) 477-4131

Tobacco Annies
8084 N. Davis Hwy.
Pensacola 32514
(904) 857-0798

Tobacco Annies
6404 N. 9th Ave.
Pensacola 32504
(904) 969-1221

Crown Liquors & Wine Merchants
7620 Peters Rd.
Plantation 33324
(305) 475-9750

Eight 'til Late
832-16 A1A North
Ponte Vedra 32082
(904) 285-5356

Smoke n' Snuff
865 Port Charlotte Town Center
1441 Tamiami Trail
Port Charlotte 33948
(941) 627-5640

Smoke n' Snuff
611 Gulfview Square Mall
9409 U.S. 19
Port Richey 34668
(813) 849-4746

Wholly Smokes & Unique Gifts
11840 U.S. Hwy. 19
Port Richey 34668
(813) 863-0374

Dangerous John Hubert's
12650 Overseas Hwy. 10
Quay Village 33050
(305) 743-9299

Smoke n' Snuff
886 Tyrone Square Mall
St. Petersburg 33710
(813) 381-9527

SARASOTA

Bennington Tobacconist
5 Filmore Dr.
Sarasota 34236
(813) 388-1562

Joe's News & Sports Card
1467 Main St.
Sarasota 34236
(813) 365-3556

The Smoke Shop
106 Crossroads Plaza
Sarasota 34239
(813) 955-6433

Seminole Smoke Shop
7884 Seminole Mall
Seminole 34642
(813) 391-2783

Mr. Bob's Pipes, Tobacco & Cigars
2279 Ridgewood Ave.
South Daytona 32119
(904) 761-1420

Caribbean Cigar Factory
760 Ocean Dr.
South Miami Beach 33139
(305) 538-6062

Beers Unlimited
1490 S. Pasadena Ave.
South Pasadena 33707
(813) 345-9905

Tobacco Depot
138 Mariner Blvd.
Spring Hill 34609
(904) 688-1500

Coffman's Tobacco Shop
4336 SE Federal Hwy.
Stuart 34997
(407) 287-5060

The Smoking Crow
23-C W. Osceola St.
Stuart 34994
(407) 287-9717

Smoker's Gallery
Sawgrass Mills
12801 W. Sunrise Blvd., #563
Sunrise 33323
(800) 226-2632, (954) 846-2631

Smoke Shop Etc.
2810-2 Sharer Rd.
Tallahassee 32312
(904) 385-9669

Smoke n' Snuff
2055 Govenor's Square Mall
Tallahassee 32301
(904) 877-8489

TAMPA

Cammarata Cigar Co.
4830 W. Kennedy, Ste. 180
Tampa 33609
(813) 287-2654

Edwards Pipe & Tobacco
3235 Henderson Blvd.
Tampa 33609
(813) 872-0723

Gonzalez Havano Cigar Co.
3304 W. Columbus Dr., Ste. C
Tampa 33607
(813) 348-0343

Regional News
101 E. Kennedy Blvd.
Tampa 33602
(813) 223-4043

Simons Market
3225 S. MacDill Ave.
Tampa 33629
(813) 839-2521

Smoke n' Snuff
2015 Tampa Bay Center
Tampa 33607
(813) 879-7071

Smoke n' Snuff
339 W. Shore Plaza
Tampa 33609
(813) 282-8776

Tampa Rico Cigars
Tampa International Aiport
3rd Floor Center Mini Mall
Tampa 33607
(813) 874-8997

Tinder Box
2133 University Square Mall
Tampa 33612
(813) 971-0623

B-21 Liquors
43380 U.S. Hwy. 19
Tarpon Springs 34689
(813) 937-5049

Don Gregory Cigars
1121 Peninsula Rd.
Tarpon Springs 34689
(813) 937-7562

The Tobacconist
119-B Bullard Pkwy.
Temple Terrace 33617
(813) 989-3133

The Pipe Den
1426 20th St.
Vero Beach 32960
(407) 569-1154

Jamestown Tobacco Co.
330 Clematis St., Ste. 118
West Palm Beach 33401
(407) 659-7273

East India Trading Co.
East India Market
610 W. Morris Blvd.
Winter Park 32789
(407) 647-7520

Liquor World
761 N. Orange Ave.
Winter Park 32789
(407) 645-3395

Tobacco Depot
36608 State Rd., 54-W
Zephyr Hills 33541
(813) 788-3806

GEORGIA

ALPHARETTA

Cigar Merchant
9850 Nesbit Ferry, Ste. 17
Alpharetta 30202
(404) 552-1942

Clubhouse Cigars
6000 Medlock Bridge Pkwy.,
    Ste. B-100
Alpharetta 30202
(770) 495-9330

Tinder Box
North Point Mall
1204 N. Point Circle
Alpharetta 30202
(770) 569-0059

Jumpin' Johnny's
1001 M.L.K. Jr. Blvd.
Americus 31709
(912) 928-2137

Fire Points Bottle Shop
1655 S. Lumpkin St.
Athens 30606
(706) 543-6989

Modern Age Tobacco & Gift
1087 Baxter St.
Athens 30606
(706) 549-6360

ATLANTA

Buckhead Fine Wine
3906 Roswell Rd., Ste. 604-167
Atlanta 30342
(404) 231-8566

Cigar Villa #2
4920 Roswell Rd., Ste. 31
Atlanta 30342
(404) 845-0801

Edward's Pipe & Tobacco
3137 Piedmont Rd.
Atlanta 30305
(404) 292-1721

Jax Liquors
5901 Roswell Rd.
Atlanta 30328
(404) 252-1443

Kroger Store
1700 Monroe Dr.
Atlanta 30324
(404) 872-0782

Roswell High Tower Beverages
8529 Roswell Rd.
Atlanta 30350
(770) 993-0810

Royal Cigar Co.
1776 Peachtree St. NE
Atlanta 30309
(404) 876-9422

Street Corner News
Underground Atlanta
50 Upper Alabama St., Ste. 134
Atlanta 30303
(404) 221-1040

Tinder Box
3393 Peachtree Rd.
Atlanta 30326
(404) 231-9853

Urban Market, Inc.
752-B N. Highland Ave.
Atlanta 30306
(404) 347-9746

Windfaire, Inc.
3885 Buford Hwy.
Atlanta 30329
(404) 634-9463

Tobacco Land
1010 Augusta Mall
3450 Wrightsboro Rd.
Augusta 30909
(706) 738-8381

Edwards Pipe & Tobacco
444 N. Indian Creek Dr.
Clarkston 30021
(404) 292-1721

Sweet Briar Smoke Shop
5592-H Whitesville Rd.
Columbus 31904
(706) 322-6467

Books, Etc.
6132 Hwy. 53 E.
Dawsonville 30534
(706) 216-0002

Tinder Box
2100 Pleasant Hill Rd., Ste. 105
Duluth 30136
(770) 813-1248

Metro News, Inc.
4686 Lake Mirror Place
Forest Park 30050
(404) 366-7742

Duke of Dixie
341 Benson St.
Hartwell 30643
(706) 376-9283

Old South Tobacco
3706 Mercer University Dr.
Macon 31204
(912) 477-5426

MARIETTA

Cigar Emporium
4719 Lower Roswell Rd.
Marietta 30068
(404) 579-8280

Cigar Villa
700 Sandy Plains Rd., Ste. A-15
Marietta 30066
(770) 919-0444

Minks Beer & Wine
2555 Delk Rd.
Marietta 30067
(404) 952-2337

Sherlock's
2156 Roswell Rd.
Marietta 30062
(770) 971-6333

Sherlock's
135 Barrett Pkwy.
Marietta 30066
(770) 426-6744

This That & the Other
2040 Cobb Pkwy. S., Ste. 44
Marietta 30060
(770) 984-8801

The Ultimate Cigar
1381 Morrow Industrial Blvd.
Morrow 30260
(404) 968-9622

SAVANNAH

Habersham Beverage
4618 Habersham St.
Savannah 31405
(912) 354-6477

O'Sullavan's
115 E. Broughton St.
Savannah 31401
(912) 232-4222

Ye Ole Tobacco Shop
131 W. River St.
Savannah 31401
(800) 596-1425, (912) 236-9384

Cigar Villa
3599 Atlanta Rd.
Smyrna 30080
(404) 433-1243

HAWAII

Kipuka Smoke Shop
308 Kamehameha Ave., Ste. 102
Hilo 96720
(808) 961-5082

HONOLULU

Ale Oke
2131 S. Beretania St., #401
Honolulu 96826
(808) 946-4805

Alfred Dunhill of London
The Sheraton Moana Surfrider Hotel
2365 Kalakaua Ave.
Honolulu 96815
(808) 971-2020

The Cigar Room
1137 12th Ave.
Honolulu 96816
(808) 627-1921

Don Pablo Cigar Co.
1430 Kona St., Ste. 102
Honolulu 96814
(808) 944-1600

The Liquor Collection
1050 Ala Moana Blvd.
Ward Warehouse
Honolulu 96814
(808) 524-8808

Oahu Home Brew Supply
856 Ilaniwai
Honolulu 96813
(808) 596-2739

R. Field Co.
1200 Ala Moana Blvd.
Honolulu 96814
(808) 596-9463

Tobacco Shack
951 N. King St.
Honolulu 96819
(808) 845-5445

Connoisseur Food & Wine
444 Hana Hwy., Unit A-1
Kahului 96732
(808) 871-9463

Stantons of Maui
Maui Mall
Kahului 96732
(808) 877-3711

Michael's Liquors II
515 Kailua Rd.
Kailua 96734
(808) 261-3433

Pali Bottle Shoppe
662 Kailua Rd.
Kailua 96734
(808) 262-5665

Kona Wine Market
75-5626 Kuakini Hwy.
Kailua Kona 96740
(808) 329-9400

Sir Wilfred's
Lahaina Cannery Ship Center
Lahaina 96761
(808) 667-1941

IDAHO

Sturman's Smoke Shop
218 N. 10th St.
Boise 83702
(208) 338-3225

Tobacco Connection
725 Vista Ave.
Boise 83705
(208) 342-6330

Resort Cellar
210 Sherman Ave., #111
Coeur d'Alene 83814
(208) 667-6127

Atkinson Market
451 4th St. E.
Ketchum 83340
(208) 726-5668

Gift World, Inc.
610½ Main St.
Lewiston 83501
(208) 746-8306

Pocatello Smoke Shop
204 N. Main St.
Pocatello 83204
(208) 234-0661

Firstop Smoke Shop
6845 W. Seltice Way
Post Falls 83854
(208) 773-4773

ILLINOIS

Payless Tobacco
709 W. Lake St.
Addison 60101
(708) 628-8177

ARP, Inc.
12332 S. Cicero Ave.
Alsip 60658
(708) 597-6535

Rick's News & Tobacco
2528 College Ave.
Alton 62002
(618) 462-7425

Arlington Pipe
3 W. Davis St.
Arlington Heights 60005
(708) 255-2263

Cigarette's Cheaper!
Southpoint Commons Shopping
   Center
708 E. Rand Rd.
Arlington Heights 60004
(708) 342-9640

John's Smoke Shop
18 S. River
Aurora 60506
(708) 897-3920

Tinder Box
1462 Fox Valley Center
Aurora 60504
(708) 898-9450

Robusto's Tobacco Shoppe
3620 N. Belt W.
Belleville 62223
(618) 277-9414

P J Discount
202 W. Irving Park Rd.
Bensonville 60106
(708) 350-2000

Smoker's Choice
1212 Towanda Ave.
Bloomington 61701
(309) 828-1581

The Cigar Exchange
470 Half Day Rd.
Buffalo Grove 60089
(847) 564-9600

Yester Year Tobacconist
200 W. Monroe
Carbondale 62901
(618) 457-8495

Egor's Tobacco & Gift Shop
2 Wisconsin Ave.
Carpentersville 60110
(708) 428-7707

Jon's Pipe Shop
509 E. Green St.
Champaign 61820
(217) 344-3459

Calliope Court
706 Jackson Ave.
Charleston 61920
(217) 348-1905

CHICAGO

Alfred Dunhill of London
Water Tower Plaza
835 N. Michigan Ave.
Chicago 60611
(312) 467-4455

Around The World
1044 W. Belmont
Chicago 60657
(312) 327-7975

Big Jim's Tobacco
1552 E. 53rd St.
Chicago 60615
(312) 288-2343

Cardinal Liquors
4905 N. Lincoln Ave.
Chicago 60625
(312) 561-0270

Casey's Liquors
1444 W. Chicago Ave.
Chicago 60622
(312) 243-2850

Cigarette's Cheaper!
The Hall Plaza
4646 W. Diversey
Chicago 60639
(312) 654-1567

Collectors Corner
750 N. Rush
Chicago 60611
(312) 943-4475

Double Corona
2058 W. Chicago Ave.
Chicago 60622
(312) 342-7820

English Pipe Shop
15 S. La Salle St.
Chicago 60603
(312) 263-3922

Up Down Tobacco • A Spectacular Cigar Smoker's Paradise!
1550 N. Wells, Chicago • (800)-5-UP-DOWN
Open late every night – 11a.m. to 11p.m.

Iwan Ries & Co.
19 S. Wabash Ave.
Chicago 60603
(312) 372-1306

Jack Schwartz Importer
175 W. Jackson Blvd.
Chicago 60604
(312) 782-7898

Old Chicago Smoke Shop
10 S. La Salle St.
Chicago 60603
(312) 236-9771

Park West Liquor & Smoke
2581 N. Lincoln
Chicago 60614
(312) 935-8197

Rubovits Cigars
320 S. LaSalle St.
Chicago 60604
(312) 939-3780

Sam's Wine & Spirits
1000 W. North Ave.
Chicago 60622
(312) 664-4394

333 Tobacco Shop
333 N. Michigan Ave.
Chicago 60601
(312) 782-4317

Up Down Tobacco
1550 N. Wells St.
Chicago 60610
(312) 337-8505

Value Most Liquors
3263 N. Pulaski Rd.
Chicago 60641
(312) 725-4151

Worldwide Tobacco
1587 N. Milwaukee
Chicago 60622
(312) 862-2226

Southtown Rx
1533 Chicago Rd.
Chicago Heights 60411
(708) 755-3500

Chiko Club Liquors
5202 W. 25th St.
Cicero 60650
(708) 656-5111

Prestige Wine & Liquor
1423 W. 55th St.
Country Side 60525
(708) 354-6969

Cardinal Liquors
305 Virginia St.
Crystal Lake 60014
(815) 459-4050

Cigarette's Cheaper!
The Grove Annex
1202 W. 75th St.
Downers Grove 60516
(708) 769-5063

Cigarette People
2900 N. Harlem Ave.
Elmwood Park 60635
(708) 453-2433

Evanston Pipe & Tobacco
923 Davis St.
Evanston 60201
(708) 328-0208

Smokey Bear
8701 S. Kedzie Ave.
Evergreen Park 60642
(708) 499-0222

Tinder Box
255 St. Clair Square
Fairview Heights 62208
(618) 632-6160

Cigarette's Cheaper!
Plaza Westlake Shopping Center
2192 Bloomingdale Rd.
Glendale Heights 60137
(708) 980-1520

Armanetti's
18244 S. Kedzie Ave.
Hazelcrest 60429
(708) 798-7700

Countyline General Store
124 Skokie Valley Rd.
Highland Park 60035
(708) 831-3310

Old Chicago Smoke Shop
Crossroads Shopping Center
200 Skokie Valley Rd.
Highland Park 66035
(708) 831-3310

Tinder Box
Joliet Mall
1034 Louis
Joliet 60435
(815) 439-1190

Cigarette's Cheaper!
Cossitt Landmark Center
8 N. La Grange
La Grange 60525
(708) 354-9611

The Marling Tobacco Shop
1383 N. Western Ave.
Lake Forest 60045
(708) 234-2232

Wine & Cheese Shoppe
884 S. Rand Rd., Ste. F
Lake Zuric 60047
(708) 438-1922

**Great World Wide Beer
 & Cigar Club**
480 Scotland Rd.
Lakemoore 60050
(800) Mr. Cigar

Suburban News
3300 W. Devon
Lincolnwood 60659
(708) 679-5577

Tinder Box
205 Yorktown Center
Lombard 60148
(708) 495-2555

Tobacco City
3281 W. 115th St.
Merrionette Park 60655
(708) 489-5700

Cut 'n Puff Pipe And Tobacco Shop
1417 5th Ave.
Moline 61265
(309) 762-1819

Tobacco Bowl
South Park Mall
4500 16th St.
Moline 61265
(309) 762-9267

Puff n' Stuff
1500 S. Lake St.
Mondelein 60060
(708) 566-8880

Gentleman's Delight
24 W. 500 Maple Ave., Ste. 104
Naperville 60540
(708) 961-2496

Gold Finger Super Sales
7227 N. Harlem Ave.
Niles 60648
(708) 647-7460

Cigarette's Cheaper!
Norridge Commons
7048 Forest Preserve Dr.
Norridge 60034
(708) 457-1820

Cigar Heaven, Inc.
2750 Dundee Rd.
Northbrook 60062
(847) 564-9600

Smoker's Haven
15806 S. Harlem Ave.
Orland Park 60462
(708) 633-8331

Tinder Box
416 Orland Square
Orland Park 60462
(708) 349-6111

Puff n' Stuff
20451 N. Rand Rd.
Palatine 60074
(708) 550-0055

World Wide Liquors
15 S. Brockway
Palatine 60067
(708) 359-0400

Royal Liquor
3714 E. State St.
Rockford 61108
(815) 235-4015

Tinder Box
Cherry Vale Mall
Rockford 61112
(815) 332-4656

Payless Tobacco & Liquor
356 E. Irving Park Rd.
Roselle 60172
(708) 980-8299

Toolland, Inc.
519 W. Rollins Rd.
Round Lake Beach 60073
(708) 740-8665

Country Sports Cards & Fine Cigars
2661 W. Schaumburg Rd.
Schaumburg 60194
(847) 539-9576

SKOKIE

Cigar King
8016 Lincoln
Skokie 60077
(708) 675-2447

Gift & Tobacco Emporium
Village Crossing Shopping Center
7140 N. Carpenter
Skokie 60077
(708) 674-4283

Gold Standard Liquors
5100 W. Dempster
Skokie 60077
(708) 831-5400

Tinder Box
125-E Old Orchard Center
Skokie 60077
(708) 677-6717

Cigars For Aficionados
717 N. Grand Ave. E.
Springfield 62702
(217) 523-4357

Epicure's Choice Smoke Shop
Myers Building
1 W. Old State Capital Plaza
Springfield 62701
(217) 523-9350

Cigarette Express
21 N. Point Plaza
Streator 61364
(815) 672-0842

Tinder Box
120 Hawthorne Center
Vernon Hills 60061
(708) 362-6655

Al's Smoke Shop Inc.
1 E. Park Blvd.
Villa Park 60181
(708) 279-2215

Schrank's Smoke 'n Gun
2010 Washington St.
Waukegan 60085
(708) 662-4034

Tinder Box
1116 Spring Hill Mall
West Dundee 60118
(708) 428-6444

Ye Olde Smoke Shoppe
1203 E. Butterfield
Wheaton 60187
(708) 682-3771

Willowbrook Dicarlo Liquors
6920 S. Rte. 83
Willowbrook 60514
(708) 654-0988

L.K. Cigars
365 Elder Lane.
Winetka 60093
(708) 501-4711

Tobacco World, Inc.
11302 S. Harlem Ave.
Worth 60482
(708) 448-0002

INDIANA

Angola Tobacco Shop
2998 N. Wayne St.
Angola 46703
(216) 665-9142

Pipe Dreams
508 Green Blvd.
Aurora 47001
(812) 926-1667

Big Red Liquors
418 N. College Ave.
Bloomington 47401
(812) 332-9495

The Briar & The Burley
2968 E. 3rd St.
Bloomington 47401
(812) 332-3300

S & N Tobacco Outlet
1711 N. College Ave.
Bloomington 47404
(812) 337-8791

Low Bob's
1911 State St.
Columbus 47201
(812) 375-9716

Judd Drugs
1200 W. Marion St.
Elkhart 46516
(219) 533-2685

Briar 'n' Bean
Eastland Mall, Ste. 121
800 N. Greenriver Rd.
Evansville 47715
(812) 479-8736

FORT WAYNE

Low Bob's
Gateway Plaza
1575-D Goshen Rd.
Fort Wayne 46808
(219) 471-3662

Low Bob's
2620 N. Clinton
Fort Wayne 46805
(219) 484-9914

Quality Liquors
3107-09 E. State Blvd.
Fort Wayne 46850
(219) 484-3201

Riegel's Pipe & Tobacco
624 S. Calhoun St.
Fort Wayne 46802
(219) 424-1429

Tobacco City
234 W. Ridge Rd.
Griffith 46319
(219) 838-5500

INDIANAPOLIS

Pipe Puffer Smoke Shop
2306 E. South County Line Rd.
Indianapolis 46227
(317) 881-2957

Tinder Box
Washington Square Mall
10202 E. Washington St.
Indianapolis 46229
(317) 899-2811

Tinder Box
6020 E. 82nd
Indianapolis 46250
(317) 845-0806

Tobacco Barn West
5302 W. 10th St.
Indianapolis 46224
(317) 481-9700

Tobacco Express
5310 N. Keystone Ave.
Indianapolis 46220
(317) 475-1444

Tobacco Farm
8059 E. 38th St.
Indianapolis 46226
(317) 895-8300

Tobacco Outlet
8613 N. Michigan Rd.
Indianapolis 46268
(317) 334-9700

The Tobacco Shop
Lafayette Square Mall
3919 Lafayette Rd.
Indianapolis 46254
(317) 299-6010

Village Smoke Shop
8910 S. Meridian St.
Indianapolis 46227
(317) 888-8122

Wine Gallery
4026 E. 82nd St., Ste. A-8
Indianapolis 46250
(317) 576-0108

Bogie's Stogies
107 N. 6th St.
Lafayette 47902
(317) 742-6771

Broadway Newstand
324 E. Broadway
Logansport 46947
(219) 753-8927

Tobacco Unlimited
3225 S. Adams
Marion 46953
(317) 664-1227

Tinder Box
2217 Southlake Mall
Merrillville 46410
(219) 769-4770

Cigarette Discount Outlet
4211 Franklin St.
Michigan City 46360
(219) 879-3300

The Golden Leaf
232 W. 4th St.
Michigan City 46360
(219) 872-9692

Tinder Box
110 University Park Mall
Mishawaka 46545
(219) 277-3440

Sal's Tobacco, Pipe & Coffee
3319 N. Everbrook Lane
Muncie 47304
(317) 286-7257

Munster Tobacco Town
17 Ridge Rd.
Munster 46321
(219) 836-0158

Men's Toy Shop
Old Colonial Bldg.
Nashville 47448
(812) 988-6590

Kaiser's Tobacco Store
415 E. Oak St.
New Albany 47150
(812) 945-2651

Kaiser's Tobacco Store
326 Pearl St.
New Albany 47150
(812) 945-5671

D.W. Cigars
917 Corner St.
Noblesville 46060
(317) 773-7776

Low Bob's
4521 National Rd. E.
Richmond 47374
(317) 935-1305

Low Bob's
1124 W. Tipton
Seymour 47274
(812) 523-3802

SOUTH BEND

Bullseye Discount Liquors
1818 S. Bend Ave.
South Bend 46637
(219) 234-6054

Landmark Liquor
4401 S. Michigan St.
South Bend 46614
(219) 291-2600

Tinder Box
1290 Scottsdale Mall, Ste. 2045
South Bend 46614
(219) 291-7342

TERRE HAUTE

Tobacco Barn
2300 Wabash Ave.
Terre Haute 47807
(812) 235-5323

Tobacco Barn
23 Southland Shopping Center
Terre Haute 47803
(812) 236-2070

Wabash Cigar Store, Inc.
815 Wabash Ave.
Terre Haute 47807
(812) 232-1249

Godfather's Liquors
107 E. Morthland (U.S. 30)
Valparaiso 46383
(215) 462-9512

Triangle Liquors
3210 N. Calumet
Valparaiso 46383
(219) 477-4849

IOWA

Hy-Vee Food Stores
3800 W. Lincoln Way
Ames 50014
(515) 292-0205

Regal Liquors
2880 Devils Glen Rd.
Bettendorf 52722
(319) 352-0957

Jefferson St. Cigar Shop
408 N. Main St.
Burlington 52601
(319) 754-6698

Hillstreet News & Tobacco
2217 College St.
Cedar Falls 50613
(319) 277-7749

DES MOINES

David's Briar Shop
944 Merle Hay Mall
Des Moines 50310
(515) 278-8701

Equitable Cigar & Pipe Store
316 6th Ave.
Des Moines 50309
(515) 243-6903

Tobacco Outlet
3814 Douglas Ave.
Des Moines 50310
(515) 279-7813

Pipe Inn
Kennedy Mall
Dubuque 52002
(319) 556-5175

The Cigar Connection
1855 A-1 Crystal Springs Lane
Fairfield 52556
(515) 469-3194

John's Grocery
401 E. Market St.
Iowa City 52245
(319) 337-2183

National Cigar
617 Sycamore St.
Waterloo 50703
(319) 234-5958

Tinder Box
177 Valley W. Mall
West Des Moines 50266
(515) 225-6011

KANSAS

Hawkins Tobacco & Gifts
1010 S. Kansas
Liberal 67901
(316) 624-3452

Street Corner News
Manhattan Town Center
100 Manhattan Rd.
Manhattan 66502
(913) 587-0597

Cigar & Tabac, Ltd.
6930 W. 105th St.
Overland Park 66212
(913) 381-5597

Street Corner News
Westridge Mall
1801 SW Wanamaker Rd., Ste. VC-9
Topeka 66604
(913) 272-8433

KENTUCKY

The Party Source
95 Riviera Dr.
Bellevue 41073
(606) 291-4007

**Bowling Green Pipe &
  Tobacco Shoppe**
434 E. Main St.
Bowling Green 42101
(502) 843-9439

Tobacco For Less
306 W. Cumberland Gap Pkwy.
Corbin 40701
(606) 526-9688

Tobacco For Less
1607 S. Green St.
Glasgow 42141
(502) 651-1679

LEXINGTON

Fayette Cigar Store
137 E. Main St.
Lexington 40507
(606) 252-6267

Liquor Barn
921 Beaumont Centre Pkwy.
Lexington 40503
(606) 223-1400

Liquor Barn
3040 Richmond Rd.
Lexington 40509
(606) 252-8800

Schwab's Pipes n' Stuff
Lexington Mall
Richmond Rd.
Lexington 40502
(606) 266-1011

Strauss Tobacconist
Hyatt Gift Shop
410 W. Vine
Lexington 40507
(606) 252-5142

LOUISVILLE

Kremer's Smoke Shoppe
333 S. Preston St.
Louisville 40202
(502) 584-3332

Liquor Outlet
1800 S. Hurstbourne Pkwy.
Louisville 40220
(502) 491-0753

Old Town Wine & Spirits
1529 Bardstown Rd.
Louisville 40205
(502) 451-8591

Oxmoor Smoke Shop
Oxmoor Center
Louisville 40222
(502) 426-4706

Up in Smoke
1431 Bardstown Rd.
Louisville 40204
(502) 456-4834

Cigar Emporium
Westland Park Plaza
2702 Fredricka St.
Owensboro 42301
(502) 691-0802

The Tobacco Barn
5023 Hinkleville Rd.
Paducah 42001
(502) 442-7633

Prospect Point Liquor
9535 U.S. Hwy. 42
Prospect 40059
(502) 228-3990

LOUISIANA

Tobacco Plus
3900 S. MacArthur Dr.
Alexandria 70130
(318) 487-2914

Phillip's Bayou Humidor
1152 S. Acadian Thruway
Baton Rouge 70806
(504) 343-1152

Jewel Caters
201 N. New Hampshire St.
Covington 70433
(504) 892-5746

Louisianna Star
409 N. Columbia St.
Covington 70433
(504) 893-8873

Tobacco Plus
115 E. 1st St.
Crowley 70526
(318) 788-0023

Tobacco Plus
100 W. Laurel
Eunice 70535
(318) 457-0214

Tobacco Plus
2611 W. Park Ave.
Houma 70360
(318) 879-1062

Tobacco Plus
14271 Hwy. 165
Kinder 70648
(318) 738-7898

LAFAYETTE

The Cigar Merchant
1001 Coolidge Blvd.
Lafayette 70503
(318) 233-9611

Tobacco Plus
3044 W. Pinhook
Lafayette 70508
(318) 237-3631

Tobacco Plus
1906 Ambassador Caffery Pkwy.
Lafayette 70560
(318) 981-3519

Shop-A-Lot
2707 Hazel St.
Lake Charles 70601
(318) 433-2846

Havana's of Louisiana
4450 Hwy. 22
Mandeville 70471
(504) 524-9631

Cohiba Cigar Emporium
102-F Metairie Heights
Metairie 70001
(803) 587-1566

Martin's Wine Cellars #2
714 Elmire Ave.
Metairie 70005
(504) 896-7300

Tobacco Plus
1005 E. Admiral Doyle Dr.
New Iberia 70560
(318) 369-9270

NEW ORLEANS

Dos Jefes
5700 Magazine St.
New Orleans 70115
(800) 863-9419, (504) 899-3030

The Epitome
729 St. Louis
New Orleans 70130
(504) 523-2844

Martin's Wine Cellar
38-27 Barronne St.
New Orleans 70115
(504) 899-7411

New Orleans Cigar Company
201 St. Charles Ave.
New Orleans 70130
(504) 524-9631

M.A.S. Smoke Shop
1736 E. 70th St., B
Shreveport 71105
(318) 797-3138

The Humidor
451 Red Oak St.
Slidell 70460
(504) 645-9060

Tobacco Plus
200 Darbonne
Sulphur 70663
(318) 527-5025

Tobacco Plus
2217 Old Hwy. 90
Vinton 70508
(318) 589-6396

MAINE

BANGOR

The Calabash
663 Stillwater Ave.
Bangor 04401
(207) 947-0100

Stillwater Convenience
340 Stillwater Ave.
Bangor 04401
(207) 990-3354

Welch's Beverage & Tobacco
546 Hammond St.
Bangor 04401
(207) 945-0112

Beal's Classics
Main St.
Northeast Harbor 04662
(207) 276-3006

PORTLAND

Joe's Smoke Shop
665 Congress St.
Portland 04101
(207) 775-3656

R. S. V. P.
887 Forest Ave.
Portland 04103
(207) 773-8803

Seaport Tobacco
10 Exchange St.
Portland 04101
(207) 775-0950

PDQ
491 Main St.
Rockland 04841
(207) 594-5010

The Calabash
407 Western Ave.
South Portland 04106
(207) 774-8673

News Shop
321 Main Mall Rd.
South Portland 04106
(207) 780-9635

Leaf and Bean
765 Roosevelt Trail
Windham 04062
(207) 892-4300

M A R Y L A N D

A. Fader & Son
Annapolis Plaza
Annapolis 21401
(410) 841-5155

The Smoke Shop
56 Maryland Ave.
Annapolis 21401
(410) 263-2066

B A L T I M O R E

A. Fader & Son
Westview Mall
Baltimore 21228
(410) 744-9090

A. Fader & Son
Eastpoint Mall
Baltimore 21224
(410) 282-6622

A. Fader & Son
107 E. Baltimore
Baltimore 21202
(410) 685-5511

Wells Liquors
6310 York Rd.
Baltimore 21212
(410) 435-2700

Decker Wine & Spirit
401 Baltimore Pike
Bel Air 21014
(410) 879-4400

J.B. Sim's Fine Tobaccos
4914 St. Elmo Ave.
Bethesda 20814
(301) 656-7123

Town & Country Liquors
28248 St. Michael's Rd.
Easton 21601
(410) 822-1433

Jason's Liquors
9339 Baltimore National Pike
Ellicott City 21402-2815
(410) 465-2424

Ronnie's Beverage Warehouse
1514 Rock Spring Rd.
Forest Hill 21050
(410) 838-4566

Tobacco Shack
Francis Scott Key Mall
Frederick 21701
(301) 662-0553

Tobacco Shack II
19328 Montgomery Village Ave.
Gaithersburg 20879
(301) 963-0330

Tobacco Shack
12615-D Wisteria Dr.
Germantown 20874
(301) 972-2905

Venice Wines & Liquors
431 Dual Hwy.
Hackerstown 21740
(301) 733-2819

Tinder Box
11301 Rockville Pike
Kensington 20895
(301) 881-8322

Capital Plaza Smoke Shop
6200 Annapolis Rd.
Landover Hills 20784
(301) 341-2614

Rolling Road Tobacco
Warehouse 1421
1421 York Rd.
Lutherville 21093
(410) 339-7072

Smoke Rings
4513 Coastal Hwy.
Ocean City 21842
(410) 289-3250

Smoke Rings
5 2nd St.
Ocean City 21842
(410) 289-1204

A. Fader & Son
Valley Village Shopping Center
Owings Mills 21117
(410) 363-7799

A. Fader & Son
25 W. Allegheny Ave.
Towson 21204
(410) 828-4555

Riverside Liquors Inc.
1811 Main St.
Agawam 01001
(413) 789-6448

Blanchard's Liquors
103 Harvard Ave.
Allston 02134
(617) 782-5588

Andover Spa
9 Elm St.
Andover 01810
(508) 475-4750

Auburndale Wine & Spirit
2102 Commonwealth Ave.
Auburndale 02166
(617) 244-2772

Mall News
480 Boston Rd.
Billerica 01821
(508) 663-5946

BOSTON

Alfred Dunhill of London
69 Newbury St.
Boston 02116
(617) 424-8600

Bauer Liquors
337 Newbury St.
Boston 02115
(617) 262-0083

Cigar Landing
Faneuil Hall Market Place
Quincy Market Bldg.
Boston 02109
(617) 723-0147

The Humidor
800 Boylston St.
Boston 02199
(617) 262-5510

The Humidor
805 E. 4th St., #2
Boston 02127
(617) 464-3153

L.J. Peretti Co.
2½ Park Square
Boston 02116
(617) 482-0218

State Street Smoke Shop, Inc.
107-A State St.
Boston 02109
(617) 227-7576

Waterfront Beer & Wine
379 Commercial St.
Boston 02109
(617) 523-4055

Brewster Package Store
2655 Main St.
Brewster 02631
(508) 896-3412

Brookline Liquor Mart
1334 Commonwealth Ave.
Boston 02134
(617) 734-7700

Brookline News & Gift
313 Harvard St.
Brookline 02146
(617) 566-9634

Busa Liquors
182 Cambridge St.
Burlington 01813
(617) 272-1050

Leavitt & Pierce
1316 Mass. Ave.
Cambridge 02138
(617) 547-0576

C.B. Perkins
95 Washington St.
Canton 02021
(617) 575-1411

Cape Cod Package Store
1495 Falmouth Rd.
Centerville 02632
(508) 775-2065

Harrington Wine & Liquors
10 Summer St.
Chelmsford 01824
(508) 256-2711

K B Tobacco
168 Everett Ave.
Chelsea 02150
(617) 889-0012

Gary's Discount Liquors
655 VFW Pkwy.
Chestnut Hill 02167
(617) 323-1122

Curtis Liquors
790 Rte. 3-A
Chief Justice Cushing Hwy.
Cohasset 02025
(617) 383-9800

Vintages at Concord, Inc.
53 Commonwealth Ave.
Concord 01742
(508) 369-2545

Heights News Cigar Pit
1006 Bennington St.
East Boston 02128
(617) 569-4450

Two Guys Smoke Shop
262 Meridian St.
East Boston 02128
(617) 561-4990

Trader Fred's
249-D State Rd.
Edgartown, Martha's Vineyard 02539
(508) 627-8004

Kappy's
296 Main St.
Everett 02149
(617) 389-7600

Two Guys Smoke Shop
423 Broadway
Everett 02149
(617) 387-6691

Jim Rogers Cigar Store
46 N. Main St.
Fall River 02720
(508) 675-0800

**The Old Firehouse Smoke
& Brew Shop**
116 Rock St.
Fall River 02720
(508) 678-2185

Norman's Liquors
21 Spring Bars Rd.
Falmouth 02540
(508) 548-2600

Tobacco Shed
400 Cochituate Rd.
Framingham 01701
(508) 875-9851

Wine Vault
2 Fairbank St.
Framingham 01701
(508) 875-6980

Franklin News
36 Main St.
Franklin 02038
(508) 528-8263

295

Liquor World
365 W. Central St.
Franklin 02038
(508) 528-0138

Trotta's
490 Main St.
Great Barrington 01230
(413) 528-3490

Four Seasons Wines & Liquors
333 Russell St.
Hadley 01035
(413) 584-8174

Tobacconist Ltd.
Hanover Mall
Hanover 02339
(617) 826-1344

Hopkinton Wine & Spirits
77 W. Main St.
Hopkinton 01748
(508) 435-1292

Cape Cod Mall Liquors
226 Falmouth Rd., Rte. 28
Hyannis 02601
(508) 790-4770

Ipswich News Co.
14 Market St.
Ipswich 01938
(508) 356-3313

Nejaime Wine & Liquor
444 Pittsfield-Lenox Rd.
Lenox 01240
(413) 637-1220

Busa Liquors
55 Bedford St.
Lexington 02173
(617) 862-1400

Pleasant Smoke Shop
428 Main St.
Malden 02148
(617) 321-3593

Rum Runner Wine & Spirit
496 Elm
Mansfield 02048
(508) 339-4795

Kappy's
10 Revere Beach Pkwy.
Medford 02155
(617) 395-8888

Liquor World
Starmarket Plaza
9 Medway Rd., Rte. 109
Milford 01757
(508) 478-1757

Power Package Store
4 South Ave.
Natick 01760
(508) 653-6832

**The Cigar Emporium at Newton
  Upper Falls Liquors**
150 Needham St.
Newton 02164
(617) 969-9200

Pipe Rack
1247 Centre St.
Newton Center 02159
(617) 969-3734

Marty's Liquor
675 Washington St.
Newtonville 02160
(617) 332-1230

The Cigar Emporium
800 Turnpike St., Ste. 300
North Andover 01845
(508) 470-0300

Den Rock Liquors
North Andover Mall
North Andover 01845
(508) 683-2216

Aurora Borealis
25 King St.
Northhampton 01060
(413) 585-9533

Jim's Package Store
Circuit Ave. Ext.
Oak Bluffs, Martha's Vineyard 02557
(508) 693-0236

Craigville Package Store
2946 Rte. 28
Osterville 02655
(508) 420-0321

Kappy's Rte. 114 Liquors
75 Andover St., Rte. 114
Peabody 01960
(508) 532-2330

Brennans & Plymouth
17 Court St.
Plymouth 02360
(508) 746-5711

Smith's
53 Main St.
Plymouth 02360
(508) 746-0496

Richard's Liquor
301 Quincy Ave.
Quincy 02169
(617) 376-0709

Salty Dog Smoke Shop
Whistle Stop Mall
Rockport 01966
(508) 546-5163

Audet's Wine & Spirits
9 Traders Way, #1
Salem 01970
(508) 744-7608

Red Lion Smoke Shop
94 Washington St.
Salem 01970
(508) 745-2050

S. Egermont Spirit Shoppe
71 Main St.
South Egermont 01258
(413) 528-1490

Curtis Liquors
486 Columbian St.
South Weymouth 02190
(617) 331-2345

Indian Smoke Shop
904 Main St.
Springfield 01103
(413) 731-6842

Phoenix Newsroom, Inc
1676 Main St.
Springfield 01103
(413) 731-8322

Yankee Spirits
376 Main St.
Sturbridge 01566
(508) 347-2231

Harringtown News & Gifts
2 Galleria Mall Dr.
Taunton 02780
(508) 880-9301

Aubut's Liquors
1768 Main St.
Tewksbury 01876
(508) 851-2031

Kelly Liquors
440 Middlesex Rd.
Tynesboro 01879
(508) 649-2243

Mark's Smoke Shop & Newsstand
360 Main St.
Wakefield 01880
(617) 592-9799

Gordon's Liquor Store
867 Main St.
Waltham 02154
(617) 893-1900

Green River Wine & Spirit
178 High St.
Waltham 02154
(617) 894-9578

Post Road Liquors
44 Boston Post Rd.
Wayland 01778
(508) 358-4300

Town & Country
1119 Riverdale St.
West Springfield 01089
(413) 736-4694

Julio's Liquor
Rte. 9, 140 Boston Tpke. Rd.
Westboro 01581
(508) 366-7380

Elliott's
191 The Strand
Winthrop 02152
N/A

G & J Smoke Shop
461 Main St.
Woburn 01801
(617) 935-2760

Tobacco Shed
Woburn Mall
300 Mishawum Rd.
Woburn 01801
(617) 933-0231

WORCESTER

The Owl Shop
416 Main St.
Worcester 01608
(508) 753-0423

Palley Cash-n-Carry
1049 Main St.
Worcester 01603
(508) 752-2811

R.A. Tiscione's Cigar Cafe
257 Shrewsbury St.
Worcester 01604
(508) 754-0067

MICHIGAN

Smokers Only
9095 Alan Rd.
Alanpark 48101
(313) 381-0480

ANN ARBOR

Big Ten Party Store Inc.
1928 Packard Rd.
Ann Arbor 48104
(313) 662-0798

Maison Edwards Tobacconist
11 Nickels Arcade
Ann Arbor 48104
(313) 662-4145

Smoker's Depot
1760 Plymouth Rd.
Ann Arbor 48105
(313) 669-9277

Village Corner
601 S. Forest Ave.
Ann Arbor 48104
(313) 995-1818

Smoky's Cigarettes & Cigars
3029 E. Walton Blvd.
Auburn Hills 48326
(810) 373-7174

Tinder Box
2050 N. Opdyke
Auburn Hills 48326
(810) 377-6840

C.J.'s Wine Cellars
18½ W. Michigan Ave.
Battle Creek 49017
(616) 964-8984

Smokers Palace - Bay City
705 N. Euclid Ave.
Bay City 48706
(517) 667-4410

Smokey's Cigarette Outlet
2727 S. Woodward
Berkley 48073
(810) 546-8431

Churchills of Birmingham
142 S. Woodward
Birmingham 48009
(810) 647-4555

Bloomfield Gourmet
1081 W. Long Lake Rd.
Bloomfield Hills 48302
(810) 647-5570

Smokers Depot
10006 E. Grand River
Brighton 48116
(810) 220-2701

Smokers Palace - Burton
6034 E. Lapeer Rd.
Burton 48509
(810) 742-8184

Bridge Street Book Shop Inc.
405 Bridge St.
Charlevoix 49720
(616) 547-7323

DEARBORN

Dearborn Tobacco Co
22085 Michigan Ave.
Dearborn 48124
(313) 562-1221

The Merchant's Warehouse
22250 Michigan Ave.
Dearborn 48124
(313) 563-8700

Wiff N. Puff
14300 Henn St.
Dearborn 48126
(519) 572-1244

- -

Smoker's Hub #4
26429 Ford Rd.
Dearborn Heights 48127
(313) 277-6015

Telegraph Cigarette Store
3965 Telegraph
Dearborn Heights 48125
(313) 565-9484

DETROIT

Gift Emporium
1000 Brush Ave.
Detroit 48226
(313) 961-4777

Hill & Hill Tobacconists Ltd.
2001 Renaissance Center
Tower 200, Level 2
Detroit 48243
(313) 259-3388

New Center Tobacco & Snacks
3011 W. Grand Blvd.
Detroit 48202
(313) 873-7833

Walters Pipe Shop
122 W. Lafayette Blvd.
Detroit 48226
(313) 965-5326

Campbells Smoke Shop, Inc.
207 Mac Ave.
East Lansing 48823
(517) 332-4269

Smokers Only
24275 Middlebelt
Farmington Hills 48336
(810) 476-8013

Paul's Pipe Shop
647 S. Saginaw St.
Flint 48502
(810) 235-0581

Port of Call
G-4225 Miller Rd.
Flint 48507
(313) 732-2793

GRAND RAPIDS

Buffalo Tobacco Traders
952 E. Fulton St.
Grand Rapids 49503
(616) 451-8090

Elliott's News & Tobacco
21 Ottawa Ave. NW
Grand Rapids 49503
(616) 235-6400

Martha's Vineyard Ltd.
200 Union NE
Grand Rapids 49503
(616) 459-0911

Smoker's Express
224-C 28th St. NW
Grand Rapids 49509
(616) 261-9456

Tuttle's
3835 28th St. SE
Grand Rapids 49512
(616) 942-6990

Hill & Hill Tobacconists Ltd.
19529 Mack Ave.
Grosse Pointe Woods 48236
(313) 882-9452

Smoker's Outlet of Highland
732 W. Highland Rd.
Highland 48357
(810) 887-2333

Butch's Dry Dock
44 E. 8th St., Ste. 100
Holland 49423
(616) 396-8227

Smoker's Depot
1235 E. Grand River
Howell 48483
(517) 546-2646

Tiffany Spirit Shoppe
1714 W. Main St.
Kalamazoo 49006
(616) 381-1414

Tinder Box
Crossroads Mall
6650 S. Westnedge
Kalamazoo 49002
(616) 327-3447

Mac's
207 S. Washington Square
Lansing 48933
(517) 487-0670

Smokers Palace - Lapeer
1045 Summit St.
Lapeer 48446
(810) 664-2020

LIVONIA

The Smoke Shop II
34710 Plymouth Rd.
Livonia 48150
(313) 266-0540

Smoky's Cigarette Outlet
16705 Middlebelt Rd.
Livonia 48154
(313) 513-2622

Wine Barrel Plus
30303 Plymouth Rd.
Livonia 48150
(313) 522-9463

Smokers Express
1460 E. 12 Mile Rd.
Madison Heights 48071
(810) 544-6818

Smokers Outlet of Madison Heights
160 W. 12 Mile Rd.
Madison Heights 48071
(810) 414-7007

Trader Toms Tobacco Shop
43249 7 Mile Rd.
Northville 48167
(810) 348-8333

Dusty Cellar Wine Bar
1839 Grand River Ave.
Okemos 48864
(517) 349-5150

Vintage Wine Shop
4137 Orchard Lake Rd.
Orchard Lake 48323
(313) 626-3235

Tobacco Etc.
7503 S. U.S. 31
Petoskey 49770
(616) 348-5808

Smokers Only
585 S. Main St.
Plymouth 48170
(313) 453-5644

Wellington Ltd.
14 Forest Pl.
Plymouth 48170
(313) 453-8966

Wine Barrel of Redford
25303 Plymouth Rd.
Redford 48239
(313) 533-9463

Serafino's
8004 N. 32nd St.
Richland 49083
(616) 629-4721

Smokers Shop
19158 Fort St.
Riverview 48192
(313) 479-0404

Lil' Havana Tobacconist
3068 Walton Blvd.
Rochester Hills 48309
(810) 375-5455

Merchant of Vino Market Place
1404 Walton Blvd.
Rochester Hills 48309
(810) 652-2100

Embassy Wine & Cigar
29010 Beaconsfield Rd.
Roseville 48066
(313) 771-7880

Smokers Outlet
18655 E. 10 Mile Rd.
Roseville 48066
(810) 772-3999

Three Ravens
210 W. 6th St.
Royal Oak 48068
(810) 545-9499

Austin's Fine Pipes & Tobaccos
4340 Bay Rd.
Saginaw 48603
(517) 792-4731

Dave's Smokin' Post
3986 Bay Rd.
Saginaw 48603
(517) 790-0066

Churchill's
21425 Great Mack Ave.
St. Clair Shores 48080
(810) 775-3181

Smokers Express
47079 Van Dyke
Shelby Township 48317
(810) 254-7272

SOUTHFIELD

Hayes Market
22580 Telegraph
Southfield 48034
(810) 352-2216

Humidor One
Panache
20000 W. 10 Mile Rd.
Southfield 48075
(313) 356-4600

J.R. Tobacco
28815 NW Hwy.
Southfield 48034
(810) 357-2340

Old Wooden Indian Tobacco
13260 Northline St.
Southgate 48195
(313) 282-1379

Churchill's JSK
14600 Lakeside Circle
Sterling Heights 48313
(810) 247-1753

Smokers Discount
33126 Dequindre
Sterling Heights 48310
(810) 268-5577

Smokers Outlet of Taylor
7150 Pardee
Taylor 48180
(313) 292-8006

Nolan's Tobacco
336 E. Front St.
Traverse City 49684
(616) 946-2640

Smokers Den
1073 S. Airport Rd.
Traverse City 49686
(616) 946-2742

TROY

Hill & Hill Tobacconists Ltd.
Oakland Mall
662 W. 14 Mile Rd.
Troy 48083
(810) 585-0621

Smokers Outlet
5086 Rochester Rd.
Troy 48098
(810) 528-8018

Tobacco Emporium
2981 E. Big Beaver Rd.
Troy 48083
(313) 689-1840

Bay Pointe Market
4100 Haggerty Market
Walled Lake 48390
(810) 360-2300

Great American Trading Post
7380 Hiland Rd.
Waterford 48327
(810) 666-7935

Smokers Only
4646 Walton Blvd.
Waterford 48329
(810) 674-1199

Lil' Havana Tobacconist
6690-A Orchard Lake Rd.
West Bloomfield 48322
(810) 539-0190

Smoker's Express
1799 Washtenaw
Yspilanti 48197
(313) 480-0705

MINNESOTA

L & M Smoke Shop
429 87th Lane
Blaine 55434
(612) 784-1140

Street Corner News
Mall of America
119 E. Broadway
Bloomington 55425
(612) 858-9826

Smoke Shoppe & Booknook
109 Washington St.
Brainerd 56401
(218) 829-5830

Tobak Shack
3950 Sibley Memorial Hwy.
Eagan 55122
(612) 454-2684

Tobacco Road
Yorktown Mall
3505 Hazelton Rd.
Edina 55435
(612) 831-2991

The Smoke Shop
809 Sibley Memorial Hwy.
Lilydale 55118
(612) 457-4953

Westside Discount Liquor
116 S. Linborg Dr.
Little Falls 56345
(612) 632-2582

MINNEAPOLIS

Depot Liquor
1010 Washington Ave. S.
Minneapolis 55415
(612) 339-4040

Golden Leaf Ltd.
Calhoun Square
3001 Hennepin Ave. S.
Minneapolis 55408
(612) 824-1867

Lewis Pipe & Tobacco
512 Niccollet Mall
Minneapolis 55402
(612) 332-9129

Madhatter's Smoke Shop
3723 Minnehaha Ave.
Minneapolis 55406
(612) 729-7949

South Lyndale Liquor
5300 Lyndale Ave. S.
Minneapolis 55420
(612) 827-5811

Surdyk's Liquors
303 E. Hennepin
Minneapolis 55414
(612) 379-3232

Tobacco Road
Foshay Tower
831 Marquette Ave.
Minneapolis 55402
(612) 333-1315

Tobacco Road
Daytona-Radisson Arcade
27 S. 7th St.
Minneapolis 55402
(612) 332-3929

Tobacco Warehouse
4727 Hiawatha Ave.
Minneapolis 55406
(612) 933-2718

Haskell's Inc.
12900 Wayzata Blvd.
Minnetonka 55305
(612) 544-4456

J.T. Tobacconists
17613 Minnetonka Blvd.
Minnetonka 55391
(612) 475-3131

Smoker's Haven
1640 Hasting's Ave.
Newport 55104
(612) 768-8310

Chundee Smoke Shop
Mistic Lake Casino
2400 Mistic Lake Blvd.
Prior Lake 55372
(612) 496-7178

TePee
2350 NW Souix Trail
Prior Lake 55372
(612) 445-8982

West End Liquors
1430 W. Main
Red Wing 55066
(612) 388-9425

A New Leaf
20 2nd Ave. SW
Rochester 55902
(507) 287-9793

Apollo Smokeshop
1513 12th St. SE
Rochester 55904
(507) 281-0888

G. & W. Coffee & Tobacco
21 Wilson Ave. NE
St. Cloud 56304
(612) 654-6111

ST. PAUL

J.R. Fielding Co.
1767 Lexington Ave.
St. Paul 55113
(612) 489-7504

Sharritt's Liquors
2389 University Ave. W.
St. Paul 55114
(612) 645-8629

Smoke 'n Gun
634 N. Snelling Ave.
St. Paul 55104
(612) 647-9397

Thomas Liquor Store
1941 Grand Ave.
St. Paul 55105
(612) 699-1860

Up in Smoke
33 N. Concord St.
St. Paul 35075
(612) 552-9559

Central Park Warehouse
8101 Hwy. 65
Spring Lake Park 55432
(612) 780-8246

Westside Discount Liquor
45 Waite Ave.
Waite Park 56387
(612) 253-9511

Treasure Island Casino Smoke Shop
5734 Sturgeon Lake Rd.
Welsh 55089
(800) 222-7077

Boozemart Wine & Spirits
131 E. Wentworth
West St. Paul 55118
(612) 457-6111

MISSISSIPPI

The Smoke Shop Ltd.
Edgewater Mall
2600 W. Beach Blvd.
Biloxi 39531
(601) 388-2022

Dyre-Kent Drug Co.
109 1st St.
Grenada 38901
(601) 226-5232

The Country Squire
1855 Lakerland Dr.
Jackson 39216
(601) 362-2233

Smokey's Discount Tobacco
2961 Bienville Blvd.
Ocean Spring 39564
(601) 872-5322

Don Johnson's Tobacco World
1420 S. Glenstone
Springfield 65804
(417) 890-1978

MISSOURI

Welcome Smokers
523 Jeffco
Arnold 63010
(314) 282-9910

Aurora Smokers Outlet
1608 S. Elliot, Unit #4
Aurora 65605
(417) 678-6333

The Wine Company
1447 Hwy. 248, Ste. G
Branson 65616
(417) 334-4551

Jon's Pipe Shop
42 N. Central Ave.
Clayton 63105
(314) 721-1480

J.R. Cigars & Fragrance
4 N. Central Ave.
Clayton 63105
(317) 727-5667

Nostalgia Shop
819 E. Walnut
Colombia 65201
(314) 874-1950

Tinder Box
147 Jamestown Mall
Florissant 63034
(314) 741-0899

Hollister Smokers Outlet
104 Ye Old Town Village
2460 S. Business 65
Hollister 65613
(417) 335-2149

JOPLIN

Automatic Cash & Carry
1902 Main St.
Joplin 64804
(417) 624-2525

Melvin's Smokers Outlet
2619 N. Rangeline
Joplin 64801
(417) 782-4711

T.J. Boggs Tobacconist
205 W. 20th St.
Joplin 64804
(417) 623-1804

KANSAS CITY

Berbiglia
1101 E. Banister
Kansas City 64131
(816) 942-0070

Diebel's Sportsmens Gallery
Country Club Plaza
426 Ward Pkwy.
Kansas City 64112
(816) 931-2988

Diebel's Sportsmens Gallery
Crown Center
2450 Grand
Kansas City 64112
(816) 474-3483

Westport Wine & Liquors
1106 Westport Rd
Kansas City 64111
(816) 561-3500

Branson West Smokers Outlet
W. Hwy. 76
Kimberling City 65686
(417) 272-8095

Welcome Smokers
176 Weldon Pkwy.
Maryland Heights 63043
(314) 569-2265

The Discount Smokes
2430 Grand Carthrage
Mission 64836
(417) 358-3455

Welcome Smokers
206 Terra Lane W.
O'Fallon 63366
(314) 978-3714

Welcome Smokers
4 Kings Plaza
Osage Beach 65065
(314) 348-4635

Republic Smokers Outlet
6938 W. U.S. Hwy. 60
Republic 65738
(417) 881-1801

Red-X Market
24-01 W. Platte Rd.
Riverside 64150
(816) 741-7200

John Dengler Tobacconist
700 S. Main St.
St. Charles 63301
(314) 946-6899

ST. LOUIS

**The Adam's Mark Hotel -
The Gift Shop**
4th & Chestnut
St. Louis 63102
(314) 241-7400

Briars & Blends
6008 Hampton Ave.
St. Louis 63109
(314) 351-1131

J.R. Cigars & Fragrance
710 Olive St.
St. Louis 63101
(314) 231-4434

Joel's Shell Food Mart
1815 Arsenal St.
St. Louis 63118
(314) 772-1977

Town & Country Tobacco
13933 Manchester Rd.
St. Louis 63011
(314) 227-0707

Welcome Smokers
19 Grasso Plaza
St. Louis 63123
(314) 631-1211

Welcome Smokers
3524 Lemay Ferry Rd.
St. Louis 63125
(314) 845-3680

Welcome Smokers
10544 Page Blvd.
St. Louis 63132
(314) 423-2264

Sedalia Cigarette & Tobacco
223-225 E. 5th St.
Sedalia 65301
(816) 826-0800

Mr. Tobacco
113 N. U.S. Hwy. 169
Smithville 64089
(816) 532-0444

SPRINGFIELD

Brown Derby
2023 S. Glenstone
Springfield 65804
(417) 866-0316

Don Johnson's Tobacco
1420 S. Glenstone
Springfield 65804
(417) 890-1978

The Humidor Ltd.
Brentwood Center
2728 S. Glenstone
Springfield 65804
(417) 887-9619

Just For Him
1328 E. Battlefield
Springfield 65804
(417) 886-8380

H.S.B. Tobacconist
6362 Delmar at Westgate
University City 63130
(314) 721-1483

Direct Source
Omis Apple House
100 N. Fisher
Versailles 65084
(800) 444-4765

Welcome Smokers
6301 Weldon Springs Rd.
Weldon Springs 63304
(314) 939-5539

MONTANA

The Cigarette Store
249 Main St.
Billings 59105
(406) 252-4279

The Cigarette Store
2646 Grand Ave., Ste. 6
Billings 59102
(406) 655-9678

The Cigarette Store
1530 Ceoar St.
Helena 59604
(406) 443-3158

Maine News
9 N. Last Chance Gulch
Helena 59601
(406) 442-6424

Tobacco Junction
1701 Hwy. 93 S.
Kalispell 59901
(406) 752-1339

Bell Pipe & Tobacco Shop
136 E. Broadway St.
Missoula 59802
(406) 728-2781

NEBRASKA

The Still
5560 S. 48
Lincoln 68516
(402) 423-1875

Ted's Tobacco
Ward's #2 Gateway
61st & O Sts.
Lincoln 68505
(402) 467-3350

White Horse Sports Cards
621 S. Dewey St.
North Platte 69101
(308) 534-9188

OMAHA

David's Briar Shop
10000 California St., Ste. 3337
Omaha 68114
(402) 397-4760

David's Briar Shop
Oak View Mall, Ste. 1113
Omaha 68114
(402) 697-0771

Nickleby's Smoke Ring
2464 S. 120
Omaha 68144
(402) 330-4556

Omaha Wine Company
701 N. 114th St.
Omaha 68154
(402) 431-8558

S.G. Roi
503 S. 11th St.
Omaha 68102
(402) 341-9264

Tobacco Hut
13766 Millard Ave.
Omaha 68137
(402) 895-1016

Sherm's Smoke Shop
100 W. 6th St.
S. Sioux City 68776
(402) 494-1412

NEVADA

Battle Mountain Indian Colony
41 Circle Way
Battle Mountain 89820
(702) 635-5866

Carsons Cigar Company
318 N. Carson, Ste. 101
Carson City 89701
(702) 884-4402

LAS VEGAS

Churchill's Tobacco Emporium
3144 N. Rainbow Blvd.
Las Vegas 89108
(702) 645-1047

Cigarette's Cheaper!
Charleston Plaza
1383 E. Charleston Blvd.
Las Vegas 89104
(702) 384-8434

Don Pablo Cigar Co.
3025 Las Vegas Blvd. S.
Las Vegas 89109
(702) 369-1818

Don Ye Yo
510 E. Fremont
Las Vegas 89101
(800) 353-YEYO

Ed's Pipes, Tobacco & Gifts
Maryland Square
3661 S. Maryland Pkwy.
Las Vegas 89109
(800) 688-6222, (702) 734-1931

Hiland
The Meadows Mall
4300 Meadows Mall
Las Vegas 89107
(702) 878-7720

Las Vegas Cigar Co.
3755 S. Las Vegas Blvd.
Las Vegas 89109
(702) 262-6100

Mr. Bill's Pipe & Tobacco Co.
4632 S. Maryland Pkwy.
Las Vegas 89119
(702) 739-8840

Mr. Bill's Pipe & Tobacco Co.
4510 E. Charleston
Las Vegas 89104
(702) 459-3400

Mr. Bill's Pipe & Tobacco Co.
4441 W. Flamingo Rd.
Las Vegas 89103
(702) 221-9771

Mr. Bill's Pipe & Tobacco Co.
4343 N. Rancho
Las Vegas 89130
new location - N/A

Royal Cigar Society
3900 S. Paradise Rd., Ste. J
Las Vegas 89109
(702) 732-4411

Scarpe
3200 Las Vegas Blvd. S.
Las Vegas 89109
(702) 369-9133

Spirits Plus Liquor Store
4880 W. Flamingo Rd.
Las Vegas 89103
(702) 873-6000

Tinder Box
3536 Maryland Pkwy.
Las Vegas 89109
(702) 737-1807

Tobacco Road Tobacco - Tobacco, Pipes and Cigars
3650 E. Flamingo Rd.
Las Vegas 89121
(702) 435-8511

Tobacco Road Tobacco #2 - Tobacco, Pipes and Cigars
1129 S. Rainbow Rd.
Las Vegas 89102
(702) 254-8511

RENO

Cigarette's Cheaper!
Mira Loma Shopping Center
3368 S. McCarren Blvd.
Reno 89502
(702) 826-9111

Cigarette's Cheaper!
Keystone Center
975 W. 5th St.
Reno 89503
(702) 348-7077
Cigarette's Cheaper!
180 W. Peckham, Ste. 1030
Reno 89509
(702) 829-0605

Cigarette's Cheaper!
1075 N. Hills Blvd., #220
Reno 89506
(702) 677-4448

Smoke Shop
2001 E. 2nd St.
Reno 89502
(702) 329-0275

Tinder Box
Park Lane Center
186 E. Plumb Lane
Reno 89502
(702) 826-2680

Cigarette's Cheaper!
Iron Horse Shopping Center
529 E. Prater St.
Sparks 89431
(702) 331-3599

NEW HAMPSHIRE

Captain's Pleasure
124 N. Main St.
Concord 03301
(603) 623-3739

The News Shop
Steeple Gate Mall
Concord 03302
(603) 226-2833

Happy Jack's Pipe & Tobacco
71 Church St.
Laconia 03246
(603) 528-4092

Captain's Pleasure
990 Elm St.
Manchester 03101
(603) 623-3739

The News Shop
1500 S. Willow St.
Manchester 03103
(603) 622-1782

Fermentation Station
4 Water St.
Meredith 03253
(603) 279-4028

The News Shop
310 Daniel Webster Hwy., Ste. 123
Nashua 03060
(603) 891-1867

The News Shop
Fox Run Mall
Newington 03801
(603) 431-5665

Federal Cigar
22 Ladd St.
Portsmouth 03801
(603) 436-5363

The News Shop
99 Rockingham Park Blvd.
Salem 03079
(603) 890-3699

Post Time Beer & Smoke
375 S. Broadway
Salem 03079
(603) 898-3704

The Gold Leaf-Tobacconist
920 Lafayette Rd., Unit 3
Seabrook 03874
(603) 474-7744

NEW JERSEY

The Trump Plaza Hotel & Casino
Mississippi Ave. & Broadway
Atlantic City 08401
(609) 441-6751

Village Tobacco
41 Clementon Rd.
Berlin 08009
(609) 768-5181

Brookdale Buy-Rite
1057 Broad St.
Bloomfield 07003
(201) 338-7090

Village Tobacco
114 Main St.
Bradley Beach 07720
(908) 774-7055

Cigars Plus
2140-1 Rte. 88
Brick 08724
(908) 295-9795

C.B. Perkins
Bridgewater Commons Mall
400 Commons Way
Bridgewater 08807
(908) 707-8787

Delmonte's News Agency
2999 Mt. Ephraim Ave.
Camden 08104
(609) 962-6929

Cape May News
8 Victorian Plaza
Cape May 08204
(609) 884-5511

Super Wines & Spirits
99 Ridgedale Ave.
Cedar Knolls 07927
(201) 267-1999

The Chatham Wine Shop
465 Main St.
Chatham 07928
(201) 635-0088

Track Town Smoke Shop
2111 Rte. 70 W.
Cherry Hill 08002
(609) 662-0214

Shop Rite Liquors
494 Anderson Ave.
Cliffside Park 07010
(201) 943-2650

Rowe-Manse Emporium
1065 Bloomfield Ave.
Clifton 07012
(201) 472-8170

Village Stationary
385 Valley Rd.
Clifton 07013
(201) 278-0746

Clinton Wine & Spirits
57 Laneco Plaza
Clinton 08809
(908) 735-9655

Puff n' Stuff
21 E. North Ave.
Cranford 07016
(908) 272-6989

C.B. Perkins
Deptford Mall
Deptford 08096
(609) 848-3363

Market Place Wines & Spirits
647-C Hwy. 18
East Brunswick 08816
(908) 432-9393

Mr. Pipe
Brunswick Square Mall
East Brunswick 08816
(908) 257-0200

Eatontown Smoke Shop
21 Main St.
Eatontown 07724
(908) 542-1855

John David Ltd.
453 Menlo Park
Edison 08837
(908) 494-8333

Smokers World Ltd.
126 Engle St.
Englewood 07631
(201) 567-1305

Burns Tobacco
2424 Fairlawn Ave.
Fairlawn 07410
(201) 797-1311

The Cigar Room
200 Main St.
Fort Lee 07024
(201) 947-5835

Franklin Park Wine & Liquors
3391 Rte. 27
Franklin Park 08823
(908) 442-2324

FREEHOLD

Mr. Pipe
Freehold Raceway Mall
3710 Hwy. 9, Ste. 1212
Freehold 07728
(908) 303-9500

Spirit Unlimited
138 Village Center Dr.
Freehold 07728
(908) 409-3060

Spirit Unlimited
611 Park Ave.
Freehold 07728
(908) 462-8100

The Jigger Shop
190 Main St.
Hackettstown 07840
(908) 852-3080

Colonial Smoke Shop
1 Mechanic St.
Haddenfield 08033
(609) 354-0999

Pipe & Tobacco Shop
797 Rte., #33
Hamilton Square 08619
(609) 587-6375

J.R. Tobacco
65 Rte. 17 S.
Hasbrouck Heights 07640
(201) 228-7676

The Smoke Shop
235 Hudson St.
Hoboken 07030
(201) 217-1701

Garden State News Village
43 Main St.
Madison 07940
(201) 939-4396

Shopper's Liquor
121 Main St.
Madison 07940
(201) 822-0200

Goodloe Liquors
Hwy. 71 & Stockton Lake Blvd.
Manasquan 08736
(908) 223-3180

Ida's Newsroom
506 Stokes Rd.
Medford 08055
(609) 654-1094

Spirit Unlimited
Rte. 9 & Adelphia Rd.
Freehold 07728
(908) 462-3738

Cigar Cafe
44 Morris St.
Morristown 07960
(201) 285-5377

Bliwise Liquors
1267 Rte. 22
Mountainside 07092
(908) 233-1133

Bottom of the Hill Newsstand
3 Easton Ave.
New Brunswick 08901
(908) 745-7983

Sell Rite Liquors
579 Rte. 22 W.
North Plainfield 07060
(908) 756-0400

Northfield News & Tobacco
Rte. 9 & Tilton Rd.
Northfield 08225
(609) 641-9112

Mister Pipe
194 Seaview Square Mall
Ocean 07712
(908) 922-9693

C.B. Perkins
39 Bergen Mall
Paramus 07652-5001
(201) 845-4384

John David Ltd.
Garden State Plaza
Paramus 07652
(201) 368-1975

Hinkle's News Shop
233 N. Broadway
Pennsville 08070
(609) 678-2460

A Little Taste of Cuba
70 Witherspoon St.
Princeton 08542
(609) 683-8988

Silver Star Trading
266 Terrace St.
Rahway 07065
(201) 344-5210

Tobacco Hut
31 Rte. 206
Raritan 08869
(908) 725-4440

The Red Pipe
39½ Broad St.
Red Bank 07701
(908) 842-6633

Tobacco Shop, Inc.
10 Chestnut St.
Ridgewood 07450
(201) 447-2204

John David Ltd.
Rockaway Town Square
Rockaway 07866
(201) 328-0603

Rumson Buy-Rite
5 W. River Rd.
Rumson 07760
(908) 842-0552

Secaucus Liquors
115 Plaza Center
Secaucus 07094
(201) 867-7428

Brick Church Collection
The Mall At Short Hills
Short Hills 07078
(201) 379-6920

Cedar Grove Wines & Liquors Inc.
120 Cedar Grove Lane
Somerset 08873
(908) 560-0009

The Spring Lake Bottle Shop
1400 3rd Ave.
Spring Lake 07762
(908) 449-5525

R Treasures
649 Morris Ave.
Springfield 07081
(908) 688-2266

E-Z Liquors
35 Rte. 37 E.
Toms River 08753
(908) 341-3444

Monaghan's Liquors
1617 Rte. 37 E.
Toms River 08753
(908) 270-6060

Princeton Avenue Cigar
1298 Princeton Ave.
Trenton 08638
(609) 396-9610

Cuban Aliados
329 48th St.
Union City 07087
(201) 348-0189

Angelbecks
621 Valley Rd.
Upper Montclair 07043
(201) 744-1375

The Tobacco Store
405 Bloomfield Ave.
Verona 07044
(201) 857-2266

Williams Continental Tobacco Shop
137 S. Delsea Dr.
Vineland 08360
(609) 692-8034

Taco Maker
61 Berdan Ave.
Wayne 07470
(201) 305-8226

Westfield Pipe Shop
214 E. Broad St.
Westfield 07090
(908) 232-2627

Stogie's Ltd.
50 Madison Ave.
Westwood 07675
(201) 666-1234

J.R. Tobacco
301 State Rte. 10 E.
Whippany 07981
(201) 887-0800

Mr. Pipe's Smoke Shop
320 Woodbridge Center
Woodbridge 07095
(908) 636-7626

NEW MEXICO

ALBUQUERQUE

Kelly Liquors
2621 Tennessee NE
Albuquerque 87110
(505) 293-3270

Palace Cigar
San Felipe Plaza
Old Town
Albuquerque 87104
(505) 247-8780

Phantom Music
2222 Central Ave. SE
Albuquerque 87806
(505) 255-2225

Pueblo Pipe Shop & Men's Gifts
2685 Louisana Blvd. NE
Albuquerque 87110
(505) 881-7999

Stag Tobacconist of Albuquerque
11200 Montgomery Blvd.
Albuquerque 87111
(505) 237-9366

Stroller's Palace Cigar
2103 Mountain Rd.
Albuquerque 87104
(505) 247-8780

Tinder Box
6600 Menaul Blvd. NE, Ste. 381
Albuquerque 87110
(505) 883-6636

Lucas Pipe & Tobacco
Holiday Inn De Las Cruces
201 E. University
Las Cruces 88001
(505) 526-3411

Tobacco Tin
700 Telsor, #1092
Las Cruces 88001
(505) 521-3593

Siano's
2400 Sudderth Dr.
Ruidoso 88345
(505) 257-9898

SANTA FE

The Santa Fe Cigar Co.
518 Old Santa Fe Trail, #3
Santa Fe 87501
(505) 982-1044

Stag Tobacconist of New Mexico
189 Devargas Center
Santa Fe 87501
(505) 982-3242

Stroller's Palace Cigar
500 Montezuma Ave.
Santa Fe 87501
(505) 982-8780

Smoke Shop
1308 Pope St.
Silver City 88061
(505) 388-5575

Smokers Discount
407 N. California St.
Socorro 87801
(505) 835-4399

Bravo Fine Wines, Foods & Spirits
1353-A Pasel del Pueblo
Taos 87571
(505) 758-8100

NEW YORK

ALBANY

Edleez Tobacco
Stuyvesant Plaza
Albany 12203
(518) 489-6872

The Smoker
136 Washington Ave.
Albany 12210
(518) 462-1302

W. J. Coulson
420 Broadway
Albany 12207
(518) 449-7577

The Village Tobacconist
76 Deer Park Ave.
Babylon 11702
(516) 661-8406

**The Great Cove Deli &
  General Store**
139 S. Clinton Ave.
Bayshore 11706
(516) 665-1372

Bedford Wine Merchants
Empire Bldg., Rte. 22
Bedford Village 10506
(914) 234-6012

One Stop Smoke Shop
2827 Jerusalem Ave.
Belmore 11710
(516) 826-8772

BUFFALO

Bernstone's Cigar Store
275 Main St.
Buffalo 14203
(716) 852-2135

Cigar Club International
369 Franklin St., 2nd Floor
Buffalo 14202
(716) 855-1200

Sans Souci
1783 Hertel Ave.
Buffalo 14216
(716) 836-3248

Valvano's Central News
185 S. Main St.
Canandaigua 14424
(716) 394-1176

Habana Premium Cigar Shop
64-B Dunsbach Rd.
Clifton Park 12065
(518) 371-0854

Michaelson's News & Variety
222 Quide Board Rd.
Clifton Park 12065
(518) 373-8703

One Stop Smoke Shop
6214 Jericho Tpke.
Commack 11725
(516) 462-9192

Hamptons Tobacco

THE FINEST SELECTION OF CIGARS, TOBACCO AND ACCESSORIES FROM AROUND THE WORLD

Please visit one of our six locations next time you are in the area.

1. 61 Jobs Lane
    Southampton, NY
    516-28-SMOKE

2. 247 Worth Avenue
    Palm Beach, Florida
    407-835-0060

3. 55D Main Street
    Easthampton, NY
    516-329-6601

4. Mizner Park
    Boca Raton, FL

5. 119 B Main Street
    Westhampton, NY
    516-288-2401

6. 2526 Montauk Highway
    Bridgehampton, NY

Coram Smoke Shop
337 Middle County Rd.
Coram 11727
(516) 736-1959

W. E. Brown & Co.
6 W. Market St.
Corning 14830
(607) 962-2612

Kristy's Smoke Shop
1836 Deer Park Ave.
Deer Park 11729
(516) 242-7421

A & D Tobacco
2031 Jericho Tpke.
East Northport 11731
(516) 499-2330

Aladdin's Tobacco Shop
260 Main St.
East Setauket 11733
(516) 689-9418

Hamptons Tobacco & News
55-D Main St.
Easthampton 11937
(516) 329-6601

**Wolcott's Beverage &
  Tobacco Center**
1007 Union Center Hwy.
Endicott 13760
(607) 754-4261

Bahama Bob's
135 Packetts Landing
Fairport 14450
(716) 223-7490

Edleez Tobacco West
4 W. Main St.
Fredonia 14063
(716) 672-4470

Tobacco Plaza
70 Forest Ave.
Glen Cove 11542
(516) 671-9037

Main Street News
14 Ridge St.
Glens Falls 12801
(518) 792-4277

Cigar Shop Ltd.
215 Middleneck Rd.
Great Neck 11021
(516) 487-4830

Tobacco Plaza
80 Northern Blvd.
Great Neck 11021
(516) 829-7134

Colonial Drugs
100 Front St.
Greenport 11944
(516) 477-1111

Tobacco King
69 Glen Cove Rd.
Greenvale 11548
(516) 484-1875

Smoke Stacks
240 N. Broadway
Hicksville 11801
(516) 938-8347

Huntington Humidor
8 New St.
Huntington 11743
(516) 423-8599

Townhouse Smoke
517-A E. Jericho Tpke.
Huntington Station 11746
(516) 351-7131

With Pipe & Book
91 Main St.
Lake Placid 12946
(518) 523-9096

Four Bees
473 Hawkins Ave.
Lake Ronkonkoma 11779
(516) 588-9148

KV's Premium Imported Cigars
470 Hawkins Ave.
Lake Ronkonkoma 11779
(516) 467-8473

Cadalso Wine & Liquors
588 New London Rd.
Latham 12110
(518) 785-3746

Coulson's
Newton Plaza
594 Loudon Rd.
Latham 12110
(518) 785-6499

Zubair Tobacco
315 Rockaway Tpke.
Lawrence 11559
(516) 371-6213

Lindy's Smoke Shop
260 E. Sunrise Hwy.
Lindenhurst 11757
(516) 957-0287

Hiram's Gas & Convenience
7669 Morgan Rd.
Liverpool 13090
(315) 652-4558

Lynbrook Smoke Shop
834 Sunrise Hwy.
Lynbrook 11563
(516) 599-4439

Boston Rd. Cigars
164 E. Boston Post Rd.
Mamaroneck 10543
(914) 831-4006

Mamaroneck Station Liquors
137 Halstead Ave.
Mamaroneck 10543
(914) 381-4006

Young's Fine Wines & Liquors
505 Plandome Rd.
Manhasset 11030
(516) 627-8955

Merrick Smoke Shop
3-A Hicksville Rd.
Massapequa 11758
(516) 799-7000

Smokes & Things Ltd.
501 Park Blvd.
Massapequa Park 11762
(516) 799-8277

S & T Smoke Shoppe
394 Old Walt Whitman Rd.
Melville 11747
(516) 549-3928

Supersale of Melville
825 Rte. 110
Melville 11746
(516) 385-0190

Fortune Smoke Shop
1701 Merrick Rd.
Merrick 11566
(516) 868-2342

Golden Embers
23 North St.
Middletown 10940
(914) 343-3373

Tobacco Junction
428 Jericho Tpke.
Mineola 11501
(516) 741-3385

Rota's Cigar Shop
288 Broadway
Monticello 12701
(914) 794-4460

Smokers Harbor
49 S. Moger St.
Mount Kisco 10549
(914) 666-2648

Jim's Smoke Shop II
331 Rte. 25-A
Mount Sinai 11766
(516) 331-4370

NEW HYDE PARK

Bambi Stationery
2127 Hillside Ave.
New Hyde Park 11040
(516) 248-6651

Smoke Stax
412 Hillside Ave.
New Hyde Park 11040
(516) 355-0915

Smoke Stax
914 Jericho Tpke.
New Hyde Park 11040
(516) 354-1166

NEW YORK CITY

MANHATTAN

Alfred Dunhill of London
450 Park Ave.
New York 10022
(212) 753-9292

Arnold's Tobacco Shop
323 Madison Ave.
New York 10017
(212) 697-1477

Barclay - Rex Inc.
70 E. 42nd St.
New York 10165
(212) 692-9680

Barclay - Rex Inc.
7 Maiden Lane
New York 10038
(212) 962-3355

Cigar Landing
South Street Seaport, Pier 17
New York 10038
(800) 9 SMOKE5

Davidoff of Geneva
535 Madison Ave.
New York 10022
(212) 751-9060

De La Concha Tobacconist
1390 Ave. of the Americas
New York 10019
(212) 757-3167

Famous Smoke Shop
55 W. 39th St.
New York 10018
(212) 221-1408

H.R. Scott
64 Exchange Place
New York 10004
(212) 422-3046

De La Concha Tobacconists

Over the last hundred years four generations of the Melendi family have been involved in the tobacco industry, from the fields to the factory to the stores in New York City and Hartford. Whether you are a novice or a connoisseur, the expertise and service at both **De La Concha** locations will complement a wide array of premium cigars and accessories.

Featuring:

- Arturo Fuente • Avo XO • Davidoff • De La Concha
- Montecristo • Por Larranaga • Puros Indios • Opus X

And the Humidors of Elie Bleu, Mastro de Paja and Savinelli

**1390 Avenue of
the Americas
New York City
212-757-3167**

**Civic Center
Hartford, CT
203-527-4291**

Member of RTDA and TAA

International Smoke Shop
153 E. 53rd St.
New York 10022
(212) 755-8339

J.R. Tobacco
219 Broadway
New York 10007
(212) 233-6620

J.R. Tobacco
11 E. 45th St.
New York 10017
(212) 983-4160

MOM'S CIGARS

- 172 Fifth Avenue
  New York, NY 10010
  212 243 1943
  800 831 8893

- 1119 Central Park Avenue
  Scarsdale, NY 10583
  914 723 3088

- 126 East Sunrise Highway
  Valley Stream, NY 11581
  516 825 0901

Mom's Cigars
(House of Oxford Distributors)
172 5th Ave.
New York 10010
(212) 243-1996

Mom's Cigars
32 W. 22nd St.
New York 10010
(212) 924-0907

Nat Sherman
500 5th Ave.
New York 10010
(800) 692-4427, (212) 764-5000

Park Avenue Liquors
292 Madison Ave.
New York 10017
(212) 685-2442

QC Cigar Company, Inc.
862 6th Ave., 2nd Floor
New York 10001
(212) 682-0660

The Stock Exchange Luncheon Club
11 Wall St., 4th Floor
New York 10005
(212) 344-6855

BROOKLYN

Barney's Cold Cut Rate
76 Court St.
Brooklyn 11201
(718) 875-8355

86 Smoke Shop
1953 86th St.
Brooklyn 11214
(718) 714-8289

Lorina's Tobacco Shop
7909 15th Ave.
Brooklyn 11228
(718) 232-6336

News Pavilion Inc.
1516 Kings Hwy.
Brooklyn 11229
(718) 375-7304

1929 Avenue U Inc.
1929 Ave. U
Brooklyn 11229
(718) 934-1451

QUEENS

The Gift Source
90-15 Queens Blvd.
Elmhurst 11373
(718) 592-0400

Max's Smoke Shop
253-22 Union Tpke.
Floral Park 11004
(718) 343-5000

Puff n' Stuff
161-10 Northern Blvd.
Flushing 11358
(718) 321-3908

Maxi's Smoke Shop
253-22 Union Tpke.
Glen Oaks 11004
(718) 343-5000

Maspeth News
69-28 Grand Ave.
Maspeth 11378
(718) 397-5633

STATEN ISLAND

Empire Smoke Shop
1398 Forest Ave.
Staten Island 10302
(718) 815-4444

Tobacco & Gift Emporium
3277 Richmond Ave.
Staten Island 10312
(718) 948-2899

Mario's
2304 Pine Ave.
Niagara Falls 14301
(716) 282-4391

Supersale of Babylon
1205 Deer Park Ave.
North Babylon 11703
(516) 242-6397

Country Tobacco
765 Rte. 25-A
Northport 11768
(516) 261-3165

Supersale of Northport
440 Ft. Salonga Rd.
Northport 11768
(516) 368-6397

Nyack Tobacco Co.
140 Main St.
Nyack 10960
(914) 358-9300

Stogey's Fine Cigar & Tobacco
112 Main St.
Nyack 10960
(914) 348-0434

Tobacco Connection
3224 Long Beach Rd.
Oceanside 11572
(516) 763-4300

Jim's Smoke Shop
582 Sunrise Hwy. W.
Patchogue 11772
(516) 289-6405

The Brown Leaf
63 E. Main St.
Pawling 12564
(914) 855-0141

Hickey's
19 S. Main St.
Pittsford 14534
(716) 385-1780

Pittsford Village Market
57 N. Main St.
Pittsford 14534
(716) 264-1060

Lee's Smoke Shop
553 Port Washington Blvd.
Port Washington 11050
(516) 883-3039

The Brewery
11 Market St.
Potsdam 13676
(315) 265-0422

O'Leary's Smoke Shop
Poughkeepsie Plaza Mall
South Rd.
Poughkeepsie 12601
(914) 471-5266

Quogue Country Market
Jessup Ave.
Quogue 11959
(516) 653-4191

United Smoke Shop
2 E. Market St.
Rhinebeck 12572
(914) 876-7185

ROCHESTER

Dewey Ave. Smoke Shop
820 Dewey Ave.
Rochester 14613
(716) 458-8824

Havana House
365 N. Washington St.
Rochester 14625
(716) 586-0620

House of Bacchus
1050 Ridge Rd. E.
Rochester 14621
(716) 266-6390

J & J Newstand
428 Greece Ridge Center
Rochester 14026
(716) 227-0270

J & J Newstand
231 Irondequoit Mall Dr.
Rochester 14622
(716) 266-1870

Park Oxford Cigar Company
365 Park Ave.
Rochester 14607
(716) 271-3850

The Smoke Shop
149 State St.
Rochester 14614
(716) 454-2180

Twelve Corners Apothecary
1832 Monroe Ave.
Rochester 14618
(716) 244-8600

P & P Smoke Shop
600 Merrick Rd.
Rockville Center 11570
(516) 536-1513

Trinity East Smoke Shop
215 Sunrise Hwy.
Rockville Center 11570
(516) 678-1822

To The Max Enterprises
366 Roslyn Rd.
Roslyn Heights 11577
(516) 621-0954

Saratoga Cigar & Pipe
130 S. Broadway
Saratoga 12866
(578) 374-6433

Cigar Box of Scarsdale
44 E. Parkway
Scarsdale 10583
(914) 722-4300

Mom's Cigars
1119 Central Park Ave.
Scarsdale 10583
(914) 723-3088

Orion Boutique
169 Jay St.
Schenectady 12305
(518) 346-4902

Street Corner News
Rotterdam Square Mall
93 W. Campbell Rd., Ste. J-142
Schenectady 12306
(518) 346-2796

Fortune Tobacco
281 Middle Country Rd.
Selden 11784
(516) 732-1701

Doc James Tobacco
Rte. 132
Shrub Oak 10588
(800) 41 SMOKE

Mr. Tobacco Store
126 E. Main St.
Smithtown 11787
(516) 724-7463

Bellezia Tobacco Shop
4549 Main St.
Snyder 14226
(716) 839-5381

Hamptons Tobacco & News
61 Job's Lane
Southampton 11968
(516) 287-6653

Market Place Smoke Shop
4924 Spring Valley Market Place
Spring Valley 10977
(914) 356-3717

Maxim Smoke
406 Jericho Tpke
Syosset 11791
(516) 921-4513

SYRACUSE

Kieffer's Cigar Store
851 N. Salinas St.
Syracuse 13208
(315) 475-3988

Mallard Tobacconist
208 Walton St.
Syracuse 13202
(315) 475-5839

Olympic News Gallery
441 S. Salinas St.
Syracuse 13202
(315) 424-1336

Rocky's Newstand
447 N. Salinas St.
Syracuse 13203
(315) 422-1997

Balls Card Shop
2 Lafayette St.
Utica 13502
(315) 733-7005

Pipes Unlimited
19 Auburn Ave.
Utica 13501
(315) 735-2588

Mom's Cigars
126 E. Sunrise Hwy.
Valley Stream 11581
(516) 825-0901

Thruway Shopping Center
78 Oak St.
Walden 12586
(914) 778-3535

Tobacco Junction
3210 Sunrise Hwy.
Wantagh 11793
(516) 783-8646

Fortune Smoke Stax
485 Hempstead Tpke.
West Hempstead 11552
(516) 481-0280

Smokers Haven
1167 Union
West Seneca 14224
(716) 675-6195

Fortune Smoke Shop
527 Old Country Rd.
Westbury 11590
(516) 997-8109

John David Ltd.
Galleria Mall
100 Main St.
White Plains 10601
(914) 761-0180

Hamptons Tobacco
121-C Main St.
Westhampton
(516) 288-2401

Tinder Box
8212 Transit Rd.
Williamsville 14221
(716) 689-2914

Broadway Humidor
1062 Broadway
Woodmere 11598
(516) 295-2626

NORTH CAROLINA

Bonnie's Little Corner
6 Patton Ave.
Asheville 28801
(704) 252-1679

Pipes Ltd.
3 S. Tunnel
Asheville 28805
(704) 298-2392

International House Ltd.
108 Holly Hill Mall
Burlington 27215
(910) 228-0024

CHARLOTTE

Arthur's Wine Shop
Belk Department Store
4400 Sharon Rd.
Charlotte 28211
(704) 366-8610

The Humidor
516 Overstreet Mall
Charlotte 28202
(704) 334-3449

McCranies Pipe Shop
4143 Park Rd.
Charlotte 28209
(704) 523-8554

Tinder Box
South Park Mall
4400 Sharon Rd.
Charlotte 28211
(704) 366-5164

Tinder Box
Eastland Mall
5521 Central Ave.
Charlotte 28212
(704) 568-8798

Island Tobacco II
Timbuk II, Ste. 100-H
Corolla 27927
(919) 453-8163

Tinder Box
242 S. Square Mall
4001 Chapel Hill Blvd.
Durham 27707
(919) 489-7765

Anstead Tobacco
337 Cross Creek Mall
Fayetteville 28303
(919) 864-5705

Tinder Box
Carolina Plaza
11025 Carolina Plaza Pkwy.
Fineville 28134
(704) 542-6115

G.S.O. Wine Warehouse
2212 Battleground Ave.
Greensboro 27408
(910) 288-2002

Pleasures & Treasures
221 Four Seasons Town Center
Greensboro 27407
(910) 855-1301

Tobacco USA
1305 Coliseum Blvd.
Greensboro 27403
(910) 292-5130

Onix Tobacco Shop
505 S. Evans St.
Greenville 27834
(919) 413-0900

Sir Tom's Tobacco Emporium
129 W. 4th Ave.
Hendersonville 28792
(704) 697-7753

Pleasures & Treasures
Oak Hollow Mall
921 Eastchester Dr., S-2340
High Point 27262
(910) 886-8666

Highlands Emporium
Towns Square
Main St.
Highland 28741
(704) 526-0433

Northwood Tobacco
Northwood Shopping Center
Jacksonville 28540
(910) 455-0629

Island Tobacco I
5000 S. Croatan Hwy.
Nags Head 27959
(800) 254-0926

RALEIGH

Harris Teeter
Cameron Village Shop Center
501 Oberlin Rd.
Raleigh 27601
(919) 828-9216

Pipes by George
1209 Hillsborough St.
Raleigh 27603
(919) 829-1167

Tinder Box
Crabtree Valley Mall
4325 Glenwood Ave.
Raleigh 27612
(919) 787-1310

Tobacconist of Raleigh
3901 Capitol Blvd., Ste. 171
Raleigh 27604
(919) 954-0020

The Wine Merchant
1214 Ridge Rd.
Raleigh 27607
(919) 828-6969

Import Gourmet & Spirits
106 Carthage St.
Sanford 27330
(919) 708-5555

J.R. Tobacco
I-95 & Rte. 70
Selma 27576
(919) 965-5055

J.R. Tobacco
1515 E. Broad St.
Statesville 28677
(704) 872-5300

Smokey Joes Inc.
145 Ebenezer Lane
Statesville 28677
(704) 876-0690

Davis and Sons Smokers Emporium
Longleaf Mall/Shipyard B
Wilmington 28403
(910) 791-6688

WINSTON-SALEM

Harris Teeter
420-22 S. Stratford Rd.
Winston-Salem 27103
(910) 723-2305

Harris Teeter
1955 N. Peace Haven Rd.
Winston-Salem 27104
(910) 760-0116

Pipes Etc.
Thruway Shopping Center
385 Lower Mall Dr.
Winston-Salem 27103
(910) 723-1269

Tinder Box
3320 Silas Creek Pkwy., Ste. 208
Winston-Salem 27103
(910) 765-9511

NORTH DAKOTA

Happy Harry's Bottle Shop
1125 19th Ave. N.
Fargo 58102
(701) 235-4661

Smoke Shop
1525 S. University Dr.
Fargo 58103
(701) 298-7824

GRAND FORKS

Happy Harry's Bottle Shop
2051 32nd Ave. S.
Grand Forks 58208
(701) 780-0902

Happy Harry's Bottle Shop
2215 Gateway Dr.
Grand Forks 58201
(701) 772-2671

Pipe Land
South Fork Plaza
1826-P S. Washington
Grand Forks 58201
(701) 772-2373

Market Place Liquor
1930 S. Broadway
Minot 58701
(701) 839-7580

Oak Park Liquors
326 16th St.
Minot 58703
(701) 838-1529

OHIO

The Pipe Rack
2200 Manchester Rd.
Akron 44314
(216) 745-9022

Village Tobacconist
Summit Mall
3265 W. Market, #202
Akron 44333
(216) 864-3929

Plaza Book & Smoke Shop
6000 Mahoning Ave.
Austintown 44515
(216) 799-2626

Tinder Box
2727 Fairfield Commons, #103
Beavercreek 45431
(513) 429-1172

Tobacco Wharf
1308 N. Fairfield Rd.
Beavercreek 45432
(513) 426-0633

Cigarette Express
4605 Market St.
Boardman 44512
(216) 782-0700

Plaza Book & Smoke Shop
271 Boardman Canfield Rd.
Boardman 44512
(216) 726-9493

Briarpatch
2870 Whipple Ave. NW
Canton 44708
(216) 477-2511

Tobacco Pouch
26 N. Main St.
Chagrin Falls 44022
(216) 247-5365

CINCINNATI

Carrousel Tobacco Shoppe
8001 Reading Rd.
Cincinatti 45237
(513) 821-5350

Cincinnati Tobacconist
617-D Vine St.
Cincinnati 45202
(513) 621-9932

Private Smoking Club
3195 Linwood Ave.
Cincinnati 45208
(513) 321-3278

Straus Tobacconist
410 Walnut Ave.
Cincinnati 45202
(513) 621-3388

Tinder Box
Tri-County Mall
11700 Princeton Pike
Cincinnati 45246
(513) 671-8966

CLEVELAND

Back Door Beverage
656 E. 185 St.
Cleveland 44119
(216) 383-0900

Cousin Cigar Co.
1828 Euclid Ave.
Cleveland 44115
(216) 781-9390

Dad's Smoke Shop
17112 Lorain Ave.
Cleveland 44111
(216) 671-3663

Huntington Building Cigar Store
Huntington Bank Building
925 Euclid Ave.
Cleveland 44115
(216) 621-5420

Old Erie Tobacco Co.
The Arcade, #150
401 Euclid Ave.
Cleveland 44114
(216) 861-0487

Sam Klein Cigar Co.
1834 E. 6th St.
Cleveland 44114
(216) 621-2673

COLUMBUS

Barclay Pipe & Tobacco
1677 W. Lane Ave., M-12
Columbus 43221
(614) 486-4243

Humidor Plus
6157 Cleveland Ave.
Columbus 43231
(614) 891-9483

Pace-Hi Carry Out
3179 N. High St.
Columbus 43202
(614) 267-1918

Pipes & Pleasures
4244 E. Main St.
Columbus 43213
(614) 235-6422

Smokers Haven
1097 Bethel Rd.
Columbus 43220
(614) 538-9534

Tinder Box
4236 Westland Mall
Columbus 43228
(614) 276-2904

Tobacco Discounters
208 Graceland Blvd.
Columbus 43214
(614) 781-0050

Vino's
6072 Busch Blvd.
Columbus 43229
(614) 431-9463

DAYTON

Kettering Pipe & Tobacco
2970 Far Hills Ave.
Dayton 45419
(513) 294-2100

Smoker's Paradise & Coffee Co.
3200 N. Main St.
Dayton 45406
(513) 277-8556

Tinder Box
2700 Miamisburg-Centerville Rd.
Dayton 45459
(513) 433-2841

Tobacco Man
4958 Springboro Rd.
Dayton 45439
(513) 298-6751

Prem Cigar Company
5187 Willowgrove Place S.
Dublin 43017
(614) 793-8012

Cigarette Express Calcutta
16485 St. Claire Ave.
East Liverpool 43920
(216) 385-3001

Boston Stoker Inc.
40 N. Broad
Fairborn 45324
(513) 878-6609

Jungle Jim's Market Inc.
5440 Dixie Hwy.
Fairfield 45014
(513) 829-1918

Girard Book & News
101 N. State St.
Girard 44420
(216) 545-8356

T.W. News Center
57 Hubbard-Brookfield Rd.
Hubbard 44425
(216) 534-2700

Doc's Smoke Shop
520 McClure Rd.
Lebanon 45036
(513) 932-5376

City News
738 Broadway
Lorain 44052
(216) 246-9097

Tobacco Road
12 S. Main St.
Mansfield 44902
(419) 522-6218

Jo Vann's Tobacco Shop
1438 Som Center Rd.
Mayfield Heights 44124
(216) 442-4775

Downtown Tobacco
44 Public Square
Medina 44256
(216) 722-9096

Molinari's Food & Wine
8900 Mentor Ave.
Mentor 44060
(216) 974-2750

Alberini's
1201 Youngstown Rd.
Niles 44446
(216) 652-5895

Carey's Smokeshop
7245 Whipple Ave. NW
North Canton 44720
(216) 494-6699

Tinder Box
434 Great Northern Mall
North Olmsted 44070
(216) 777-1066

Wild Berry
15 W. High St.
Oxford 45056
(513) 523-4345

Parma Heights Smoke Shop
6647 Pearl Rd.
Parma Heights 44130
(216) 886-3449

Knobby Shop
333 N. Main St.
Piqua 45356
(513) 773-0081

Arisen Merchandise
26 W. Main St.
Springfield 45506
(513) 323-1791

Herald Square Cigar Store
183 N. 4th St.
Steubenville 43952
(614) 282-2241

El Fumidor
3065 W. Bancrost, Ste. B
Toledo 43606
(419) 535-9990

Port Royale
3301 W. Central
Toledo 43606
(419) 537-1491

City News
135 S. Market St.
Wooster 44691
(216) 262-5151

Cigarette Express
3814 Belmont Ave.
Youngstown 44502
(216) 759-0034

OKLAHOMA

Francesca
737 W. Danforth
Edmond 73003
(404) 341-6566

Dave's Pipe & Tobacco Shop
216 W. Maple St.
Enid 73701
(405) 237-1666

Plantations
Sooner Fashion Mall
3335 W. Main
Norman 73072
(405) 364-5152

Royal Pipe & Tobacco
105 E. Boyd St.
Norman 73069
(405) 364-5151

OKLAHOMA CITY

ABC Tobacco
4508 S. May Ave.
Oklahoma City 73119
(405) 685-1716

Jose's Party Stand
10902 N. Penn Ave.
Oklahoma City 73120
(405) 752-7380

Plantations
Crossroads Mall
7000 Crossroads Blvd., Ste. 1128
Oklahoma City 73149
(405) 631-2511

R & K Cigars
Quail Plaza Shopping Center
10904-J N. May Ave.
Oklahoma City 73120
(405) 752-2772

Tobacco Exchange
French Market Mall
2828 NW 63rd
Oklahoma City 73116
(405) 843-1688

The Tobacco Room
7400 N. May Ave.
Oklahoma City 73116
(405) 843-1010

Potawatomi Tribal Store
214 E. Walnut
Pecunsch 74873
(405) 598-2012

Ted's Pipe Shop
2002 Utica Square
Tulsa 74114
(918) 742-4996

Tobacco Pouch
5800 S. Lewis Ste., 117
Tulsa 74105
(918) 742-1660

OREGON

OREGON

Timber Valley Tobaccos
3355 SW Cedar Hills Blvd.
Beaverton 97005
(503) 644-3837

Specialty Cigar
550 SW Industrial Way, #28
Bend 97709
(541) 389-1001

The Briar Shoppe
278 Valley River Center
Eugene 97401
(503) 343-4738

Browser's Books
1591 Willamette St.
Eugene 97401
(503) 302-9209

News & Smokes
1330 NW 6th St.
Grants Pass 97526
(503) 479-3790

Rick's Smoke Shop
124 S. 11th St.
Klamath Falls 97601
(503) 884-0313

News & Smokes
259-C Barnett Rd.
Medford 97501
(503) 779-3900

News & Smokes
2295 W. Main
Medford 97526
(503) 779-5449

Cascade News & Tobacco
11103 SE Main St.
Milwaukee 97222
(503) 786-3607

Pappy's Tobacco Road
910-A N. Coast Hwy.
Newport 97635
(503) 265-8384

PORTLAND

Bertha Station News
6446 SW Capital Hwy.
Portland 97201
(503) 246-6225

Burlingame Grocery
8502 SW Terwilliger Blvd.
Portland 97219
(503) 246-0711

Cascade News & Tobacco
528 SW Madison
Portland 97204
(503) 790-9045

82nd Ave Tobacco & Pipe
400 SE 82nd Ave.
Portland 97216
(503) 255-9987

Paul's Trading Co.
9986 SE Washington St.
Portland 97216
(503) 255-4471

Paul's Trading Co.
1409 Jantzen Beach Center
Portland 97217
(503) 283-4924

Rich's Cigar Store
706 NW 23rd Ave.
Portland 97210
(503) 227-6907

Rich's Cigar Store
801 SW Alder St.
Portland 97205
(503) 228-1700

Stroheckers
2855 SW Patton Rd.
Portland 97201-1699
(503) 223-7391

T. Whittaker Tobaccos
1123 Lloyd Center
Portland 97232
(503) 654-4812

The Tobacco Shack
6835 N. Fessenden
Portland 97203
(503) 286-4527

Redmond Smoke & Gift
245 SW 6th
Redmond 97756
(503) 923-6307

News & Smokes
457 NW Garden Valley
Roseburg 97470
(503) 673-1601

Salem's Vintage House
559 Court St. NE
Salem 97301
(503) 363-4014

Tinder Box
9614 SW Washington Square Rd.
Tigard 97223
(503) 639-8776

PENNSYLVANIA

Tobacco Taverne
519 E. 25th Ave.
Altoona 16601
(814) 949-9007

Tinder Box Internationale
3 Bala Plaza East, Ste. 102
Bala Cynwyd 19004
(610) 668-4220

Tobacco World
638-B Rostraver Rd.
Belle Vernon 15012
(412) 930-0112

Keystone News
2854 Street Rd.
Bensalem 19020
(215) 638-3605

Pat's News
327 S. New St.
Bethlehem 18015
(215) 865-6233

Tinder Box
3926 Linden St.
Bethlehem 18017
(610) 882-9195

Johnsons Pipe Shop
151 S. Hanover St.
Carlisle 17013
(717) 243-8260

Country Food Market
203 W. State St.
Doylestown 18901
(215) 348-8845

Lu-Co
247 N. Hampton St.
Easton 18042
(610) 258-3561

Silicone Indian Cigars
1213 Washington St.
Easton 18042
(610) 515-9991

Tobacco Land
330 Mill Creek Mall
Erie 16565
(814) 868-8413

Magikal Garden
1174 Wyoming Ave.
Exeter 18643
(717) 655-0924

SMOKIN' JOE'S
TOBACCO SHOP, INC.

ROUTE 209 NORTH
EAST STROUDSBURG, PENNSYLVANIA

INTRODUCING:

CAOBA

MANUFACTURED BY

Monte Cristi De Tobacos, e.x.a.
Dominican Republic

Available in the following sizes, boxes of 24

Coaba #1 6 3/4 x 48	Coaba #5 4 x 42
Coaba #2 6 1/4 x 46	Coaba Pan #1 7 1/2 x 40
Coaba #3 5 1/2 x 42	Coaba Pan #2 6 3/4 x 38
Coaba #4 5 x 44	Coaba Pan #3 6 x 38

OFFERING A FULL LINE OF PREMIUM CIGARS

CALL 1-800-441-7584

We accept American Express, Visa, Mastercard

Ichabod's News
511 E. Lincoln Hwy.
Exton 19341
(610) 363-5908

J.M. Cigars
27 Marchwoood Rd.
Exton 19341
(610) 363-3063

Smoke Shop
114 S. Easton Rd.
Glenside 19038
(215) 886-7415

Jernigan's Tobacco Village
Westmoreland Mall
Rte. 30
Greensburg 15601
(412) 838-1090

Smokin' Joe's Tobacco Shop
Rte. 11
Great Bend (Halsted) 18822
(717) 879-8059

HARRISBURG

Hilton Hotel & Towers Gift Shop
1 N. 2nd St.
Harrisburg 17102
(717) 579-0674

Pipe Den
Harrisburg E. Mall
Harrisburg 17111
(717) 564-8425

Tinder Box
219 N. 2nd St.
Harrisburg 17101
(717) 232-7166

Burdicks Hatboro News
206 S. York Rd.
Hatboro 19040
(215) 675-9960

Tinder Box Internationale
391 W. Lancaster Ave.
Haverford 19041
(610) 896-4511

Quik Pick & Pak, Inc.
217 Lourel Mall
Hazleton 18201
(717) 459-3099

Ken's Cigar & Tobacco
517 Allegheny
Hollidaysburg 16648
(814) 695-6650

Widmers Tobacco Shop
Macdade Mall
Holmes 19043
(610) 586-3857

Pavilion News
Bent Fox Pavilion
Jenkintown 19046
(215) 885-1881

Ye Olde Tobacco Barrel
King of Prussia Plaza
King of Prussia 19406
(610) 265-4544

Tobacco Palace, Inc.
311 Park City Center
Lancaster 17601
(717) 397-7569

Tobacco Road
154 N. Prince St.
Lancaster 17603
(717) 293-8688

Tobacco Land
Lebanon Valley Mall
422 W. Cumberland St.
Lebanon 17042
(717) 228-0262

Wingenroth Pipe Shop
638 Cumberland St.
Lebanon 17042
(717) 273-7727

The General Store
5323 New Falls Rd.
Levittown 19056
(215) 547-7762

Tobacco Mart
900 Market St.
Leymone 17043
(717) 975-0994

Rose's Newstand
117 S. Olive
Media 19063
(215) 565-9015

The County Boys
624 W. Herford St.
Milford 18337
(717) 296-5000

Jernigan's Tobacco Village
Monroeville Mall
Monroeville 15146
(412) 372-4114

Tobacco Outlet
Rte. 63 (¾ mi. West of Rte. 309)
Montgomeryville 18936
(215) 643-2575

Pennsylvania News & Tobacco
Mill Pond Shopping Center
Morrisville 19067
(215) 295-4004

United Cut-Rate Stores
19 E. Bridge St.
Morrisville 19067
(215) 295-3835

Klafter's Cigar Express
216 N. Beaver St.
New Castle 16101
(800) 801-2697, (412) 658-6561

Neds Cigar Store
4 S. State St.
Newtown 18940
(215) 968-6337

Black Horse Cigars
1515 Ridge Pike
Norristown 19401
(610) 279-7676

Hillcrest Tobacco
120 W. Germantown Pike
Norristown 19401
(610) 279-8610

Discount Tobacco Shop
1129 Main St.
Peckville 18452
(717) 383-6944

PHILADELPHIA

Artifax
2446 Cottman Ave.
Philadelphia 19149
(215) 331-0306

Chestnut Smoke Shop
27 S. 8th St.
Philadelphia 19106
(215) 923-1699

Harry's Smoke Shop
15 N. 3rd St.
Philadelphia 19106
(215) 925-4770

Holts Cigar Store, Inc.
1522 Walnut St.
Philadelphia 19102
(215) 732-8500

J.R. Cigars
1518 Sansom St.
Philadelphia 19102
(215) 563-9850

Max's Tobacconists
The Pipe Rack
8433-C Germantown Ave.
Philadelphia 19118
(215) 242-3625

Tobacco Junction
9961 Bustleton Ave.
Philadelphia 19115
(215) 464-2484

Tobacco Village
NE Plaza, #231
7300 Bustleton Ave.
Philadelphia 19152
(215) 745-7040

Twin Smoke Shop
1537 S. 10th St.
Philadelphia 19147
(215) 334-0970

Continental Smoke Shop
2210 Murray Ave.
Pittsburgh 15217
(412) 422-4444

Jernigan's Tobacco Village
The Galleria
1500 Washington Rd.
Pittsburgh 15228
(412) 531-5881

Poor Richard's
Freight House Shops
Station Square
Pittsburgh 15219
(412) 281-1133

Ross Park News
1000 Ross Park Mall Dr.
Pittsburgh 15237
(412) 366-0160

Save-More Beer & Pop Warehouse
4516 Browns Hill Rd.
Pittsburgh 15217
(412) 421-8550

Smoke Signals
120 S. River St.
Plains 18705
(717) 822-5058

Tobacco Outlet
201 Station Rd.
Quakertown 18951
(215) 538-3665

Smokin' Joe's Tobacco Shop
312 N. Elmira St.
Sayre 18840
(717) 888-9332

Markowitz Bros
256 Wyoming Ave.
Scranton 18503
(717) 342-0315

Montage Tobacco
632 Davis St.
Scranton 18505
(717) 342-3388

One Stop Tobacco
725 S. Main Ave.
Scranton 18503
(717) 343-3393

Ye Olde Tobacco Barrel
Susquehanna Valley Mall
Selingrove 17870
(717) 374-9453

The Cigar Shop
231 E. Beaver Ave.
State College 16801
(814) 231-0828

Tobacco Taverne
256 E. Calder Way
State College 16801
(814) 237-8252

Lancaster Cigar Aficionado
1 Historic Dr.
Strasburg 17579
(717) 687-7691

Pipe Shop
23 Garrett Rd.
Upper Darby 19082
(610) 352-8478

The Smoke Shop
Franklin Mall
Washington 15301
(412) 228-3266

Smokin' Joe's Tobacco Shop
RR 2 Box 41-B1
Waymart 18472
(717) 282-9085

Tinder Box
Century III Mall
3075 Clairton Rd.
West Mifflin 15122
(412) 653-1177

Collins Tobacco
205 Lehigh Valley Mall
Whitehall 18052
(215) 264-7911

Tobacco Village
Outside Shop
598 Whitehall Mall
Whitehall 18052
(610) 264-5371

Leo Matus
46 Public Square
Wilkes Barre 18701
(717) 822-3613

Tobacco Center
21 Church St.
Williamsport 17701
(717) 322-7766

Tobacco Land
Berkshire Mall
Wyomissing 19610
(610) 372-6571

Custom Blends
2559 S. Queen St.
York 17402
(717) 741-4972

Hain's Pipe Shop
225 S. George St.
York 17403
(717) 843-2237

R H O D E   I S L A N D

Humidor
1500 Oaklawn Ave.
Cranston 02920
(401) 463-5949

Barbato & Sons Candy Co.
65 Newport Ave.
East Providence 02916
(401) 434-3004

Dapper Dare's Smoke Shop
1465 Atwood Ave.
Johnston 02919
(401) 751-8499

Bag Piper Smoke Shoppe
8-A Pier Market Place
Nargansett 02882
(401) 783-0555

Wellington Square Liquors
580 Thames St.
Newport 02840
(800) 898-WINE

Cooper's Smoke Shop
742 Broadway
Pawtucket 02860
(401) 727-3198

Moriarty Liquor Locker
624 Park Ave.
Portsmouth 02871
(401) 683-4441

P R O V I D E N C E

Headlines
270 Wickenden St.
Providence 02903
(401) 274-6397

Olde Smoke Shoppe
130 Westminster St.
Providence 02903
(401) 272-4699

Red Carpet Smoke Shop
108½ Waterman St.
Providence 02906
(401) 421-4499

Red Lantern Smoke Shop
1903 Mineral Spring Ave.
Providence 02904
(401) 353-4860

Sir Winston Tobacco Emporium
341 S. Main St.
Providence 02903
(401) 861-5700

Town Wine & Spirits
179 Newport Ave.
Rumford 02916
(401) 434-4563

SOUTH CAROLINA

Pipe Dreams
Aiken Mall
2441 Whiskey Rd. S.
Aiken 29803
(803) 642-0080

Harris Teeter
290 E. Bay St.
Charleston 29401
(803) 722-6821

The Smoking Lamp
197 E. Bay St.
Charleston 29401
(803) 577-7339

Tinder Box Internationale
177 Meeting St.
Charleston 29401
N/A

Intermezzo
2015 Devine St.
Columbia 29205
(803) 799-2276

Boda Pipes
McAllister Square Mall
225 S. Pleasantburg
Greenville 29607
(803) 242-1545

Leaf n' Match
5 Hammond Square
233 N. Main St
Greenville 29601
(803) 271-9080

The Lodge
Hilton Head Plaza, 7-C
Greenwood Dr.
Hilton Head 29928
(803) 842-8966

Low Country Outfitters
1533 Fording Island Rd., Ste. 316
Hilton Head 29926
(803) 837-6100

Hilton Head Brewing Co.
Hilton Head Plaza
7-C Greenwood Dr.
Hilton Head Island 29928
(803) 783-2739

MYRTLE BEACH

Owen's Liquors, Inc.
8000 N. King's Hwy.
Myrtle Beach 29572
(803) 449-6835

Tinder Box
2501 N. Kings Hwy.
Myrtle Beach 29577
(803) 626-2654

Tinder Box
10177 N. Kings Hwy.
Myrtle Beach 29577
(803) 272-2336

Smokey's Tobacco Shop
5720 Northwood Mall
North Charleston 29418
(803) 553-4447

General Store
1985 E. Main
Spartanburg 29307
(803) 585-6328

The Tobacco Merchant
1600 Reidville Rd.
Spartanburg 29301
(803) 587-1566

SOUTH DAKOTA

Doc James Tobacco
668 Main St.
Deadwood 57732
(605) 578-1969

Miller Liquors
101 Military Rd.
North Sioux City 57049
(605) 232-4616

Eastwood Smokeshop
136 S. Phillips Ave.
Sioux Falls 57102
(605) 332-2701

Tobacco Road Smoke Shop
901 Broadway
Yankton 57078
(605) 665-7057

TENNESSEE

Tobacco Harbor
6942 Doefield Trail
Bartlett 38135
(901) 382-8286

CHATTANOOGA

Chattanooga Billiard Club, Downtown
725½ Cherry St.
Chattanooga 37402
(615) 267-7740

Chattanooga Billiard Club, East
110 Jordan Dr.
Chattanooga 37421
(615) 499-3883

Signal Mountain Tobacco and Beer Mart
425 Signal Mountain
Chattanooga 37405
(615) 266-9453

Smokin' Joe's
Ringgold Rd.
Chattanooga 37412
(423) 490-0344

Tinder Box
2100 Hamilton Place Blvd., #215
Chattanooga 37421
(423) 894-7843

Tobacco Mart
4011 C-3 Brainerd Rd.
Chattanooga 37411
(615) 493-9056

Briar & Bean
Governor's Square Mall
Clarksville 37040
(615) 552-6465

Fred Stokers & Sons, Inc.
Hwy. 89 S.
Dresden 38225
(901) 364-5419

Smokin' Joe's
6501 Ring Gold Rd.
East Ridge 37412
(423) 490-0344

Street Corner News
1800 Galleria Blvd., Ste. 3110
Franklin 37067
(615) 771-7278

Uptown's Smoke Shop
1745 Galleria Blvd.
Franklin 37064
(615) 771-7036

The Gatlin-Burlier Tobacconist
603 Skyline Dr.
Gatlinburg 37738
(615) 436-9177

Shamrock Beverage & Tobacco
300 W. Walnut St.
Johnson City 37604
(615) 926-8511

Plugh's Tobacco Rd.
325 Clinchfield St.
Kingsport 37660
(615) 246-5417

KNOXVILLE

Jim's Pipes & Gifts
6925-B Maynardville Hwy.
Knoxville 37918
(615) 922-3914

Smokey's Pipe & Tobacco
143 Montvue Center
Knoxville 37919
(423) 693-8371

Smokin' Joe's
5236 N. Broadway
Knoxville 37918
(423) 281-2002

Smokin' Joe's
6110 Papermill Rd.
Knoxville 37919
(423) 584-9010

The Smoke Shop
1011 South Galitin Pike
Madison 37115
(615) 860-8253

MEMPHIS

Select Smoke Shop
5100 Poplar Ave., Ste. 163
Memphis 38137
(905) 685-7788

Tinder Box
4477 Mall Of Memphis
Memphis 38118
(901) 795-0360

The Tobacco Bowl
152 Madison Ave.
Memphis 38103
(901) 525-2310

Tobacco Corner, Ltd.
669 S. Mendenhall
Memphis 38117
(901) 682-3326

Panther Pipe Shop
2037 S. Economy Rd.
Morristown 37813
(615) 581-7473

Three-Ten Pipe Shop
109 E. Main St.
Murfreesboro 37130
(615) 893-3100

NASHVILLE

Arcade Smoke Shop
11 Arcade
Nashville 37219
(615) 726-8031

Elliston Place Pipe & Tobacco
2204 Elliston Place, H (Upstairs)
Nashville 37203
(615) 320-7624

Mosko's Inc.
2204 Elliston Place (Downstairs)
Nashville 37203
(615) 327-2658

Tobacco Road Smoke Shop
Harding Mall
4050 Nolansville Rd.
Nashville 37211
(615) 331-7139

Uptowns Smoke Shop
3900 Hillsboro Rd.
Nashville 37215
(615) 292-6866

TEXAS

Bradley's Pipe & Gift Gallery
202 Cypress St.
Abilene 79601
(915) 673-9215

Cigar Shop & More
4285 Beltline Rd.
Addison 75244
(214) 661-9136

Cowan Pipe & Tobacco
Wolftin Square N.
2497 I-40 W.
Amarillo 79109
(806) 355-2821

The Smoke Shop
2201 S. Western St.
30 Western Plaza
Amarillo 79109
(806) 353-6331

ARLINGTON

Pipe Dream Cigar & Tobacco
1308 S. Cooper St.
Arlington 76013
(817) 469-8986

Pipeline Tobacco
839 NE Green Oaks Blvd.
Arlington 76006
(817) 461-7473

Tobacco Lane
2911 E. Division St., #318
Arlington 76011
(817) 640-3210

Tobacco Lane
Parks Mall, Ste. 2136
3811 S. Cooper
Arlington 76015
(817) 784-0022

Smoke Signals
414 E. Maine St.
Atlanta 75551
(903) 796-8893

AUSTIN

Austin Wine & Spirits
5505 Balconies
Austin 78731
(512) 458-2244

BR News
3208 Guadalupe
Austin 78705
(512) 454-9110

Cedar Valley Liquor
12009 Hwy. 290 W., #2
Austin 78737
(512) 288-4937

Cigar Palace
121 W. 8th St.
Austin 78701
(512) 472-2277

Pipe World
2160 Highland Mall
Austin 78752
(512) 451-3713

Ruta-Maya
218 W. 4th St.
Austin 78701
(512) 472-9637

Texas Tobacconist
115-T E. 6th
Austin 78701
(512) 479-8741

Twin Liquors
8030 Mesa Dr.
Austin 78731
(512) 346-1861

Wiggy's
1130 W. 6th
Austin 78703
(512) 474-9463

Gray's Discount Tobacco Store
1412 Chico Hwy.
Bridgeport 76426
(817) 683-6592

Alessandra Imports
1867 Briarcrest Dr.
Bryan 77802
(409) 774-0044

JJ's Package
1219 N. Texas Ave.
Bryan 77803
(409) 822-1042

JJ's Package
1600 S. Texas Ave.
College Station 77840
(409) 693-2627

Cigar Specialist
10123 Stidham Blvd.
Conroe 77302
(800) CIGAR 66

Mr. Smoke's
1029 N. Loop 336 W.
Conroe 77301
(409) 760-2727

International Tobacconist
6710 White Wing
Corpus Christi 78413
(512) 880-4100

Tobacco World
1220 Airline Rd., Ste. 270
Corpus Christi 78412
(512) 992-4427

D's Pipes Etc.
200-N 15th St.
Corsicana 75110
(903) 874-8661

DALLAS

Edward's Pipe & Cigar
338 Spanish Village
Dallas 75248
(214) 774-1658

Edward's Pipe & Cigar
3307 Oak Lawn Ave.
Dallas 75219
(214) 522-1880

Lone Star Cigar, Inc.
13305 Montfort Dr.
Dallas 75240
(214) 392-4427

Marty's
3316 Oak Lawn
Dallas 75219
(214) 526-0900

Perry's Wine Shop
9669 N. Central Expy., Ste 90
Dallas 75231
(214) 373-7646

Dallas' Largest Selection of Premium Cigars at Low Prices

13305 Montfort Drive
Dallas, TX 75240

Call 39-CIGAR
(214) 392-4427
Fax (214) 458-0743

WE SMOKE THE COMPETITION

Pogo's Wine & Spirits
Inwood Village Shopping Center
5360 W. Lovers Lane
Dallas 75209
(214) 350-8989

Red Colemans
2030 Empire Central
Dallas 75235
(214) 350-4300

Servi Cigar Inc.
3840 West NW Hwy., Ste. 430
Dallas 75220
(214) 350-1496

Sigel's Beverages, L.P.
2960 Anode Lane
Dallas 75220
(214) 350-1271

Sir Elliot's Tobacco
18101 Preston Rd., Ste. 203
Dallas 75252
(214) 250-4630

Tobacco Club, Inc.
4043 Trinity Mills Rd., Ste. 112
Dallas 75287
(214) 306-2880

Tobacco Lane
Preston Wood Mall
5301 Belt Line Rd.
Dallas 75240
(214) 239-1521

Up In Smoke
2315 Galleria Mall
Dallas 75240
(214) 458-7501

Up In Smoke
2032 Valley View Center
Dallas 75240
(214) 934-3618

Tobacco Lane
Triangle Mall
2201 I-35 E.
Denton 76205
(817) 566-6421

Papa's
6315 N. Mesa
El Paso 79912
(915) 585-8965

Pipes & Gifts
6254 Edgemere
El Paso 79925
(915) 778-5950

FORT WORTH

Puff n' Stuff
107 Hulen Mall
Fort Worth 76132
(817) 294-0600

The Smoke Shop
Tandy Center Mall
100 Throckmorton St.
Fort Worth 76102
(817) 877-5212

Smokes Etc!!
3014 Alta-Mere Dr.
Fort Worth 76116
(817) 244-9394

Tobacco Lane
Ridgmar Mall
2090 Green Oaks Rd.
Fort Worth 76116
(817) 738-6806

Carol's Pipe Pub
19020 Gulf Fwy.
Friendswood 77546
(713) 488-7300

Hollywood Tobacco
1660 Westheimer St.
Hollywood 77006
(713) 528-0456

HOUSTON

Alfred Dunhill of London
Galleria
5085 Westheimer Rd.
Houston 77056
(713) 961-4661

Antique Pipe Shoppe
6366 Richmond Ave.
Houston 77057
(713) 785-4080

Avalon Liquors
2880 Westheimer
Houston 77098
(713) 520-5550

Avalon Liquors
3135 Hokum
Houston 77025
(713) 662-3800

The Briar Shoppe
2412 Times Blvd.
Houston 77005
(713) 529-6347

Carol's Pipe Pub
13236-A NW Fwy.
Houston 77040
(713) 690-9346

Cigars Pipes & More
14520 Memorial Dr., Ste. 22
Houston 77079
(713) 493-9196

Greenway Pipe & Tobacco
5 Greenway Plaza E., Ste. C-4
Houston 77046
(713) 626-1613

Heart's Stone Tobacco Mart
6176 N. Hwy. 6
Houston 77084
(713) 385-9199

Jeffrey Stone Ltd.
9694 Westheimer
Houston 77063
(713) 783-3555

Lone Star Tobacco
3741 FM 1960 W
Houston 77068
(713) 444-2464

Mandalas Warehouse Liquors
4310 Richmond
Houston 77027
(713) 621-5314

McCoy's Fine Cigars & Tobacco
1201 Louisiana, B-204
Houston 77002
(713) 739-8110

Paradise Gift Store
1200 Mckinney, Ste. 481
Houston 77010
(713) 650-8708

Richard's Liquors & Fine Wines
1701 Brun St., Ste. 200
Houston 77019
(713) 529-6266

Richard's Liquors & Fine Wines
2411 S. Gessner
Houston 77063
(713) 780-9750

Richard's Liquors & Fine Wines
2124 S. Shepherd
Houston 77019
(713) 529-4849

Richard's Liquors & Fine Wines
2514 Rice Blvd.
Houston 77005
(713) 522-3881

Richard's Liquors & Fine Wines
5630 Richmond
Houston 77057
(713) 783-3344

Richard's Liquors & Fine Wines
5050 FM 1960 W.
Houston 77069
(713) 893-5080

Richard's Liquors & Fine Wines
6532 San Felipe
Houston 77057
(713) 781-0022

Richard's Liquors & Fine Wines
5750 Woodway
Houston 77057
(713) 975-6859

Richard's Liquors & Fine Wines
3268 Westheimer
Houston 77098
(713) 523-7405

Richard's Liquors & Fine Wines
4000 Bissonnet
Houston 77005
(713) 661-8770

Richmond Ave. Cigar
3301 Fondren at Richmond
Houston 77063
(713) 975-9057

Spec's Warehouse
2410 Smith St.
Houston 77006
(713) 526-8787

Tinder Box
Kroger Food Market
1801 Voss
Houston 77057
(713) 978-7443

Wines of America
6530 Woodway
Houston 77057
(713) 461-4497

Wines of America
2055 Westheimer Rd., Ste. 155
Houston 77098
(713) 524-3397

Atlascocita Liquors
5311 FM 1960 E.
Humble 77346
(713) 852-4845

Tobacco Lane
2220 North East Mall
Hurst 76053
(817) 284-7251

Up In Smoke
3621 Irving Mall
Irving 75062
(214) 255-8812

Clubs Are Us
22704 Ste. F, Loop 494
Kingwood 77339
(713) 358-5040

Tobacco Tin
Brazos Mall, #1070
Lake Jackson 77566
(409) 297-5771

House of Tobacco
Mall Del Norte
Laredo 78041
(210) 723-9961

Up In Smoke
2086 Vista Ridge Mall
Lewisville 75067
(214) 315-1300

Nothin Butt Smokes
317 University
Lubbock 79415
(806) 747-1311

Smokers Haven
1915 19th St.
Lubbock 79405
(806) 744-0017

Magnolia Foods
619 Magnolia Blvd.
Magnolia 77355
(713) 356-2700

Casa Petrides
306 S. Broadway
McAllen 78501
(210) 631-5219

Sir Elliot's Tobacco
2176 Town East Mall
Mesquite 75150
(214) 681-4959

Martin Pipe & Tobacco
2004 W. Front St.
Midland 79701
(915) 682-2301

Old Town Mercantile
201 W. Ave. G
Midlothian 76065
(214) 775-3115

J. Morgan's Tobacco
2407-A W. Arkansas Lane
Pantego 76013
(817) 860-2343

Puff n' Stuff
311 Pasadena Plaza S.C.
Pasadena 77504
(713) 943-0170

Beverage City #2
1100 Preston Pkwy.
Plano 75093
(214) 964-8660

Discount Smoke Shop & More
Aroppho Village #2, Ste. A
Richardson 75080
(214) 238-8806

Market Wine & Spirit
110 N. Interstate Hwy. 35, Ste. 175
Round Rock 78681
(512) 310-0486

Colonel's Pipe Shop
3544 Knickerbocker Rd.
San Angelo 76904
(800) 497-7533

SAN ANTONIO

Gabriel's Wine & Spirits
4445 Walden Rd.
San Antonio 78218
(210) 654-1123

The Humidor
6900 San Pedro, Ste. 111
San Antonio 78216
(210) 824-1209

The Humidor
112 N. Star Mall
San Antonio 78216
(210) 308-8545

Joe Saglinbeni Fine Wine
638 W. Rhaposdy, #1
San Antonio 78216
(210) 349-5149

Tobacco Bowl of Texas
622 NW Loop 410, Ste. 276
San Antonio 78216
(210) 349-7708

Hill Country Humidor
122 N. LBJ
San Marcos 78666
(512) 396-7473

Tobacco Gallery
4800 N. Pkwy., Ste. 722
Sherman 75090
(903) 892-8854

The Beverage Shoppe
4775 W. Panther Creek, Ste. C-300
Spring 77381
(713) 363-9463

Cynthia's Rose Garden
1918 W. Ave H
Temple 76504
(817) 771-3388

Cigar International
505 Mason St.
Tomball 77375
(713) 351-7488

Don's Humidor and Coffee Beans
1412 N. Valley Mills Dr.
Waco 76710
(817) 772-3919

The Smoke Ring
17050 Hwy. 3
Webster 77598
(713) 332-9871

Cigars, Tobacco Etc.
3401 Kemp Blvd., Ste. G
Wichita Falls 76308
(817) 691-2347

Aroma's
4936 Windsor Hill
Windcrest 78239
(210) 590-1802

UTAH

Tobacco Products Int'l.
4227 S. Highland Dr., #8
Holladay 84117
(801) 278-8508

Crawford-Bennett Trading
419 Main St.
Park City 84060-0337
(801) 649-0101

Jeanie's Smoke Shop
156 S. State St.
Salt Lake City 84111
(801) 322-2817

Tinder Box
2A26 Crossroads Plaza
50 S. Main Street
Salt Lake City 84144
(801) 355-7336

VERMONT

Smoker's Den & Discount
214 Hunt St.
Bennington 05201
(802) 442-2861

Garcia Tobacco Shop
Burlington Square Mall
Burlington 05401
(802) 658-5737

Howie's Humidor
1174 Williston Rd., #5
South Burlington 05403
(802) 862-5745

Lilydale Inc.
1350 Shelburn Rd., Ste. 270
South Burlington 05403
(802) 658-5896

Discount Beverage
157 Marlboro Rd.
West Brattleboro 05301
(802) 254-4950

The Hermitage
Cold Brook Rd.
Wilmington 05363
(802) 464-3511

VIRGINIA

ALEXANDRIA

Cigar Club International
2869 Duke St.
Alexandria 22314
(703) 823-2234

John Crouch Tobacconist
215 King St.
Alexandria 22314
(703) 548-2900

Total Beverage
Landmark Plaza
240 Little River Tpke.
Alexandria 22312
(703) 941-1133

The Cigar Vault
1500 Wilson Blvd.
Arlington 22209
(703) 276-7225

Tobacco Barns - Pentagon City
1100 S. Hayes St.
Arlington 22202
(703) 415-5554

Tobacco Alley
120 Wilson St.
Blacksburg 24060
(840) 951-3154

Side Track Tobacco Shop
Train Station Market Place
Bristol 24201
(703) 466-8450

Total Beverage
Greenbriar Town Center
13055-C Lee Jackson Hwy.
Chantilly 22035
(703) 817-1177

CHARLOTTESVILLE

Artesanias Mexicanas Carmelita's
316 E. Main St.
Charlottesville 22902
(804) 979-0936

Cavalier Pipe Shop
1100 Emmet St.
Charlottesville 22901
(804) 293-6643

Tobacconist & Gift
214 Zan Rd.
Charlottesville 22905
(804) 923-9065

John B. Hayes
11755-l Fair Oaks Mall
Fairfax 22033
(703) 385-3033

Tobacco Barn
6208-K Leesburg Pike
Falls Church 22044
(800) 999-6882, (703) 536-5588

The Tobacco Bar
Westwood Center
1915 Plank Rd.
Fredricksburg 22401
(703) 373-4533

Stogies
4040-F Cox Rd.
Glen Allen 23060
(804) 527-1919

The Wine Seller
9912-C Georgetown Pike
Great Falls 22066
(703) 759-0430

Peace Pipe Inc.
Dukes Plaza
2193 S. Main St.
Harrisburg 22801
(540) 433-7473

Leesburg Emporium & Smoke Shop
205 Harrison St. SE
Leesburg 22075
(703) 777-5557

Special Somethings
6604 Richmond Rd.
Lightfoot 23090
(804) 564-8346

Cafe France
3225 Old Forest Rd.
Lynchburg 24501
(804) 385-8989

Tobacco Barn
8300 Sudley Rd.
Manassas 22110
(703) 330-9753

Georgetown Tobacco
Tysons Corner Center
McLean 22102
(703) 893-3366

Total Beverage
1451-B Chain Bridge Rd.
McLean 22101
(703) 745-0011

NORFOLK

Emerson's Fine Tobacco
Military Circle Center
Norfolk 23502
(804) 461-6848

Emerson's Fine Tobacco
116 Granby St.
Norfolk 23510
(804) 624-1520

West Side Wine Shop
4702 Hampton Blvd.
Norfolk 23508
(804) 440-7600

RICHMOND

Island Tobacco & Gifts
1601 Willow Lawn Dr., Ste. 229
Richmond 23230
(804) 285-5604

Tinder Box
Three James Center
1051 E. Cary St.
Richmond 23219
(804) 343-1827

Tobacco House, Ltd.
3138 W. Cary St.
Richmond 23221
(804) 353-4675

Tobacconist of Richmond
11521-H Midlothian Tpke.
Richmond 23235
(804) 378-7756

Harris Teeter
Tower Shopping Center
2721 Colonia Ave. SW
Roanoke 24015
(703) 342-1017

Milan Bros.
106 S. Jefferson St.
Roanoke 24011
(703) 344-5191

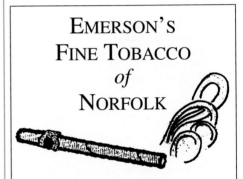

Tobacco Barn
6568 Springfield Mall
Springfield 22150
(703) 971-1933

York Tobacco Co.
1520 George Washington Memorial
  Hwy., Rte. 17
Tabb 23693
(804) 596-2120

J & M Imports
2973 Shore Dr., Unit 104
Virginia Beach 23451
(804) 496-5500

Big G Tobacco Shop
14836 Build America Dr.
Woodbridge 22191
(703) 494-1299

Total Beverage
Smoketown Stations
2904 Prince William Pkwy.
Woodbridge 22192
(703) 878-1188

WASHINGTON

Tinder Box
10150 Main St.
Bellevue 98004
(800) 68-CIGAR

Fairhaven Smoke Shop
1213 Harris Ave.
Bellingham 98225
(360) 647-2379

M & R Tobacco
202 S. Tower St.
Centralia 98531
(360) 736-4933

International Cigar Store
31840 Pacific Hwy. S., Ste. A
Federal Way 98003
(206) 946-5016

Wine, Beer, Etc...
710 NW Gilman Blvd., Ste. D-112
Issaquah 98027
(206) 392-6242

The Briar Shop
313 Columbia Center
Kennewick 99336
(509) 783-6928

Smoker's Choice
24817 Pacific Hwy. S., Ste. 203
Kent 98032
(206) 941-8730

Smoker's Choice
13520 100th Ave. NE, Ste. 40
Kirkland 98034
(206) 823-9232

Le Bon Vie
5826 Ste. A Pacific Ave. SE
Lacey 98503
(360) 493-1454

H.G. Tobacco & Snuff
5800 198th St., J
Lynnwood 98036
(206) 774-4002

Tinder Box
222 Alderwood Mall
3000 184th St. SW
Lynnwood 98037
(206) 771-8418

Smokin' Deal #1
1227 A State Ave.
Marysville 98270
(360) 653-0182

Valley Blends
1722 Riverside Dr.
Mount Vernon 98273
(360) 424-6365

Oz's Pipe & Tobacco
319 W. Louis
Pasco 99301
(509) 545-6386

Smoker's Choice
15161 NE 24th St.
Redmond 98052
(206) 641-8421

SEATTLE

Alfred Dunhill of London
409 Pike St.
Seattle 98101
(206) 223-0234

Arcade Smoke Shop
610 Pine St.
Seattle 98101
(206) 587-0159

Downtown Cigar Store
310 Columbia St.
Seattle 98104
(206) 624-2794

G & G Cigar Co.
Smith Tower
504 Second Ave.
Seattle 98104
(206) 623-6721

Kirsten Pipe Co., Inc.
W. Knickerson, Ste. 112
Seattle 98119
(206) 286-0851

Larry's Market
100 Mercer St.
Seattle 98109
(206) 213-0778

Nickel Cigar
89 Yesler Way
Seattle 98104
(206) 622-3204

Pete's Supermarket
58 E. Lynn
Seattle 98102
(206) 322-2660

Smoke Plus
1432 4th Ave., #622
Seattle 98101
(206) 622-1521

Tom's University Smoke Shop
4140 University Way NE
Seattle 98105
(206) 632-9260

Tobacco World
W-621 Mallon Ave.
Spokane 99201
(509) 326-4665

University Pipe Square
703 University City Mall
Spokane 99206
(509) 928-9531

TACOMA

Indian Smoke Shop
7402 Pacific Hwy. E.
Tacoma 98424
(206) 922-3001

Mike's Smoke Shop
101 Pioneer Way E.
Tacoma 98404
(206) 627-8959

Puromundo
763 Broadway
Tacoma 98402
(206) 272-0565

Queen Anne's Thriftway
2420 N. Proctor
Tacoma 98406
(206) 761-3663

Tinder Box
Tacoma Mall, #1131
4502 S. Steele St.
Tacoma 98409
(206) 472-9993

Tinder Box
751 S. Center
Tukwila 98188
(206) 243-3443

Little Brown Smoke Shack
3201 Goodman Rd.
Yakima 98903
(509) 457-6404

WEST VIRGINIA

Multi-Sound Music
3708 McConkle Ave.
Charleston 25304
(304) 925-8273

The Squire
30 Capitol St.
Charleston 25301
(304) 345-0366

La Fontaines Tobacco & Gift
940 4th Ave.
Huntington 25701
(304) 523-7879

Stephen Street Emporium
306 W. Stephen St.
Martinsburg 25401
(800) 249-9130

Crumbakers
292 Grand Central Mall
Parkersburg 26101
(304) 422-3393

WISCONSIN

Edward's Pipe & Tobacco
13825 Capitol Dr.
Brookfield 53005
(414) 783-7473

V. Richards
17165 W. Bluemound Rd.
Brookfield 53005
(414) 784-8303

The Coffee Grounds
2925 London Square Mall
Eau Claire 54701
(715) 834-1733

Elm Grove Liquor
15380 Watertown Plank
Elm Grove 53122
(414) 784-3545

Bosse's News & Tobacco
220 Cherry St.
Greenbay 54301
(414) 432-8647

Tobacco World
4818 S. 76th St.
Greenfield 53220
(414) 281-1935

Andrea's Tobacconist
2401 60th St.
Kenosha 53140
(414) 657-7732

Tenuta's
3203 52nd St.
Kenosha 53144
(414) 657-9001

Briar Patch
519 Main St.
La Crosse 54601
(608) 784-8839

Gerhardt Drugs
4620 Cottage Grove Rd.
Madison 53716
(608) 221-3888

The Tobacco Bar
6613 Seybold Rd.
Madison 53719
(608) 276-7668

MILWAUKEE

East Town Pharmacy
788 N. Jefferson St., Ste. 103
Milwaukee 53202
(414) 271-4441

Edward's Pipe & Tobacco
400 W. Silver Spring Dr.
Milwaukee 53217
(414) 964-8212

Green Tree Liquors
6945 N. Pt. Washington Rd.
Milwaukee 53217
(414) 352-8282

Uhle's Pipe Shop
114 W. Wisconsin Ave.
Milwaukee 53203
(414) 273-6665

The Tasting Room
6325 Monona Dr.
Monona 53716
(414) 223-1641

Country Gentlemans Smoke Shop
216 S. Main St.
River Falls 54022
(715) 425-7478

Tobacco Hut, Inc.
1005 Michigan Ave.
Sheboygan 53081
(414) 452-1790

Swan-Serve U Pharmacy
9130 W. North Ave.
Wauwatosa 53226
(414) 258-9550

WYOMING

Lane's Tobacco & Gifts
Eastridge Mall
601 SE Wyoming Blvd.
Casper 82609
(307) 577-5209

Smoker Friendly
1453 Sheridan Ave.
Cody 82414
(307) 527-6926

Tobacco Row
120 N. Cache
Jackson 83001
(307) 733-4385

INTERNATIONAL

ANDORRA

La Casa del Habano
Gallery Roc Blanc (White Rock)
Plaza del Coprinceps
Escaldes
376 869 255

ARGENTINA

La Casa del Habano
Víamontes No. 524 1er. Piso Apt. 1
Buenos Aires
54 1 315 4085

ARUBA

La Casa del Habano
Royal Plaza
Oranjestaad
297 825 355

RC Gift Shop & Drug Store
Windham Aruba Resort-Lower Lobby
Shopping Arcade
Oranjestaad
297 832 699

AUSTRALIA

J & D of Alexanders
Shop 7A (Tok H Centre)
459 Toorak Rd.
Toorak Village Vic. 3142
61 3 9827 1477

BAHAMAS

Graycliff Hotel
W. Hill St.
Nassau
(809) 322-2796

Pink Flamingo Trading Co.
Bay and Charlotte St.
Nassau
(809) 322-7391

La Casa del Habano
W. Hill St.
Nassau
(809) 322-2796

Tropique International Smoke Shop
Marriot Crystal Palace Casino
   Shopping Arcade
W. Bay St.
Nassau
(809) 327-7292

BAHRAIN

La Casa del Habano
Le Royal Meridiem, Shop No. 8
Manama
973 580400

BERMUDA

Tobacco Associates, Ltd.
Corner of Victoria & Parliament Sts.
Hamilton
(441) 292-4411

BRAZIL

La Casa del Habano
Havana Cigars
Almeida Lorena, 1821
Sao Paulo 01424-002
55 11 883 7344

Ranieri Pipes
Almeida Lorena, 1221
Sao Paulo 01424
55 11 577 5420

BRITISH VIRGIN ISLANDS

Fort Wine & Spirits
1 Chalwell St., Road Town
Tortola
(809) 494-2388

CANADA

BRITISH COLUMBIA

Shefield & Sons Tobacconist
320-A 4741 Lakelse Ave.
Terrace V8G 1R5
(604) 635-9661

Shefield & Sons Tobacconist
712 Park Royal N.
West Vancouver V7T 1H9
(604) 926-7011

Memory of Whistler
4249 Village Stroll
Whistler VON 1B0
(604) 932-6439

MANITOBA

Thomas Hinds Tobacconist
98-185 Carlton St.
Winnipeg R3C 3J1
(204) 942-0203

ONTARIO

Smalley's Cigar Store
132 Hurontario St.
Collingwood L9Y 2L8
(705) 445-1666

Havana Tobacconist
Stone Road Mall
435 Stone Rd.
Guelph N1G 2X6
(519) 837-9193

International News
Lime Ridge Mall
999 Upper Wentworth St.
Hamilton L9A 4X5
(905) 318-5872

Lake of the Woods Tobacco
131 Matheson St.
Kenora P9N 4L8
(807) 468-3949

The King City Outpost
Hwy. 400 N.
King City L0G 1K0
(905) 832-2305

Real Fakes
13 Queen St.
Niagara-on-the-Lake L0S 1L0
(905) 468-0957

Celebrity Tobacco & Gift
Trafaldar Village
125 Cross Ave.
Oakville L6J 2W7
(905) 849-3845

Sharkskin
112 Michigan Ave.
Point Edward N7V 1E6
(519) 332-3550

Havana House
87 Avenue Rd.
Toronto M5R 3R9
(416) 927-9070

House of Salgado
Royal Bank Plaza
200 Bay St.
Toronto M5J 2J3
(416) 865-0094

Thomas Hinds Tobacconist
8 Cumberland St.
Toronto M4W 1J5
(416) 757-0237

Thomas Hinds Tobacconist
392 Eglinton Ave. W.
Toronto M5N 1A2
(416) 481-6909

Touch of Class
630 Mt. Pleasant
Toronto M4S 2N1
(416) 487-5535

Havana Tobacconist
Bayview Village Shopping Center
2901 Bayview Ave.
Willowdale M2K 1E6
(416) 733-9736

La Casa del Habano
473 Ouellette Ave.
Windsor N9A 4J2
(519) 254-0017

QUEBEC

Davidoff
1452 rue Sherbrooke W.
Montreal H3G 1K4
(514) 289-9118

CUBA

La Casa del Habano
Mercaderes No. 120
La Habana Vieja (Old Havana)
N/A

La Casa del Habano
Partagas Factory
Industria No. 520
La Habana Vieja (Old Havana)
537 33 80 60

La Casa del Habano
Ave. 1ra. esq. 64
Varadero, Matanzas
537 56 67 843

CYPRUS

La Casa del Habano
Higa Fereou Str. No. 4
Limmassol
357 5 747 341

CZECH REPUBLIC

La Casa del Habano
Hotel Intercontinental
Nan. Curieovych 43/5
11000 Prague 1
42 2 488 1544

DENMARK

W.O. Larsen A/S
9 Amagertorv
Copenhagen DK - 1160
45 3 312 2050

Alfred & Christian Petersen A/S
Norgesvej 10
Horsens DK - 8700
45 75 61 20 00

FRANCE

La Casa del Habano
169 Boulevard St. Germain
Paris 75006
33 1 45 49 24 30

La Civette des Quatre Temp
Centre Commercial Des 4
Casier 102 Cedex 25
Paris 92092
33 1 47 74 75 28

GERMANY

Hotel-Restaurant Landsknecht
Post Str. 70, Meerbusch
40667 Düsseldorf
49 21 325 947

Dachauer
Filiale Bauerstr 1 U
Turkenstr 43
80335 Munich
49 89 550 4448

Alte Tabakstube
Schillerplatz 4
D-70173 Stuttgart
49 711 292 729

Pfeifen Archiv
Calwer Passage
70173 Stuttgart
fax 49 711 299 1555

GREECE

La Casa del Habano
1-3 Spyromiliov St.
10564 Athens
30 1 32 35 325, 33 10 189

IRELAND

The Decent Cigar
Ballsbridge, 4
Dublin
353 1 885 49363

J.J. Fox
119 Grafton St., 2
Dublin
353 1 677 0533

Terroirs Ltd.
103 Morehampton Rd.,
Donnybrook, 4
Dublin
353 1 667 1311

LUXEMBOURG

La Civette
22-B Av. Porte-Neuve
1-2227 Luxembourg
352 221 321

MALAYSIA

Havana Club Sdn Bhd
Level 6 Annex Blk Lt 10 S/C, 50
Jalan Sultan Ismail
Kuala Lumpor 50250
60 3 211 3222

MEXICO

La Casa del Habano
Plaza Flamingo, L-233, Zona Hotelera
Cancun, Quintana Roo 77500
52 988 529 29

La Casa del Habano
Plaza Loreto Altamirano, #46, L-119
Ave. Revolucion
Colonia Tizapan San Angel
Mexico City D.F. 01090
52 5 616 1430

La Casa del Habano
Presidente Mazaryk 393, Local 28
Colonia Polanco
Mexico City D.F. 11560
52 5 282 1184, 282 1046

Amigos Smoke Shop
Calle M Doblado y Morelos
San Jose Del Cabo
52 114 24 055

NETHERLANDS ANTILLES

The New Amsterdam Store
66 Front St.
Philipsburg
St. Maarten
599 5 22787, 22788

PHILIPPINES

Tabac, Inc.
Grand Boulevard Hotel
1990 Roxas Blvd.
Manila 1057
63 2 521 0004

PORTUGAL

Empor-Importacao e Export
Rua Joao Dos Santos, Lote 2
1300 Lisbon
fax 351 1 364 6820

PUERTO RICO

International House of Cigars
1595 Jesus T. Pinero Ave.
Caparra Heights
(809) 782-6871

Fun Times
152 Barbosa Ave.
Catano 00962
(809) 788-3588

International House of Cigars
B-2 Tabonuco St.
Guaynabo 00968-3004
(809) 782-6871

The Smokers Suite
Pisa De Capassa Ste.
Guaynabo 00966
(809) 720-1200

Good Times Smoke Shop
Mckinley #74 - Oeste
Mayaguez 00680
(809) 265-2380

Smoker's Suite
El San Juan Hotel & Casino
La Galeria
6073 Isla Verde Ave.
San Juan 00979
(809) 791-6002

International House of Cigars
1203 Americo Miranda Ave.
Reparto Metropolitano
San Juan
(809) 782-6871

SAUDI ARABIA

La Casa del Habano
Palestine Rd.
Al Hamra - Jeddah
966 2 665 8227

La Casa del Habano
Saladin St.
Al Malaz - Riyadh
966 1 476 3114

La Casa del Habano
Prince Sultan St.
Olaya - Riyadh
966 1 465 037

SOUTH AFRICA

Wesley's - The Cock 'n Bull
20 Tyger Valley Centre
Bellville Cape
27 21 948 2400

Wesley's
Sanlam Plaza, Shop 14
Bloemfontein
27 51 484 658

Wesley's
Gardens Shopping Centre, 5-A
(Upper Level)
Cape Town
27 21 45 1890

Wesley's
Golden Acre, 7 Plaza Level
Cape Town
27 21 21 5090

Wesley's - The Cock 'n Bull
G-40 Cavendish Square
Cape Town
27 21 61 1432

Wesley's - The Cock 'n Bull
143 V & A Waterfront
Cape Town
27 21 21 1860

Wesley's - Zoggy's Durban
87 Gardiner St.
Durban
27 31 304 0866

Wesley's
Vincent Park Centre, 40-A
East London
27 431 57873

Wesley's
Rosebank Mall, Shop 170
Johannesburg 2196
27 11 880 1150

Wesley's
G-39 Garden Pavillion, Carlton
Centre
Johannesburg
27 11 331 1050

Wesley's
Bank City, Pritchard St.
Johannesburg
27 11 633 2510

**Wesley's Pipe & Tobacco -
Swaziland Jewellers**
The Mall
Mbabane
27 9268 42460

Wesley's
Boster Brown Centre, 22-C
Nelspruit
27 1311 53308

Wesley's - The Cock 'n Bull
8 The Square
Plettenberg Bay
27 4457 30335

Wesley's
24 Shoprito Chockers Mall,
Greenacres
Port Elizabeth
27 41 34 2036

Tabak L'Art - Wesley's
109 Brooklyn Mall, Mucklaneuk
Pretoria
27 12 46 7781

Wesley's
124 Sanlam Centre
Randburg
27 11 787 6358

Wesley's
The Boardwalk, Shop 49-A
Richards Bay
27 351 98 7271

Wesley's
The Pavilion, Shop 234
Westville
27 31 265 0735

SWEDEN

Broberg's Tobakshandel AB
Arkaden, Box 111 10
Göteborg S-404 23
46 31 15 36 14

Broberg's Tobakshandel AB
Sturegallerian 39
Stockholm 114 46
46 31 611 69 00

SWITZERLAND

Eden Tabac Cigares
rue du Grand Lancy 6
Acacias 1227
41 22 342 27 57

Davidoff
Steinenvorstadt 2
Basel 4051
41 61 22 87 37

Davidoff
Centralbahnplatz 9
Basel 4052
41 61 23 11 52

Kagi
2 place du Theatre
Berne
41 22 31 37 03

Alfred Dunhill
rue de Rhône 100
Geneva 1204
41 22 312 42 60

Comptoirs du Rhône
rue de Rhône 59
Geneva 1204
41 22 312 14 22

Davidoff
2 rue de Rive
Geneva 1204
41 22 310 90 41

Eden Confederation Emile SA
rue de la Confederation 8
Geneva 1204
41 22 311 96 41

Fradkoff Cigares
Quai des Berques 29
Geneva 1201
41 22 342 27 57

Raffi's
2-4 place Longemalle
Geneva 1204
41 22 31 97 40

Tabac Rhein
1 rue du Mont-Blanc
Geneva 1204
41 22 32 97 64

Davidoff
Hotel Savoy, Poststrasse 12
Zürich
41 1 211 48 00

Durr
Bahnhofplatz 6
Zürich
41 1 211 63 23

La Casa del Habano
Kuttelgasse 4
Zürich 8001
41 1 212 04 44

Tabak Schwarzenbach
Hauptbahnof
Zürich 8000
41 1 211 63 25

THAILAND

The Davidoff Shop
Hilton International Hotel
Bangkok
66 2 253 0123

TURKEY

POGEP Inc.
Sulunlu Sok No: 3 80620 I. Levent
Istanbul
90 1 212 264 1929

UNITED KINGDOM

Berry Bros. & Rudd Ltd.
Terminal 3 - Heathrow Airport
Hounslow, Middlesex TW6 1JH
44 181 564 8361

Alfred Dunhill Ltd.
30 Duke St., St. James
London SW1 Y6DL
44 171 499 9566

Benson & Hedges
13 Old Bond St.
London W1X 4QP
44 171 493 1825

Davidoff of London
35 St. James's St.
London SW1 1HD
44 171 930 3079

Harvey Nichols
109-125 Knightsbridge
London SW1 X7RJ
44 171 235 5000

J.J. Fox
19 St. James's St.
London SW1 A1ES
44 171 930 3787

Monte's on Sloane St.
164 Sloane St.
London SW1 X9QB
44 171 245 0892

Sautter of Mayfair
106 Mount St.
London W1Y 5HE
44 171 499 4866

U.S. VIRGIN ISLANDS

Baci Duty Free
55 Company St.
Christiansted
St. Croix 00820
(809) 773-5040

Steeles Smokes & Sweets
1102 Strand St.
Christiansted
St. Croix 00820
(809) 773-3366

Gregory's
PO Box 9071
St. Thomas
(809) 777-5480

WEST INDIES

La Casa del Habano
Heritage Quay No. 45
St. Johns
Antigua
(809) 462-2677

La Casa del Habano
Centre St. John Perse No. 54
97110 Pinte A. Pitre
Guadeloupe
590 89 42 16

La Casa del Habano
Villa Creole
St. Jean
St. Barthelemy
590 27 78 73

Le Comptoir du Cigare
6 General de Gaulle, Gustavia
St. Barthelemy 97133
590 27 50 62

La Casa del Cigarro
Marina Port La Royale
Marigot, BP 445
St. Martin 97150
590 87 90 48

La Casa del Habano
71, Port La Royale
Marigot
St. Martin 97150
590 87 58 94

Le Cigare
rue de la Liberté
Marigot, BP 1020
St. Martin 97061
590 87 79 10

CHAPTER 15

Cigar-friendly Restaurants

The cigar-friendly restaurants that follow are divided into two sections: United States and International. Restaurants in the United States are listed by state, and then alphabetically by city. International restaurants are listed by country, and then alphabetically by city. Each listing details where cigar-smoking is allowed inside the restaurant.

A number of cigar-friendly establishments are private clubs, some offer more than the typical restaurant and others are simply bars or coffeehouses. These establishments are indicated by a ▲.

The restaurant information was provided by the restaurants themselves in a questionnaire prepared by Cigar Aficionado. *Each listing was checked as close to the publication date as possible, but changes occur all the time, so it's best to call ahead.*

UNITED STATES

ALABAMA

Basil's Grill & Wine Bar
1318 20th St. S.
Birmingham 35205
(205) 933-9222
•Bar only.

▲ Grayson Valley Country Club
2201 Grayson Valley Dr.
Birmingham 35235
(205) 854-5420
fax (205) 854-8468
•All areas.
•Private club open to the public for a
Sunday buffet and brunch only.

▲ North River Yacht Club
New Watermelon Rd.
Tuscaloosa 35404
(205) 345-0202
•All areas.
•Private club.

ALASKA

Chena Hot Springs Resort
206 Driveway
Fairbanks 99707
(907) 369-4111
fax (907) 456-3122
•Smoking area.

ARIZONA

▲ The Discovery Lounge at Boulders
34631 N. Tom Darlington Dr.
Carefree 85377
(602) 488-9009
•Lounge serving hors d'œuvres only.

Wigwam Resort
300 E. Indian Pool
Litchfield Park 85340
(602) 935-3811
•Bar, lounge and patio only.

Doubletree Paradise Valley Resort
Loggia Lobby Bar
5401 N. Scottsdale Rd.
Paradise Valley 85250
(602) 947-5400
fax (602) 946-1524
•Bar and lounge only.

PHOENIX

Another Pointe in Tyme
South Mountain Hilton
7777 S. Pointe Pkwy.
Phoenix 85044
(602) 431-6472
fax (602) 431-6525
•Bar, private rooms and patio only.

Christopher's
Christopher's Bistro
2398 E. Camelback Rd.
Phoenix 85016
(602) 957-3214
fax (602) 381-0203
•Cigar room and patio only.

Different Pointe of View
Pointe Hilton Tapatio Cliff
11111 N. 7th St.
Phoenix 85020
(602) 863-0912
fax (602) 866-6358
•Bar, lounge, private rooms and patio only.

Morton's of Chicago
Shops at the Esplanade
2501 E. Camelback Rd., Ste. 1
Phoenix 85016
(602) 955-9577
•Smoking section, bar and patio.

Pointe in Tyme
Pointe Hilton Tapatio Cliff
11111 N. 7th St.
Phoenix 85020
(602) 866-6348
•Smoking section and lounge.

Ritz-Carlton
2401 E. Camelback Rd.
Phoenix 85016
(602) 468-0700
•Bar before 6 p.m. and after 9 p.m. only.

Tarbell's
3213 E. Camelback Rd.
Phoenix 85018
(602) 955-8100
fax (602) 955-8181
•Private room only.

Wrong Number Lounge
4041 N. 40th St.
Phoenix 85018
(602) 955-9886
•All areas.

SCOTTSDALE

Marquessa
Scottsdale Princess Hotel
757 E. Princess Dr.
Scottsdale 85255
(602) 585-4848
fax (602) 585-0086
•Dining room and lounge.

Mary Elaine's
Phoenician Resort
6000 E. Camelback Rd.
Scottsdale 85251
(602) 941-8200
fax (602) 947-4311
•Private rooms and patio only.

Remington's
The Scottsdale Plaza Resort
7200 N. Scottsdale Rd.
Scottsdale 85253
(602) 951-5101
fax (602) 998-5971
•Lounge and patio/sidewalk only.

Lakes Club
10484 W. Thunderbird Blvd.
Sun City 85351
(602) 974-6041
fax (602) 933-2883
•Bar, lounge, private rooms and patio
only.

TUCSON

Anthony's in the Catalinas
6440 N. Campbell
Tucson 85718
(520) 299-1771
fax (520) 299-6635
•Bar, lounge, private rooms and patio
only.

Charles Restaurant
6400 E. El Dorado Circle
Tucson 85715
(602) 296-7173
fax (602) 296-7050
•Smoking section.

Daniel's Restaurant
4340 N. Campbell, #107
Tucson 85718
(602) 742-3200
•Smoking section.

El Charro Cafe
311 N. Court Ave.
Tucson 85701
(520) 622-1922
fax (520) 628-4188
•Bar only.

ARKANSAS

James at the Mill
3906 Greathouse Springs Rd.
Johnson 72741
(501) 443-1400
fax (501) 575-0295
•Smoking areas and private dining room
(14 seats) designed for cigar and wine
tasting.

Cafe Saint Moritz
225 E. Markham
Little Rock 72201
(501) 372-0411
fax (501) 376-4633
•Dining room, bar and private rooms.

The Capital Bar
  Capital Hotel
111 W. Markham
Little Rock 72201
(501) 374-7474
fax (501) 370-7091
•Bar only and not at lunch.

CALIFORNIA

Mr. Stox
1105 E. Katella Ave.
Anaheim 92805
(714) 634-2994
fax (714) 634-0561
•Lounge and outside garden room only.

The Ballard Store Restaurant & Bar
2449 Baseline Ave.
Ballard 93463
(805) 688-5319
•Wine cellar only.

BEVERLY HILLS

Armani Cafe
9533 Brighton Way
Beverly Hills 90210
(310) 271-9940
fax (310) 271-9031
•*After dinner only.*

Beverly Hilton Hotel
9876 Wilshire Blvd.
Beverly Hills 90210
(310) 274-7777
•*Bar and lounge only (separate from restaurant).*

Canon Liquor Cafe
338 N. Canon Dr.
Beverly Hills 90210
(310) 246-9463
fax (310) 246-1514
•*Patio only.*

▲ **Hamiltons at The Wine Merchant**
9701 Santa Monica Blvd.
Beverly Hills 90210-4294
(310) 278-0347
fax (310) 278-6158
•*All areas.*
•*Bar with an appetizer menu and jazz entertainment six nights a week.*

Lawry's The Prime Rib
100 N. La Cienega Blvd.
Beverly Hills 90211
(310) 652-2827
fax (310) 657-5463
•*Bar only.*

Maple Drive
345 N. Maple Dr.
Beverly Hills 90210
(310) 274-9800
fax (310) 274-2782
•*Bar after 3 p.m only.*

The Peninsula Beverly Hills
9882 Santa Monica Blvd. S.
Beverly Hills 90212
(310) 551-2888
fax (310) 788-2319
•*Bar only.*

La Vie en Rose
240 S. State College Blvd.
Brea 92622
(714) 529-8333
fax (714) 529-2751
•*Bar, lounge and private rooms only.*

CARMEL

Covey at Quail Lodge Resort
8205 Valley Greens Dr.
Carmel 93921
(408) 624-1581
•*Lounge, private rooms and patio only.*

**Pacific's Edge Restaurant
Highlands Inn**
Hwy. 1
Carmel 93921
(408) 624-3801
fax (408) 626-1574
•*Lounge, private rooms and patio only.*

Rio Grill
101 Crossroads
Carmel 93921
(408) 625-5436
fax (408) 625-2950
•*Patio only.*

COSTA MESA

Amici Trattoria
655 Anton Blvd., Ste. C
Costa Mesa 92626
(714) 850-9399
fax (714) 850-0116
•*Patio/sidewalk only.*

The Golden Truffle
1767 Newport Blvd.
Costa Mesa 92627
(714) 645-9858
fax (714) 645-7831
•Patio only.

Habana Restaurant & Bar
2930 Bristol St.
Costa Mesa 92626
(714) 556-0176
fax (714) 556-5862
•Bar area and patio only.

Ritz-Carlton
33533 Ritz Carlton Dr.
Dana Point 92629
(714) 240-2000
fax (714) 240-1061
•Library only.

Brix Dining Cafe and Bar
6763 N. Palm Ave.
Fresno 93704
(209) 435-5441
fax (209) 435-0154
•Bar and heated patio only.

The Cellar
305 N. Harbor Blvd.
Fullerton 92632
(714) 525-5682
fax (714) 525-3853
•Bar only.

Fresco Ristorante
514 S. Brand Blvd.
Glendale 91204
(818) 247-5541
•Bar only.

Bistango
19100 Von Karman Ave.
Irvine 92715
(714) 752-5222
fax (714) 851-7849
•Bar only.

Chanteclair
18912 MacArthur Blvd.
Irvine 92715
(714) 751-8001
•Bar and patio only.

Top O' The Cove
1216 Prospect St.
La Jolla 92037
(619) 454-7779
fax (619) 454-3783
•Front patio only.

Wente Vineyards Restaurant
5050 Arroyo Rd.
Livermore 94550
(510) 447-3696
fax (510) 447-0970
•Private rooms and veranda only.

LONG BEACH

Moose McGillycuddy's Pub & Cafe
190 Marina Dr.
Long Beach 90803
(310) 596-8108
fax (310) 596-5328
•Lounge and patio only.

Nino's Ristorante Italiano
3853 Atlantic Ave.
Long Beach 90807
(310) 427-1003
•Patio and private parties only.

Phil Trani's
3490 Long Beach Blvd.
Long Beach 90807
(310) 426-3668
•Bar only.

LOS ANGELES

Bel-Air Hotel Dining Room
701 Stone Canyon Rd.
Los Angeles 90077
(310) 472-1211
•Lounge and terrace only.

Cafe Pinot
700 W. 5th St.
Los Angeles 90071
(213) 239-6500
fax (213) 239-6514
•Patio only.

Campanile
624 S. La Brea Ave.
Los Angeles 90036
(213) 938-1447
fax (213) 938-5840
•Bar only.

**Cardini Ristorante
  Los Angeles Hilton**
930 Wilshire Blvd.
Los Angeles 90017
(213) 227-3464
fax (213) 612-3987
•Bar, private rooms and patio only.

Checkers
535 S. Grand Ave.
Los Angeles 90071
(213) 624-0000
fax (213) 626-9906
•Lounge only.

Fénix at the Argyle
8358 Sunset Blvd.
Los Angeles 90069
(213) 848-6677
•Patio only.

Four Seasons Hotel
9500 Wilshire Blvd.
Los Angeles 90212
(310) 275-5200
•Bar only.

▲ **Friars Club of California**
9900 Santa Monica Blvd.
Los Angeles 90212
(310) 553-0850
•Bar and card room only.
•Private club.

**Gardens Restaurant, Window's
  Bar & Lounge
  Four Seasons Hotel Beverly Hills**
300 S. Doheny Dr.
Los Angeles 90048
(310) 273-2222
fax (310) 274-3891
•All areas of Window's Bar & Lounge;
Gardens bar and patios only.

Il Ristorante Rex
617 S. Olive St.
Los Angeles 90014
(213) 627-2300
fax (213) 627-6957
•Bar only.

L'Orangerie
903 N. La Cienega Blvd.
Los Angeles 90069
(310) 652-9770
fax (310) 652-8870
•Bar area only.

Lunaria
10351 Santa Monica Blvd.
Los Angeles 90025
(310) 282-8870
fax (310) 282-0502
•Bar and in cigar club only.

**McCormick & Schmick's
  Seafood Restaurant**
633 W. 5th St.
Los Angeles 90071
(213) 629-1929
•Bar after 8 p.m. and on the patio
anytime.

Monty's Steak House
1100 Glendon Ave.
Los Angeles 90024
(310) 208-8787
fax (310) 208-6727
•Bar only.

Morton's of Chicago
435 S. LaCienega
Los Angeles 90048
(310) 246-1501
•*Bar only.*

Orleans
11705 National Blvd.
Los Angeles 90064
(310) 479-4187
•*Patio only.*

Pinot Hollywood
1448 N. Gower St.
Los Angeles 90028
(213) 461-8800
fax (213) 461-3949
•*Patio only.*

Revival Cafe
7149 Beverly Blvd.
Los Angeles 90036
(213) 930-1210
fax (213) 932-0114
•*Patio only.*

Taix French Restaurant
1911 Sunset Blvd.
Los Angeles 90026
(213) 484-1265
•*Bar, lounge and private rooms only.*

The Tower
1150 S. Olive St. atop the
    TransAmerica Center
Los Angeles 90015
(213) 746-1554
fax (213) 742-4593
•*Bar only.*

Ritz-Carlton
4375 Admiralty Way
Marina del Rey 90292
(310) 823-1700
fax (310) 823-2403
•*Library bar and lobby lounge only.*

Dal Baffo Restaurant
878 Santa Cruz Ave.
Menlo Park 94025
(415) 325-1588
fax (415) 326-2780
•*Lounge and private rooms only.*

Jordan's Chateau
408 W. Main St.
Merced 95340
(209) 384-1607
fax (209) 384-7811
•*Bar only.*

Terrace Cafe
1100 El Camino Real
Millbrae 94030
(415) 742-5588
•*Bar, lounge and patio only.*

Casa Munras Garden Hotel
700 Munras Ave.
Monterey 93940
(408) 375-2411
•*Private rooms only.*

The Whaling Station Inn
763 Wave St.
Monterey 93940
(408) 373-3778
fax (408) 373-2460
•*Bar, lounge and private rooms only.*

Bistro Don Giovanni
4110 St. Helena Hwy.
Napa 94558
(707) 224-3300
fax (707) 224-3395
•*Patio only.*

Mustards Grill
7399 St. Helena Hwy.
Napa 94558
(707) 944-2424
fax (707) 944-0828
•*Outside patio only.*

NEWPORT BEACH

Antoine
Le Meridien Hotel
4500 MacArthur Blvd.
Newport Beach 92660
(714) 476-2001
fax (714) 250-7191
•*Private area only.*

John Dominis Restaurant
2901 W. Coast Hwy.
Newport Beach 92663
(714) 650-1220
•*Patio and private rooms only.*

The Ritz
880 Newport Center Dr.
Newport Beach 92660
(714) 720-1800
fax (714) 720-3973
•*Bar and private dining room only.*

Twin Palms Newport Beach
630 Newport Center Dr.
Newport Beach 92660
(714) 721-8288
fax (714) 721-8460
•*Bar and patio only.*

The Hobbit
2932 E. Chapman Ave.
Orange 92669
(714) 997-1972
•*Cigar lounge and patio only.*

Il Sogno
863 Swarthmore Ave.
Pacific Palisades 90272
(310) 454-6522
•*Patio/sidewalk only.*

Morton's of Chicago
74-880 Country Club Dr.
Palm Dessert 92260
(619) 340-6865
fax (619) 340-2645
•*Bar only.*

Empire Grill & Tap Room
651 Emerson St.
Palo Alto 94301
(415) 321-3030
fax (415) 462-9006
•*All areas, but only after dinner.*

PASADENA

Bistro 45
45 S. Mentor Ave.
Pasadena 91106
(818) 795-2478
•*Needs advance notice, but will accomodate cigar smokers.*

Parkway Grill
510 S. Arroyo Pkwy.
Pasadena 91105
(818) 795-1001
fax (818) 796-6221
•*Bar and lounge from 3 p.m. to 5 p.m. only.*

Twin Palms Pasadena
101 W. Green St.
Pasadena 91105
(818) 577-2567
fax (818) 577-1306
•*Bar and patio only.*

▲ Zona Rosa Caffe
15 S. El Molino Ave.
Pasadena 91101
(818) 793-2334
•*Patio only.*
•*Coffeehouse that welcomes cigars on the patio and also has cigar events.*

The Bay Club/Inn at Spanish Bay
Pebble Beach Resort
2700 17 Mile Dr.
Pebble Beach 93953
(408) 647-7433
•*Lounge, private rooms and patio only.*

Iberia Restaurant
190 Ladera-Alpine Rd.
Portola Valley 94028
(415) 854-1746
•Bar only.

Magic Lamp Inn
8189 Foothill Blvd.
Rancho Cucamonga 91730
(909) 981-8659
•Bar, lounge and private rooms only.

Sycamore Inn
8318 Foothill Blvd.
Rancho Cucamonga 91730
(714) 982-1104
•Lounge only.

Ritz-Carlton
68900 Frank Sinatra Dr.
Rancho Mirage 92270
(619) 321-8282
fax (619) 321-6928
•Bar only.

Auberge du Soleil
180 Rutherford Hill Rd.
Rutherford 94573
(707) 963-1211
•Bar only.

SACRAMENTO

A Tabola
2627 Town & Country Place
Sacramento 95821
(916) 973-1800
fax (916) 973-9632
•Patio/sidewalk only.

Ciao Yama
  Hyatt Regency Sacramento
1209 L St.
Sacramento 95814
(916) 443-1234
•Patio/sidewalk only.

Harlows Restaurant
2708 J St.
Sacramento 95816
(916) 441-4693
•Cigar lounge over the bar only.

Mace's
501 Pavillion Lane
Sacramento 95825
(916) 922-0222
fax (916) 922-0201
•Bar, lounge, private rooms and patio/sidewalk only.

Morton's of Chicago
521 L St.
Sacramento 95814
(916) 442-5091
•Bar only.

The Pig's Ear Pub
1987 S. Diners Court
San Bernardino 92408
(909) 889-1442
•Bar and smoking restaurant (where drinks are primary and food is secondary).

SAN DIEGO

Baci's
1955 W. Morena Blvd.
San Diego 92110
(619) 275-2094
•Bar and lounge only.

El Bizcocho
17550 Bernardo Oaks Dr.
San Diego 92128
(619) 487-1611
•Lounge only.

Grant Grill
326 Broadway
San Diego 92101
(619) 239-6806
fax (619) 239-9517
•*Lounge only.*

Osteria Panevino
722 5th Ave.
San Diego 92101
(619) 595-7959
•*Bar and patio only.*

Prego Ristorante
1370 Frazee Rd.
San Diego 92108
(619) 294-4700
•*Bar, lounge, private rooms and patio only.*

Trattoria Portobello
715 4th Ave.
San Diego 92101
(619) 232-4440
•*Bar and patio only.*

SAN FRANCISCO

Alioto's Restaurant
8 Fisherman's Wharf
San Francisco 94133
(415) 673-0183
fax (415) 673-3894
•*Lounge only.*

The Big Four
Huntington Hotel
1075 California St.
San Francisco 94108
(415) 771-1140
fax (415) 474-6227
•*Bar only.*

Bistro "M"
Milano Hotel
55 5th St.
San Francisco 94103
(415) 543-8555
fax (415) 543-5843
•*Bar only.*

Cafe Tiramisu
28 Belden Lane
San Francisco 94114
(415) 421-7044
•*Private room only.*

Cypress Club
500 Jackson St.
San Francisco 94133
(415) 296-8555
fax (415) 296-9250
•*Bar, lounge, private rooms and patio/sidewalk only.*

Fournou's Ovens
905 California St.
San Francisco 94108
(415) 989-3500
fax (415) 986-8195
•*Lounge only.*

George's Global Kitchen &
Take-Out Cafe
340 Division St.
San Francisco 94103
(415) 864-4224
fax (415) 864-2332
•*Dining room during smoker nights only and patio.*

J.T.'s
555 Golden Gate Ave.
San Francisco 94102
(415) 861-7827
fax (415) 554-0351
•*Special facility, the "Stellar Cigar Society Smoke Room."*

Morton's of Chicago
400 Post St.
San Francisco 94102
(415) 986-5830
•*Bar only.*

The Occidental Grill
453 Pine St.
San Francisco 94104
(415) 834-0484
•*Bar and lounge only.*

Palio d'Asti
640 Sacramento St.
San Francisco 94111
(415) 395-9800
fax (415) 362-6002
•*Bar, lounge and private rooms only.*

The Park Grill
  Park Hyatt Hotel
333 Battery St.
San Francisco 94111
(415) 296-2933
fax (415) 296-2919
•*Bar only.*

Redwood Room
  Clift Hotel
495 Gedry St.
San Francisco 94102
(415) 775-4700
•*Lounge only.*

Ritz-Carlton
600 Stockton St.
San Francisco 94108
(415) 296-7465
•*Ritz-Carlton Bar from 6 p.m. until closing only.*

Stars
150 Redwood Alley
San Francisco 94102
(415) 861-7827
fax (415) 554-0351
•*Special facility, the "Stellar Cigar Society Smoke Room," which Stars shares with J.T.'s.*

Timo's
842 Valencia St.
San Francisco 94110
(415) 647-0558
•*Bar, lounge and patio only.*

▲ **Vendetta**
12 Tillman Place
San Francisco 94108
(415) 397-7755
•*Cigar smoking room—members only.*
•*Membership smoking club in retail store that sells cigars and men's accessories.*

Yoshida-Ya
2909 Webster St.
San Francisco 94123
(415) 346-3431
fax (415) 346-0907
•*Bar only.*

Cafe Roma
1819 Osos St.
San Luis Obispo 93401
(805) 541-6800
•*Patio only.*

Barley & Hopps
201 S. B St.
San Mateo 94401
(415) 348-7808
•*Parlor area only.*

Morton's of Chicago
1661 W. Sunflower Ave., Ste. C-5
Santa Ana 92704
(714) 444-4834
fax (714) 444-4836
•Bar and private dining only.

La Sala Lounge
1260 Channel Dr.
Santa Barbara 93108
(805) 969-2261
fax (805) 969-4212
•Lounge after 5 p.m. only.

Wine Cask
813 Anacapa St.
Santa Barbara 93101
(805) 966-9463
fax (805) 568-0664
•Patio/sidewalk only.

SANTA MONICA

Abiquiu
1413 5th Ave.
Santa Monica 90401
(310) 395-8611
•Bar and patio only.

Drago Ristorante
2628 Wilshire Blvd.
Santa Monica 90403
(310) 828-1585
•Bar and private rooms only.

Michael's
1147 3rd St.
Santa Monica 90403
(310) 451-0843
•Bar and garden after 10 p.m. only.

Remi
1451 3rd St. Promenade
Santa Monica 90401
(310) 393-6545
fax (310) 394-8851
•Private rooms and patio/sidewalk only.

Röckenwagner
2435 Main St.
Santa Monica 90405
(310) 399-6504
•Patio only.

Schatzi on Main
3110 Main St.
Santa Monica 90405
(310) 399-4800
fax (310) 399-6868
•Bar and patio/sidewalk only.

Valentino
3115 Pico Blvd.
Santa Monica 90405
(310) 829-4313
•Garden and private parties only.

Romeo et Juliette
1198 Pacific Coast Hwy., Ste. E
Seal Beach 90740
(310) 430-2331
•Cigar divan and outdoor patio only.

Spaghettini Rotisserie & Grill
3005 Old Ranch Pkwy.
Seal Beach 90740
(310) 596-2199
fax (310) 596-6573
•Bar only.

The Restaurant at Meadowood
  Meadowood Resort
900 Meadowood Lane
St. Helena 94574
(707) 963-3646
•Bar and private rooms only.

Showley's at Miramonte
1327 Railroad Ave.
St. Helena 94574
(707) 963-1200
•Private rooms only (please call).

Eureka Restaurant
445 W. Weber Ave.
Stockton 95203
(209) 462-2996
fax (209) 462-9052
•*Bar only.*

STUDIO CITY

The Bistro Garden at Coldwater
12950 Ventura Blvd.
Studio City 91604
(818) 501-0202
fax (818) 501-2244
•*Bar only.*

Pinot Bistro
12969 Ventura Blvd.
Studio City 91604
(818) 990-0500
fax (818) 990-0540
•*Patio only.*

Sportsmen's Lodge-Caribou
12833 Ventura Blvd.
Studio City 91604
(818) 984-0202
•*Bar only.*

Vintage Press Restaurant
216 N. Willis St.
Visalia 93991
(209) 733-3033
fax (209) 738-5262
•*Bar, lounge, private rooms and patio/sidewalk.*

Cicada
8478 Melrose Ave.
West Hollywood 90669
(213) 655-5559
•*Private room only.*

Provencia
945 N. Fairfax Ave.
West Hollywood 90046
(213) 654-4594
fax (213) 654-6275
•*Bar and patio only.*

Napa Valley Grille
6795 Washington St.
Yountville 94599
(707) 944-8686
•*Patio/sidewalk only.*

COLORADO

Marie's Inn
400 Mountain Ave.
Berthoud 80513
(970) 532-2648
•*Smoking room only.*

Laudicio
2785 Iris Ave.
Boulder 80304
(303) 442-1300
•*Private cigar room only.*

DENVER

Avenue Grill
630 E. 17th Ave.
Denver 80203
(303) 861-2820
•*Bar, private rooms and late night in the dining room.*

Morton's of Chicago
1710 Wynkoop St.
Denver 80202
(303) 825-3353
•*Smoking section.*

Mr. D's
2121 S. Sheridan Blvd.
Denver 80214
(303) 985-1518
•*Bar and patio/sidewalk only.*

Palace Arms
  Brown Palace Hotel
321 17th St.
Denver 80202
(303) 297-3111
fax (303) 297-3928
•Smoking section.

Papillon
250 Josephine St.
Denver 80206
(303) 333-7166
fax (303) 333-4820
•Bar only.

The Parlour
846 Broadway
Denver 80203
(303) 837-0660
•Bar area downstairs only.

▲ **Shakespeare's**
2375 15th St.
Denver 80202
(303) 433-6000
fax (303) 964-9445
•All areas.
•Billiard hall, pub and restaurant.

Tante Louise
4900 E. Colfax Ave.
Denver 80220
(303) 355-4488
fax (303) 321-6312
•Select areas of the dining room and lounge.

Trinity Grille
1801 Broadway
Denver 80202
(303) 293-2288
•Bar area only.

Nico's Catacombs
115 S. College Ave.
Fort Collins 80524
(970) 484-6029
•Bar, lounge and private rooms after 9:30 p.m. only.

The Left Bank Restaurant
183 Gore Creek Dr.
Vail 81657
(970) 476-3696
•Bar only.

C O N N E C T I C U T

Callahan's Restaurant
1027 S. Main St.
Cheshire 06410
(203) 271-1993
•All areas.

McDoogles Restaurant & Tap Room
19 Derby Ave., Rte. 34
Derby 06418
(203) 735-0049
fax (203) 734-1924
•All areas.

Restaurant Jean-Louis
61 Lewis St.
Greenwich 06830
(203) 622-8450
fax (203) 622-5845
•Late night in the dining room only.

Morgan Restaurant
265 Glenville Rd.
Greenwich 06831
(203) 531-5100
fax (203) 531-5103
•Bar only.

Peppercorn's Grill
357 Main St.
Hartford 06106
(860) 547-1714
•Lounge after dinner and bar only.

Tollgate Hill Inn
Rte. 202 & Tollgate Rd.
Litchfield 06759
(860) 567-4545
fax (860) 567-8397
•*Dining room (if other diners do not complain) and bar area.*

Eli Cannon's Tap Room
695 Main St.
Middletown 06457
(860) 347-3547
• *Tap room and outdoor courtyard only.*

Scribner's
31 Village Rd.
Milford 06460
(203) 878-7019
fax (203) 878-2238
•*Lounge/bar only.*

Flood Tide
Junction Rtes. 1 & 27
Mystic 06365
(203) 536-8140
•*Bar, lounge and private rooms only.*

Le Bon Coin
223 Litchfield Tpke.
New Preston 06777
(203) 868-7763
•*Bar only.*

Old Lyme Inn
85 Lyme St.
Old Lyme 06371
(860) 434-2600
•*Bar only.*

Georgies
232 Leavenworth Rd.
Shelton 06484
(203) 929-7343
•*Dining room and bar.*

La Bretagne Restaurant
2010 W. Main St.
Stamford 06902
(203) 324-9539
•*Bar and lounge only.*

Bacco's Restaurant
1230 Thomaston Ave.
Waterbury 06704
(203) 755-0635
•*Bar only.*

Cafe 4 Fifty 7
457 W. Main St.
Waterbury 06702
(203) 574-4507
•*Bar only.*

The Meeting Street Grill
1563 Post Rd. E.
Westport 06880
(203) 256-3309
•*Bar only.*

DISTRICT OF COLUMBIA

The Capital Grille
601 Pennsylvania Ave.
Washington, D.C. 20037
(202) 737-6200
•*Smoking sections and bar.*

The City Club of Washington, D.C.
555 13th St. NW
Washington, D.C. 20004
(202) 347-0818
fax (202) 737-4341
•*Lounge area only.*

i Ricchi
1220 19th St. NW
Washington, D.C 20036
(202) 835-0459
fax (202) 872-1220
•*Smoking areas.*

J. Paul's
3218 M St. NW
Washington, D.C. 20007
(202) 333-3450
fax (202) 342-6721
•*Smoking section and bar.*

John Hay Room
  Hay Adams Hotel
800 16th St. NW
Washington, D.C. 20006
(202) 638-6600
fax (202) 638-2716
•*Lounge only.*

La Brasserie
239 Massachusetts Ave. NE
Washington, D.C. 20001
(202) 546-9154
fax (202) 546-5183
•*Private rooms only (must be reserved in advance).*

La Colline
400 N. Capitol St. NW
Washington, D.C. 20001
(202) 737-0400
fax (202) 737-3026
•*Dining room.*

Les Halles Restaurant
1201 Pennsylvania Ave. NW
Washington, D.C. 20004
(202) 347-6848
fax (202) 347-6911
•*3rd level dining room and bar/lounge.*

The Monocle on Capitol Hill
107 D St. NE
Washington, D.C. 20002
(202) 546-4488
•*Dining room and bar.*

Morton's of Chicago
3251 Prospect St. NW
Washington, D.C. 20007
(202) 342-6258
fax (202) 338-8033
•*Smoking section.*

Nathan's
3150 M St. NW
Washington, D.C. 20007
(202) 338-2000
fax (202) 333-2509
•*Bar only.*

Ozio
1835 K St. NW
Washington, D.C. 20006
(202) 822-6000
fax (202) 822-6003
•*All areas.*

Renaissance Hotel
999 9th St. NW
Washington, D.C. 20001
(202) 898-9000
fax (202) 789-4213
•*Bar only.*

Ritz-Carlton
2100 Massachusetts Ave. NW
Washington, D.C. 20008
(202) 293-2100
fax (202) 293-0641
•*Jockey Club bar only.*

Roma Restaurant
3419 Connecticut Ave. NW
Washington, D.C. 20008
(202) 363-6611
•*Bar, private rooms and patio only.*

Sam & Harry's
1200 19th St. NW
Washington, D.C. 20036
(202) 296-4333
•*Smoking section.*

Seasons Restaurant
  Four Seasons Hotel
2800 Pennsylvania Ave. NW
Washington, D.C. 20007
(202) 342-0810
fax (202) 342-1673
•*Smoking section.*

Sesto Senso
1214 18th St. NW
Washington, D.C. 20036
(202) 785-9525
fax (202) 785-9522
•*Smoking section, bar and upstairs
lounge.*

Sfuzzi Washington
50 Massachusetts Ave. NE
Washington, D.C. 20001
(202) 842-4141
fax (202) 842-2760
•*Specially designated area only.*

Sheraton Carlton
923 16th St. NW & K St.
Washington, D.C. 20006
(202) 638-2626
fax (202) 347-6961
•*Lounge only.*

Tunnicliff's Restaurant
222 7th St. SE
Washington, D.C. 20003
(202) 546-3663
fax (202) 544-7479
•*Bar, living room, patio and front tables
in the restaurant.*

Washington Grill
1143 New Hampshire Ave. NW
Washington, D.C. 20037
(202) 775-0800
•*Dining room, bar and private rooms.*

DELAWARE

Blue Coat Inn
800 N. State St.
Dover 19901
(302) 674-1776
•*Designated smoking sections.*

Columbus Inn
2216 Pennsylvania Ave.
Wilmington 19806
(302) 571-1492
fax (302) 571-1111
•*Bar, adjoining club room and 3 private
dining rooms.*

Harry's Savoy Grill
2020 Naaman's Rd.
Wilmington 19810
(302) 475-3000
fax (302) 475-9990
•*Bar, private rooms and patio/sidewalk
only.*

FLORIDA

Maison & Jardin
430 S. Wymore Rd.
Altamonte Springs 32714
(407) 862-4410
•*Lounge, patio and private dining rooms
only.*

Ritz-Carlton
4750 Amelia Island Pkwy.
Amelia Island 32034
(904) 277-1100
fax (904) 277-1145
•*Lobby and lounge only.*

Sheldon's
9501 Harding Ave.
Bal Harbour 33154
(305) 866-6251
•*Bar only.*

Boca Raton Hotel & Club
501 E. Camino Real
Boca Raton 33432
(407) 395-3000
fax (407) 447-3483
•Bar and lounge only.

Maxwell's Chophouse
501 E. Palmetto Park Rd.
Boca Raton 33432
(407) 347-7077
fax (407) 347-7079
•Bar and Club Room only.

Bobby's Bistro & Wine Bar
(located directly behind Bob Heilman's
  Beachcomber Restaurant)
447 Mandalay Ave.
Clearwater Beach 34630
(813) 446-WINE
•Smoking section, bar and patio.

Churchill's Restaurant & Pub
Pine Lake Plaza
10076 Griffin Rd.
Cooper City 33328
(954) 680-0226
•Pub and private dining room only.

Caffe Abbracci
318 Aragon Ave.
Coral Gables 33134
(305) 441-0700
fax (305) 442-0061
•Bar only.

Yuca
177 Giralda Ave.
Coral Gables 33134
(305) 444-4448
fax (305) 441-8617
•Smoking section, bar and lounge.

FORT LAUDERDALE

Burt & Jack's
Berth 23, Port Everglades
Fort Lauderdale 33316
(954) 522-5225
fax (954) 522-2048
•Cocktail lounge and patio only.

**Harbor Beach
  Marriott Hotel**
3030 Holiday Dr.
Fort Lauderdale 33316
(954) 525-4000
•Bar only.

**Smoke Chophouse and Cigar
  Emporium**
2863 E. Commercial Blvd.
Fort Lauderdale 33308
(954) 489-1122
fax (954) 771-1597
•All areas.

Studio One Cafe
2447 E. Sunrise Blvd.
Fort Lauderdale 33304
(954) 565-2052
•Dining room after 9 p.m. and
patio/sidewalk only.

▲ **Up-In-Smoke**
2863 E. Commercial Blvd.
Fort Lauderdale 33308
(954) 489-1122
fax (954) 771-1597
•All areas.
•Cocktail lounge and bar above Smoke
Chophouse and Cigar Emporium.

The Blue Anchor Pub
10550 Old St. Augustine Rd.
Jacksonville 32257
(904) 262-1592
•All areas.

Rusty Pelican Restaurant
3201 Rickenbacker Causeway
Key Biscayne 33149
(305) 361-3818
•*Dining room, bar and lounge.*

**Snook's Bayside Restaurant and
Patrick's Waterfront Bar**
M.M. 99.9 (behind Largo Honda)
Key Largo 33037
(305) 453-3799
•*Bars and outside only.*

KEY WEST

**Angler's Seafood & Steak
Restaurant**
3618 N. Roosevelt Blvd.
Key West 33040
(305) 294-4717
•*Separate dining room and bar only.*

Louie's Backyard
700 Weddell Ave.
Key West 33040
(305) 294-1061
fax (305) 294-0002
• *"Afterdeck Bar"—a transom's height
above the water.*

The Ocean View
1435 Simonton St.
Key West 33040
(305) 296-5000
fax (305) 296-2830
•*Lounge only.*

**The Colony Restaurant
The Colony Beach Hotel**
1620 Gulf of Mexico Dr.
Longboat Key 34228
(941) 383-5558
fax (941) 387-0250
•*Lounge only.*

Ritz-Carlton
100 Ocean Blvd.
Manalapan 33462
(407) 533-6000
fax (407) 588 4202
•*Lobby lounge only.*

MIAMI

Casa Juancho Restaurant
2436 SW 8th St.
Miami 33135
(305) 642-2452
fax (305) 642-2524
•*Dining room, bar, lounge and private
rooms.*

**Grand Cafe
Grand Bay Hotel**
2669 S. Bayshore Dr.
Miami 33133
(305) 858-9600
fax (305) 854-3057
•*Bar, lounge, private rooms and
patio/sidewalk only.*

Hotel Casa de Campo
2600 SW 3rd Ave., #300
Miami 33129
(809) 523-3333
fax (809) 523-8510
•*Lounge only.*

Le Pavillon Restaurant
100 Chopin Plaza
Miami 33131
(305) 577-1000
•*Salon only.*

Victor's Cafe
2340 SW 32nd Ave.
Miami 33145
(305) 445-1313
fax (305) 445-2372
•*Bar and lounge only.*

MIAMI BEACH

Alfredo the Original of Rome
  Doral Ocean
4833 Collins Ave.
Miami Beach 33140
(305) 532-3600
•*Bar and lounge only.*

Brasserie Le Coze
2901 Florida Ave.
Miami Beach 33140
(305) 444-9697
fax (305) 444-7651
•*Bar only.*

Cafe Royal
  Hotel Sofitel Miami
5800 Blue Lagoon Dr.
Miami Beach 33126
(305) 264-4888
fax (305) 261-7871
•*"Le Fumoir" cigar lounge and bar;
private parties in the Limoges room.*

Colony Bistro
736 Ocean Dr.
Miami Beach 33139
(305) 673-0088
fax (305) 532-0762
•*Patio only.*

▲ **The Forge/Cuba Club**
432 Arthur Godfrey Rd.
Miami Beach 33140
Forge: (305) 538-8533
Cuba Club: (305) 604-9798
•*All areas.*
•*Forge is open to the public; Cuba Club
is a private cigar club—new members
are always welcome.*

i Paparazzi
940 Ocean Dr.
Miami Beach 33139
(305) 531-3500
•*Patio only.*

Joe's Stone Crab
227 Biscayne St.
Miami Beach 33139
(305) 673-0365
fax (305) 673-0295
•*Bar and smoking area only.*

Le Festival
2120 Salzedo St.
Miami Beach 33134
(305) 442-8545
fax (305) 445-5563
•*Private room only.*

The Strand
671 Washington St.
Miami Beach 33133
(305) 532-2340
fax (305) 532-1342
•*All areas.*

Versailles
3555 SW 8th St.
Miami Beach 33135
(305) 445-7614
fax (305) 445-9469
•*Smoking section.*

NAPLES

The Chef's Garden
1300 3rd St. S.
Naples 33940
(941) 262-5500
•*Lounge and private room only.*

▲ **Heaven**
The Hibiscus Center
2950 N. Tamiami Trail
Naples 33940
(941) 649-6373
fax (941) 649-5330
•*All areas.*
•*Wine bar and beer list; "clublike"
atmosphere; highly ventilated.*

Villa Pescatore
8920 N. Tamiami Trail
Naples 33963
(941) 597-8119
•Lounge only.

Chef Allen's
19088 NE 29th Ave.
North Miami Beach 33160
(305) 935-2900
fax (305) 935-9062
•Bar only.

The Leopard Room
  Restaurant & Supper Club
  Chesterfield Hotel
363 Cocoanut Row
Palm Beach 33480
(407) 659-5800
fax (407) 659-6707
•All areas.

Fisherman's Wharf
222 Pompano Beach Blvd.
Pompano Beach 33062
(305) 941-5522
•Smoking section.

▲ **TPC (Tournament Players Club)**
  at Sawgrass
110 TPC Blvd.
Ponte Vedra 32082
(904) 273-3242
fax (904) 285-7970
•Throughout the clubhouse.

Cafe L'Europe
431 St. Armand Circle
Sarasota 34236
(941) 388-4415
fax (941) 388-2362
*•Front dining room and private rooms
only.*

Gecko's Grill & Pub
4870 S. Tamiami Trail
Sarasota 34231
(813) 923-8896
•All areas.

Johnny's
13079 Park Blvd.
Seminole 34642
(813) 398-0780
fax (813) 398-0696
•Smoking section lounge and bar.

TAMPA

Armani's
  Hyatt Regency Westshore
6200 Courtney Campbell Causeway
Tampa 33607
(813) 281-9165
•Lounge and terrace only.

Bern's Steakhouse
1208 S. Howard Ave.
Tampa 33606
(813) 251-2421
fax (813) 251-5001
*•Bar, lounge and the Harry Waugh
Dessert Room only.*

Columbia Cafe Cigar Bar
2117 E. 7th Ave.
Tampa 33605
(813) 248-4961
fax (813) 247-5581
•Cigar bar only.

Le Bordeaux
1502 S. Howard Ave.
Tampa 33606
(813) 254-4387
fax (813) 254-5485
•Bar and bistro only.

O'Keefe's Irish Pub Restaurant
115 S. Rockingham Ave.
Tavares 32778
(904) 343-2157
•*All areas.*

Morton's of Chicago
777 S. Flagler
West Palm Beach 33401
(407) 835-9664
•*Smoking section, lounge and private rooms.*

GEORGIA

▲ **The Golf Club of Georgia**
1 Golf Club Dr.
Alpharetta 30202
(770) 664-8644
fax (770) 664-0044
•*The Men's Grill Room only.*
•*Private golf club.*

ATLANTA

The Abbey
163 Ponce de Leon Ave.
Atlanta 30308
(404) 876-8532
fax (404) 876-8832
•*Bar, lounge and private rooms only.*

Bone's Restaurant
3130 Piedmont Rd.
Atlanta 30305
(404) 237-2663
•*Dining room, bar and private rooms.*

Bugatti Restaurant
100 CNN Center
Atlanta 30335
(404) 659-0000
•*Smoking area of dining room and lounge.*

Cafe Intermezzo
1845 Peachtree Rd.
Atlanta 30309
(404) 355-0411
fax (404) 350-8158
•*In Loggia (special smoking room— dining available), bar and patio.*

Cassis
   Hotel Nikko
3300 Peachtree Rd.
Atlanta 30305
(404) 365-8100
•*Smoking section.*

Chops
70 W. Paces Ferry Rd.
Atlanta 30305
(404) 262-2675
•*Smoking area and lounge.*

Florencia
75 14th St.
Atlanta 30309
(404) 881-9898
fax (404) 888-8610
•*Segovia bar only.*

The Mansion
179 Ponce de Leon Ave.
Atlanta 30308
(404) 876-0727
fax (404) 876-7322
•*Smoking section.*

Morton's of Chicago
303 Peachtree St. NE
Atlanta 30308
(404) 577-4366
•*Smoking section, bar and lounge.*

Morton's of Chicago, Buckhead
Peachtree Lenox Building
3379 Peachtree Rd. NE
Atlanta 30326
(404) 816-6535
•*Smoking area, bar and boardrooms.*

103 West
103 W. Paces Ferry Rd.
Atlanta 30305
(404) 233-5993
•*Lounge/bar only.*

Ritz-Carlton, Atlanta
181 Peachtree St. NE
Atlanta 30303
(404) 659-0400
•*Bar only.*

Ritz-Carlton, Buckhead
3434 Peachtree Rd.
Atlanta 30326
(404) 237-2700
•*Lobby lounge only.*

Tongue & Groove
3055 Peachtree Rd.
Atlanta 30305
(404) 261-2325
fax (404) 261-4137
•*All areas.*

Winfield's
Galleria Mall
1 Galleria Pkwy.
Atlanta 30339
(770) 955-5300
fax (770) 953-1343
•*Smoking section.*

Santa Fe Flats
  Embassy Suites
4700 Southport Rd.
College Park 30337
(404) 767-1988
•*Smoking section.*

The Captain's Roost
2873 Main St.
East Point 30344
(404) 761-9468
•*Smoking section.*

Hackett's
  Holiday Inn Skytop Convention
20 U.S. 411 E.
Rome 30161
(706) 295-1100
fax (706) 291-7182
•*Smoking area.*

45 South at the Pirate's House
20 E. Broad St.
Savannah 31401
(912) 233-1881
fax (912) 233-5757
•*Lobby, private parties and late night in the dining room.*

HAWAII

HONOLULU

▲ **Caffe Pronto**
131 Kaiulani Ave.
Honolulu 96815
(808) 923-0111
•*Outside patio seating only.*
•*Coffeehouse offering pastries, desserts, cigars, etc...*

Gordon Biersch
1 Aloha Tower Dr.
Honolulu 96813
(808) 599-4877
fax (808) 537-3287
•*Smoking section and outside bar.*

Han Tree Lanai
2863 Kalakaua Ave.
Honolulu 96815
(808) 923-1555
fax (808) 922-9404
•*All areas.*

Johnny's Restaurant
500 Ala Moana Blvd.
Honolulu 96813
(808) 536-2566
•*Outside bar only.*

Kapalua Bay Club
1 Kapalua Bay Dr.
Honolulu 96761
(808) 669-8008
fax (808) 669-4620
•Poolside only.

L'Italiano
1330 Ala Moana Blvd.
Honolulu 96814
(808) 591-0105
fax (808) 591-1362
•All areas.

O'Tooles Irish Pub
902 Nuuanu
Honolulu 96813
(808) 536-6360
•Bar only.

Swan Court
  Hyatt Regency Maui
200 Nohea Kai Dr.
Lahaina 96761
(808) 661-1234
fax (808) 661-4499
•Lounge only.

ILLINOIS

University Inn - Sneakers Lounge
302 E. John St.
Champaign 61820
(217) 384-2100
fax (217) 322-2298
•Smoking section.

CHICAGO

Barney's Market Club Steakhouse
741 W. Randolph St.
Chicago 60661
(312) 372-6466
fax (312) 372-6013
•Bar only.

Bice Ristorante
158 E. Ontario St.
Chicago 60611
(312) 664-1474
•Bar, private rooms and patio/sidewalk only.

Binyon's Restaurant
327 S. Plymouth Court
Chicago 60604
(312) 341-1155
•All areas.

▲ **B.L.U.E.S. Etc...**
1124 W. Belmont
Chicago 60657
(312) 549-9416
•All areas.
•Blues bar with live music, dancing and pool tables.

Cafe Ba Ba Reeba!
2024 N. Halsted St.
Chicago 60614
(312) 935-5000
•Cigar lounge, bar and private rooms only.

Cafe Gordon
100 E. Chestnut
Chicago 60611
(312) 280-2100
fax (312) 467-9782
•Bar only.

Carlucci
2215 N. Halsted St.
Chicago 60614
(312) 281-1220
•Bar, lounge, private rooms and patio/sidewalk only.

Chez Paul
1300 Astor
Chicago 60610
(312) 944-6680
fax (312) 944-6685
•Bar and cigar room only.

Chicago Chop House
60 W. Ontario St.
Chicago 60610
(800) 229-2356, (312) 787-7100
•*Bar only.*

Coco Pazzo
300 W. Hubbard
Chicago 60610
(312) 836-0900
•*Bar and limited tables in dining room only.*

Cuisine's
  Stouffer Riviere Hotel
W. Wacker
Chicago 60601
(312) 372-7200
•*Cafe only.*

Danilo's

**464 NORTH HALSTED
CHICAGO, IL 60622
(312) 421-0218**

Danilo's, a family owned and operated steakhouse and Italian restaurant in the River West area, proudly serves large USDA prime aged steaks, chops, fresh fish and pasta. We are particularly well-known for our Pepper Steak, Veal Chops and Chicken Vesuivo, as well as a beautiful restored original 1920's art-deco bar. A lovely outdoor garden, and private room accommodates up to 80 people.

FREE PARKING
OPEN TUESDAY THROUGH FRIDAY
11:30 AM TO 11 PM,
SATURDAY 3:30 - 11 PM,
CLOSED SUNDAY AND MONDAY.

Danilo's
464 N. Halsted St.
Chicago 60622
(312) 421-0218
fax (312) 421-9417
•*Bar only.*

Distant Mirror Cafe
7007 N. Sheridan Rd.
Chicago 60626
(312) 761-3776
fax (312) 761-3069
•*All areas.*

Drink & Eat, Too!
541 W. Fulton
Chicago 60606
(312) 441-0818
fax (312) 441-9811
•*All areas.*

Entre Nous
  Fairmont Hotel
200 N. Columbus Dr.
Chicago 60601
(312) 565-7997
•*Bar at all times; Monday nights in the restaurant; Metropole lounge at all times.*

Four Seasons Hotel
120 E. Delaware
Chicago 60611
(312) 280-8800
•*Bar and private rooms only.*

Frontera Grill
445 N. Clark St.
Chicago 60601
(312) 661-1434
fax (312) 661-1830
•*Bar only.*

Gene & Georgetti
500 N. Franklin St.
Chicago 60610
(312) 527-3718
•*Bar only.*

392

Gibsons
1028 N. Rush St.
Chicago 60611
(312) 266-8999
fax (312) 787-5649
•Bar and private dining rooms only.

Harry's Velvet Room
534 N. Clark St.
Chicago 60610
(312) 828-0770
fax (312) 828-0775
•Bar after 9 p.m. and smoking lounge
only.

Jaxx
  Park Hyatt Hotel
800 N. Michigan Ave.
Chicago 60611
(312) 280-2230
fax (312) 280-1963
•Smoking area, bar and lobby lounge.

Jesse Livermore's
401 S. LaSalle St.
Chicago 60605
(312) 786-5272
•Bar only.

Mambo Grill
412 N. Clark St.
Chicago 60610
(312) 467-9797
fax (312) 755-0993
•Bar only.

The Marc
311 W. Superior
Chicago 60610
(312) 642-3810
fax (312) 642-0703
•After 10 p.m. only.

Morton's of Chicago
1050 N. State St.
Chicago 60610
(312) 266-4820
•Smoking section, bar, lounge and
private rooms.

Mr. D's Villa
10468 S. Indianapolis Blvd.
Chicago 60617
(312) 374-6089
fax (312) 734-8874
•Dining room.

Nick's Fishmarket
1 First National Plaza
Chicago 60603
(312) 621-0200
fax (312) 621-1118
•Cocktail lounge only.

O'Brien's
1528 N. Wells St.
Chicago 60610
(312) 787-3131
fax (312) 787-3990
•Bar only.

The Outpost Restaurant & Bar
3438 N. Clark
Chicago 60657
(312) 244-1166
email www.The-Outpost.com
•Dining room after service, bar and
outdoor cafe (weather permitting).

Printer's Row Restaurant
550 S. Dearborn St.
Chicago 60605
(312) 461-0780
•Lounge only.

The Pump Room
  The Ambassador East Hotel
1301 N. State Pkwy.
Chicago 60610
(312) 266-0360
fax (312) 266-7098
•*Bar and lounge only.*

Reminiscent Bar & Grill
3614 N. Damen Ave.
Chicago 60618
(312) 281-2118
•*Dining room and bar.*

Rigoletto
293 E. Illinois
Chicago 60045
(708) 234-7675
fax (708) 234-7688
•*Dining area in the bar only.*

Ritz-Carlton
160 E. Pearson St.
Chicago 60611
(312) 266-1000
fax (312) 266-9623
•*Bar, lounge and terrace only.*

Savoy Bar & Grill
440 S. LaSalle St.
Chicago 60605
(312) 663-8800
•*Bar only.*

Scoozi!
410 W. Huron St.
Chicago 60610
(312) 943-5900
fax (312) 943-8969
•*Bar only.*

Seasons Bar
120 E. Delaware
Chicago 60611
(312) 280-8800
•*Bar only.*

Shaw's Crab House
21 E. Hubbard St.
Chicago 60611
(312) 527-2722
fax (312) 527-4740
•*Bar only.*

Sorriso
321 N. Clark
Chicago 60610
(312) 644-0283
fax (312) 644-0318
•*Dining room and bar.*

Tania's Restaurant
2659 N. Milwaukee Ave.
Chicago 60647
(312) 235-7120
fax (312) 235-7954
•*Dining room, bar, lounge and private rooms.*

Mitchell's
9932 W. 55th St.
Countryside 60525
(708) 352-6840
•*Bar only.*

Pete Miller's Steakhouse
1557 Sherman Ave.
Evanston 60201
(708) 328-0399
fax (708) 332-2997
•*Smoking area, bar, jazz lounge and billiard room.*

Benjamin's
103 N. Main St.
Galena 61036
(815) 777-0467
•*Bar area only.*

Maurie's Table
2360 Glenwood Ave.
Joliet 60435
(815) 744-2619
•*Dining room, bar and patio/sidewalk.*

Uptown Bar & Grill
613 1st St.
LaSalle 61301
(815) 224-4545
fax (815) 224-3877
•*Smoking section.*

Ken's Guest House
9848 SW Hwy.
Oaklawn 60453
(708) 422-4014
•*Bar, lounge and private rooms only.*

R O C K F O R D

Cafe Patou
3929 Broadway
Rockford 61108
(815) 227-4100
fax (815) 227-0778
•*Bar area only.*

The City Club of Rockford
501 7th St.
Rockford 61104
(815) 966-6966
fax (815) 966-6969
•*Bar, lounge and private rooms only.*

Giovanni's Restaurant
610 N. Bell School Rd.
Rockford 61107
(815) 398-6411
fax (815) 398-6416
•*Bar and special private rooms only.*

Morton's of Chicago
9525 W. Bryn Mawr
Rosemont 60018
(847) 678-5155
fax (847) 678-5193
•*All areas.*

Scalawag's
313 W. State
Sycamore 60178
(815) 895-4333
•*Bar only.*

Jumer's Castle Lodge - Urbana
209 S. Broadway
Urbana 61801
(217) 384-8800
fax (217) 384-9001
•*Smoking section and bar.*

Morton's of Chicago
1 Westbrook Corporate Center
  22nd & Wolf Rds.
Westchester 60153
(708) 562-7000
fax (708) 562-7073
•*Smoking section, bar and private dining
rooms.*

I N D I A N A

I N D I A N A P O L I S

Graffiti's
50 S. Capital
Indianapolis 46204
(317) 231-3970
fax (317) 231-3986
•*All areas.*

Keystone Grill
8650 Keystone Crossing
Indianapolis 46240
(317) 848-5202
fax (317) 575-0068
•*Dining room.*

The Marker Restaurant
  Adam's Mark Hotel
2544 Executive Dr.
Indianapolis 46241
(317) 248-2481
fax (317) 381-6170
•*Private room only.*

St. Elmo Steak House
127 S. Illinois St.
Indianapolis 46225
(317) 635-0636
•*Bar and private rooms only.*

La Salle Grill
115 W. Colfax
South Bend 46601
(800) 382-9323, (219) 288-1155
•*Bar, cigar salon, late evenings in the dining room and patio/sidewalk.*

Orion's Restaurant
1700 Rozella Rd.
Warsaw 46580
(219) 269-9100
•*Lounge only.*

IOWA

Des Moines Eight Hundred One Steak & Chop House
801 Grand Ave., Ste. 200
Des Moines 50309
(515) 288-6000
fax (515) 288-4083
•*Bar and special cigar and wine room (35 seats).*

▲ Embassy Club
801 Grand Ave.
Des Moines 50309
(515) 244-2582
•*Lounge only.*
•*Private club.*

Metz Continental Cuisine
303 Locust St.
Des Moines 50309
(515) 246-1656
fax (515) 246-8718
•*Lounge and atrium only.*

KANSAS

Lucky Bar & Grille
710 N. Manhattan Ave.
Manhattan 66502
(913) 776-9090
•*All areas.*

KENTUCKY

Dagwood's
204 N. 3rd St.
Bardstown 40004
(502) 348-4029
•*All areas.*

Coach House Restaurant
855 S. Broadway
Lexington 40504
(606) 252-7777
fax (606) 252-7778
•*Lounge only.*

LOUISVILLE

Azalea
3612 Brownsboro Rd.
Louisville 40207
(502) 895-5493
•*Private dining room and patio.*

Bobby J's
3220 Frankfort Ave.
Louisville 40206
(502) 899-7142
•*Bar, after dinner and at cigar dinners. (Moving to a new location July '96.)*

Deitrich's in the Cresent
2862 Frankfort Ave.
Louisville 40206
(502) 897-6076
•*Lounge only.*

Flagship Restaurant Galt House Hotel
140 N. 4th Ave.
Louisville 40202
(502) 589-5200
fax (502) 585-4266
•*Dining room, bar and lounge.*

▲ **Illusions — A Nightclub**
  and Restaurant
1506 Lake Shore Court
Louisville 40223
(502) 425-7339
•*Smoking section of restaurant, "Pier 1506" and all areas of nightclub.*

The Oakroom
  Seelbach Hotel
500 4th Ave.
Louisville 40202
(502) 585-3200
fax (502) 585-9240
•*"Derby Winners Anteroom" and private room.*

LOUISIANA

Charley G's Seafood Grill
111 Veterans Blvd.
Metairie 70005
(504) 837-6408
fax (504) 837-2466
•*Dining room, bar and private rooms.*

Crozier's Restaurant
3216 W. Esplanade Ave. N.
Metairie 70002
(504) 833-8108
•*After late dinners and cigar nights only.*

NEW ORLEANS

Antoine's
713 St. Louis St.
New Orleans 70130
(504) 581-4422
•*Main dining room and private banquet rooms.*

Arnaud's Restaurant
813 Bienville St.
New Orleans 70112
(504) 523-5433
fax (504) 581-7908
•*Bars and private rooms only.*

Brennan's
417 Royal St.
New Orleans 70130
(504) 525-9711
•*Smoking areas.*

Brossard's Restaurant
819 Conti St.
New Orleans 70112
(504) 581-3866
fax (504) 581-3873
•*Bar, courtyard and banquet rooms at all times; main dining room late in the evening.*

Cafe Rue Bourbon Restaurant
241 Rue Bourbon at Bienville
New Orleans 70130
(504) 524-0114
fax (504) 524-0146
•*All areas.*

The Court of Two Sisters
613 Royal St.
New Orleans 70130
(504) 522-7261
fax (504) 581-5804
•*Smoking area.*

Emeril's Restaurant
800 Tchoupitoulas
New Orleans 70130
(504) 528-9393
•*Bar and dining room.*

Galatoire's
209 Bourbon St.
New Orleans 70130
(504) 525-2021
•*Dining room.*

The Grill Room
300 Gravier St.
New Orleans 70130
(504) 522-1992
fax (504) 596-4513
•*Polo lounge only.*

Kabby's
  Riverside Hilton
2 Poydras
New Orleans 70140
(504) 584-3880
•*Smoking section.*

Louis XVI Restaurant
730 Rue Bienville
New Orleans 70130
(504) 581-7000
fax (504) 524-8925
•*Piano bar dining area and courtyard
dining area.*

Maximo's Italian Grill
1117 Decatur St.
New Orleans 70116
(504) 586-8883
fax (504) 586-8891
•*Smoking section and bar.*

The Rib Room
  Omni Royal Orleans Hotel
621 St. Louis St.
New Orleans 70130
(504) 529-5333
•*Bar and smoking room "Escoffier"
adjacent to restaurant.*

Versailles
2100 St. Charles Ave.
New Orleans 70130
(504) 524-2535
fax (504) 527-5036
•*Lounge only.*

Windsor Court Hotel
300 Gravier St.
New Orleans 70130
(504) 523-6000
fax (504) 596-4713
•*Polo Lounge only.*

Sazerac Bar
  The Fairmont Hotel
123 Barrone St.
New Orleans 70140
(504) 529-7111
•*Bar only.*

MAINE

The Greenhouse Restaurant
193 Broad St.
Bangor 04401
(207) 945-4040
•*Dining room, lounge and private
rooms.*

La Conque
  The Manor Inn
Battle Ave., Box 276
Castine 04421
(207) 326-4335
fax (207) 326-4066
•*Smoking section.*

Lincoln House Country Inn
Rtes. 1 & 86
Dennysville 04628
(207) 726-3953
•*Pub only.*

MARYLAND

BALTIMORE

Baltimore Brewing Company
104 Albemarle St.
Baltimore 21202
(410) 837-5000
fax (410) 837-5024
•*Bar & cocktail area and indoor terrace
only.*

The Brass Elephant
   Victor's
924 N. Charles St.
Baltimore 21201
(410) 547-8480
fax (410) 783-2933
•*Lounge only.*

Da Mimmo Finest Italian Cuisine
217 S. High St.
Baltimore 21202
(410) 727-6876
fax (410) 727-1927
•*Bar, lounge, private rooms and
patio/sidewalk only.*

The Fishery Restaurant
1717 Eastern Ave.
Baltimore 21231
(410) 327-9340
fax (410) 327-9569
•*Bar and private rooms only.*

▲ **Max's on Broadway**
737 S. Broadway
Baltimore 21231
(410) 276-2850
fax (410) 276-4807
•*All areas.*
•*Offers 62 beers on draft, cigars,
satellite sports and bar food.*

The Prime Rib
1101 N. Calvert St.
Baltimore 21202
(410) 539-1804
•*Bar only.*

Ruth's Chris Steak House
600 Water St.
Baltimore 21202
(410) 783-0033
fax (410) 783-0049
•*Dining room and lounge/cigar room
(seats 50).*

Savannah
   Admiral Fell Inn
888 S. Broadway
Baltimore 21231
(410) 522-2195
fax (410) 522-0707
•*Wine Cellar and English Pub only.*

Windows
202 E. Pratt St.
Baltimore 21202
(410) 547-1200
fax (410) 752-2857
•*Lounge only.*

Nick's Airport Inn
Rte. 11 N.
Hagerstown 21742
(301) 733-8560
•*Lounge only.*

Old Angler's Inn
10801 McArthur Blvd.
Potomac 20854
(301) 365-2425
fax (301) 983-0630
•*Bar, lounge, private rooms and
patio/sidewalk.*

The Inn at Perry Cabin
308 Watkins Lane
St. Michael's 21663
(800) 722-2949, (410) 745-2200
fax (410) 745-3348
•*Everywhere except dining room.*

Antrim 1844 Country Inn
30 Treventon Rd.
Taneytown 21787
(410) 756-6812
fax (410) 756-2744
•*Pub and veranda only.*

Hersh's Orchard Inn
1528 E. Joppa Rd.
Towson 21286
(410) 823-0384
•Bar and lounge only.

Westminster Inn
5 S. Center St.
Westminster 21157
(410) 857-4445
*•Cigar lounge/shop and Courtyard
Restaurant (when lounge/shop is closed).*

MASSACHUSETTS

BOSTON

Anthony's Pier 4
140 Northern Ave.
Boston 02210
(617) 682-6262
•Smoking areas.

Biba Restaurant
272 Boylston St.
Boston 02116
(617) 426-7878
•Bar and lounge only.

Four Seasons Hotel
200 Boylston St.
Boston 02116
(617) 338-4400
•Bristol Lounge smoking area.

The Capital Grille
359 Newbury St.
Boston 02115
(617) 262-8900
fax (617) 262-9449
•Dining rooms, bar and private rooms.

Grill 23 & Bar
161 Berkeley St.
Boston 02116
(617) 542-2255
fax (617) 542-5114
•Dining room, bar and lounge.

Jimmy's Harborside
242 Northern Ave.
Boston 02210
(617) 423-1000
fax (617) 423-1937
•Bar and cocktail lounge only.

Locke-Ober
3 Winter Place
Boston 02108
(617) 542-1340
•Dining room and lounge.

Morton's of Chicago
1 Exeter Plaza
Boston 02116
(617) 266-5858
•Smoking section.

Ritz-Carlton
15 Arlington St.
Boston 02116
(617) 536-5700
•Lounge and private rooms only.

Seasons
  The Bostonian Hotel
Faneuil Hall Market Place
Boston 02109
(617) 523-3600
fax (617) 523-3981
•Smoking area.

Upstairs at the Pudding
10 Holyoke St.
Cambridge 02138
(617) 864-1933
*•Bar, herb garden terrace and waiting
area only.*

The Barley Neck Inn & Lodge
5 Beach Rd.
East Orleans 02643
(508) 255-0212
fax (508) 255-3626
•*Dining room (on special occasions) and bar.*

Joe's Beach Road Bar & Grille
5 Beach Rd.
East Orleans 02643-0486
(508) 255-0212
fax (508) 255-3626
•*Grille Room only.*

Down Under Restaurant
91 Purchase St.
Fall River 02720
(508) 672-6951
•*All areas.*

Castle Restaurant
1230 Main St.
Leicester 01524
(508) 892-9090
•*Bar, lounge, private rooms and patio/sidewalk only.*

Blantyre Hotel
16 Blantyre Rd.
Lenox 01240
(413) 637-3556
•*Lounge, private rooms and patio only.*

Two Fabulus Guys One Swell Buritow
164 Circuit Ave.
Oak Bluffs, Martha's Vineyard 02557
(508) 696-6494
•*Smoking area.*

The Chanticleer
9 New St.
Siaconset, Nantucket 02554
(508) 257-6231
fax (508) 257-4154
•*Bar and patio only.*

Union Market Station
17 Nichols Ave.
Watertown 02172
(617) 923-0480
•*Dining room and bar.*

Moby Dick Wharf Restaurant & Marina
1 Bridge Rd.
Westport Point 02791
(508) 636-6500
fax (508) 636-3935
•*West deck only.*

MICHIGAN

Holiday Inn
501 Saginaw St.
Bay City 48708
(517) 892-3501
•*Lobby only.*

Fox & Hounds
1560 N. Woodward
Bloomfield Hills 48304
(810) 644-4800
•*Pub/bar only.*

DETROIT

Carl's Chop House
320 Grand River
Detroit 48201
(313) 833-0700
fax (313) 831-2390
•*Smoking section.*

Caucus Club
150 W. Congress
Detroit 48226
(313) 965-4970
•*Dining room and bar.*

Gertie's Garden
3031 W. Grand Blvd.
Detroit 48202
(313) 874-2246
•*Bar only.*

Joe Muer's
1000 Gratiot Ave.
Detroit 48207
(313) 567-1088
fax (313) 567-6665
•*2 of 5 dining rooms are smoking.*

Opus One
565 E. Larned
Detroit 48226
(313) 961-7766
•*Bar and lounge only.*

The Rattlesnake Club
300 River Place
Detroit 48207
(313) 567-4400
fax (313) 567-2063
•*Bar only.*

Vivio's
2460 Market St.
Detroit 48207
(313) 393-1711
fax (313) 393-1343
•*Bar and bar room only.*

The Whitney
4421 Woodland Ave.
Detroit 48201
(313) 832-5700
fax (313) 832-2159
•*3rd floor lounge and 2nd floor guest hall only.*

Chesapeake Crab House
300 M.A.C. Ave.
East Lansing 48823
(517) 337-4440
•*Lounge only.*

Rowe Inn
6303 C-48 Ellsworth
E. Jordan Rd.
Ellsworth 49729
(616) 588-7351
fax (616) 588-2365
•*Wine cellar only.*

Ginopolis' on the Grill
27815 Middlebelt Rd.
Farmington Hills 48334
(810) 851-8222
fax (810) 851-7193
•*Bar and lounge only.*

Glen Oaks Golf Club
30500 W. 13 Mile Rd.
Farmington Hills 48334
(810) 626-2600
•*Dining room and bar.*

Lakos Downtown
188 Monroe NW
Grand Rapids 49503
(616) 459-4135
fax (616) 774-0272
•*Bar and lounge only.*

Arboretum
7075 S. Lakeshore Dr.
Harbor Springs 49740
(616) 526-6291
•*Bar, lounge and private rooms.*

▲ **Bar Harbor**
100 State St.
Harbor Springs 49740
(616) 526-2671
•*All areas.*
•*A tavern.*

Whirligig
2000 Holiday Inn Dr.
Jackson 49202
(517) 783-2681
•*All areas.*

The Black Swan
3501 Greenleaf Blvd.
Kalamazoo 49008
(616) 375-2105
fax (616) 375-1346
•*Martell's Tavern lounge only.*

Vannelli Gus' Steak House
801 S. Lapeer, M-24
Lake Orion 48362
(810) 693-8882
•*Smoking areas.*

Knight Cap
320 E. Michigan Ave.
Lansing 48933
(517) 484-7676
•*All areas.*

Herman's Garland Resort
Rte. 1, Box 364 M
Lewiston 49756
(517) 786-2211
fax (517) 786-2254
•*Lounge only.*

Fonte d'Amore
32030 Plymouth Rd.
Livonia 48150
(313) 422-0770
fax (313) 422-1377
•*Dining room and lounge.*

The Pink Pony
PO Box 250
Mackinac Island 49757
(906) 847-3341
•*Restaurant after 11 p.m. and bar only.*

▲ **Muskegon Country Club**
2801 Lakeshore Dr.
Muskegon 49441
(616) 755-3737
•*Bar and lounge only.*
•*Private club.*

MacKinnon's Restaurant
126 E. Main St.
Northville 48167
(810) 348-1991
fax (810) 348-9470
•*Bar only.*

Pike Street Restaurant
18 W. Pike
Pontiac 48342
(313) 334-7878
•*Bar, lounge and private rooms only.*

Treasure Island
924 N. Niagara St.
Saginaw 48602
(517) 755-6577
fax (517) 755-3103
•*Main dining room and lounge.*

SOUTHFIELD

Chianti Villa Italiana
28565 Northwestern Hwy.
Southfield 48034
(810) 350-0055
•*Bar only.*

Excalibur Restaurant
28875 Franklin Rd.
Southfield 48034
(810) 358-3355
fax (810) 358-3227
•*Dining room and bar.*

Golden Mushroom
18100 W. 10 Mile Rd.
Southfield 48075
(810) 559-4230
fax (810) 559-7312
•*Bar and lounge only.*

Morton's of Chicago
One Towne Square
Southfield 48076
(810) 354-6006
fax (810) 354-6012
•*Smoking area and bar.*

Andiamo Lakefront Bistro
24026 Jefferson Ave.
St. Clair Shores 48080
(810) 773-7770
•*Bar only.*

TROY

Grub Street Hermit
2865 W. Maple
Troy 48084
(810) 435-5858
•*Dining room, bar and patio/sidewalk.*

Spectadium
2511 Livernois
Troy 48083
(810) 362-4030
fax (810) 362-2099
•*In two-thirds of the restaurant only.*

Stelline
The Somerset Collection
2801 W. Big Beaver
Troy 48084
(810) 649-0102
•*Bar only.*

Cass Avenue Cafe
45199 Cass Ave.
Utica 48317
(810) 726-0770
•*2 of 4 rooms.*

MINNESOTA

Shorewood
6161 Hwy. 65 NE
Fridley 55432
(612) 571-3444
•*Smoking section and lounge.*

MINNEAPOLIS

Brit's Pub & Eating Establishment
1110 Nicollet Mall
Minneapolis 55403
(612) 332-3908
fax (612) 332-8032
•*Upstairs dining area, bar, lounge and fireplaces.*

Crown Plaza North South
618 2nd Ave. S.
Minneapolis 55402
(612) 338-2288
fax (612) 338-6194
•*Smoking section and lounge.*

D'Amico Cucina
100 N. 6th St.
Minneapolis 55403
(612) 338-2401
fax (612) 337-5130
•*Lounge only.*

Huberts
601 Chicago Ave.
Minneapolis 55415
(612) 332-6062
•*Bar, lounge, private room and patio/sidewalk only.*

Manny's Steak House
  Hyatt Regency
1300 Nicollett Mall
Minneapolis 55403
(612) 339-9900
•*Bar only.*

Morton's of Chicago
555 Nicollet Mall
Minneapolis 55402
(612) 673-9700
•*Smoking section and bar.*

Murray's
26 S. 6th St.
Minneapolis 55402
(612) 339-0909
•*Front lounge only.*

Nye's Polonaise Room
112 E. Hennepin
Minneapolis 55414
(612) 379-2021
•*Bar only.*

Schiek's Palace Royale
115 S. 4th St.
Minneapolis 55401
(612) 341-0054
fax (612) 341-0521
•*Library area only.*

Town & Country Club
300 Mississippi River Blvd. N.
Minneapolis 55104
(612) 646-7121
•*Bar, lounge and private rooms only.*

ST. PAUL

Chang O'Hara's Bistro
498 Selby
St. Paul 55102
(612) 290-2338
fax (612) 290-0371
•*All smoking areas.*

Forepaugh's
276 S. Exchange St.
St. Paul 55102
(612) 224-5606
fax (612) 224-5607
•*Lounge only.*

The St. Paul Hotel
350 Market St.
St. Paul 55102
(612) 22 GRILL
fax (612) 228-3810
•*Bar and private rooms only.*

Sweeney's Saloon
96 N. Dale St.
St. Paul 55102
(612) 221-9157
•*All areas.*

Wabasha Boatworks
10 Church Ave.
Wabasha 55981
(612) 565-2752
•*Smoking section and bar.*

MISSOURI

Annie Gunn's
16806 Chesterfield Airport Rd.
Chesterfield 63005
(314) 532-7684
fax (314) 532-7642
•*Smoking section, bar, wine bar and patio.*

Morton's of Chicago
7822 Bonhomme Ave.
Clayton 63105
(314) 725-4008
fax (314) 725-1261
•*Dining room and bar.*

Seven Gables Inn
26 Meramec
Clayton 63105
(314) 863-8400
fax (314) 863-3346
•*Bar and patio/sidewalk only.*

KANSAS CITY

American Restaurant
25th & Grand
Kansas City 64108
(816) 426-1133
•*Lounge only.*

Cafe Allegro
1815 W. 39th St.
Kansas City 64111
(816) 561-3663
•*Bar and lounge only.*

Fedora Cafe & Bar
210 W. 47th St.
Kansas City 64112
(816) 561-6565
fax (816) 561-2663
•*Bar and lounge only.*

Harry's Bar & Tables
501 Westport Rd.
Kansas City 64111
(816) 561-3950
•*All areas.*

Il Caffe
7510 Wornall Rd.
Kansas City 64114
(816) 361-0900
fax (816) 363-2284
•*Bar and lounge only.*

Jasper's
405 W. 75th St.
Kansas City 64114
(816) 363-3003
fax (816) 363-2284
•*Bar, lounge and private rooms only.*

Majestic Steakhouse
931 Broadway
Kansas City 64105
(816) 471-8484
fax (816) 471-8686
•*Main dining room, jazz club and private dining room.*

Marco Polo's
7514 Wornall
Kansas City 64114
(816) 361-0900
fax (816) 363-2284
•*Bar, private rooms and coffee shop.*

Minsky's Cafe
5105 Main St.
Kansas City 64114
(816) 561-5100
•*Dining room and private rooms.*

Plaza III
4749 Pennsylvania St.
Kansas City 64112
(816) 753-0000
•*Bar only.*

The Woodlands
9700 Leavenworth Rd.
Kansas City 66112
(913) 299-9797
fax (913) 299-9804
•*Smoking areas.*

ST. LOUIS

Cardwell's
8100 Maryland
St. Louis 63105
(314) 726-5055
•*Bar and patio only.*

Dierdorf & Harts Steak House
323 Westport Plaza
St. Louis 63146
(314) 878-1801
•*Bar only.*

Jake's Steaks
707 Clamorgan Alley
St. Louis 63102
(314) 621-8184
fax (314) 621-1098
•*Smoking area of dining room and bar.*

Kemoll's of Saint Louis
211 N. Broadway
St. Louis 63102
(314) 421-0555
fax (314) 421-5171
•*Lounge only.*

LoRusso's Cucina
3121 Watson
St. Louis 63139
(314) 647-6222
•*Lounge and private rooms only.*

▲ **Noonday Club**
1 Metropolitan Square
St. Louis 63102
(314) 231-8452
•*All areas.*
•*Private city club.*

Ritz-Carlton
100 Carondelet Plaza
St. Louis 63105
(314) 863-6300
fax (314) 863-7486
•*Lounge only.*

Tony's
410 Market St.
St. Louis 63102
(314) 231-7007
•*Lounge only.*

Nearly Famous Deli & Pasta House
1828 S. Kentwood
Springfield 65804
(417) 883-3403
•*Smoking section and patio/sidewalk.*

Station Grill
  Hyatt Regency
1 St. Louis
Union Station 63103
(314) 231-1234
fax (314) 923-3971
•*2 public lounges and the Link Room.*

MONTANA

The Grand Hotel
139 McLeod St.
Big Timber 59011
(406) 932-4459
•*Bar only.*

NEBRASKA

Misty's Restaurant & Lounge
6235 Havelock Ave.
Lincoln 68507
(402) 466-8424
fax (402) 466-7222
•*Bar, lounge and private rooms only.*

Top Hat
736 W. Cornhusker
Lincoln 68521
(402) 479-9935
•*All areas.*

OMAHA

The Aquarium
1830 S. 72nd St.
Omaha 66124
(402) 392-0777
fax (402) 392-2835
•*Lounge (piano bar) only.*

Le Cafe de Paris
1228 S. 6th St.
Omaha 68108
(402) 344-0227
•*Dining room.*

Omaha Prime
415 S. 11th St.
Omaha 68102
(402) 341-7040
fax (402) 341-7808
•*Glass-enclosed dining room and lounge.*

NEVADA

LAS VEGAS

Bally's Casino Resort
3645 Las Vegas Blvd. S.
Las Vegas 89109
(702) 739-4111
•*All areas of the 8 restaurants.*

The Fiore
  Rio Hotel
3700 W. Flamingo
Las Vegas 89114
(702) 252-7777
•*Terrace only.*

Morton's of Chicago
3200 Las Vegas Blvd. S.
Las Vegas 89109
(702) 893-0703
•*Lounge only.*

Spago Las Vegas
  Caesar's
3500 Las Vegas Blvd. S.
Las Vegas 89109
(702) 369-0360
fax (702) 369-0361
•*Dining room (late night only), bar, cafe
and private rooms.*

Suzette's
  Santa Fe Hotel
4949 N. Rancho Dr.
Las Vegas 89130
(702) 658-4900
•*Smoking section and bar.*

The Tillerman
2245 E. Flamingo Rd.
Las Vegas 89119
(702) 731-4036
•*Bar, lounge and patio/sidewalk only.*

RENO

**The Brasserie—"A Country
  French Grill"**
1695 S. Virginia St.
Reno 89502
(702) 785-7910
•*Bar and bistro only.*

Harrah's Steak House
219 S. Center St.
Reno 89504
(702) 788-2929
•*Lounge only.*

▲ **The Men's Club of Reno**
270 Lake St.
Reno 89501
(702) 786-7800
fax (702) 786-7373
•*All areas.*
•*A gentlemen's club featuring topless
entertainment.*

Rapscallion
1555 S. Wells
Reno 89502
(702) 323-1211
fax (702) 323-6096
•*Bar, lounge and private rooms.*

Harvey's Resort, Hotel and Casino
Hwy. 50
Stateline 89449
(702) 588-2411
•*Bars and lounges only.*

NEW HAMPSHIRE

Water Works
1 Nashua Dr.
Nashua 03060
(603) 882-4433
fax (603) 882-1611
•*Full-service lounge only.*

Scottish Lion Inn & Restaurant
Rte. 16
North Conway 03860
(603) 356-6381
•*Special cigar and pipe room in
Blackwatch Pub only.*

Barnstormers Restaurant
27 International Dr.
Pease International Trade Port
Portsmouth 03801
(603) 433-6700
•*Lounge only.*

Legends 1291
Town Square
Waterville Valley 03215
(603) 236-4678
•*All areas.*

NEW JERSEY

The Ram's Head Inn
9 W. White Horse Pike
Absecon 08201
(609) 652-1700
fax (609) 748-1588
•*Bar, lounge, private rooms, gallery and patio/sidewalk.*

Sands Hotel & Casino
Indiana Ave. & Brighton Park
Atlantic City 08401
(800) 257-8580
•*All smoking areas of Brighton Steakhouse, Medici and Chinamoon.*

Trump Plaza Hotel & Casino
Boardwalk at Mississippi
Atlantic City 08401
(609) 441-6800
fax (609) 441-6249
•*All smoking areas of Ivana's, Max's, Fortune's and Roberto's.*

Seven Hills Restaurant
88 Washington St.
Bloomfield 07003
(201) 743-5331
•*Bar and private rooms only.*

Azúcar
10 Dempsey Ave.
Edgewater 07020
(201) 886-0747
fax (201) 886-0747
•*All areas.*

Conservatory
   The Madison Hotel
1 Convent Rd.
Morristown 07960
(201) 285-1800
•*Smoking section and bar.*

Village Dugout
6118 New Kirk Ave.
North Bergen 07047
(201) 854-1489
•*Dining room and bar.*

The Park Steakhouse
151 Kinderkamack Rd.
Park Ridge 07656
(201) 930-1300
fax (201) 573-4941
•*Private dining room for smokers only and bar.*

Ray's Cabaret
1793 Rte. 206
Southampton 08088
(609) 859-9676
•*All areas.*

Bond Street Club
1300 Princeton Ave.
Trenton 08638
(609) 392-1765
fax (609) 392-2111
•*Dining room, bar and lounge.*

Diamond's
132 Kent St.
Trenton 08611
(609) 393-1000
fax (609) 393-1672
•*All areas.*

Season's Restaurant
644 Pascack Rd.
Washington Township 07675
(201) 664-6141
•*Lounge area only.*

The Taco Maker
61 Berdan Ave.
Wayne 07470
(201) 305-8226
fax (201) 305-3969
•*Dining room only.*

The Ryland Inn
Rte. 22 W.
Whitehouse 08888
(908) 534-4011
fax (908) 534-6592
•*In the special cigar & brandy room and the bar/lounge; entire restaurant during cigar dinners only.*

NEW MEXICO

Ranchers Club
  Albuquerque Hilton
1901 University Blvd. NE
Albuquerque 87102
(505) 884-2500
•*Lounge only.*

The Double A
331 Sandoval St.
Santa Fe 87501
(505) 982-8999
•*Bar only.*

Billy Crews
1200 Country Club Rd.
Santa Teresa 88008
(505) 589-2071
fax (505) 589-9463
•*Dining room and lounge.*

NEW YORK

Mansion Hill Inn
115 Philip St.
Albany 12202
(518) 465-2038
fax (518) 434-2313
•*Dining room, private rooms and patio/sidewalk.*

Lock, Stock & Barrel
35 Bardonia Rd.
Bardonia 10954
(914) 623-6323
•*Dining room and bar.*

Hoppfields Restaurant
954 Old Post Rd., Rte. 121
Bedford 10506
(914) 234-3373
fax (914) 234-7692
•*Private dining room only.*

▲ **E.T. Quigg's**
2807 Merrick Rd.
Bellmore 11710
(516) 785-9559
•*All areas.*
•*Primarily a bar, but pub-style cuisine is available.*

Cavanaugh's
255 Blue Point Ave.
Blue Point 11715
(516) 363-2666
•*All areas.*

Adam's Steak & Seafood
204 Como Park Blvd.
Buffalo 14227
(716) 683-3784
•*Bar and private rooms only.*

Crabtree's Kittle House
11 Kittle Rd.
Chappaqua 10514
(914) 666-8044
fax (914) 666-2684
•*Bar only.*

Louisiana Cajun Cafe
25 Cedar St.
Dobbs Ferry 10522
(914) 693-9762
fax (914) 674-0706
•*Bar only.*

Old Drovers Inn
Old Rte. 22
Dover Plains 12522
(914) 832-9311
fax (914) 832-6356
•*Private rooms, patio and the park only.*

The White Inn
52 E. Main St.
Fredonia 14063
(716) 672-2103
fax (716) 672-2107
•*Bar, lounge and patio/sidewalk only.*

Jonathan's American Grill
3000 Jericho Tpke.
Garden City Park 11530
(516) 742-7300
fax (516) 742-7346
•*Bar, lounge and private rooms only.*

▲ Nassau Country Club
St. Andrews Lane
Glen Cove 11542
(516) 676-0554
•*Main bar and adjoining lounge areas only.*
•*Private club.*

Depuy Canal House
Rte. 213
High Falls 12440
(914) 687-7700
•*Bar only.*

Marco
Rte. 6
Lake Mahopac 10541
(914) 621-1648
fax (914) 265-7931
•*Lounge only.*

Riverside Inn
115 S. Water St.
Lewiston 14092
(716) 754-8206
fax (716) 754-8352
•*Smoking areas.*

Beardslee Castle
Rte. 5
Little Falls 13365
(315) 823-3000
fax (315) 823-3000
•*All areas.*

Brick Cafe
157 Lakeview Ave.
Lynbrook 11563
(516) 599-9669
•*Dining room and bar.*

The Dock
1 Town Rd.
Montauk 11954
(516) 668-9778
•*Bar only.*

NEW YORK CITY

MANHATTAN

Ahnell
177 Prince St.
New York 10012
(212) 254-1260
fax (212) 254-3099
•*Dining area and front bar only.*

The Alamo
304 E. 48th St.
New York 10017
(212) 759-0590
•*Bar only.*

Alva
36 E. 22nd St.
New York 10010
(212) 228-4399
•*Bar only.*

An American Place
2 Park Ave.
New York 10016
(212) 684-2122
•*Bar only.*

The Assembly Restaurant
630 5th Ave.
New York 10021
(212) 581-3580
fax (212) 489-5714
•*Separate smoking dining room ("Cigar Room") and bar area.*

Bayamo
704 Broadway
New York 10003
(212) 475-5151
•*Bar only.*

Beefsteak Charlie's
2 Penn Plaza
New York 10001
(212) 630-0301
•*Bar area only.*

▲ **Beekman Bar and Books featuring The Cigar Bar**
889 1st Ave.
New York 10022
(212) 980-9314
•*Bar and cigar lounge serving elegant light fare.*

Ben Benson's Steakhouse
123 W. 52nd St.
New York 10019
(212) 581-8888
fax (212) 581-1170
•*Bar and dining tables in the bar room only.*

Bice
7 E. 54th St.
New York 10022
(212) 688-1999
•*Bar and lounge area only.*

BlackFinn Bar and Restaurant
994 2nd Ave.
New York 10022
(212) 355-6993
fax (212) 207-3864
•*All areas.*

The Box Tree Restaurant
250 E. 49th St.
New York 10017
(212) 593-9810
fax (212) 308-3899
•*Bar and private rooms only.*

Boxers
190 W. 4th St.
New York 10014
(212) 633-BARK
•*Smoking section and bar.*

Brew's
156 E. 34th St.
New York 10016
(212) 889-3369
fax (212) 889-3386
•*Bar only.*

Brothers Bar-B-Q
225 Varick St.
New York 10014
(212) 727-2775
•*Bar only.*

Bull and Bear Restaurant
301 Park Ave.
New York 10022
(212) 872-4900
fax (212) 486-5107
•*Bar only.*

Butlers Restaurant
1407 Broadway
New York 10018
(212) 575-1407
•*Upstairs only.*

▲ Cafe Aubette
119 E. 27th St.
New York 10016
(212) 686-5500
•*All areas, but encouraged in the back
room.*
•*Bar serving innovative American
appetizers and dessert at night; European
espresso bar in the afternoon, serving
pastries, sandwiches and salads.*

Cafe Pierre
  The Pierre Hotel
2 E. 61st St.
New York 10021
(212) 940-8185
fax (212) 940-8109
•*Bar only.*

Cal's
22 W. 21st St.
New York 10010
(212) 929-0740
fax (212) 631-1212
•*Bar only.*

Campagna
24 E. 21st St.
New York 10010
(212) 460-0900
•*Bar, lounge and patio only.*

Cellini
65 E. 54th St.
New York 10022
(212) 751-1555
fax (212) 753-2848
•*Private room only.*

Charltons
922 3rd Ave.
New York 10022
(212) 688-4646
fax (212) 644-6651
•*Bar only.*

Christo's Steakhouse & Grill
541 Lexington Ave.
New York 10022
(212) 355-2695
•*Bars and semi-private room.*

The Cigar Room at Trumpets
  Grand Hyatt Hotel
Grand Central Station
New York 10017
(212) 850-5999
fax (212) 697-3772
•*All areas.*

Circus
808 Lexington Ave.
New York 10021
(212) 223-2566
fax (212) 593-5421
•*Smoking area after 10 p.m.*

Cité
120 W. 51st St.
New York 10020
(212) 956-7100
•*Bar only.*

City Crab & Seafood Co.
235 Park Ave. S.
New York 10003
(212) 529-3800
fax (212) 533-7596
•*Private dining room and bar only.*

Coco Pazzo
23 E. 74th St.
New York 10021
(212) 794-0205
•*Bar only.*

The Conservatory
Mayflower Hotel
15 Central Park W.
New York 10023
(212) 641-1173
•*Bar area only.*

Dakota Bar & Grill
1576 3rd Ave.
New York 10128
(212) 427-8889
fax (212) 534-5685
•*Bar area only.*

Dix et Sept
181 W. 10th St.
New York 10014
(212) 645-8023
•*Bar only.*

Drake Bar & Restaurant
Drake Swiss Hotel
440 Park Ave.
New York 10022
(212) 756-3925
•*Bar only.*

Eight and One Half Restaurant
208 E. 52nd St.
New York 10022
(212) 759-7373
•*Bar and lounge only.*

Elaine's Restaurant
1703 2nd Ave.
New York 10028
(212) 534-8114
•*Dining room and bar.*

Felix
340 W. Broadway
New York 10013
(212) 431-0021
•*Bar only.*

Ferrier
29 E. 65th St.
New York 10021
(212) 772-9000
fax (212) 861-0655
•*Bar only.*

Filli Ponte Ristorante
39 Debrosses St.
New York 10013
(212) 226-4621
fax (212) 226-3115
•*Cigar lounge and bar.*

Florio's of Little Italy
192 Grand St.
New York 10013
(212) 226-7610
fax (212) 274-9414
•*Bar and separate dining areas only.*

Flowers
21 W. 17th St.
New York 10011
(212) 691-8888
fax (212) 647-9698
•*Front room and upstairs only.*

Four Seasons Hotel
57 E. 57th St.
New York 10022
(212) 758-5700
•*Bar, lounge and private rooms only.*

Frank's Restaurant
85 10th Ave.
New York 10014
(212) 243-1349
fax (212) 243-1868
•*Lounge and bar only.*

Frankie & Johnnie's
269 W. 45th St.
New York 10036
(212) 997-9494
fax (212) 997-6851
•*Bar only.*

Fresch
143 Perry St.
New York 10014
(212) 243-9287
•*One at a time only.*

Fresco by Scotto
34 E. 52nd St.
New York 10019
(212) 935-3434
fax (212) 935-3436
•*Bar and lounge area only.*

Gallagher's Steak House
228 W. 52nd St.
New York 10019
(212) 245-5336
fax (212) 245-5426
•*Smoking section.*

Ginger Thai
363 Greenwich St.
New York 10013
(212) 226-4565
•*Bar only.*

Giovanni
47 W. 55th St.
New York 10019
(212) 262-2828
fax (212) 262-0179
•*Cigar room only.*

The Grange Hall
50 Commerce St.
New York 10014
(212) 924-5246
•*Bar during non-dining hours only.*

Halcyon
151 W. 54th St.
New York 10019
(212) 468-8736
fax (212) 468-8816
•*Bar and lounge only.*

Harbour Lights
South Street Seaport, Pier 17, 3rd Fl.
New York 10004
(212) 227-2800
fax (212) 227-3984
•*Separate room for smokers only.*

Harry's at Hanover Square
1 Hanover Square
New York 10004
(212) 425-3412
•*Bar only.*

Home
20 Cornelia St.
New York 10014
(212) 243-9579
•*Garden only.*

▲ **Hudson Bar and Books**
636 Hudson St.
New York 10014
(212) 229-2642
•*Bar and cigar lounge serving elegant
light fare.*

Hudson River Club
4 World Financial Center
New York 10281
(212) 786-1500
•*Bar, lounge and private rooms only.*

Il Monello
1460 2nd Ave.
New York 10021
(212) 535-9310
•*Bar and private room only.*

Il Toscanaccio
7 E. 59th St.
New York 10022
(212) 935-3535
•*Smoking area, bar and lounge.*

Il Vagabondo
351 E. 62nd St.
New York 10021
(212) 832-9221
fax (212) 832-9234
•*Bar only.*

Joe Mayo's Pub
41 Madison Ave.
New York 10010
(212) 679-8316
•*Bar only.*

Jubilee
347 E. 54th St.
New York 10022
(212) 888-3569
•*Smoking area near the bar only.*

Keens Steakhouse
72 W. 36th St.
New York 10018
(212) 947-3636
•*Bar only.*

L'Auberge du Midi
310 W. 4th St.
New York 10014
(212) 242-4705
•*Bar only.*

La Granita
1470 2nd Ave.
New York 10021
(212) 717-5500
•*Special separate room only.*

La Taverne
525 Broome St.
New York 10013
(212) 343-2321
•*Bar and certain areas of the restaurant only.*

Le Bar Bat
311 W. 57th St.
New York 10019
(212) 307-7228
fax (212) 307-7234
•*All areas.*

Le Madri
168 W. 18th St.
New York 10011
(212) 727-8022
•*Bar and patio only.*

Le Veau d' Or
129 E. 60th St.
New York 10022
(212) 838-8133
•*All areas.*

**Les Célébrités
  Hotel Nikko**
155 W. 58th St.
New York 10019
(212) 484-5113
fax (212) 484-4680
•*Lounge and private dining rooms only.*

▲ **Lexington Bar and Books
  featuring The Cigar Bar**
1020 Lexington Ave.
New York 10021
(212) 717-3902
•*Bar and cigar lounge serving elegant light fare.*

Lipizzana
987 2nd Ave.
New York 10022
(212) 753-4858
•*Bar only.*

Lola
30 W. 22nd St.
New York 10010
(212) 675-6700
fax (212) 645-6738
•*Lounge only.*

Mad. 61
10 E. 61st St.
New York 10022
(212) 833-2200
•*Lounge only.*

Maggie's Place
21 E. 47th St.
New York 10017
(212) 753-5757
fax (212) 753-5765
•*Downstairs at night only.*

Manhattan Cafe
1161 1st Ave.
New York 10021
(212) 888-6556
fax (212) 832-2956
•*Separate cigar smoking dining room
(seats 60-70).*

Mark's Restaurant and Bar
25 E. 77th St.
New York 10021
(212) 879-1864
fax (212) 744-2749
•*Bar and private rooms only.*

Marti Kebab
1269 1st Ave.
New York 10021
(212) 737-6104
•*Private room only.*

Michael's
24 W. 55th St.
New York 10019
(212) 767-0555
•*Bar and lounge area only.*

Minetta Tavern
113 MacDougal St.
New York 10012
(212) 475-3850
•*Bar only.*

Monkey Bar
60 E. 54th St.
New York 10022
(212) 838-2600
fax (212) 838-4595
•*Bar only.*

Moran's Restaurant
146 10th Ave.
New York 10011
(212) 627-3030
•*Bar and private rooms only.*

Morton's of Chicago
551 5th Ave.
New York 10017
(212) 972-3315
•*Bar and lounge only.*

North Star Pub
93 South St.
New York 10038
(212) 509-6757
•*All areas.*

**Oak Room & Bar
Plaza Hotel**
768 5th Ave.
New York 10019
(212) 546-5330
fax (212) 546-5234
•*Cigar bar only.*

Oceana
55 E. 54th St.
New York 10022
(212) 759-5941
fax (212) 759-6076
•*Bar only.*

The Odeon
145 W. Broadway
New York 10013
(212) 233-0507
•*Bar only.*

Old Homestead
56 9th Ave.
New York 10011
(212) 242-9040
fax (212) 727-1637
•*Bar and cocktail area only.*

Oyster Bar
Grand Central Station
New York 10017
(212) 490-6650
fax (212) 949-5210
•Saloon only.

Palio
151 W. 51st St.
New York 10019
(212) 245-4850
fax (212) 397-7814
•Bar only.

Palm
837 2nd Ave.
New York 10021
(212) 687-2953
•Bar and a limited number of tables only.

Park Avenue Cafe
100 E. 63rd St.
New York 10021
(212) 644-1900
•Bar only.

The Pearl Room
131 Duane St.
New York 10013
(212) 693-1333
fax (212) 693-1191
•Bar and lounge only.

Pen & Pencil
205 E. 45th St.
New York 10017
(212) 682-1580
•Smoking areas.

The Post House
28 E. 63rd St.
New York 10021
(212) 935-2888
fax (212) 371-9264
•Bar only.

Rainbow Room
30 Rockefeller Plaza
New York 10112
(212) 632-5000
•The Rainbow Promenade bar only.

Raoul's
180 Prince St.
New York 10012
(212) 966-3518
fax (212) 966-0205
•Garden room and bar only.

Remi
145 W. 53rd St.
New York 10019
(212) 581-4242
fax (212) 581-7182
•Bar area of main dining room, atrium and garden only.

Runyon's
305 E. 50th St.
New York 10019
(212) 223-9592
•Bar and some tables only.

Russian Samovar
256 W. 52nd St.
New York 10022
(212) 757-0168
fax (212) 765-2133
•Smoking section.

Ruth's Chris Steak House
148 W. 51st St.
New York 10019
(212) 245-9600
fax (212) 245-0460
•Smoking lounge (where dining is also available) and private rooms only.

St. Regis Hotel - King Cole Bar &
  Astor Court
2 E. 55th St.
New York 10022
(212) 753-4500
fax (212) 787-3447
•Bar and Cognac Room only.

San Domenico
240 Central Park S.
New York 10019
(212) 459-9016
fax (212) 397-0844
•Bar and bar lounge only.

Sardi's
234 W. 44th St.
New York 10036
(212) 221-8444
•Bar only.

SettaMoMA
  Museum of Modern Art
12 W. 54th St.
New York 10009
(212) 708-9710
fax (212) 333-1109
•Bar and terrace only.

Slaughtered Lamb Pub
182 W. 4th St.
New York 10014
(212) 727-3350
•Smoking section.

Smith & Wollensky
201 E. 49th St.
New York 10017
(212) 753-1530
fax (212) 751-5446
•Bar only.

The Stanhope
995 5th Ave.
New York 10028
(212) 288-5800
•Lounge and Gerard's Bar only.

▲ **Stringfellows**
35 E. 21st St.
New York 10010
(212) 254-2444
fax (212) 254-7630
•Dining room, bar and lounge.
•A gentlemen's club.

Tatou
151 E. 50th St.
New York 10022
(212) 753-1144
fax (212) 355-4392
•Cigar bar and near the bar in main
dining room.

Torremolino's Restaurant
230 E. 51st St.
New York 10022
(212) 755-1862
fax (212) 755-1877
•Bar only.

Tse Yang
34 E. 51st St.
New York 10022
(212) 688-5588
fax (212) 980-2081
•Bar and private rooms only.

The 21 Club
21 W. 52nd St.
New York 10019
(212) 582-7200
fax (212) 586-5065
•Cocktail lounge and banquet rooms
only.

Victor's Cafe 52
236 W. 52nd St.
New York 10019
(212) 586-7714
fax (212) 247-7052
•Bar only.

The Water Club
500 E. 30th St.
New York 10016
(212) 683-3333
•*Bar only.*

West 63rd Street Steakhouse
44 W. 63rd St.
New York 10023
(212) 246-6363
fax (212) 765-4913
•*Bar, lounge and private rooms.*

BROOKLYN

Ferdinando's Focacceria
151 Union St.
Brooklyn 11231
(718) 855-1545
•*All areas.*

Lundy Bros. Restaurant
1901 Emmons Ave.
Brooklyn 11235
(718) 743-0022
fax (718) 743-6896
•*Bar and mezzanine only.*

The River Cafe
1 Water St.
Brooklyn 11201
(718) 522-5200
fax (718) 875-0037
•*Bar and lounge only.*

QUEENS

Piccola Venezia Ristorante
42-01 28 Ave.
Astoria 11103
(718) 721-8470
fax (718) 721-2110
•*Bar and private rooms only.*

Caffe on the Green
201-10 Cross Island Pkwy.
Bayside 11360
(718) 423-7272
•*Bar, lounge, private rooms and patio/sidewalk only.*

Polo Club Bar & Grill
1575 Montauk Hwy.
Oakdale 11769
(516) 567-0055
•*Bar only.*

The Saloon
45 W. Central Ave.
Pearl River 10965
(914) 735-5300
•*Smoking area.*

La Pavillon
230 Salt Point Tpke.
Poughkeepsie 12603
(914) 473-2525
•*Bar, private rooms and patio/sidewalk only.*

ROCHESTER

Moretti's of San Francisco
4671 Ridge Rd. W.
Rochester 14626
(716) 352-4000
•*Lounge, private rooms and patio/sidewalk only.*

Thendara Inn & Restaurant
4356 E. Lake Rd.
Rochester 14424
(716) 394-4868
fax (716) 396-0804
•*Bar and patio/sidewalk only.*

Water Street Grill
175 Water St.
Rochester 14604
(716) 546-4980
fax (716) 546-4173
•*Bar, lounge and patio/sidewalk only.*

Bryant & Cooper Steakhouse
2 Middleneck Rd.
Roslyn 11576
(516) 627-7270
•*Large bar area only.*

American Hotel
25 Main St.
Sag Harbor 11963
(516) 725-3535
fax (516) 725-3573
•*Bar and lounge only.*

The Canterbury
500 Union Ave.
Saratoga Springs 12866
(518) 587-9653
fax (518) 587-0526
•*Bar, private rooms and Club Room only.*

Forty Three Phila Bistro
43 Phila St.
Saratoga Springs 12866
(518) 584-2720
•*Bar only.*

The Inn at Speculator
Rte. 163
Speculator 12164
(518) 548-3811
•*Bar, lounge and private rooms only.*

SYRACUSE

Danzer's Restaurant
153 Ainsley Dr.
Syracuse 13210
(315) 422-0089
•*Smoking section.*

For the Fun of It
312 Park St.
Syracuse 13203
(315) 471-7111
•*Bar only.*

Pascale Restaurant
204 W. Fayette St.
Syracuse 13202
(315) 471-3040
fax (315) 471-3060
•*Bar only.*

Jack Appleseed's Tavern
147 N. Genesee
Utica 13502
(315) 797-7979
•*Smoking section and bar.*

Yesterday's
907 Vestal Pkwy. E.
Vestal 13850
(607) 785-3313
•*Small part of dining room, bar and lounge only.*

Gregory's Steak Pub
324 Central Ave.
White Plains 10606
(914) 684-8855
•*Bar only.*

NORTH CAROLINA

Prestonwood Country Club
300 Prestonwood Pkwy.
Cary 27513
(919) 467-2566
fax (919) 469-1195
•*Bar, lounge, private rooms and patio/sidewalk only.*

CHARLOTTE

H. Dundee's Steakhouse
8128 Providence Rd.
Charlotte 28277
(704) 543-6299
And
4508 Independence Blvd.
Charlotte 28277
(704) 536-5003
•*Dining room, bar and lounge.*

The Lamplighter Restaurant
1065 E. Moorehead St.
Charlotte 28202
(704) 372-5343
fax (704) 372-5354
•*Bar and private rooms only.*

Morton's of Chicago
227 W. Trade St.
Charlotte 28202
(704) 333-2602
fax (704) 333-3204
•*All areas.*

University Place Restaurant
9005 J.M. Keynes Dr.
Charlotte 28262
(704) 547-1985
fax (704) 547-1986
•*Bar, lounge, private rooms and patio/sidewalk only.*

The City Club of Gastonia
532 S. New Hope Rd.
Gastonia 28054
(704) 865-1980
fax (704) 865-1998
•*All areas.*

House of Wang
710 W. Vernon Ave.
Kinston 28501
(919) 527-7897
•*Lounge only.*

RALEIGH

Angus Barn
U.S. 70 W. at Aviation Pkwy.
Raleigh 27612
(919) 787-3505
fax (919) 783-5568
•*Wild Turkey lounge only.*

The Capital City Club
411 Fayetteville Street Mall
Raleigh 27603
(919) 832-5526
fax (919) 829-1721
•*Lounge and private rooms only.*

It's Prime Only
5509 Edwards Mill Rd.
Raleigh 27612
(919) 420-0224
fax (919) 420-0845
•*Smoking section and cigar room.*

**Provence Restaurant
Radisson Plaza Hotel**
421 S. Salisbury St.
Raleigh 27601
(919) 834-9900
fax (919) 833-1217
•*Smoking section, bar and lounge.*

Vinnie's Steak House & Tavern
7440 Six Forks Rd.
Raleigh 27615
(919) 847 7319
fax (919) 676-6818
•*Most areas.*

Gisele Fine Foods
226 N. Marshall St.
Winston-Salem 27101
(910) 761-0674
fax (910) 761-0041
•*All areas.*

OHIO

Ristoranti Giovanni's
25550 Chagrin Blvd.
Beachwood 44122
(216) 831-8625
fax (216) 831-4338
•Lounge only.

CINCINNATI

Celestial Restaurant
1071 Celestial St.
Cincinnati 45202
(513) 241-4455
•Bar, lounge and private rooms only.

Cricket Lounge
601 Vine St.
Cincinnati 45215
(513) 381-3000
fax (513) 657-0256
•Bar, lounge and private rooms only.

**Hartwell Recreation Center &
   Golf Club**
59 Caldwell Dr.
Cincinnati 45216
(513) 821-9257
fax (513) 821-6208
•Bar and private rooms only.

The International Bar & Grill
6708 Sandalwood Lane
Cincinnati 45224
(513) 671-6600
•Smoking section, bar and lounge.

**Montgomery Inn
   The Boathouse**
925 Eastern Ave.
Cincinnati 45202
(513) 721-7427
fax (513) 345-3712
•All areas.

Morton's of Chicago
Tower Place, 28 W. 4th St., #105
Cincinnati 45202
(513) 241-4104
fax (513) 241-3666
•Smoking section, bar and private rooms.

Orchids
35 W. 5th St.
Cincinnati 45202
(513) 421-1772
•Bar, lounge and private rooms only.

CLEVELAND

Baricelli Inn
2203 Cornell Rd.
Cleveland 44106
(216) 791-6500
fax (216) 791-9131
•Private rooms and lobby only.

John Q's Steakhouse
55 Public Square
Cleveland 44113
(216) 861-0900
fax (216) 861-1237
•Bar and lounge only.

The Lincoln Inn
75 Public Square
Cleveland 44113
(216) 621-9085
fax (216) 621-2544
•Bar, lounge and private rooms only.

Morton's of Chicago
230 Huron Rd. NW
Cleveland 44114
(216) 621-6200
•Smoking section and lounge.

Ninth Street Grill
100 Erieview Plaza
Cleveland 44114
(216) 579-9919
fax (216) 579-0919
•*Bar area only.*

The River View Room
1515 W. 3rd St.
Cleveland 44113
(216) 623-1300
•*Lounge only.*

COLUMBUS

Bravo! Cucina
3000 Hayden Rd.
Columbus 43235
(614) 791-1245
fax (614) 764-1577
•*Bar only.*

Deibels
263 E. Whittier St.
Columbus 43206
(614) 444-1139
•*Everywhere except non-smoking area.*

Morton's of Chicago
2 Nationwide Plaza
Columbus 43215
(614) 464-4442
•*Smoking section and lounge.*

The Refectory
1092 Bethel Rd.
Columbus 43220
(614) 451-9774
•*Lounge, private rooms and patio only.*

**Miss Kitty's Steakhouse and
  Grand Saloon**
4336 Medina Rd.
Copley 44321
(216) 666-7429
•*Bar only.*

**Mad Anthony's
  Greenville Inn**
851 E. Martin St.
Greenville 45331
(513) 548-3613
fax (513) 548-5851
•*Smoking section and lounge.*

The White House Inn
4940 Muhlhausern Rd.
Hamilton 45011
(513) 860-1110
fax (513) 860-9050
•*Tavern only.*

Courthouse Cafe
110 S. Broadway
New Philadelphia 44663
(216) 343-7896
fax (216) 364-9189
•*Smoking area.*

Alberini's
1201 Youngstown Rd.
Niles 44446
(216) 652-5895
•*Private cigar smoking room, bar and
lounge only.*

**The Olde Loyal Oak Tavern &
  Restaurant**
3044 Wadsworth Rd.
Norton 44203
(216) 825-8280
fax (216) 825-0432
•*Specified area of the main dining room,
bar, lounge and private rooms.*

Town Crier Restaurant
2293 Wadsworth Rd.
Norton 44203
(216) 745-8110
•*Bar only.*

Rider's Inn
792 Mentor Ave.
Painesville 44077
(216) 354-8200
•Pub only.

The Bogey Inn Lounge &
Restaurant
6013 Glick Rd.
Powell 43065
(614) 889-0150
fax (614) 792-0893
•Most areas.

Chez Francois
555 Main St.
Vermilion 44089
(216) 967-0630
•Bar and patio/sidewalk only.

Eddie's Place
28601 Chagrin Blvd.
Woodmere 44122
(216) 591-1545
•Smoking section and bar.

Boat Yard Ltd.
3163 Belmont Ave.
Youngstown 44505
(216) 759-7892
•Bar and patio/sidewalk only.

Mr. P's Cafe & Bakery
7325 South Ave.
Youngstown 44512
(216) 726-2442
•Bar only.

OKLAHOMA

Old Germany Restaurant
15920 SE 29th
Choctaw 73020
(405) 390-8647
•Bar and lounge only.

OREGON

PORTLAND

The Heathman Hotel
1001 SW Broadway at Salmon
Portland 97205
(503) 241-4100
fax (503) 790-7110
•Mezzanine library only

Jake's Famous Crawfish
401 SW 12th Ave.
Portland 97205
(503) 226-1419
•Bar only.

McCormick & Schmick's Seafood
Restaurant
235 SW 1st Ave.
Portland 97214
(503) 224-7522
•Bar on a regular basis; dining room on
"smoker nights" only.

The Sports Den
Shilo Inn
9900 SW Canyon Rd.
Portland 97225
(503) 297-6125
fax (503) 297-7708
•Cigar bar only.

PENNSYLVANIA

Hartefeld National
1 Hartefeld Dr.
Avondale 19311
(800) 240-7373, (610) 268-8800
fax (610) 268-7425
•Irish Pub and Walking Cup dining
room

**Wooden Angel Restaurant &
  Casual Cafe**
Sharon Rd./Leopard Lane,
Bridgewater
Beaver 15009
(412) 774-7880
fax (412) 774-7994
•*Smoking section bar, lounge and private
rooms.*

Country Squire Diner/Restaurant
2560 W. Chester Pike
Broomall 19008
(610) 356-3030
fax (610) 356-0555
•*Dining room and lounge.*

Central Bar & Grille
39 Morris Ave.
Bryn Mawr 19010
(610) 527-1400
•*Bar only.*

Log Cabin Inn
430 Perry Hwy.
Harmony 16037
(412) 452-4155
•*Smoking room and bar.*

Nick's 1014 Cafe
1014 N. 3rd St.
Harrisburg 17102
(717) 238-8844
fax (717) 238-5088
•*All areas.*

Scotts' Bar & Grille
212 Locust St.
Harrisburg 17101
(717) 234-7599
•*Dining room and bar.*

The Park Ridge at Valley Forge
480 N. Gulph Rd.
King of Prussia 19406
(610) 337-1800
•*Mad Anthony's Tavern only.*

Strawberry Hill
128 W. Strawberry St.
Lancaster 17603
(717) 393-5544
•*Bar and private rooms only.*

Chetremon Golf Club
1416 Clearview Dr.
Latrobe 15650
(412) 537-5535
•*Bar only.*

D'Ignazio's Town House Restaurant
117 Veterans' Square
Media 19063
(610) 566-6141
fax (610) 566-3840
•*Bar only.*

Alfred's Victorian
38 N. Union St.
Middletown 17057
(717) 944-4929
•*Bar, private rooms and patio/sidewalk
only.*

East Wind
1418 Butler Ave.
New Castle 16101
(412) 658-7175
•*Dining room, bar and private rooms.*

Charlotte's Restaurant
3207 W. Chester Pkwy.
Newtown Square 19073
(610) 356-7100
fax (610) 359-1552
•*Lounge seating only.*

D'Ignazio's Nottingham Inn
Old U.S. 1 & Rte. 272
Nottingham 19323
(610) 932-4050
•*Back of dining room and bar area only.*

PHILADELPHIA

Chris's Cafe
1421 Sansom St.
Philadelphia 19102
(215) 568-3131
•*All areas.*

Ciboulette
  The Bellevue Building
200 S. Broad St.
Philadelphia 19102
(215) 790-1210
fax (215) 790-1209
•*Bar only.*

Dickens Inn
421 S. 2nd St.
Philadelphia 19147
(215) 928-9307
•*Dining room, bar and private rooms.*

Dilullo Centro
1407 Locust St.
Philadelphia 19102
(215) 546-2000
fax (215) 546-8639
•*Lounge only.*

The Bellevue
1415 Chancellor Ct.
Philadelphia 19102
(215) 893-1776
fax (215) 893-9868
•*Library lounge only.*

The Happy Rooster
119 S. 16th St.
Philadelphia 19102
(215) 563-1481
•*All areas.*

Jack's Firehouse
2130 Fairmount Ave.
Philadelphia 19130
(215) 232-9000
fax (215) 765-7920
•*Bar area only.*

Le Bec Fin
1523 Walnut St.
Philadelphia 19102
(215) 567-1000
fax (215) 568-1151
•*Bar Lyonnais after 9:30 p.m.*

London Grill
2301 Fairmount Ave.
Philadelphia 19130
(215) 978-4545
fax (215) 978-4915
•*Bar only.*

McGillin's Olde Ale House
1310 Drury Lane
Philadelphia 19107
(215) 735-5562
fax (215) 735-4144
•*Dining room, bar and lounge.*

Morton's of Chicago
1 Logan Square
Philadelphia 19103
(215) 557-0724
fax (215) 557-9741
•*Smoking section, bar and private rooms.*

Palm Restaurant
200 S. Broad St.
Philadelphia 19102
(215) 546-7256
fax (215) 546-3088
•*Dining room and bar.*

Philip's Italian Restaurant
1145 S. Broad St.
Philadelphia 19147
(215) 334-0882
•*Dining room, lounge and private rooms.*

Ritz-Carlton
17th & Chestnut Sts. at Liberty Plaza
Philadelphia 19103
(215) 563-1600
fax (215) 564-9559
•*Bar only.*

Seventeen Hundred One Restaurant
  The Warwick Hotel
1701 Locust St.
Philadelphia 19103
(215) 735-6000
fax (215) 790-7766
•*Lounge only.*

Zoot
126 Chestnut St.
Philadelphia 19147
(215) 925-6220
•*Smoking section after 11 p.m. and bar.*

Seven Stars Inn
Rte. 23 & Hoffecker Rd.
Phoenixville 19460
(610) 495-5205
fax (610) 495-5340
•*Special dining room (seats 12-18), bar
and lounge.*

PITTSBURGH

American Harvest Restaurant
  Doubletree Hotel
1000 Penn Ave.
Pittsburgh 15222
(412) 281-3700
fax (412) 227-4501
•*Smoking section.*

The Carlton
One Mellon Bank Center
Pittsburgh 15206
(412) 391-4099
fax (412) 391-4240
•*Smoking section, bar and lounge.*

Cliffside
1208 Grandview Ave.
Pittsburgh 15237
(412) 431-6996
•*Bar only.*

Fox Chapel Yacht Club
1366 Old Freeport Rd.
Pittsburgh 15238
(412) 963-8881
•*Smoking area.*

Grandview Saloon
1212 Grandview Ave.
Pittsburgh 15211
(412) 431-1400
fax (412) 431-1471
•*Bar only.*

Le Mont
1114 Grandview Ave.
Pittsburgh 15211
(412) 431-3100
•*Front dining room, lounge and private
rooms.*

Morton's of Chicago
625 Liberty Ave.
Pittsburgh 15222
(412) 261-7141
fax (412) 261-7153
•*All areas.*

Roland's Seafood Grill
1904 Pennsylvania Ave.
Pittsburgh 15222
(412) 261-3401
fax (412) 261-3426
•*Bar and private rooms only.*

Siena
430 Market Square
Pittsburgh 15222
(412) 338-0945
fax (412) 338-0243
•*All areas.*

Tink's Cafe
519 Linden St.
Scranton 18509
(717) 346-8465
•*Bar and patio only.*

The Washington House
  The Historic Strasburg Inn
1 Historic Dr.
Strasburg 17579
(717) 687-7691
fax (717) 687-6098
•*Tavern only.*

R H O D E   I S L A N D

Atomic Grill
99 Chestnut St.
Providence 02903
(401) 621-8888
fax (401) 521-9021
•*Smoking area and bars.*

The Capital Grille
1 Cookson Place
Providence 02903
(401) 521-5600
fax (401) 331-8997
•*Dining room, bar and lounge.*

S O U T H   C A R O L I N A

Pasta House
404 N. Lake Condo
Anderson 29631
(803) 231-8811
fax (803) 231-6622
•*Dining area, bar, cocktail lounge and patio.*

Le Midi
337 King St.
Charleston 29401
(803) 577-5571
•*Bar only.*

Restaurant Million
2 Unity Alley
Charleston 29401
(803) 577-7472
fax (803) 853-0684
•*Lounge and atrium only.*

Austin's and Beau's
  Greenville Marriott
1 Parkway E.
Greenville 29615
(803) 297-0300
•*Dining room, bar and private rooms
(Beau's open after 5 p.m.).*

Inn on the Square
104 Court St.
Greenwood 29646
(803) 223-4488
fax (803) 223-7067
•*Pub only.*

New York Prime
405 28th Ave. N.
Myrtle Beach 29577
(803) 448-8081
fax (803) 448-7726
•*Smoking section and bar area.*

Ship's Bounty Restaurant
PO Box 3326
North Myrtle Beach 29582
(803) 272-7485
•*Bar and lounge only.*

H. Dundee's Steakhouse
2455 Cherry Rd.
Rock Hill 29732
(803) 325-7661
•*Dining room, bar and lounge.*

SOUTH DAKOTA

Alcester Steakhouse
PO Box 438
Alcester 57001
(605) 934-2974
•*Dining room and lounge.*

Theo's Great Food
601 W. 33rd St.
Sioux Falls 57105
(605) 338-6801
fax (605) 338-8025
•*Smoking section, bar and lounge.*

TENNESSEE

NASHVILLE

Arthur's
  Grand Heritage Hotel
1001 Broadway
Nashville 37203
(615) 255-1494
fax (615) 255-1496
•*Atrium of the hotel only.*

Belle Meade Brasserie
101 Page Rd.
Nashville 37205
(615) 356-5450
fax (615) 356-5456
•*Smoking area.*

The Bound'ry
711 20th Ave. S.
Nashville 37212
(615) 321-3043
fax (615) 321-0984
•*Bar and lounge only.*

F. Scott's
2210 Crestmoore Dr.
Nashville 37215
(615) 269-5861
fax (615) 269-8948
•*Bar only.*

Mario's
2005 Broadway
Nashville 37203
(615) 327-3232
fax (615) 321-2675
•*Bar and lounge only.*

The Merchants Restaurant
401 Broadway
Nashville 37203
(615) 254-1892
fax (615) 254-3012
•*All areas.*

Mere Bulles
152 2nd Ave. N.
Nashville 37201
(615) 256-1946
fax (615) 726-0751
•*Lounge only.*

Morton's of Chicago
641 Church St.
Nashville 37219
(615) 259-4558
•*Smoking section, bar area and private rooms.*

Ruth's Chris Steak House
2100 W. End Ave.
Nashville 37202
(615) 320-0163
fax (615) 320-0540
•*Bar only; smokers are welcome to dine in the bar.*

Sunset Grill
2001-A Belcourt Ave.
Nashville 37212
(615) 386-3663
fax (615) 386-0579
•*Bar, lounge and patio/sidewalk only.*

Valentino's
1907 W. End Ave.
Nashville 37203
(615) 327-0148
fax (615) 327-9482
•Smoking section and bar.

Wild Boar
2014 Broadway
Nashville 37203
(615) 329-1313
fax (615) 329-4930
•Bar, lounge and private rooms only.

▲ **Chattanooga Billiard Club**
110 Jordan Dr.
Chattanooga 37421
(423) 499-3883
 And
725½ Cherry St.
Chattanooga 37402
(423) 267-7740
•All areas.
•Besides billiards, offers lunch, dinner, a large humidor and much more.

▲ **Cafe Elliston Coffee House**
Elliston Place
210 Louise Ave.
Nashville 37203
(615) 329-0024
•Humidor room and outside patio only.
•Gourmet light fare, desserts, appetizers, coffee drinks and fine wines.

T E X A S

Morton's of Chicago
14831 Midway Rd.
Addison 75244
(214) 233-5858
fax (214) 233-6197
•All areas.

Louis 106 Grill & Tapas Bar
106 E. 6th St.
Austin 78701
(512) 476-1997
fax (512) 477-4304
•Private rooms only.

Hoffbrau Steaks
2310 N. 11th St.
Beaumont 77703
(409) 892-6911
fax (409) 899-3100
•Bar and outdoor beer garden only.

D A L L A S

Bob's Steak & Chop House
4300 Lemmon Ave.
Dallas 75219
(214) 528-9446
fax (214) 526-8159
•All areas.

Cabaret Royale
10723 Composite Dr.
Dallas 75220
(214) 350-0303
•VIP room.

▲ **Dallas Country Club**
4100 Beverly Dr.
Dallas 75205
(214) 521-2151
•Smoking section.
•Private club.

Del Frisco's Double Eagle Steakhouse
5251 Spring Valley Rd.
Dallas 75240
(214) 490-9000
fax (214) 934-0867
•Dining room and bar.

Four Seasons Resort & Club
4150 N. MacArthur Blvd.
Dallas 75038
(214) 717-0700
•Smoking section and separate bar and
lounge.

The French Room
  The Adolphus Hotel
1321 Commerce
Dallas 75202
(214) 742-8200
•Lounge only.

Hoffbrau Steaks
3205 Knox St.
Dallas 75205
(214) 559-2680
fax (214) 520-9415
•Bar only.

Les Saisons
165 Turtle Creek Village
Dallas 75219
(214) 528 1102
•Bar area only.

Mansion on Turtle Creek
2821 Turtle Creek Blvd.
Dallas 75219
(214) 559-2100
fax (214) 526-5345
•Bar and lounge area only.

Morton's of Chicago
50l Elm St.
Dallas 75202
(214) 741-2277
fax (214) 748-6360
•Smoking section, bar and private rooms
only.

Mr. G's
  Hyatt Regency DFW
DFW International Pkwy.
DFW Airport
Dallas 75261
(214) 453-1234
fax (214) 615-6829
•Smoking section.

Nana Grill
2201 Stemmons Fwy.
Dallas 75208
(214) 761-7459
fax (214) 761-7516
•Bar and private dining rooms only.

Newport's Seafood Restaurant
703 McKinney Ave.
Dallas 75202
(214) 954-0220
•Bar and private room only.

The Palm
701 Ross Ave.
Dallas 75202
(214) 698-0470
fax (214) 742-4410
•Smoking section.

Pyramid Room
  Fairmont Hotel
1717 N. Akard St.
Dallas 75201
(214) 720-5249
•Lounge only.

Trail Dust Steak House
10841 Composite Dr.
Dallas 75220
(214) 357-3862
fax (214) 357-1287
•Smoking section.

Watel's
1923 McKinney Ave.
Dallas 75201
(214) 720-0323
•Patio/sidewalk only.

Carmen's
  Radisson Hotel
2211 I-35E N.
Denton 76201
(817) 381-0263
•*Smoking section.*

Cafe Central
109 N. Oregon
El Paso 79901
(915) 545-CAFE
fax (915) 545-2255
•*Bar, private rooms and patio/sidewalk only.*

Michael's
3413 W. 7th St.
Fort Worth 76107
(817) 877-3413
fax (817) 877-3430
•*Dining room after meals, bar, lounge and patio/sidewalk.*

Gaido's Restaurant
3800 Seawall
Galveston 77550
(409) 762-9625
•*Smoking section only.*

Grey Moss Inn
19010 Scenic Loop Rd.
Grey Forest 78023
(210) 695-8301
fax (210) 695-3237
•*Private rooms and patio only.*

HOUSTON

▲ **Big John's Neighborhood Bar**
6150 Wilcrest
Houston 77072
(713) 498-3499
fax (713) 498-3147
•*All areas of bar.*
•*Bar serves pub food at lunch; dinner specials at times.*

Brennan's
3300 Smith St.
Houston 77006
(713) 522-9711
fax (713) 522-9142
•*Bar only.*

The Brownstone
2736 Virginia
Houston 77098
(713) 520-5666
fax (713) 520-7001
•*Private room, gallery and terrace.*

Charley's 517
517 Louisiana St.
Houston 77002
(713) 224-4438
fax (713) 229-8112
•*Bar, lounge and private rooms only.*

▲ **Colorado Bar & Grill**
6710 SW Fwy.
Houston 77074
(713) 781-1122
fax (713) 565-9777
•*All areas.*
•*A gentlemen's club—world's largest topless sports bar and grill.*

Four Seasons Hotel
1300 Lamar St.
Houston 77002
(713) 650-1300
•*Dining room of Terrace Cafe during low occupancy only.*

La Colombe d'Or
3410 Montrose Blvd.
Houston 77006
(713) 524-7999
fax (713) 524-8923
•*Bar and library only.*

La Reserve
  Omni Houston
4 Riverway
Houston 77056
(713) 871-8177
•*Bar, lounge and private rooms only.*

Montesano Ristorante Italiano
6009 Beverly Hill Lane
Houston 77057
(713) 977-4565
fax (713) 977-6855
•*Smoking area only.*

Morton's of Chicago
Centre at Post Oak
5000 Westheimer
Houston 77056
(713) 629-1946
fax (713) 629-4348
•*All areas.*

Pappas Bros. Steakhouse
5839 Westheimer
Houston 77056
(713) 780-7352
•*Smoking section, all private dining areas, bar and lounge.*

Rainbow Lodge
1 Birdsall
Houston 77007
(713) 861-8666
•*Bar, lounge and private rooms only.*

Ritz-Carlton
1919 Briar Oaks Lane
Houston 77027
(713) 840-7600
fax (713) 840-0616
•*Dining room, bar, lounge and private rooms.*

Ruggles
903 Westheimer
Houston 77006
(713) 524-3839
fax (713) 527-8341
•*Smoking section.*

Ruth's Chris Steak House
6213 Richmond
Houston 77057
(713) 789-2333
fax (713) 789-4136
•*Bar only.*

The Velvet Elvis
3303 Richmond
Houston 77098
(713) 520-0434
fax (713) 520-0036
•*All areas.*

Marcello's Italian Restaurant
110 N. Tarmada
Port Isabel 78578
(210) 943-7611
fax (210) 943-1200
•*Smoking section.*

SAN ANTONIO

Morton's of Chicago
849 E. Commerce St.
San Antonio 78205
(210) 228-0700
fax (210) 228-0778
•*Smoking section, bar and private rooms.*

Polo's
  Fairmont Hotel
401 S. Alamo
San Antonio 78205
(210) 224-8800
fax (210) 224-2767
•*Bar only.*

Pour La France
7959 Broadway, 204
San Antonio 78215
(210) 826-4333
•*Smoking section, bar and patio.*

Rock Bottom Brewery
4050 Beltline Rd.
West Addison 75240
(214) 404-7456
fax (214) 404-7454
•*Bar only.*

VERMONT

Main Street Grill & Bar
118 Main St.
Montpelier 05602
(802) 229-9202
fax (802) 223-0634
•*Smoking room only.*

La Poule a Dents
Main St.
Norwich 05055
(802) 649-2922
•*Bar only.*

Ye Olde England Inne
433 Mountain Rd.
Stowe 05672
(802) 253-7064
fax (802) 253-8944
•*Patio and private dining rooms only.*

Hermitage Inn
Coldbrook Rd.
Wilmington 05363
(802) 464-3511
fax (802) 464-2688
•*Bar only.*

VIRGINIA

Bullfeathers
112 King St.
Alexandria 22314
(703) 836-8088
fax (703) 836-3426
•*Bar area only.*

Morrison House
116 S. Alfred St.
Alexandria 22314
(703) 838-8000
fax (703) 684-6283
•*Wine room only.*

Coco's Casa Mia Ristorante
3111 Columbia Pike
Arlington 22204
(703) 920-5450
fax (703) 979-9647
•*Bar, lounge and private rooms only.*

Ritz-Carlton
1250 S. Hayes St.
Arlington 22202
(703) 412-2760
fax (703) 415-5061
•*Lounge only.*

Tavern at Boar's Head Inn & Sports Club
Rte. 250 W.
Charlottesville 22903
(804) 296-2181
fax (804) 922-6016
•*Service lounge only.*

Key West Holiday Inn
725 Woodlake Dr.
Chesapeake 23320
(804) 523-1500
fax (804) 523-0683
•*All areas.*

AJ's on the Creek
6585 Maddox Blvd.
Chincoteague 23336
(804) 336-5888
fax (804) 336-3358
•Bar from 2 p.m. - 4 p.m.; patio after
10 p.m.

Cafe France
3225 Old Forest Rd.
Lynchburg 24501
(804) 385-8989
•Dining room after 9:45 p.m. only.

**Evans Farm Inn and The Sitting
  Duck Pub**
1696 Chain Bridge Rd.
McLean 22101
(703) 356-8000
•Sitting Duck Pub dining room and 5
banquet rooms.

Ritz-Carlton
1700 Tysons Blvd.
McLean 22102
(703) 506-4300
•Bar and lounge only.

Havana '59
16 N. 17th St.
Richmond 23219
(804) 649-2822
fax (804) 648-2951
•All areas.

The Tobacco Co. Restaurant
1201 E. Cary St.
Richmond 23219
(804) 782-9431
•Dining room, bar and lounge.

Morton's of Chicago
8075 Leesburg Pike
Vienna 22182
(703) 883-0800
fax (703) 883-0673
•Smoking section and lounge.

The Lighthouse Restaurant
1st St. & Atlantic Ave.
Virginia Beach 23451
(804) 428-7974
•Smoking dining rooms.

Ford's Colony Country Club
240 Ford's Colony Dr.
Williamsburg 23188
(804) 258-4107, -4100 (Grill Room)
fax (804) 258-4168
•Most areas.

WASHINGTON

The Courtyard Bistro
419 Commercial Ave.
Anacortes 98221
(206) 299-2923
•Garden/patio area only; all areas on
cigar nights.

Palmer's Restaurant & Pub
201 E. Washington St.
LaConner 98257
(360) 466-4261
fax (360) 466-3270
•Bar, lounge and patio/sidewalk only.

The Spar Cafe & Bar
114 4th Ave. E.
Olympia 98501
(360) 357-6444
fax (360) 352-2969
•Restaurant and bar.

SEATTLE

Bandoleone
2241 Eastlake Ave. E.
Seattle 98103
(206) 329-7559
fax (206) 329-3122
•Lounge area only.

Bookstore Bar
  The Alexis Hotel
1007 1st Ave.
Seattle 98104
(206) 382-1506
•*All areas.*

Daniel's Broiler
200 Lake Washington Blvd.
Seattle 98114
(206) 329-4191
•*Bar only.*

F. X. McRory's Steak, Chop &
  Oyster House
419 Occidental Ave. S., #501
Seattle 98104
(206) 623-4800
•*All areas.*

Georgian Room
  Four Seasons Hotel
411 University St.
Seattle 98101
(206) 621-7889
fax (206) 623-2271
•*Terrace Lounge and private rooms only.*

McCormick's Fish House and Bar
722 4th Ave.
Seattle 98104
(206) 682-3900
•*Bar and patio/sidewalk only.*

Metropolitan Grill
820 2nd Ave.
Seattle 98104
(206) 624-3287
fax (206) 389-0042
•*Lounge and private dining rooms only.*

Ray's Boathouse
6049 Seaview NW
Seattle 98107
(206) 789-3770
fax (206) 781-1960
•*Lounge, private rooms and
patio/sidewalk only.*

John Horan House
2 Horan Rd.
Wenatchee 98801
(509) 663-0018
fax (509) 662-2228
•*Outside dining area only (weather
permitting).*

WEST VIRGINIA

The Anvil Restaurant
1270 Washington St.
Harpers Ferry 25425
(304) 535-2582
•*Bar only.*

Greenbrier Hotel
Main St.
White Sulphur Springs 24986
(304) 536-1110
fax (304) 536-7854
•*Bar, lounge, private rooms and
patio/sidewalk only.*

WISCONSIN

Jimmie's White House Inn
5776 Main St.
Butte des Morts 54927
(414) 582-7211
•*Bar and private rooms only.*

Fountain Blue
5133 S. Lake Dr.
Cudahy 53110
(414) 481-1482
fax (414) 744-6379
•*Bar room only.*

Studio Grille
1318 Racine St.
Delavan 53115
(414) 728-0456
•*Smoking section and lounge only.*

Alfred's Supper Club
506 Hill St.
Green Lake 54941
(800) 664-3631, (414) 294-3631
•*Dining room, bar and private rooms.*

The Fox & Hounds
1298 Friess Lake Rd.
Hubertus 53033
(414) 251-4100
fax (414) 628-2440
•*Bar and private rooms only.*

Horse & Plow
  The American Club
Highland Dr.
Kohler 53044
(414) 457-8000
•*Dining room and bar.*

Kirsch's Restaurant
Hwy. 50 W.
Lake Geneva 53191
(414) 245-5756
•*Bar, lounge, private rooms and patio only.*

The Bistro
  Madison Concourse Hotel
1 W. Dayton St.
Madison 53703
(608) 257-6000
•*Bar and Solitaire Room only.*

▲ **The Cardinal Bar & Dance Club**
418 E. Wilson St.
Madison 53703
(608) 251-0080
•*All areas.*
•*Bar and dance club.*

Inn on Maritime Bay
101 Maritime Dr.
Manitowoc 54220
(414) 682-7000
•*Smoking section.*

Johnny's Bar & Grill
3161 Hwy. 51
Mercer 54547
(715) 476-2516
•*All areas.*

Shaker's Cigar Bar
422 S. 2nd St.
Milwaukee 53204
(414) 272-4222
fax (414) 271-4370
•*All areas.*

Snug's Restaurant
  The Shorecrest Hotel
1962 N. Prospect Ave.
Milwaukee 53202
(414) 278-8480
•*All areas.*

Fifty Two Stafford,
  An Irish Guest House
52 Stafford St.
Plymouth 53073
(414) 893-0552
fax (414) 893-1800
•*Restaurant and bar.*

Cavalier Room Restaurant &
  Lounge
70 N. Stevens St.
Rhinelander 54501
(715) 362-7100
•*Lounge and private rooms only.*

▲ **Wausau Club**
309 McClellan St.
Wausau 54403
(715) 845-2131
fax (715) 848-5115
•*Private dining club.*

Steakhouse 100
10725 W. Greenfield Ave.
West Allis 53214
(414) 771-2223
fax (414) 771-8781
•*Bar only.*

WYOMING

Gros Ventre River Ranch
18 Gros Ventre Rd.
Moose 83012
(307) 733-4138
fax (307) 733-4272
•*Bar, lounge, private rooms and
patio/sidewalk.*

INTERNATIONAL

AUSTRIA

Gottfried
Untere Viaduktgasse 45
Vienna A1010
43 1 71 38 256
fax 43 1 71 38 257
•*All areas.*

Korso
  Bristol Hotel
Karntner Ring 1
Vienna A1010
43 1 51 51 60
fax 43 1 51 51 65 50
•*All areas.*

La Scala
  The Vienna Plaza
Schottenring 11
Vienna A1010
43 1 31 39 00
fax 43 1 31 39 01 60
•*Smoking section.*

Restaurant Steirereck
Rasumofskygasse 2
Vienna A1010
43 1 71 33 168
fax 43 1 71 35 16 82
•*Dining room and bar.*

BAHAMAS

Graycliff
W. Hill St.
Nassau
(809) 322-2797
fax (809) 326-6110
•*All areas.*

BELGIUM

De Matelote
Haarstraat 9
Antwerp 2000
32 2 23 13 207
fax 32 2 23 13 207
•*All areas.*

'T Fornuis
Reyndersstraat 24
Antwerp 2000
32 3 23 36 270
fax 32 3 23 39 903
•*Bar and after dinner only.*

Bruneau
ave. Broustin 75
Brussels 1080
32 2 42 76 978
fax 32 2 42 59 726
•*All areas.*

Comme Chez Soi
23 place Rouppe
Brussels 1000
32 2 51 22 921
fax 32 2 51 18 052
•*Dining room and private rooms.*

La Maison du Cygne
Grand Place 9
Brussels 1000
32 2 51 18 244
fax 32 2 51 43 148
•*All areas.*

La Truffe Noire
12 blvd. de La Cambre
Brussels 1050
32 2 64 04 422
fax 32 2 64 79 704
•*All areas.*

**Les 4 Saisons
  Royal Windsor**
rue Duquesnoy 5
Brussels 1000
32 2 50 55 100
fax 32 2 50 55 500
•*Smoking section.*

Maison du Boeuf
blvd. du Waterloo 38
Brussels 1000
32 2 50 41 111
fax 32 2 50 42 111
•*All areas.*

Sea Grill
J. Le Divellec, rue Fossé-aux-Loups 47
Brussels 1000
32 2 22 73 120
fax 32 2 21 96 262
•*Smoking section, bar and atrium
lounge.*

Villa Lorraine
ave. du Vivier d'Oie 75
Brussels 1180
32 2 37 43 163
fax 32 2 37 20 195
•*Dining room after 9:30 p.m. only.*

Carême
Koningin Astridlaan 114
Kontich 2500
32 3 45 76 304
fax 32 3 45 79 302
•*All areas.*

Rudy's Fonduehuisje
St. Maartenstraat 12-C
Leuven 3000
32 16 20 44 20
fax 32 16 22 32 82
•*All areas.*

B R A Z I L

Cafe Ideal
Inconfidentes 312
Belo Horizonte
55 31 223 9986
fax 55 31 221 3837
•*All areas.*

C A N A D A

A L B E R T A

▲ **Tasmanian Ballroom & Havana's
  Cigar Lounge**
1215 1st St. SW
Calgary T2R OB3
(403) 266-1824
fax (403) 263-7987
•*All areas.*
•*Nightclub and private club (with guests
welcome)*

B R I T I S H C O L U M B I A

Deep Cove Chalet
11190 Chalet Rd.
Vancouver Island
Sidney V8L 4R4
(604) 656-3541
fax (604) 656-2601
•*All areas.*

The Cannery Seafood Restaurant
2205 Commissioner St.
Vancouver V5L 1A4
(604) 254-9606
fax (604) 254-1820
•*Lounge only.*

**Chartwell
  Four Seasons Hotel**
791 W. Georgia St.
Vancouver V6C 2T4
(604) 689-9333
fax (604) 689-3466
•*Bar, lounge and private rooms only.*

La Gavroche
1616 Alberni St.
Vancouver V6G 1A6
(604) 685-3924
•*Private rooms only.*

NOVA SCOTIA

Joe's Warehouse & Food Emporium
424 Charlotte St.
Sydney B1P 1E2
(902) 539-6686
fax (902) 539-2070
•*Smoking section, bar and private dining room.*

ONTARIO

Barberian's Steak House Tavern
7 Elm St.
Toronto M5G 1H1
(416) 597-0335
fax (416) 597-1407
•*Smoking section.*

Black Peter Buffet
221 Dufferin Rd.
Toronto M6K 1Y9
(416) 534-5846
•*At 3 tables only.*

Estonian House Restaurant
958 Broadview Ave.
Toronto M4K 2R6
(416) 463-3321
•*Smoking section and bar.*

George Bigliardi's
463 Church St.
Toronto N4Y 2C5
(416) 922-9594
•*Dining room, bar and private rooms.*

Mary Johns Restaurant
91 Gerard St. W.
Toronto M5G 2A7
(416) 595-1475
•*Smoking section.*

Opus Restaurant
37 Prince Arthur Ave.
Toronto M5R 1B2
(416) 921-3105
•*Bar only.*

Prego della Piazza
150 Bloor St. W.
Toronto M5S 2X9
(416) 920-9900
fax (416) 920-9949
•*Wine bar "Enoteca" at all times; dining room after 10:30 p.m.*

The Senator
249 Victoria St.
Toronto M5B 1T8
(416) 364-7517
fax (416) 364-3784
•*Dining room and nightclub.*

Shark City Bar & Grill
117 Eglinton Ave. E.
Toronto M4P 1H4
(416) 488-7899
fax (416) 486-3316
•*Dining area and billiards lounge.*

The School of Fine Dining
4121 14th Ave.
Unionville L3R 2J2
(905) 477-1161
fax (905) 479-2388
•*Lounge only.*

QUEBEC

Four Seasons Hotel
1050 Scherook St.
Montreal H3A 2R6
(514) 284-1110
•*Smoking section of piano bar.*

L'Inox
37 St. André
Quebec City G1K 8T3
(418) 692-2877
•*All areas.*

La Mas des Oliviers
1216 rue Bishop
Montreal H3G 2E3
(514) 861-6733
fax (514) 861-7838
•*Special room only.*

Le Lutetia
1430 rue de La Montagne
Montreal H3G 125
(514) 288-5656
•*Special smoking area in lobby.*

Bistro à Champlain
75 Chemin Masson
Sainte-Marguerite du Lac
Masson J0T 1L0
(514) 228-4988
fax (514) 228-4893
•*Special cigar room.*

D E N M A R K

Restaurant Kanalen
Wilders Plads
Copenhagen 1403
45 1 329 51330
fax 45 1 329 51338
•*All areas.*

Kommandanten
NY Adelgade 7
Copenhagen 1104
45 3 312 0990
fax 45 3 393 1233
•*All areas.*

Nouvelle
Gammel Strand 34
Copenhagen 1202
45 3 313 5018
fax 45 3 332 0797
•*All areas.*

Restaurationen
Montergade 19
Copenhagen
45 1 3314 9495
•*Dining room.*

F I N L A N D

Lord a la Carte
Lönnrotinkatu 29
Helsinki 00180
358 0 68 01 680
fax 358 0 68 01 315
•*All areas.*

F R A N C E

Restaurant La Belle Otéro/Carlton
  Casino Club
  Hôtel Carlton International
58 blvd. Croisette
Cannes 06400
33 93 68 00 33
fax 33 93 39 09 06
•*Dining room and near the piano bar.*

La Côte
  Hôtel Carlton International
58 blvd. Croisette
Cannes 06400
33 93 06 40 06
fax 33 93 38 20 90
•*Private room only.*

La Palme d'Or
73 blvd. Croisette
Cannes 06400
33 93 29 87 414
fax 33 93 39 03 38
•*Smoking section.*

Royal Gray
  Hôtel Gray d'Albion
6 rue êtats-Unis
Cannes 06408
33 92 99 79 60
fax 33 93 99 26 10
•*Dining room and bar.*

Les Millésimes
25 rue Eglise
Gevrey-Chambertin 21220
33 8 05 18 424
fax 33 8 03 41 273
•*Lounge only.*

A La Côte St. Jacques
14 Paris
Joigny
33 86 62 09 70
fax 33 86 91 49 70
•*Bar and lounge only.*

Léon de Lyon
1 rue Pleney
Lyons 69001
33 7 828 1133
fax 33 7 839 8905
•*Bar only.*

Paul Bocuse
Collonges-au-Mont-d'Or
Lyons 69660
33 7 24 29 090
fax 33 7 22 78 587
•*All areas.*

Le Petit Nice
Anse de Maldorme
Marseilles
33 91 59 25 92
fax 33 91 59 28 08
•*All areas.*

Gastronomique
42 ave. Charles de Gaulle
Neuilly-sur-Seine 92200
33 14 62 44 261
•*Dining room.*

Restaurant Chantecler
  Hôtel Négresco
37 Promenade des Anglais
Nice Cedex 1
33 93 16 64 00
•*Dining room, bar and private rooms.*

Amphyclés
78 ave. Ternes
Paris 75017
33 1 40 68 01 01
•*All areas.*

Apicius
122 ave. Villiers
Paris 75007
33 1 43 80 19 66
•*All areas.*

Arpäge
84 rue Varenne
Paris 75007
33 1 45 51 47 33
fax 33 1 44 18 98 39
•*All areas.*

Bristol
  Hôtel Bristol
112 rue Faubourg St-Honoré
Paris 75008
33 1 42 66 91 45
fax 33 1 42 66 68 68
•*All areas.*

Carre des Feuillants
14 rue de Castiglione
Paris 75001
33 1 42 86 82 82
fax 33 1 42 86 07 71
•*Private rooms only.*

Chez Pauline
5 rue Villédo
Paris 75001
33 1 42 96 20 70
•*All areas.*

Chiberta
3 rue Arsène-Houssaye
Paris 75008
33 1 45 63 77 90
•*All areas.*

Drouant
18 place Gaillon
Paris 75002
33 1 42 65 15 16
•*All areas.*

Duquesnoy
6 ave. Bosquet
Paris 75007
33 1 47 05 96 78
fax 33 1 44 18 90 57
•*Smoking tables only.*

Espadon
  Hotel Ritz
15 place Vendôme
Paris 75041
33 43 16 30 80
fax 33 43 16 33 67
•*Smoking areas.*

Faucher
123 ave. de Wagram
Paris 75017
33 1 42 27 61 50
fax 33 1 46 22 25 72
•*All areas.*

Ferme St. Simon
6 rue St. Simon
Paris 75007
33 1 45 48 35 74
fax 33 1 40 49 07 31
•*All areas.*

Fifteen Montaigne Maison Blanche
15 ave. Montaigne
Paris 75008
33 1 47 23 55 99
fax 33 1 47 20 09 56
•*All areas.*

Gérard Besson
5 rue Coq Héron
Paris 75001
33 1 42 33 14 74
•*All areas.*

Goumard-Prunier
9 rue Duphot
Paris 75001
33 1 42 60 36 07
•*All areas.*

Grand V'efour
17 rue Beaujolais
Paris 75001
33 1 42 96 56 27
fax 33 1 42 86 80 71
•*All areas.*

Grande Cascade
Alleé de Longchamp, Bois de
  Boulogne
Paris 75016
33 1 45 27 33 51
fax 33 1 44 28 89 906
•*Dining room.*

Guy Savoy
18 rue Troyon
Paris 75017
33 1 43 80 40 61
fax 33 1 44 62 24 309
•*All areas.*

Hemingway Bar
  Hôtel Ritz
15 Place Vendôme
Paris 75041
33 43 16 33 65
fax 33 43 16 33 67
•*All areas of the bar.*

Jacques Cagna
14 rue Grands Augustins
Paris 75006
33 1 43 26 49 39
•*Dining room.*

Joël Robuchon
59 ave. Raymond Poincare
Paris 75116
33 1 47 27 12 27
fax 33 1 47 27 31 22
•*All areas.*

Joséphine
117 rue Cherche-Midi
Paris 75006
33 1 45 48 52 40
fax 33 1 42 84 06 38
•*Lounge only.*

Jules Verne
Eiffel Tower, 2nd Platform
Paris 75007
33 1 45 55 61 44
fax 33 1 47 05 94 40
•*Bar only.*

L'Ambroisie
9 place des Vosges
Paris 75004
33 1 42 78 51 45
•*All areas.*

L'Espadon
15 place Vendìme
Paris 75001
33 1 42 60 38 30
•*All areas.*

La Boule d'Or
13 blvd. La Tour Maubourg
Paris 75007
33 1 47 05 50 18
•*Smoking section.*

La Cagouille
10 place Constantin Brancusi
Paris 75014
33 1 43 22 09 01
fax 33 1 45 38 57 29
•*Dining room.*

La Couronne
  Hôtel Warwick
5 rue Berri
Paris 75008
33 1 45 63 78 49
fax 33 1 45 63 75 81
•*Smoking section.*

La Mare
1 rue Daru
Paris 75008
33 1 43 80 20 00
fax 33 1 48 88 04 04
•*Dining room.*

La Table d'Anvers
2 place d'Anvers
Paris 75009
33 1 48 78 35 21
fax 33 1 45 26 66 67
•*All areas.*

La Table du Gouverneur
Pavillon Elysée
10 ave. des Champs Elysées
Paris 75008
33 1 42 65 85 10
fax 33 1 42 65 76 23
•*Smoking areas.*

Lasserre
17 ave. Franklin D. Roosevelt
Paris 75008
33 1 43 59 53 43
fax 33 1 45 63 72 25
•*Smoking section.*

Laurent
41 ave. Gabriel
Paris 75008
33 1 42 25 00 39
fax 33 1 45 62 45 21
•*Dining room.*

Le Bellecour
22 rue Surcouf
Paris 75007
33 1 45 51 46 93
fax 33 1 45 50 30 11
•*Throughout the restaurant.*

Le Céladon
  Hôtel Westminster
15 rue Daunou
Paris 75002
33 1 47 03 40 42
fax 33 1 42 60 30 66
•*All areas.*

Le Clos Longchamp
81 blvd. Gouvion-St-Cyr
Paris 75017
33 1 40 68 00 70
fax 33 1 40 68 30 81
•*Smoking areas.*

Le Divellec
107 rue Université, Invalide
Esplenade
Paris 75007
33 1 45 51 91 96
fax 33 1 45 51 31 75
•*All areas.*

Le Grand V'efour
17 rue de Beaujolais
Paris 75001
33 1 42 96 56 27
fax 33 1 42 86 80 71
•*All areas.*

Le Meurice
  Hôtel Meurice
228 rue Rivoli
Paris 75001
33 1 44 58 10 50
fax 33 1 44 58 10 15
•*All areas.*

Le Petit Colombier
42 rue Acacias
Paris 75017
33 1 43 80 28 54
fax 33 1 44 40 04 29
•*Fireplace salon only.*

Le Sormani
4 rue Gén-Lanrezac
Paris 75017
33 1 43 80 13 91
•*Dining room.*

Ledoyen
Carré Champs-Elysées
Paris 75008
33 1 47 42 23 23
fax 33 1 47 42 55 01
•*All areas.*

Les Ambassadeurs
  Hôtel Crillon
10 place Concorde
Paris 75008
33 1 44 71 16 16
fax 33 1 44 71 15 02
•*Smoking section.*

Les Elysées
  Hôtel Vernet
25 rue Vernet
Paris 75008
33 1 44 31 98 98
fax 33 1 44 31 85 69
•*Under the Tiffel Coupole.*

Lucas-Carton
9 place Madeleine
Paris 75008
33 1 42 65 22 90
fax 33 1 42 65 06 23
•*Smoking section.*

Manoir de Paris
6 rue Pierre Demours
Paris 75017
33 1 45 72 25 25
fax 33 1 45 74 80 98
•*Bar only.*

Mercure Galant
15 rue Petits-Champs
Paris 75001
33 1 42 96 98 89
fax 33 1 42 96 08 89
•*All areas.*

Michel Rostang
20 rue Rennequin
Paris 75017
33 1 47 63 40 77
fax 33 1 47 63 82 75
•*Smoking area.*

Montparnasse 25
  Hôtel Méridien Montparnasse
19 rue Cdt Mouchotte
Paris 75014
33 1 44 36 44 25
fax 33 1 44 36 49 00
•*Smoking section.*

Restaurant Morot-Gaudry
8 rue de la Cavalerie
Paris 75015
33 1 45 67 06 85
fax 33 1 45 67 55 72
•*All areas.*

Restaurant Opéra-Café de la Paix
  Grand Hôtel Inter-Continental
5 place Opéra
Paris 75009
33 1 40 07 30 10
fax 33 1 42 66 12 51
•*Smoking section.*

Petite Bretonniere
2 rue Cadix
Paris 75015
33 1 48 28 34 39
•*Dining room (if nobody complains).*

Pharamond
24 rue Grande-Truanderie
Paris 75001
33 1 42 33 06 72
fax 33 1 40 28 01 81
•*First floor of restaurant.*

Pile ou Face
52 bis rue Notre-Dames-des-Victoires
Paris 75002
33 1 42 33 64 33
fax 33 1 42 36 61 09
•*Dining room.*

Port Alma
10 ave. New York
Paris 75116
33 1 47 23 75 11
•*Smoking section.*

Pré Catelan
Route de Suresnes
Paris 75016
33 1 45 24 55 58
fax 33 1 45 24 43 25
•*One dining room*

Récamier
4 rue Récamier
Paris 75007
33 1 45 48 86 58
fax 33 1 42 22 84 76
•*All areas.*

Régence
  Hôtel Plaza Athénée
25 ave. Montaigne
Paris 75008
33 1 47 23 78 33
fax 33 1 47 20 20 70
•*Dining room.*

Relais Louis XIII
1 rue Pont de Lodi
Paris 75006
33 1 43 26 75 96
fax 33 1 44 07 07 80
•*Dining room.*

Taillevent
15 rue Lamennais
Paris 75008
33 1 45 61 12 90
fax 33 1 42 25 95 18
•*Dining room.*

Toit de Passy
94 ave. P. Doumer
Paris 75016
33 1 45 24 55 37
fax 33 1 45 20 84 57
•*Smoking area.*

Tour d'Argent
15 quai Tournelle
Paris 75005
33 1 43 54 23 31
fax 33 1 44 07 12 04
•*Special cigar smoking section only.*

Vivarois
192 ave. Victor Hugo
Paris 75116
33 1 45 04 04 31
fax 33 1 45 03 09 84
•*All areas.*

Les Crayéres
64 blvd. Vasnier
Rheims 51100
33 26 82 80 80
fax 33 26 82 65 52
•*Bar only.*

Troisgros
22 cour Républíque
Roanne 42300
33 77 71 66 97
fax 33 77 70 03 977
•*Bar only.*

Côte d'Or
2 rue Argentine
Saulieu 21210
33 80 90 53 53
•*Dining room (except on Saturdays).*

Buerehiesel
4 parc de L'Orangerie
Strasbourg 67000
33 88 61 62 24
•*All areas.*

Le Crocodile
10 rue Outre
Strasbourg 67000
33 88 32 13 02
fax 33 88 75 72 01
•*Smoking section.*

Georges Blanc
Vonnas 01540
33 74 50 90 90
fax 33 74 50 08 80
•*All areas.*

FRENCH POLYNESIA

Bali Hai Huahine
Sare
Huahine, Tahiti
689 68 84 77
fax 689 68 82 77
•*All areas.*

Bali Hai Moorea
BP26 Maharepa
Moorea, Tahiti
689 56 13 59
fax 689 56 19 22
•*All areas.*

GERMANY

**Brenner's Park Restaurant &
Oleander Bar
Schwarzwald**
Schillerstrasse 6, Lichtenthaler Allee
Baden Baden 76530
49 7 221 9000
•*All areas.*

**Schloss Thiergarten Hotel &
Restaurant**
Oberthiergärtnerstrasse 36
Bayreuth
49 9 209 9840
•*All areas.*

Rino Casati
Ebertplatz 3-5
Cologne 50668
49 221 721108, after August 1 call
7201108
fax 49 221 728097
•*All areas.*

Im Schiffchen
Kaiserswerther Markt 9
Düsseldorf
49 21 140 1050
fax 49 21 140 3667
•*All areas.*

Hotel & Restaurant Landsknecht
Post Str. 70, 40667 Meerbusch
Düsseldorf
49 21 325 947
fax 49 21 321 0978
•*All areas.*

Victorian
Königstrasse 3-A
Düsseldorf
49 21 186 550 20
fax 49 21 186 550 13
•*All areas.*

**Schassberger Ebnisee Spa &
Resort Hotel**
Winnender 10
Ebnisee 73667
49 7 184 2920
fax 49 7 184 292 204
•*Bar, lounge, private rooms and
patio/sidewalk only.*

La Grappa
Rellinghauserstrasse 4
Essen 0201
49 20 123 1766
•*All areas.*

Restaurant Français
Bethmannstrasse 33
Frankfurt 60311
49 69 215 806
fax 49 69 275 903
•*All areas.*

Weinhaus Brückenkeller
Schützenstrasse 6
Frankfurt
49 69 29 80 070
fax 49 69 29 60 68
•*Bar and lounge only.*

**Wald-und Schlosshotel
Friedrichsruhe**
Friedrichsruhe
49 79 41 608 70
•*All areas.*

Hotel & Restaurant Zur Traube
Bahnstrasse 47
Grevenbroich 41515
49 21 816 8767
fax 49 21 816 1122
•*All areas.*

Le Canard
Elbchaussee 139
Hamburg 22763
49 40 88 05 057
fax 49 40 47 24 13
•*All areas.*

Hessler
Bootshaferam 4
Maintal M474
49 61 814 3030
•All areas.

Boettner
Theatinerstrasse 8
Munich 80333
49 89 221 210
•All areas.

Hilton Grill
  Hotel Park Hilton
Am Tucherpark 7
Munich 80538
49 89 384 5261
fax 49 89 384 51845
•All areas.

Kônigshof
Karlsplatz 25
Munich 80335
49 89 551 360
•All areas.

Le Gourmet Schwarzwälder
Hartmannstrasse 8
Munich 80333
49 89 212 0993
fax 49 89 2120 906
•All areas of garden/restaurant.

Tantris
Johann-Fichtestrasse 7
Munich 80805
49 89 362 061
•All areas.

Rüdesheimer Schloss
Drosselgasse
Rüdesheim am Rhein 65385
49 6 722 90500
fax 49 6 722 47960
•All areas.

Landgasthof-Metzgerei Paulus
Prälat-Faber Straße 2-4
Sitzerath/Saar D-66620
49 6 873 91011
fax 49 6 873 64222
•All areas.

Restaurant Backmulde
Karmeliterstrasse 11-13
Speyer 67346
49 62 32 715 77
fax 49 62 32 709 03
•Bar and after dinner only.

Die Ente vom Lehel
Kaiser-Friedrichplatz 3/4
Wiesbaden 65183
49 61 113 3666
fax 49 61 113 3683
•Restaurant bar all night and after
dinner only.

Kiefernweg 12
Winterberg 59955
49 2 981 2042
fax 49 2 981 3670
•All areas.

GUATEMALA

Jake's
17 Calle 10-40
Guatemala City
502 2 680 351
•All areas.

HONG KONG

Brown's Restaurant & Wine Bar
Exchange Square Tower II
Central Hong Kong
852 2523 7003
fax 852 2521 7799
•All areas.

Petrus
Island Shangri-La Hotel
Pacific Place
Supreme Court Rd.
Hong Kong
852 2877 3838
•*Smoking section.*

Panorama Western
Fine Dining Room
4/F New World Hotel
22 Salisbury Rd.
Tsimshatsui, Kowloon
852 2369 4111
fax 852 2369 9387
•*Smoking section.*

The Peninsula Hotel
Salisbury Rd.
Tsimshatsui Kowloon
852 2366 6251
fax 852 2722 4170
•*Smoking section.*

I R E L A N D

Le Coq Hardi
35 Pembroke Rd., Pallsbridge
Dublin 4
353 1 668 4130
•*Dining room, bar, lounge and private rooms.*

I T A L Y

La Taverna
Piazza Castello 2
Colloredo 33010
39 43 28 89 045
•*Dining room, bar and patio.*

Enoteca Pinchiorri
Via Ghibellina 87
Florence 50122
39 55 24 27 77/2
fax 39 55 24 49 83
•*Private room only.*

Lorenzo
Via Carducci 61
Forte dei Marmi
39 5 848 4030
fax 39 5 84 84 030
•*All areas.*

A Riccione
Via Taramelli 70
Milan 20124
39 2 66 86 807
fax 39 2 66 80 36 16
•*All areas.*

Alfredo-Gran San Bernardo
Via Borgese 14
Milan 20154
39 2 33 19 000
fax 39 2 40 09 06 52
•*All areas.*

Peck
Via Victor Hugo 4
Milan 20121
39 2 87 67 74
fax 39 2 87 04 08
•*Bar only.*

Ristorante Sadler
Troilo 14
Milan 20136
39 2 58 10 44 51
fax 39 2 58 11 23 43
•*All areas.*

Scaletta
Piazza Stazione Genova 3
Milan 20144
39 2 58 10 02 90
•*All areas.*

Checchino dal 1887
Via Monte Testaccio 30
Rome 00153
39 6 57 46 318
fax 39 6 57 43 816
•Principal room of the restaurant.

Papa Giovanni
Via dei Sediari 4
Rome 00186
39 6 68 80 48 07, 68 65 308
fax 39 6 68 65 308
•After dessert only.

Relais le Jardin
  Hotel Lord Byron
Via G. De Notaris 5
Rome 00197
39 6 32 20 404
fax 39 6 32 20 405
•Smoking section and bar.

Restaurant Sans Souci
Via Sicilia 20/24
Rome 00187
39 6 48 21 814
fax 39 6 48 21 771
•Dining room (on request), bar and lounge.

JAPAN

Chez Wada
2-10-14 Nishi Shinsaibashi Chou-Ku
Osaka
81 6 212 1780
•All areas.

LUXEMBOURG

Patin d'Or
40 route de Bettembourg
Luxembourg 1899
352 226 499
fax 352 404 011
•All areas.

St-Michel
rue Eau 32
Luxembourg
352 223 215
fax 352 462 593
•All areas.

MEXICO

Champs Elysees
Reforma 316
Mexico City 06600
52 5 514 0450, 333 698
fax 52 5 208 2302
•Dining room and bar.

Circulo del Sureste
Lucerna 12
Mexico City 06600
52 5 535 2704
fax 52 5 535 6462
•Smoking section.

Delmonico's
Londres 91
Mexico City 06600
52 5 207 4949
fax 52 5 207 9892
•Smoking section.

Fonda del Recuerdo
Bahia de las Palmas 37
Mexico City
52 5 260 1292
fax 52 5 260 1670
•All areas.

Fonda del Refugio
Liverpool 166
Mexico City 06600
52 5 207 2732
fax 52 5 207 8802
•All smoking rooms.

Restaurante Fouquet's de Paris
Hotel Camino Real
Mariano Escobebo 700
Mexico City 11590
52 5 203 2121
fax 52 5 254 4332
•*Smoking section.*

La Hacienda de Los Morales
Vazquez de Mella 525
Mexico City 11510
52 5 281 4554
fax 52 5 282 1342
•*Smoking section.*

Les Moustaches
Rio Sena 88
Mexico City
52 5 533 3390, 535 3440
•*Smoking section.*

Passy
Amberes 10
Mexico City
52 5 208 2087
•*Smoking section.*

San Angel Inn
Diego Rivera 50
Mexico City
52 5 616 0973
•*Smoking section.*

El Dorado Bar & Grill
Belden and Ocampo 401
Nuevo Laredo, Tamaulipas 88000
52 87 120 015
fax 52 87 120 015
•*All areas.*

Fashion City Cafe
Andres Bello 10
Polanco
52 5 282 0062
•*Smoking section.*

MONACO

Grill de l'Hôtel de Paris
place du Casino
Monte Carlo 98002
33 92 16 3002
fax 33 92 16 3840
•*Bar only.*

La Coupole
Hôtel Mirabeau
1 ave. Princess Grace
Monte Carlo 98000
33 92 16 6565
fax 33 93 50 8485
•*Special area only.*

Restaurant Louis XV
Hôtel de Paris
place du Casino
Monte Carlo 98000
33 92 16 30 01
fax 33 92 16 69 21
•*Dining room, bar and lounge.*

NETHERLANDS

Christophe
Leliegracht 46
Amsterdam 1015DR
31 20 625 0807
fax 31 20 638 9132
•*All areas.*

Halvemaan
van Leyenberghlaan 320
Amsterdam 1082GM
31 20 644 0348
fax 31 20 644 1777
•*All areas.*

Le Restaurant Tout Court
Runstraat 13
Amsterdam 1016GG
31 20 625 8637
•*Dining room.*

Vermeer
Prins Hendrikkade 59-72
Amsterdam 1012AD
31 20 556 4885
•*Smoking lounge and restaurant.*

Kaatje bij de Sluis
Browerstraat 20
Blokzijl 8356DF
31 527 291833
fax 31 527 291836
•*All areas.*

De Bokkedoorns
Zeeweg 53
Eboverveen 2153
31 23 26 3600
•*All areas.*

Restaurant/Hotel Sauelberg
Oosteinde 14
Eh Voorburg 2271EH
31 70 387 2081
•*Dining room, lounge and private rooms.*

De Oude Rosmolen
Duinsteeg 1
Hoorn 1621ER
31 22 901 4752
fax 31 22 921 4938
•*All areas.*

NETHERLANDS ANTILLES

Antoine's
103 Front St.
Phillipsburg, St. Maarten
599 5 229 64
•*All areas.*

Shivsagar
16 Front St.
Phillipsburg, St. Maarten
599 5 222 99
•*Bar only.*

NORWAY

Bagatelle
Bygdy Alle 3
Oslo 0257
47 2 244 0990
fax 47 2 243 6420
•*Bar and lounge only.*

PORTUGAL

Casa da Comida
Travessa das Amoreiras 1
Lisbon
351 1 388 5376
fax 351 1 387 5132
•*All areas.*

Coventual
Praça das Flores 45
Lisbon
351 1 609 196
fax 351 1 609 9196
•*All areas.*

Tagide
Largo da Academia Nacional
de Belas Artes 1820
Lisbon 1200
351 1 342 0720
fax 351 1 347 1880
•*Dining room, bar, lounge and private rooms.*

PUERTO RICO

Perichi's
Hotel Parador
Carr 102, KN 14.3
HC01 Box 16310
Cabo Rojo 00623
(809) 851-0620
•*Lounge only.*

▲ The Cigar Bar
  El San Juan Hotel & Casino
6063 Isla Verde Ave.
San Juan 00979
(809) 791-1000
•*All areas.*

S P A I N

Botafumeiro
Grand de Gràcia 81
Barcelona 08012
34 3 218 4230
fax 34 3 415 5848
•*All areas.*

Ca L'Isidre
Les Flors 12
Barcelona 08001
34 3 441 1139
fax 34 3 442 5271
•*All areas.*

Gaig
Passeig de Maragall 402
Barcelona 08031
34 3 429 1017
fax 34 3 429 7002
•*All areas.*

Jaume de Provença
Proven a 88
Barcelona 08029
34 3 430 0029
•*All areas.*

La Dama
Ave. Diagonal 423
Barcelona 08036
34 3 202 0686
fax 34 3 200 7299
•*All areas.*

Neichel
Ave. de Pedralbes 16 bis.
Barcelona 08034
34 3 203 8408
fax 34 3 205 6369
•*All areas.*

Via Veneto
Ganduxer 10-12
Barcelona 08021
34 3 200 7244
fax 34 3 201 6095
•*All areas.*

Cabo Mayor
37 Ramayor Madrid 28036
34 3 350 8776
fax 34 1 359 1621
•*All areas.*

Café de Oriente
Plaza de Oriente 2
Madrid 28013
34 3 541 3974
fax 34 1 547 7707
•*All areas.*

Casa d'a Troya
Emiliano Barral 14
Madrid
34 1 416 4455
•*All areas.*

El Cenador del Prado
Prado 4
Madrid 28014
34 1 429 1561
•*All areas.*

El Olivo
General Gallegos 1
Madrid 28036
34 1 359 1535
fax 34 1 345 9183
•*All areas.*

El Pescador
José Ortega y Gasset 75
Madrid 28006
34 1 402 1290
•*All areas.*

Goizeko Kabi
Comandante Zorita 37
Madrid 28020
34 1 533 0185
fax 34 1 533 0214
•*All areas.*

Jockey
Amador de Los Ríos 6
Madrid 28010
34 1 319 2435
•*All areas.*

La Trainera
Lagasca 60
Madrid 28001
34 1 576 0575
fax 34 1 575 0637
•*All areas.*

Las Cuatro Estaciones
General Ibàñez Ibero 5
Madrid 28003
34 1 553 6305
•*All areas.*

Luculo
Génova 19
Madrid 28004
34 1 319 4029
fax 34 1 319 4029
•*All areas.*

Señoría de Bertiz
Comandante Zorita 6
Madrid 28020
34 1 533 2757
fax 34 1 534 5090
•*All areas.*

Viridiana
Juan de Mena 14
Madrid 28014
34 1 523 4478
•*All areas.*

S W I T Z E R L A N D

The Griffins Club
36 blvd. Helvetique
Geneva 1207
41 22 735 12 18
fax 41 22 736 75 46
•*All areas.*

La Cigogne
  Hôtel de la Cigogne
17 place Longemalle
Geneva 1204
41 22 818 40 40
•*All areas.*

Le Chat Botte
  Hôtel Beau Rívage
13 Mont-Blanc
Geneva 1201
41 22 731 65 32
•*All areas.*

Le Cygne
19 Quai Mont-Blanc
Geneva 1201
41 22 908 90 81
fax 41 22 908 90 90
•*All areas.*

Restaurant Steinbock & Le Pavillon
85 Hauptstrasse
Tagerwilen 8274
41 22 669 11 72
fax 41 71 669 17 52
•*All areas.*

Restaurant Wiesental
Zürichstrasse 25
Winkel 8185
41 1 860 15 00
•*Dining room, bar and private rooms.*

Gourmet Hôtel Zürich
Neumuhlequai 42
Zürich 8006
41 1 363 63 63
fax 41 1 363 60 15
•*Smoking section, bar and lounge.*

Taverna Catalana
Glockengasse 8
Zürich 8001
41 1 221 12 62
•*All areas.*

UNITED KINGDOM

Terrace
  Waldos
Cliveden Taplow
Berkshire SL6 0JS
44 1628 668 561
fax 44 1628 661 837
•*Private sitting rooms only.*

The New Mill Restaurant and Grill
New Mill Rd., Eversley
Hampshire RG2 7ORA
44 173 473 2105
fax 44 173 432 780
•*Bar, lounge, private rooms and patio/sidewalk.*

Albero & Grana
  Chelsea Cloisters
Sloane Ave.
London SW3 3DW
44 171 225 1048
fax 44 171 581 3259
•*All areas.*

▲ **Annabel's**
44 Berkeley Square
London
44 171 629 1096
•*All areas.*
•*Private nightclub since 1963.*

Bentleys Seafood Restaurant
Swallow St.
London W1R 7HD
44 171 734 4756
fax 44 171 287 2972
•*All areas.*

The Berkley Restaurant
Wilton Place
London SW1 X7RL
44 171 235 6000
fax 44 171 235 4330
•*Dining room, bar, lounge and private rooms.*

Bibendum
  Michelin House
81 Fulham Rd.
London SW3 6RD
44 171 581 5817
•*All areas.*

Blue Print Cafe
  The Deskin Museum
Butlers Wharf
London SE1 2YD
44 171 378 7031
•*Dining room.*

Bombay Brasserie
Courtfield Rd.
London SW7 4UH
44 171 370 4040
fax 44 171 835 1669
•*Smoking section.*

The Butlers Wharf Chop-House
The Butlers Wharf Building, 36-E
Shad Thames
London SE1 2YE
44 171 403 3403
fax 44 171 403 3414
•*All areas.*

Cafe Nico
  Grosvenor House
Grosvenor Park Lane
London
44 171 499 6363
•*Smoking section.*

Cantina del Ponte
The Butlers Wharf Building, 36-C
Shad Thames
London SE1 2YE
44 171 403 5403
fax 44 171 403 0267
•*Back area of dining room only.*

Caviar House
161 Piccadilly
London W1V 9DF
44 171 409 0445
fax 44 171 493 1667
•*All areas.*

Cecconi Restaurant
5-A Burlington Gardens
London W1X 1LE
44 171 434 1509
fax 44 171 494 2440
•*All areas.*

Christopher's/The American Grill
28 Wellington St.
London WC2 E7DD
44 171 240 4222
fax 44 171 240 3357
•*All areas.*

City Circle
10 Basinghall St.
London EZ2
44 171 600 8479
fax 44 171 600 2446
•*All areas.*

▲ **Corney & Barrow**
44 Cannon St.
London EZ4 6JJ
44 171 248 1700
fax 44 171 329 8012
•*All areas.*
•*A wine bar.*

Cornucopia
6 Garrick St.
Covent Garden
London WC2 9EH
44 171 240 4866
fax 44 171 878 0763
•*Dining room, bar and patio/sidewalk.*

Elephant on the River
129 Grosvenor Rd.
London SW1 V354
44 171 834 1621
fax 44 171 834 4232
•*All areas.*

The English Garden Restaurant
10 Lincoln St., Chelsea
London SW3 2TS
44 171 584 7272
fax 44 171 581 2848
•*Smoking areas.*

The English House Restaurant
3 Milner St., Chelsea
London SW3
44 171 584 3002
fax 44 171 581 2848
•*Smoking areas.*

Fifth Floor Restaurant Bar Cafe
  Harvey Nichols
109 Knightsbridge
London SW1 7RJ
44 171 235 5250
fax 44 171 823 2207
•*Café, bar and dining room (with consideration to other diners).*

Finos Wine Cellar
123 Mount St.
London W1Y 5HD
44 171 491 1640
•*All areas.*

Four Seasons Hotel
Hamilton Place, Park Lane
London W1A 1AZ
44 171 499 0888
fax 44 171 493 6629 (hotel)
•*All areas.*

Gattis Restaurant
1 Finsbury Ave.
London EZ2 M2PA
44 171 247 1051
•*Small area only.*

Green's Restaurant & Oyster Bar
36 Duke St., St. James's
London SW1 Y6DF
44 171 930 4566
fax 44 171 491 7463
•*All areas.*

Greenhouse Restaurant
27-A Hays Mews
London W1X 7RJ
44 171 499 3331
fax 44 171 499 5368
•*All areas.*

The Grill Room - Dorchester
53 Park Lane
London W1A 2HJ
44 171 629 8888
fax 44 171 317 6464
•*All areas.*

Grill St. Quinten
3 Yeomans Row
London SW3
44 171 581 8377
fax 44 171 584 6064
•*Most areas.*

Halcyon Hotel & Restaurant
81 Holland Park
London W17 3RZ
44 171 727 7288
fax 44 171 229 8516
•*One half of the restaurant.*

▲ **Harry's Bar**
26 S. Audley St.
London W1Y 5DJ
44 171 499 0844
fax 44 171 491 1860
•*All areas.*
•*Private luncheon and dining club.*

Howard Hotel
Temple Place
London WC2 R2PR
44 171 836 3555
fax 44 171 379 4547
•*All areas.*

La Tante Claire Restaurant
68 Royal Hospital Rd.
London SW3 4HP
44 171 352 6045
fax 44 171 352 3257
•*All areas.*

The Lanesborough
1 Lanesborough Place
London SW1 X7TA
44 171 259 5599
fax 44 171 259 5606
•*All areas (but not at breakfast).*

Le Pont de la Tour
The Butlers Wharf Building, 36-D
Shad Thames
London SE1 2YE
44 171 403 8403
fax 44 171 403 0267
•*All areas.*

Les Saveurs
37-A Curzon St., Mayfair
London W1Y 7AF
44 171 491 8919
fax 44 171 491 3658
•Lounge area and late night in dining room.

Lindsay House Restaurant
21 Romilly St.
London W1
44 171 439 0450
fax 44 171 581 2848
•Smoking areas.

▲ **Mark's Club**
46 Charles St.
London W1X 7PB
44 171 499 2936
•All areas.
•Private luncheon and dining club.

Mezzo
100 Wardour St.
London W1V 3LE
44 171 314 4000
fax 44 171 314 4040
•All areas.

Montes on Sloane St.
164 Sloane St.
London SW1 X9QB
44 171 245 0892
•All areas.

Mosimann's
Belgrave Square/11-B W. Halkin St.
London SW1 X8JL
44 171 235 9625
fax 44 171 245-6354
•Dining room, bar and private rooms.

Motcombs The Club
5 Halkin Arcade
London SW1 X8JT
44 171 235 5532
fax 44 171 245 6125
•All areas.

Overtons Restaurant
5 St. James's St.
London SW1
44 171 839 3774
fax 44 171 839 4330
•Dining room, bar and private rooms.

Pine Bar
 Britannia Intercontinental
Grosvenor Square
London
44 171 629 9400
fax 44 171 408 0899
•Pine Bar; Adams Restaurant.

Poissonnerie de l'Avenue
82 Sloane Ave.
London SW3 3D2
44 171 589 2457
fax 44 171 581 3360
•All areas.

Quaglino's
16 Bury St.
London SW1 Y6AL
44 171 930 2605
•All areas.

Rules Restaurant
35 Maiden Lane
London WC2 E7LB
44 171 836 5314
fax 44 171 497 1081
•All areas.

Sale e Pepe Restaurant
9 Pavilion Rd.
London SW1 XOHD
44 171 235 0098
•All areas.

Savoy Grill
1 Savoy Hill
London
44 171 836 4343
fax 44 171 240 6040
•All areas.

Scalini Restaurant
1-2-3 Walton St.
London SW3 2JD
44 171 225 2301
•*All areas.*

Scott's Restaurant
20 Mount St.
London W16 HE
44 171 629 5248
fax 44 171 499 8246
•*Bar only.*

Sheekey's Restaurant
28/32 St. Martins Court
London WC2 N4AL
44 171 240 2565
fax 44 171 379 1417
•*All areas.*

Signor Sassi
14 Knightsbridge Gardens
London SW1 8LG
44 171 584 2277
•*All areas.*

Simpsons-in-the-Strand
100 Strand
London WC2 ROEW
44 171 836 9112
•*All areas.*

The Square
32 Kings St. - St. James
London SW1 45RJ
44 171 839 8787
fax 44 171 321 2124
•*All areas.*

Toto Restaurant
  Walton House
Walton St.
London SW1
44 171 589 2062
•*All areas.*

Trader Vic Restaurant
  The London Hilton
Park Lane
London W1Y 4BE
44 171 208 4113
•*All areas.*

Tramp
40 Jermyn St.
London SW1 Y6DN
44 171 734 0565
•*All areas.*

Walsh's Seafood & Shellfish
  Restaurant
5 Charlotte St.
London W1P 1HD
44 171 637 0222
fax 44 171 637 0224
•*All areas.*

Waltons Restaurant
121 Walton St.
London SW3 2HB
44 171 584 0204
fax 44 171 581 2848
•*All areas.*

Wig & Pen Club
229 Strand
London WC2 R1BA
44 171 583 7255
fax 44 171 583 6608
•*All areas.*

Wiltons Restaurant
55 Jermyn St.
London 6LX
44 171 629 9955
fax 44 171 495 6233
•*All areas (with consideration to other diners).*

Hambleton Hall
Hambleton, Oakham
Rutland LE1 58TH
44 1572 756 991
fax 44 1572 724 721
•Bar and lounge only.

The Whitehorse at Chilgrove
Chichester
West Sussex P01 89HX
44 1243 535 219
•Bar, lounge and private rooms only.

U.S. VIRGIN ISLANDS

The Galleon
PO Box 24669 GBS
St. Croix 00820
(809) 773-9949
•Bar only.

The Grea House at Villa Madeleine
Box 3109, Christiansted
St. Croix 00820
(809) 778-7377
fax (809) 773-7518
•All areas.

WEST INDIES

La Vie en Rose
On the Waterfront
Marigot
St. Martin
596 87 54 42
fax 596 87 58 26
•Restaurant and balcony.

Banana Boat/Wahoo Grill
Turtle Cove Marina
Providenciales
Turks & Caicos
(809) 941-5706
•All areas.

Tiki Hut Cabana Bar and Grill
Turtle Cove Marina
Providenciales
Turks & Caicos
(809) 941-5341
•All areas.

Cigar Notes